Economic Change in Eastern Europe since 1918

Economic Change in Eastern Europe since 1918

Derek H. Aldcroft

Research Professor in Economic History
Manchester Metropolitan University

and Steven Morewood

Lecturer in Economic History
University of Birmingham

Edward Elgar

Published by
Edward Elgar Publishing Limited
Gower House
Croft Road
Aldershot
Hants GU11 3HR
England

Edward Elgar Publishing Company
Old Post Road
Brookfield
Vermont 05036
USA

British Library Cataloguing in Publication Data
Aldcroft, Derek H.
   Economic Change in Eastern Europe Since
   1918
   I. Title   II. Morewood, Steven
   330.947

Library of Congress Cataloguing in Publication Data
Aldcroft, Derek Howard.
    Economic change in Eastern Europe since 1918 / by Derek H.
Aldcroft and Steven Morewood.
       p.   cm.
    Includes bibliographical references and index.
    1. Europe, Eastern—Economic conditions—1945–1989.   2. Europe,
Eastern—Economic conditions—1989–   3. Europe—Economic
conditions—20th century.   I. Morewood, Steven, 1955–
II. Title.
    HC244.A622 1994
    330.947′084—dc20   94–16370
                                                                                  CIP

ISBN 1 85278 819 4
       1 85278 823 2 (paperback)
Printed and bound in Great Britain by
Hartnolls Limited, Bodmin, Cornwall

Contents

List of tables		vii
Preface		ix
Introduction		xi
1	The legacy of war and the peace settlements	1
2	Inflation, reconstruction and stabilization	22
3	Indebtedness and instability in the later 1920s	42
4	Policies to combat depression	58
5	War and the emergence of new regimes	86
6	A new start under socialism in the 1950s and 1960s	105
7	Eastern Europe within the Soviet orbit	128
8	Economic slowdown and renewed pressure for reform	156
9	The road to revolution	177
10	An uncertain fate	206
References		237
Index		263

Tables

1.1	Territorial and population changes in Eastern Europe, 1914–21	3
1.2	Population dependent on agriculture and population change	18
1.3	Agricultural undertakings by hectare size, circa 1930	19
2.1	Industrial production and mining in Europe, 1913–25	23
2.2	Currency stabilization in Eastern Europe	38
3.1	Indices of industrial production for selected regions, 1925–29	43
3.2	Indices of manufacturing output, 1913–29	44
3.3	Debt servicing as a percentage of exports	56
4.1	Declines in per capita GNP and manufacturing production, 1929–33	61
4.2	Germany's share of East European trade	67
4.3	Indices of manufacturing output, 1929–38	79
4.4	GNP per capita levels (1960 US dollars) and percentage changes, 1913–38	84
5.1	Per capita levels of national income, industrial production and agricultural production in 1949	103
6.1	First five-year plans of the East European countries	107
6.2	Share of investment by branch, 1953–55	109
6.3	National income, 1956–65	114
6.4	The socialist sector in Eastern Europe	121
7.1	Soviet and East European imports, various years	134
7.2	Eastern Europe: trade with the USSR as a percentage of total trade, 1960–78	136
7.3	Military expenditure as a share of net material product	142
8.1	Distribution of the CMEA region's trade with the West by countries	156
8.2	East European indebtedness in the 1970s: gross debt in billions of current US dollars	161
8.3	Destination by country of communist high-tech imports from the industrial West	163
8.4	Comparative inflation in selected countries, 1971–77	166
9.1	Eastern Europe and the Soviet Union: share of CMEA countries in total trade, 1988	184
9.2	European patents by country of origin	186

9.3   Eastern Europe and the Soviet Union: external debt, 1989   193
10.1 Real growth of GDP in Eastern Europe   208
10.2 Indices of GDP per capita in Europe and the United States,
      1870, 1910, 1987   232

Preface

Recent developments in Eastern Europe have given a new dimension to the history of the region. Much has been written on the political history of the region but the economic aspects have been less well documented. We believe however that long-term economic and social factors are very relevant to the recent dramatic changes in the political and economic structures of Eastern Europe. In this volume therefore we attempt to show how these have influenced and shaped the course of events since the First World War, culminating in the breakdown of the communist regimes in 1989. We further believe that future stability in the region is very much dependent on success in the economic sphere.

The preparation of this study has been divided equally between the two authors, with Professor Aldcroft taking major responsibility for the period up to 1950 and Dr Morewood for the subsequent period. However, at all stages of the work we have successively read, commented upon and amended each other's draft.

We should like to thank Professor David Good of the Center for Austrian Studies at the University of Minnesota, who so kindly provided us with his revised data on long-term output estimates for Eastern Europe and allowed us to reproduce some of the data in Chapter 10.

Derek H. Aldcroft
Steven Morewood

Introduction

While it might be unjust to reduce the economic history of Eastern Europe to a mere footnote, as Doreen Warriner (1964, 75) suggests, there can be little doubt that, along with Southern Europe, it remained very much a backward region throughout the nineteenth century and for much of the twentieth. The industrial transformation of the West in the nineteenth century had led to a widening gap in income levels and economic structures within Europe with the result that by 1914 much of Eastern Europe could be classed as underdeveloped. This was especially the case the further east one went. Of the six countries which form the main subject matter of this study, the three Balkan countries (Yugoslavia, Romania and Bulgaria) remained overwhelmingly agrarian with some 80 per cent of their populations dependent on the land for a livelihood (Deldycke, Gelders and Limbor 1968). Per capita industrial production was but a fraction of the levels in Britain, Belgium and Germany and income per head averaged less than a third that of Britain (Berend and Ranki 1982, 144). Hungary and Poland were somewhat better situated structurally with two-thirds to three-quarters of their active populations in the primary sector though income levels were only marginally higher. Only the Czech lands could in any way compare with the West with one-third of the active population engaged in industry and income levels about half those of Great Britain (Bairoch 1976, 307; 1991, 33).

This does not mean that modern economic growth or industrial development completely bypassed these countries. Indeed, modern scholarship has shown (Good 1984; Komlos 1983, 1989; Berend and Ranki 1982; Sylla and Toniolo 1991) that in most cases economic change of some sort was fairly pervasive throughout the European continent before the war. This was certainly the case in the lands incorporated within the Austro-Hungarian Empire, especially the western half, while even the more outlying areas of the region experienced some economic awakening in the latter half of the nineteenth century, often as a result of the infiltration of Western interests. Even so, modern capitalism in scale and scope could not match that of the West; often it was little more than an island or two in a sea of primitivism, heavily concentrated spatially, for example around Budapest in Hungary and Sofia in Bulgaria. Moreover, industry proper still accounted for a very small share of national income and employment. Agricultural systems, though by no means

static, were very primitive and retained many feudal characteristics, especially in the Balkans, so that productive efficiency was very much lower than
in the countries of Western Europe (Bairoch 1991).

It is important to stress the relatively low level of development achieved
by the early twentieth century, not only in terms of the level of incomes, but
also in the context of the poor infrastructure facilities, low social overhead
capital provision and unfavourable institutional systems. This is partly because most of these countries were to experience very strong population
pressure at a time when they were least able to cope with it. Whereas most
Western countries were sufficiently advanced to surmount the population
pressures which occurred in the late eighteenth and early nineteenth centuries
(Komlos 1989), this was very much less the case with Eastern Europe in the
first half of the twentieth century. Low levels of development and accumulation and land shortages, coupled with unyielding agrarian systems, made it
difficult to accommodate the burden of increasing numbers. Moreover, the
problem was compounded by the unfavourable external environment – two
world wars and a great depression – which undermined the agrarian sector
and left a legacy of destruction and immiseration. In fact, against this appall-
ing background it is surprising that they managed to survive at all, let alone
register any form of progress.

The situation is even more remarkable, perhaps, when one takes into
account the fissiparous nature of political and social structures which can
scarcely have been the most conducive to economic progress. Eastern Europe
was, and still is, riddled with nationalities, religions and political factions,
always very close to the surface waiting to burst the bonds of containment.
Up to 1914 containment was achieved largely through the benevolent despot-
ism of the great powers and the ministrations of the Austro-Hungarian Empire which managed, not always completely successfully, to subjugate the
forces of protest in the region. From its very inception the Austro-Hungarian
Empire found nationality disputes a perennial problem and only loyalty to the
monarchy and its claims to 'supernationality' held the disjointed kingdom
together.

When the great power control disintegrated following the First World War
the fragile equilibrium was undermined and a power vacuum emerged. The
peace treaty settlements did more to exacerbate the problems of the region
than to restore stability since by their emphasis on self-determination and
nationality they gave free rein to latent forces of nationalism. Ethnic, reli-
gious and political diversity could not be accommodated harmoniously within
the new nation states that emerged partly because they were, rather like some
of the subsequent ex-colonial states, not fully prepared for self-government,
parliamentary democracy and free expression. There had been, it is true,
some experience in these areas before 1914 but what was notable was the

extensive corruption which pervaded representative institutions and the narrow base for which these catered. Such characteristics were inevitably carried over into the more liberal atmosphere of the postwar period and hence parliamentary institutions were weak, corrupt and vulnerable to infiltration and takeover, first by indigenous forms of authoritarian control often of a monarchical variety, and later by external forces, first Germany and then the Soviet Union. The latter once again put the lid on irredentist forces but it did not crush or eliminate them. It was only a matter of time before they exploded once again.

While Western Europe was able to turn to the United States for aid to facilitate postwar reconstruction, the East European countries chose or were compelled by Soviet pressure to adopt communist forms of government and install command economic systems. These new socialist regimes, under the watchful eye of the Soviet Union, did achieve quite spectacular results initially, but it is now apparent that their economic progress was based on very shaky foundations. The Achilles heel of these cumbersome economies, with their emphasis on heavy industry and armaments, was their failure to improve significantly the living standards of the population and their neglect of the agrarian sector. As awareness of Western consumption patterns and norms increased, so too did the demand increase for concessions and reform. Unfortunately the political and administrative regimes could not readily adapt to the pressures exerted by changing economic and social circumstances. Attempts at reform were half-hearted and incomplete, and as economic and living conditions deteriorated from the late 1970s the pressures built up and led to the explosive climax of general revolution throughout the region in 1989, a traumatic year which marked another milestone in the history of this troubled region. Chaos reigned as these countries once again lurched from one type of regime to another and sought to graft market structures on to an alien environment. As in the case of the parliamentary democracies of the 1920s, time is now not on their side given the internal pressures which could well force further changes in political structures in the future.

Any study of economic change and development in Eastern Europe must therefore take account of the political and social factors which have helped to shape the region's history. Nor can one neglect the agrarian and land issues which have dominated the scene for so much of the time. But first we turn to the circumstances surrounding the creation of the six states following the catharsis of the First World War, since it is from this time that many later problems were to emerge.

1. The legacy of war and the peace settlements

The First World War marked the end of an era for Europe both economically and politically. On the eve of hostilities Sir Edward Grey, the then British foreign secretary, had prophesied that the lamps would not be 'lit again in our lifetime', and in fact for a generation or more they were to remain extinguished as far as Europe was concerned.

The war destroyed the unity of Europe and undermined her economic strength, while the political and social order had never before in modern times been so disturbed (Boyce and Robertson 1989, 11). Europe's influence in the world economy declined as the centre of gravity shifted westwards, while the reshaping of the map of Europe arising from the peace settlement fragmented the former power base of the continent. The great empires which had orchestrated the European system in the nineteenth century were no more; in their place there emerged greatly weakened national powers together with a collection of new and reconstituted states whose rivalry for a place in the sun was matched only by that of the machinations of the major powers to influence their affairs.

Six of these states form the subject matter of this volume. Collectively referred to as Eastern Europe, or East–Central Europe or the Danubian states, they were carved out of the former Austro-Hungarian, Romanov, German and Turkish Empires. Three were new creations: Czechoslovakia, Yugoslavia and Poland; the other three (Hungary, Bulgaria and Romania) were reconstituted either through gains or losses of territory and population following the postwar boundary changes. Since the provisions of the postwar settlement effectively brought them into existence and were also the cause of many later problems it is appropriate that we begin by looking at the terms of that settlement as they affected Eastern Europe.

THE PEACE SETTLEMENT

The peacemaking exercise comprised two main features: first, heavy penalties and exactions including reparations were imposed on the vanquished, and second, extensive territorial changes were made, especially in Central

1

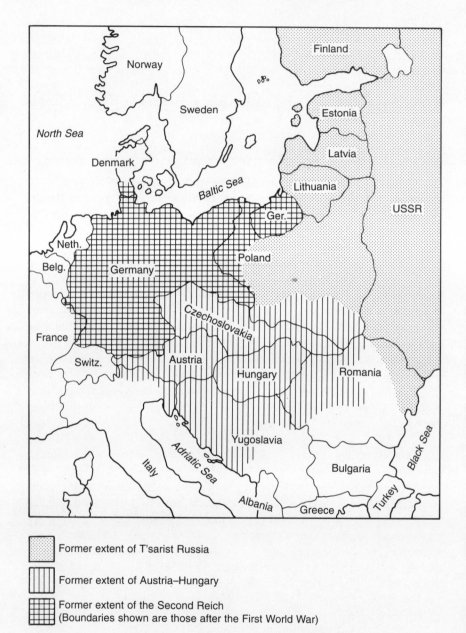

Former extent of T'sarist Russia

Former extent of Austria–Hungary

Former extent of the Second Reich
(Boundaries shown are those after the First World War)

Source: J. Lee, *The European Dictatorships*, London: Methuen, 1987.

Map 1   The impact of the First World War

and Eastern Europe. Few countries remained completely unaffected by these changes and they represented the biggest reshaping of the political geography of the European continent ever undertaken (Thompson 1966, 626). Effectively it led to the political disintegration of Europe and undermined the former balance of power.

The main provisions of the peace settlement were contained in a series of treaties concluded with the former enemy countries: Germany (Versailles 28 June 1919), Austria (St Germain 10 September 1919), Bulgaria (Neuilly 27 November 1919), Hungary (Trianon 4 June 1920 and Turkey (Sèvres 10 August 1920, superseded in 1923 by the Treaty of Lausanne). To a large extent these treaties merely confirmed the broad territorial outlines of the new Europe which the emerging nations had already marked out and laid claim to on the basis of the Wilsonian concept of national self-determination following the collapse of the former empires, especially the Austro-Hungarian, in the latter half of 1918 (Macartney 1939, 16–17). In the frantic rush of events the allied powers missed the opportunity to formulate a coherent plan for the reshaping of Europe and so they were forced to accede to the initiatives taken by the newly emerging nations. Thus 'instead of facing a tabuyla [sic] rasa in Central and Eastern Europe, the Allies found that the nations themselves were hurriedly and avidly endeavouring to fill in the white spots on the political map of Europe' (Perman 1962, 70). The size and composition of the new formations in Eastern Europe can be seen from the data in Table 1.1.

Table 1.1   Territorial and population changes in Eastern Europe, 1914–21

	Area (sq. kil.)		Population ('000s)	
	1914	1921	1914	1921
Aust.-Hung. Mon.	676 443		51 390*	
Austria		85 533		6 536
Hungary		92 607		7 600
Czechoslovakia		140 394		13 613
Bulgaria	111 800	103 146	4 753	4 910
Poland		388 279		27 184
Romania	137 903	304 244	7 516	17 594
Serbia	87 300		4 548	
Yugoslavia		248 987		12 017

*   Includes Bosnia and Herzegovina

Source: Berend and Ranki (1969, 170)

Austria and Hungary suffered by far the worst fate following the collapse of their empire since they emerged but a quarter of their former size in terms of area and only a little larger in population. Slabs of the former monarchy were distributed unevenly among no less than seven states: Czechoslovakia, Yugoslavia, Romania, Poland, Italy and the two rumps of the old regime. The new state of Czechoslovakia was forged out of the Austria provinces of Bohemia, Moravia and Austrian Silesia together with Slovakia and Ruthenia ceded by Hungary. The latter also gave up Croatia and Slovenia which, along with Bosnia and Herzegovina, went to join Serbia and later Montenegro to form the Kingdom of Serbs, Croats and Slovenes, officially renamed Yugoslavia in 1929. A very much enlarged Romania gained acquisitions from neighbouring countries including Transylvania from Hungary, Bessarabia from Russia, the Dobrudja from Bulgaria and Bukovina from Austria. The other major beneficiary was Poland, back on the map after more than a century of suspension. She secured substantial chunks of territory from the original partitioning powers Austria, Germany and Russia (Butler 1968, 222–3). Finally, Bulgaria was dealt with relatively lightly, losing Western Thrace to Greece, the Dobrudja to Romania and parts of Macedonia to Yugoslavia. Otherwise the Treaty of Neuilly confirmed the frontiers existing in 1914 which had been cut back severely the previous year following the conclusion of the Balkan Wars (Temperley 1921, 459).

The peacemaking exercise can scarcely be hailed as a resounding success and it has had few apologists. Howerd (1989, 50) felt that the settlement was not too bad given the circumstances of the time, but then goes on to list a series of issues to which solutions were never found. Most commentators however have been critical of the outcome and rightly so. Thompson (1966, 633) reckoned that it created more problems than it removed, while Mitrany (1936, 182) felt that the dislocation caused by the peace settlement was greater than that caused by the war itself because it destroyed many former contacts and patterns of communication. Certainly at the time there were few countries, if any, which were entirely happy with the result, and Keynes's vitriolic denunciation of the settlement only served to fan the flames of discontent (Keynes 1919; 1922).

The reorganization of boundaries created several new and weak states, it greatly increased the length of European political frontiers and the number of separate customs units, and it left many national minorities under alien rule which inevitably led to revisionist demands for the transfer of territory. It also posed enormous problems of economic integration and left unresolved the question of the balance of power in Europe. Some of these difficulties were of course the inevitable outcome of trying to satisfy a series of incompatible objectives simultaneously, namely ethnic delineation, national self-determination, the reconstruction of historic frontiers and economic rationale, since to satisfy one often required the modification of another. For example, to provide Poland with access to the sea she had to be given territory that included a German-speaking element, while the predominantly German Sudetenland was incorporated into Czechoslovakia in order to give the latter a defensive frontier for Bohemia and Moravia. But given the complex mix of nationalities within Eastern Europe, ethnic problems of this sort were bound to arise even had national self-determination been followed to the letter of Wilson's doctrine.

From the longer-term point of view perhaps the most serious issue was the power vacuum that emerged in East–Central Europe. The former Austro-Hungarian Monarchy was replaced by several new and reconstituted states all of which suffered from acute political and social tensions. Newly created parliamentary institutions, based on best Western democratic practice, proved a disappointment. As Sontag (1971, 68) put it, the seed of democracy fell on stony ground in Eastern Europe. Lacking any real experience of political pluralism, political instability arising from graft, corruption and inter-ethnic rivalry was widespread and endemic from the start and, with the sole exception of Czechoslovakia, the Eastern European states all drifted in time towards authoritarian regimes (Lee 1987, 254; Gilberg 1992, 278–83). Schwartz (1973, 11–12) expresses amazement that anyone should have expected democracy to flourish in the region after the war because of so little experience with democratic institutions and the acute internal divisions based on class or nationality. These, along with other factors responsible for the later anti-democratic reaction, have been analysed in depth by Newman (1970, 21–2, 33–40, 77, 91–3, 111, 153). The former monarchy may not have been perfect but it did at least have some semblance of political and economic coherence while acting as a bulwark between Eastern and Western powers. Indeed, more recent work has been much kinder to the old empire (Good 1984; Komlos 1983) and its destruction has been described as 'one of the greatest diplomatic errors in history' (Kiraly, Pastor and Sanders 1982, 39–40). In fact the allied powers themselves were reluctant until near the very last to dispense with the empire's existence, but it was largely the march of events that sealed its fate. Its replacement by the successor states shattered the political and economic unity of Europe, leaving a vacuum which effectively provided the seedbed for the Second World War (Aldcroft 1991a).

The situation was exacerbated by the fact that cohesion and cooperation among the new states was minimal, partly because of frictions and rivalry arising from the territorial adjustments and hostile relations at common borders, and partly because of the activities of the major powers in the area for purposes of their own self-interest. None of the European powers was prepared to back the new system or to promote the cause of Danubian federation, despite a British proposal for a Danubian customs union (Dockrill and

Goold 1981, 128–30; Stambrook 1963; League of Nations 1932a). In contrast to the position after 1945, national sovereignties dominated the scene in the 1920s to the extent that there was little prospect of achieving unity and stability in Europe (Jacobson 1983, 630, 644). The new states in fact became little more than pawns in a game of European high politics and were therefore allowed 'to exist and function as sovereign units for reasons which had little in common with economic considerations' (Momtchiloff 1944, 84). It is true that the inherent weakness of the new states and their incompetent governments together with the corruption of many state officials left them vulnerable to loss of independence, but it has also been argued that the lack of understanding and foresight on the part of the allied nations as to the significance of the region in terms of the future balance of power ultimately 'paved the way for Hitler's aggressive policy in Eastern Europe and eventually opened wide the door for Russian penetration' (Kiraly, Pastor and Sanders 1982, 43). In short, there were, according to Ross (1983, 53), 'few good Europeans'.

The failure to resolve the balance of power could have but one outcome, namely renewed conflict. Newman (1968, 27, 58, 105–6, 201) frequently stresses the crucial role of the region in determining the future distribution of power throughout the whole of Europe and, ultimately, the fate of the continent. In time the vacuum in Europe was bound to be filled by a predator nation since the new and reconstituted states were 'extremely weak reeds to place in the path of Germany, and they possessed few features that would lead to any hope of their being anything but satellites ... of Germany, Hitler or no Hitler'. The battle for control of the region enjoined France and Germany almost from the first moment of peace, with Germany's claims fortified by her ignominious treatment at the peace table. But that is part of another story.

The weakness of the East European states bore testimony to their economic deprivation for which the new European configuration could provide few answers. Economically the new states were worse off than before the war, since they not only inherited a 'gigantic backlog of backwardness' (Spulber 1966, 75) from the past, but to which should be added the chaos following hostilities, the loss of a large internal market and the impact of new boundaries. Komlos (1983, 6; cf. Jaszi 1929) claims that the consequences of the destruction of the Central European market for the splintered territories was little short of disastrous, and this view would seem to be strengthened by what we now know about the economic viability of the former Habsburg Empire (Good 1984, 256). The potential trade losses might not have been so serious had economic factors been accorded greater priority when redefining the shape of the new Europe. It is true that they were not totally ignored but they were certainly never at the top of the agenda. Nor were the treaty provisions drafted with the intent of promoting any pan-European objective, economic or otherwise, and, in Friedman's (1974, 12) view, they caused the maximum disruption to the European productive system.

Consequently, the new territorial formations lacked economic logic since their economic potential bore little relation to their inheritance of land and people (Berend and Ranki 1969, 170). Apart from Czechoslovakia, which acquired a large proportion of the industrial assets of the former monarchy, most of the states fared rather badly in this respect. Each nation received whatever resources and equipment happened to be located in the lands assigned to it. This frequently meant the complete break-up of former trading patterns and lines of communication and the splitting of mutually dependent branches of industry. Yugoslavia, for example, inherited five railway systems with four different gauges; each system served different centres so that they were practically unconnected with each other, and unifying the disparate parts took the best part of half a decade. The textile industry of Austria was split apart. The spindles were located in Bohemia and Moravia which became part of the new Czech Republic, while the weaving looms were located mainly in and around Vienna (Pasvolsky 1928, 527, 548).

In the case of Hungary, the main problem was the loss of raw material sources to service her developing industries. She was left with about half of her industrial undertakings, including the important manufacturing centre of Budapest, but was deprived of many important raw materials, including 84 per cent of her forests, a similar proportion of iron ore, all her salt, copper and other non-ferrous metals, 90 per cent of her water power and 30 per cent of her lignite. Losses of industrial capacity were very uneven, ranging from 89 per cent in the case of saw-mills to 18 per cent of the machine industries. The net result was that Hungary retained proportionately more industrial activities than raw materials so she actually emerged from the war in a more advanced state than previously (Macartney 1937, 461–2; Janos 1982, 205–6; Berend and Ranki 1974b, 92–3). Regional concentration of industrial activities also increased markedly, with Greater Budapest accounting for some two-thirds of the gainfully occupied workers in manufacturing in 1920 compared with about one-quarter in prewar Hungary. Such heavy geographical concentration, which increased further in the interwar years, tended to restrict the subsequent industrialization of the more backward areas of the country (Bencze and Tajti 1972, 19–28). In addition, the Treaty of Trianon destroyed Hungary's integrated transport system, especially the waterway network, the major part of the management of which was transferred to Prague, Bucharest and Belgrade (Halasz 1928, 26). Such changes did more to hinder than to promote economic recovery after the war, and in the longer term they created resentment and frustration which added strength to the forces of nationalism and revisionism in the interwar years.

Perhaps even more problematic for the successor states was the task of building new economic systems and integrating the various segments of territory. The new states acquired fragments of territory at different stages of development, comprising varied fiscal and monetary systems, and different legal and administrative practices, which were very difficult to weld into viable economic units. In practice it entailed the creation of new administrative systems, new currency and fiscal systems, new lines of communication, and the forging of fresh economic and trading links to replace those that had been destroyed. The Poles, for example, had the difficult task of integrating three very different segments of territory previously owing allegiance to alien rulers into one single state. Zweig (1944, 13) described the situation as follows:

> On the day of their political unification the three parts of Poland did not constitute a single economic unit. They had different systems of civil, commercial, and fiscal legislation. They belonged to differing customs units, to differing money and credit systems. Nor did they constitute a unity in the sense that they had developed after an organised pattern by constant and mutual testing. On the contrary some parts were over- and some under-developed.

The task was complicated further by the fact that Poland was in conflict with all her neighbours after the war, she had no natural frontiers, no government agencies to serve the whole country, very few established financial and monetary institutions to meet the needs of the new state and little in the way of highly developed industry except for that part of Upper Silesia awarded to her by the plebiscite of 1921 (Kitchen 1988, 106).

The new Kingdom of Serbs, Croats and Slovenes (Yugoslavia) had an even greater diversity of interests to assimilate and consolidate: six customs areas, five currencies, five railway systems, three divergent banking systems and a host of different nationalities and religions (Lampe 1980, 139). For Czechoslovakia the main task was that of reconciling the Czech lands with the less developed Slovak and Ruthenian territories, while Romania had to integrate its greatly enlarged domain. Austria and Hungary, on the other hand, had the reverse task of making sense of the remnants left to them of their old empire, shorn of some of the most valuable assets. Only Bulgaria was spared large-scale integration problems arising from territorial changes and ethnic heterogeneity, though she did have a large number of refugees from ceded lands to accommodate and a substantial reparations bill equivalent to one-quarter of her total national wealth (Bell 1977, 164, 194).

One problem which defied solution throughout the postwar period was the ethnic composition of Eastern Europe. Though the postwar settlement is said to have reduced by about half the number of people living under alien rule in Europe, this still left some 30 million people in Central and Eastern Europe with minority status, and on average one-quarter of the population of the East European states consisted of minorities (Pearson 1983, 147–8; Sharp 1991, 155). 'The ethnographic map of Eastern Europe in 1919 resembled a complicated and irregularly patterned mosaic, reflecting the historic interminglings and movements of populations in the region.' (Sharp 1991, 132). All countries were poly-ethnic and in some cases, notably in Yugoslavia, Czechoslovakia and Romania, up to a dozen nationalities and as many religions comingled together. Significantly, pockets of Germans resided in all the new states (Polonsky 1975, 158–63). Czechoslovakia and Yugoslavia had by far the highest concentration of minorities, Romania and Poland were above average, while Bulgaria and Hungary had the smallest incidence. In addition, some countries had large expatriate populations arising from the relocation of boundaries. Altogether over 21 million people or 7.8 per cent of the dominant populations of Central and Eastern Europe lived outside the state of their inherited nationality, about half of whom consisted of Germans, Magyars and Bulgarians (Macartney 1934, 268). Apart from the Albanians, the Hungarian expatriate situation was by far the worst, with one in three Hungarians living under foreign rule compared with one in sixteen Bulgars and approximately one in ten Germans (Pearson 1983, 148, 170–71; Kiraly, Pastor and Sanders 1982, 73).

This 'ethnological soufflé' as Tiltman (1934, 266) called it, was bound to give rise to serious problems some of which have persisted until the present day, most notably in Yugoslavia and Czechoslovakia. Though most countries were enjoined to observe good behaviour towards their alien residents under the League of Nations minority treaties, they were generally reluctant to abide by their obligations. Generally speaking, 'the states were mainly concerned with interpreting the provisions in the most restrictive possible sense and used every device to vitiate their effect'. (Robinson 1943, 264). In few cases were minority groups accorded equality of treatment with the dominant nationality in terms of politics, education and economics. The situation was particularly bad in the multinational states of Czechoslovakia, Yugoslavia and Romania (Donald 1928, 131). In the case of the first two countries there was not even a majority nationality since the Czechs and the Serbs accounted for less than half the respective populations. The Czechs were probably the most ruthless, though the Serbs probably came a very close second. As Pearson (1983, 155) observes: 'In operating what was in practice a Czech empire, the Czechs broke all their earlier promises to their "subordinate minorities" in a manner almost calculated to antagonise them.' They managed to alienate virtually all their important minorities – the Germans, Magyars, Slovaks, Ruthenes and Poles – by their discriminatory policies. The worst friction was probably between the Czechs and Slovaks. The Czechs regarded the Slovaks as ignorant 'hillbillies', while in turn the latter saw the Czechs as arrogant oppressors who were unwilling to recognize Slovakia's just claims. Conversely, it was the Sudeten Germans who regarded the Czechs to be the inferior race, while the Czechs for their part looked on the Germans as invaders intent on subjugating the Czechs (Schwartz 1973, 11; Wiskemann 1938, 118–20). The Germans and also the Magyars were particularly incensed by their loss of status and it is scarcely surprising that Hitler took the opportunity to exploit the cause of the Sudeten Germans as a prelude to his acquisition of Czechoslovakia in 1938 (Pearson 1983, 153).

The Yugoslav situation was yet more complex, with an even greater diversity of nationalities than Czechoslovakia. The ethnic breakdown consisted of 43 per cent Serbians, 23 per cent Croatians, 8.5 per cent Slovenes, 6 per cent Bosnian Muslims, 5 per cent Macedonian Slavics, 3.6 per cent Albanians, 3.6 per cent Germans and 3.4 per cent Magyars, with the remainder being made up of Romanians, Jews, Gypsies, Vlachs and Turks (Jelavich 1983, 151). None of these peoples considered themselves as belonging to one nation and hence a distinct Yugoslav identity failed to materialize. From the beginning the minority Serbs, who were weaker than their Czech brethren and inferior economically to the Croats and Slovenes, sought to dominate the new state by imposing centralized control, while the Croats and other minorities struggled to gain greater autonomy and power. While apologists have sought to mitigate the charge of Serbian exploitation, the fact remains that ethnic conflict was a serious source of weakness from the start (Dragnich 1983, 135–51). The most bitter rivalry occurred between the Serbs and Croats which at times paralysed the nation and left it vulnerable to external takeover (Jelavich 1983, 151).

The conflict and rivalry between different ethnic groups, the roots of which went far back in time (Job 1993, 53; Banac 1988), not only seriously weakened the states in question, but also gave rise to irredentism on the part of expatriate groups, incited in turn by the revisionist policies of the ex-enemy countries, most notably Germany and Hungary. Refugees from the lost territories also added weight to the claim for boundary revisions and at the same time caused problems of assimilation for the host countries. Bulgaria, for example, faced an influx of 450 000 refugees from territories ceded to Greece and Yugoslavia, while 426 000 Hungarians returned from Czechoslovakia, Romania, Yugoslavia and Austria between 1918 and 1924 (Bell 1977, 164; Mocsy 1983, 10; cf. Donald 1928, 266). The Hungarian refugees remained fully committed to the restoration of lost territories even though there was little prospect of the successor states agreeing to a revision of the Trianon boundaries (Apponyi 1928). For the longer term the situation was fraught with danger since as Mocsy (1983, 195) points out: 'The resulting cool relations between Hungary and its neighbours weakened them all, increased their isolation, and prepared the way for domination of the entire region by a great power.'

The peace settlement clearly had many defects which could not be easily rectified even had the successor states been willing to accede to some of the claims of the revisionist powers. Apart from the serious long-term consequences for the future of Central and Eastern Europe, it undoubtedly made the task of postwar reconstruction that much more difficult.

DEVASTATION AND DESTRUCTION

Eastern Europe emerged from the war in a much weaker state than the West. It would be little exaggeration to say that by the close of the war the economic and social systems of the region were on the point of collapse (Rothschild 1974, 16). Most countries had been totally exhausted by the war effort and it is doubtful whether they could have withstood another wartime winter. Output levels were but a fraction of prewar; impoverishment and famine were widespread; food, raw materials and capital equipment were desperately short; transport systems were completely disorganized and badly in need of repair and re-equipment; and fiscal and currency systems were running out of control (League of Nations 1920; 1922; 1943a; 1945d). There had, too, been very heavy asset losses, both physical and human. The social and political turmoil following the armistice as new states were in the making, plus the continuation of several border conflicts only added to the general problems.

Of the six countries, probably Serbia (soon part of Yugoslavia) and Poland can lay claim to have been the most severely affected. Yovanovich (1930, 302) described the war losses in Serbia as 'overwhelming' and by far the worst of any country. From the point of view of mortality this was certainly the case. No other country mobilized on such an extensive scale; virtually the whole of the male population aged between 18 and 55 was drafted into the forces, 822 000 in total, of whom one half eventually perished. If to this figure is added civilian deaths due to war-induced causes such as occupation, deportation, disease and famine, then the total loss approaches one million, or nearly one-quarter of the prewar population. If account is also taken of the wartime birth deficits, that is estimates of children unborn as a result of military mobilization, then the final tally is well over a million, equivalent to some 31 per cent of the peacetime population (Notestein 1944, 75). In addition, some 250 000 were wounded or incapacitated in some way. In relative terms human losses in most other countries pale into insignificance. Romania, with the second highest casualty list, suffered a total population deficit of 14 per cent, Austro-Hungary 9.5 per cent, Bulgaria 9.2 per cent, while the proportions for the Western powers were even lower: France 7.7 per cent, Belgium 5.4 per cent, Germany 8 per cent and the United Kingdom 3.9 per cent (Notestein 1944, 75). Further loss of life also occurred in many countries after the armistice as a result of famine and starvation, disease including the influenza epidemic of 1918–19, and massacres of various nationalities in the extensive postwar border conflicts in Eastern Europe.

Material and physical losses in Serbia were equally devastating. In total they amounted to nearly half the national wealth and three times the current income (Yovanovich 1930, 302). Following the Austro-Hungarian retreat nearly all the factories and industrial establishments were in a useless condition. The saw-mills, cement works and brick kilns had been totally wrecked, while the farms had been stripped of most of their livestock and implements. Total livestock losses probably amounted to about half. Some of the damage done to the land was almost beyond repair and the production of food was only 30–40 per cent of prewar levels, while food consumption was little better. The railways were rendered unworkable and in some districts many of the houses had been been gutted of fixtures and furniture (Berend 1985, 151; Yovanovich 1930, 298; Temperley 1920, 147).

Apart perhaps from Serbia and northern France and possibly Latvia, no other country was devastated as severely as Poland. At some time 80–90 per cent of Polish territory had been the scene of prolonged and destructive military operations (Wellisz 1938, 39–40). The occupying powers – Russia, Germany and Austria – literally ransacked the country, destroying or stripping it of cash, securities, factories, buildings, livestock, farm implements and other assets. Direct material losses have been estimated at more than 11 per cent of prewar national property, though this is probably an underestimate judging by the damage done (Roszkowski 1986, 287). Probably over half the bridges, station buildings, machinery workshops and locomotives were destroyed and over 1.7 million of houses, including 75 per cent of farm buildings, were lost by fire or other means. Many villages, especially in the eastern provinces, were levelled to the ground. Damage to the land and its assets was enormous. Nearly 11 million acres (4.45 million hectares) of agricultural land were rendered useless, 6 million acres (2.43 million hectares) of forest totally destroyed and 7600 million cubic feet (215 million cubic metres) of timber were removed by alien forces. In addition, large tracts of agricultural land were laid waste and 60 per cent of the livestock disappeared, including 2 million cattle, 1 million horses, 1.5 million sheep and 2.5 million pigs (Berend 1985, 151; Roszkowski 1986, 287–9). As in other countries, Polish agriculture also suffered from a loss of male labour to the armed forces and the requisition of horses for military purposes. By the end of the war, therefore, production levels in agriculture had slumped heavily.

Industrial operations came almost to a standstill in many areas, though there were considerable regional and sectoral variations. The worst affected area was the former Kingdom of Poland within the Russian sector due to the

Russian evacuation of 1915 and the subsequent German occupation (Roszkowski 1986, 288). The metallurgical industry was completely immobilized and industry in and around Warsaw was severely crippled (Wynot 1983, 57; Kitchen 1988, 106; Rose 1939, 110). Industrial production at the beginning of 1919 was little better than that in the Soviet Union, at a mere 15 per cent of the prewar level, and it had only risen to 30 per cent by the end of the year (Teichova 1985, 224). To make matters worse the administrative and financial apparatus was in a state of extreme chaos because of the different fiscal and currency systems in operation; the virtual collapse of the former banking system based on links with Berlin, St Petersburg and Vienna; the immobilization of the transport system; and the pernicious effects of rampant inflation. Continued border hostilities, especially in the east, also led to further losses and destruction (Leslie 1980, 140; Roszkowski 1989, 106; Zweig 1944, 29–33; Taylor 1952, 140–42). Moreover, Poland, along with other successor states of the Austro-Hungarian Monarchy apart from Hungary and Austria, had to bear the cost of liberation payments, which were in the nature of indemnities to be paid by the nationalities of the former monarchy to the victors to defray the cost and damages sustained in liberating them (Moulton and Pasvolsky 1932, 140).

Poland was therefore in a desperate situation in the immediate postwar period. Everything, and especially food, was in short supply, unemployment was high and malnutrition and disease were widespread. For some years after the war the country verged on the brink of civil war, such were the conditions of life as described by the British Director of Relief:

> The country ... had undergone four or five occupations by different armies, each of which combed the land for supplies. Most of the villages had been burnt down by the Russians in their retreat [of 1915]; land had been uncultivated for four years and had been cleared of cattle, grain, horses and agricultural machinery by both Germans and Bolsheviks. The population here was living upon roots, grass, acorns and heather. The only bread obtainable was composed of those ingredients, with perhaps about 5 per cent of rye flour. Their clothes were in the last stages of dilapidation; the majority were without boots and shoes and had reached the lowest depths of misery and degradation. The distribution of food in the towns was very unequal. It was possible to buy almost anything in the restaurants at a price, and cafés and cake shops were well supplied, but in other parts of the same towns it was impossible to obtain food. (Quoted in Clough, Moodie and Moodie 1969, 100)

The returning soldiers swelled the ranks of the unemployed, exacerbated the food problem and spread disease. Half the population of Warsaw was in receipt of unemployment relief, as was nearly all that of Lodz. In some areas children were dying for lack of milk and in many parts of eastern Poland famine conditions prevailed. Disease was also fairly general, especially typhus brought in by returning soldiers, and up to 60 per cent of the population was affected in some way. Malnutrition and disease pushed up the rate of mortality to more than 40 per thousand, while birth rates in Warsaw dropped to just under 12 per thousand.

The Hungarian situation appeared to be only marginally better even though physical destruction was less intense than in the case of Poland. By the end of the war it had become almost impossible to feed and clothe either the civilian population or the forces in combat. Agricultural and industrial production in 1918–19 was but a fraction of prewar levels (15–30 per cent) and even by 1920 had barely recovered to half the previous volumes. Mounting inflation and budgetary deficits coupled with the loss of former markets and resources left Hungary's economy on the point of collapse, matched by the political instability following defeat, including a short-lived Soviet Republic under Bela Kun between March and August of 1919, which caused further loss of life and assets (Berend and Ranki 1974b, 92–8; Volgyes 1991). Furthermore, as part of the former enemy camp Hungary, along with Germany, Austria and Bulgaria, had to make reparations payments. She was not treated as leniently as Austria, though no final determination was actually made of her share in the total bill for reparations. Nevertheless, deliveries and cessions were made in the early postwar years and a regular schedule of payments was implemented in 1924 (Moulton and Pasvolsky 1932, 237).

The other countries of the region fared somewhat better though none of them escaped lightly. Romania was badly ravaged and looted by the German occupation and by the end of the war industrial output was running at about one-third the prewar level. The transport system was also badly disorganized as a result of the destruction of many miles of track and fixed installations and a severe shortage of rolling stock due to destruction and lack of repair. The locomotive stock was down to a quarter of the prewar level, passenger coaches 35 per cent and as low as 14 per cent for freight wagons (Teichova 1985, 225). Agriculture also suffered severely from the occupation with the loss of many farm buildings, 30 per cent of the agricultural equipment and up to a half of the livestock (Berend 1985, 152).

Czechoslovakia undoubtedly came off the best. The Czech lands benefited from the demand for military supplies on behalf of the monarchy and it was only towards the end of the war, with the impending collapse of the empire, that shortages of fuel and raw materials began to present problems. Industrial production sagged to around half its peacetime level, recovering to 70 per cent in 1920. In compensation, however, the new republic inherited the bulk of the industrial capacity (70 per cent) of the monarchy and nearly half its labour force, compared with territory and population shares of no more than a quarter. The chief snag was that its domestic market was now much more limited (Teichova 1985, 225–65).

Bulgaria's agricultural production was just over half the prewar level at the end of the war but recovered to 80 per cent in 1920. This was a creditable achievement given the extensive mobilization of the country's manpower and the subsequent losses, and the fact that the economy was on the point of collapse by the end of the war with the country facing famine and starvation (Pundeff 1992, 79–80; Bell 1977, 122–3). Industrial production received a stimulus from German demand during the war, though by 1918 Bulgaria was severely handicapped by labour and raw material shortages (Lampe 1986, 43–5; Danaillow 1932).

Thus, aside from the task of consolidating the revised territorial arrangements, the successor states had a more immediate and pressing problem on their hands – that of staving off economic collapse and averting famine. By the end of 1918 the spectre of famine prevailed over a wide area of Central and Eastern Europe since stocks and production levels were but a fraction of those of normal times. The countries had little means to pay for imports since they had lost many former export markets, and in any case their supply capability had been severely impaired by wartime destruction, shortages of equipment and materials and by general disorganization. Mounting budgetary deficits through rising expenditure commitments coupled with an eroding tax base caused governments to resort to monetary financing of the public sector which, in conjunction with the seriously impaired supply potential, led to rising inflation and currency depreciation. Continued military conflict after the war and social and political upheavals in the successor states only added to the difficulties of controlling public expenditure.

RELIEF AND RECONSTRUCTION

The situation prevailing in many parts of Europe at the war's end urgently required a substantial relief programme to aid the stricken countries and to facilitate reconstruction. But apart from famine and relief deliveries in the armistice period, which were totally inadequate, there was little attempt to plan the reconstruction of Europe (Silverman 1982, 230). The United States had no desire to get embroiled in the affairs of Europe on a permanent basis, while allied cooperation disintegrated soon after the war because of Anglo-American rivalry (Artaud 1973, 17). The sharp boom followed by deflationary policies in the Anglo-Saxon countries between 1919 and 1921 further complicated the problems of war-torn Europe.

What relief aid there was consisted mainly of food and clothing supplies, the bulk of which was provided by or through American organizations, principally the American Relief Administration which had been set up early in 1919 as the executive agency of the Allied Supreme Council responsible for relief. Under these arrangements food to the value of $1250 million was delivered to some 20 European countries, most of it being provided on a credit basis rather than as an outright gift. After the middle of 1919 the official aid programme was sharply curtailed and subsequently relief activities were confined largely to private and semi-official organizations. These managed to distribute a further $500 million of foodstuffs over a period of two to three years, mostly in the form of gifts (League of Nations 1943b, 34). Of these amounts Poland, Czechoslovakia, Romania and Yugoslavia received $336 million and $70 million respectively under the two arrangements. The majority of the relief was credit-financed though Bulgaria had to pay cash for all deliveries, while Hungary received very little (Nötel 1974, 69–70). Additional small sums were disbursed to cover clothing needs.

The whole programme was clearly inadequate given the scale of requirements and it came to an abrupt halt long before the problems of poverty and hunger had been solved. On average every child in Central and Eastern Europe was fed for one month only by the American relief organization which accounted for some 80 per cent of the total aid disbursed. Child poverty alone therefore remained extremely acute in many areas. Even in the most advanced country of Czechoslovakia, one medical inquiry carried out in March 1921 found that 60 per cent of the children were undernourished or lacking in vitality (League of Nations 1943d, 21–3). The real extent of the problem was never properly surveyed, the whole relief exercise was hastily improvised, and there were difficulties in coordinating the relief efforts of the allied powers. Ex-enemy states, moreover, were discriminated against in that they were expected to pay cash for any deliveries received.

Relief of famine was of course only the first step in the process of reconstruction. European countries were equally in need of raw materials and capital equipment to facilitate recovery of production. In this field international action was conspicuous by its absence despite official recognition that something ought to be done. In its absence countries had to struggle as best they could to obtain imports by arranging credits with willing lenders on a private basis. The situation was not made any easier for them by the frantic scramble for raw materials in the boom of 1919–20 when commodity prices soared. Not surprisingly, therefore, many countries secured only minimal supplies. In both 1919 and 1920 Germany and Eastern Europe obtained only one-third of their 1913 level of imports by volume, whereas the Western allies slightly exceeded their peacetime levels and the neutrals fell short by 20 per cent (Orde 1990, 111).

This inability to secure essential supplies largely explains the very slow recovery in production after the war. Though some improvement was achieved from the very low levels recorded at the end of hostilities, by 1920 industrial output still barely averaged half that of 1913. Agriculture held up a little better but even here there was a serious shortfall compared with 1913 (League of Nations 1943a, 12, 1943b, 7–10).

Thus, having brought into being the successor states, the allied powers largely withdrew from the scene and left them to fend for themselves. One of the tragedies of this period was undoubtedly the failure to organize a proper reconstruction programme to assist the devastated regions of Europe. The consequences for Eastern Europe were particularly serious. Rehabilitation was much retarded, the successor states were weakened further and, in order to cope with an almost impossible situation, governments were forced into extreme measures such as trade control, inflation and currency depreciation. These may have provided temporary relief, but the longer-term consequences could be disastrous, as the experience of Hungary and Poland was later to demonstrate (see Chapter 2). As the League of Nations (1943e, 70) observed in one of its later reports, the whole economic and social fabric of some countries was allowed to rot away and 'when it was finally faced, it had ceased to be a general problem of transition and reconstruction and had become a problem of cutting the gangrene out of the most affected areas one by one'.

LAND REFORM

One issue demanding prompt attention immediately after the war was land reform. Many predominantly agrarian countries undertook land reorganization in this period. Altogether twelve European countries passed reform measures involving 60 million acres (25.28 million hectares), equivalent to 11 per cent of the total area redistributed. Of this amount more than half was allocated to former tenants, landless labourers and owners of tiny plots, about a quarter was acquired by the state, and the remainder was retained by the former landlords (Woytinsky and Woytinsky 1953, 497). All the East European countries promulgated land reform laws between 1918 and 1921.

The motives behind land reform were primarily political and social rather than economic. As Baumont (1946, 101) saw it: 'Les partages des terres étaient inévitable pour le maintien de la paix sociale.' The sheer size of the agrarian population and the political enfranchisement of the masses under the new postwar constitutions meant that the long-standing aspirations of the peasantry could no longer be ignored. The proportion of the population dependent on agriculture was as high as 75–80 per cent in the Balkan countries and well over half in Poland and Hungary. Population was also growing very much faster than in the West, so that there was a pressing need to provide land for the additional numbers (Table 1.2). At the same time the turbulent political and social conditions at the end of the war, the severe

Table 1.2   Population dependent on agriculture and population change

	% population dependent on agriculture (1921)	% increase in population (1920–39)
Czechoslovakia	40	14.0
Hungary	56	14.2
Poland	64	29.9
Romania	75–80	28.2
Yugoslavia	75–80	31.0
Bulgaria	75–80	32.3
NW and Central Europe	–	11.2

Sources: Kirk (1946, 24); Spulber (1959, 266–8)

privations suffered by the peasantry during wartime hostilities and the grow-ing threat of the Bolshevik menace following the Russian revolution of 1917, all conspired to make the danger of a peasant revolt a very real one if land hunger went unsatisfied. Expropriation of foreign estate owners – the Rus-sians, Germans, Turks, Austrians and Hungarians – in the successor states was a further powerful motive which made for change and provided a con-venient way of satisfying nationalist sentiments (Seton-Watson 1946, 78–9; Munting 1972, 4).

The main objectives of the land reforms were to sweep away many of the feudal or semi-feudal remnants of society, to break up large estates and provide the peasants with land to secure their economic independence, and to prevent the re-emergence of large estates by setting a limit to the amount of land owned by any one person. It was envisaged that such measures would create a self-sufficient and contented peasantry that would provide a stable basis for the new regimes (Mitrany 1948, 104; Seton-Watson, 1946, 80).

In practice things turned out somewhat differently. The reforms were car-ried out piecemeal and over a lengthy period of time, and in most cases they were never fully implemented to the letter of the law. Infringement of the statutes was quite common with the result that land available for redistribu-tion was not always passed on to the peasants, while the maximum permitted holdings were frequently exceeded. In Czechoslovakia, for example, the 500 hectare limit was frequently disregarded and over 40 per cent of the land originally put under sequester was eventually returned to the former owners. Thus large estates continued to flourish including some of Sudeten origin – the Schwarzenburg family retained over 50 000 hectares – despite the inten-tion to dispossess the big German landowners, while the Roman Catholic

Church managed, needless to say, to hang on to extensive territories (Wiskemann 1938, 159). The terms of the reform also varied considerably from country to country. They were least extensive in Hungary and Bulgaria. In the latter case much of the land was already in peasant ownership as a result of earlier reforms, while the Hungarian outcome reflected the reactionary response to the short-lived rule of Bela Kun. In contrast, Yugoslavia and Romania carried out extensive and radical reform with some 30 per cent of the land area being redistributed in the latter case (Mitrany 1930). In Czechoslovakia and Poland the scale of reform was more moderate (Berend and Ranki 1974a, ch. 8).

From the data in Table 1.3 it can be seen that the reforms had not everywhere produced a revolution in the distribution of landownership. Large-scale holdings still accounted for a significant share of the agricultural land in Hungary, Poland and Romania by 1930. Only in Bulgaria and Yugoslavia had large estates been virtually swept away. The second notable feature is that in terms of undertakings, small-scale enterprises (1–5 hectares) clearly predominated in all cases, even though they owned less than a third of the land area. This was one of the most unsatisfactory aspects of the reform. By concentrating on tenurial rights and equality in distribution it gave many peasants a stake in the land, but one which was often insufficient to satisfy their basic needs and which placed impediments in the way of improved efficiency. Many of the holdings consisted of scattered plots, while the holdings themselves became tinier over time as subdivision through particle inheritance took place under the growing pressure of population expansion (Ponikowski 1930, 291). The reforms did little to prevent the fragmentation of holdings, nor did they tackle the problem of consolidation of land holdings.

Table 1.3   Agricultural undertakings by hectare size, circa 1930

	% of undertakings		% of agricultural land	
	1–5 hectares	over 50 hectares	1–5 hectares	over 50 hectares
Bulgaria	57.4	0.1	29.1	1.6
Czechoslovakia	59.7	1.0	20.0	21.1
Hungary	67.7	1.7	14.6	51.3
Poland	64.2	0.5	14.8	47.3
Romania	75.0	0.7	28.1	32.2
Yugoslavia	67.8	0.3	28.0	9.7

Source: Moore (1945, 82)

Dovring (1965, 40) estimated that some 50 per cent of the land in Eastern Europe was in need of consolidation.

In other respects the reforms did little to help the peasant improve his lot. Though the state sometimes provided compensation to former estate owners for expropriation of their lands, more often than not it was the peasantry which shouldered this burden. Negotiations over compensation terms dragged on for many years and the delay only added to the uncertainty of the peasants' commitments. Thus, having eventually acquired some land the peasant often lacked the essential means to put it to good use. Many peasants were in need of tools, equipment, farm stock, technical knowledge and other resources to make a successful start but they could not afford to buy such means. Hence they rapidly ran into debt and, as Baumont (1946, 102) explained, servitude to the lord was replaced by servitude to the moneylender:

> La révolution agraire faisait litière des considérations économiques et agricoles. Après des siècles de grande propriété, le paysan était mal préparé à son rôle nouveau. Tout lui manquait: capital, outillage, éducation technique, connaissances et resources. Sans outils, sans bétail, sans bâtiments d'exploitation, il n'avait que la terre. Les crédits mis à sa disposition étaient minimes. Devenu propriétaire, il a emprunté à des taux dont l'exagération s'expliquait par la pénurie de capitaux et par les risques que couraient les prêteurs. De la servitude du locataire, il est tombé dans la servitude du débiteur auprès d'usuriers locaux.

Reform did not therefore produce a fully employed, self-sufficient, landowning peasantry. Except in Bulgaria, landless workers still constituted a significant proportion of the gainfully occupied population – one-third or more in Hungary and around 15 per cent in Czechoslovakia and Poland (Moore 1945, 86–7; Kérek 1940, 477). Under-employment of the rural population was extensive, especially in the Balkans, where it accounted for 50 per cent or more of the workforce in 1930 (Jelavich 1983, 240). In many cases farm holdings were too small to ensure self-sufficiency. Of the total peasant population of Eastern Europe about one-quarter did not produce enough to satisfy basic household needs, with the most acute deficiences in southern and eastern Poland, Transylvania and Ruthenia (Warriner 1964, 87–8). The immediate impact of the reforms, moreover, was not encouraging since reorganization and fragmentation of holdings reduced the marketable surpluses of agrarian products. As we shall see in later chapters, the agrarian issue and peasant poverty remained a problem throughout the interwar years and beyond.

A FRESH START

By the beginning of the 1920s the prospects for the new republics were far from bright. Though some recovery had taken place from the very low levels of output recorded at the close of the war, there was still some way to go before peacetime rates of activity were regained. Reconstruction had barely begun in the sense of making good war losses, and the process was obviously set back by the curtailment of relief aid and the downturn of the business cycle in Western countries, especially Britain, the United States and Sweden, in 1920–21. The task of integrating the new territorial groupings and of reconciling the conflicting interests within them would also take some time to complete even under the most favourable conditions. But these were clearly what were lacking. The new states were faced with a host of internal problems at a time when the international climate had turned sour. Accordingly, drastic action was required to ensure their very survival.

2. Inflation, reconstruction and stabilization

It is not easy to generalize about the economic performance of Europe in the decade of the 1920s partly because of the unreliability of the data for this period, and partly because there were wide disparities between regions and countries and also between the first and second halves of the decade. Much of the first part of the period was devoted to reconstruction and recovery from the war and the immediate postwar slump and it was not until 1924–25 that the prospects for general sustained expansion appeared more promising (Davis 1924, 242). Lewis (1949, 34) describes the year 1925 as a cheerful one: 'The dark days of postwar dislocation seemed to have been left behind, and the prospects seemed good.' The political situation was by that time much better and a large part of the wartime physical destruction in Europe had been made good. The level of economic activity in many European countries had reached or surpassed the former peacetime levels. The fall in commodity prices had been reversed and primary producers were beginning to feel the benefits of increased industrial activity and the recovery in world trade which had already exceeded prewar levels. Some of the worst inflations had run their course and Britain's return to the gold standard in April 1925 gave a boost to currency stabilization more generally. The improved climate was also favourable to a revival of foreign lending. The spirit of anxiety, pessimism and even despair which had prevailed in the post-armistice years at last gave way to restrained confidence and determination (Davis 1925, 61).

THE SCOPE OF EUROPEAN RECOVERY

What is particularly striking in the postwar recovery period is how Europe lagged behind the rest of the world. Estimates based on the League of Nation's data suggest that by 1925 world indices of manufacturing and commodity production (food and raw materials) were some 20 per cent above prewar levels whereas for Europe as a whole they were barely back to parity (Svennilson 1954, 204–5; Loveday 1931, 7; Woytinsky and Woytinsky 1953, 1002). A similar pattern can be observed in the trade statistics. Most regions of the world surpassed their prewar trade volumes whereas Europe was some

10 per cent down on 1913. Thus the effect of the war and its aftermath was to shift the balance of economic power away from the European continent.

Within Europe itself there was also a marked difference between Central and Eastern Europe and the West. Most of the countries in the former region, including Germany, failed to attain their prewar levels of activity. This was especially the case in industrial production as can be seen from the data in Table 2.1. By 1925 industrial production in the region was some 13 per cent below that of 1913 whereas the western allies and the neutral countries recorded gains of a similar magnitude. In the eastern sector Czechoslovakia stands out as an exception with an increase of manufacturing activity more than a third greater than the prewar level.

*Table 2.1　Industrial production and mining in Europe, 1913–25
(1913=100)*

	1920	1921	1922	1923	1924	1925
Western allies*	70.3	60.2	85.1	94.6	112.2	114.9
Neutrals[†]	98.7[≠]	87.3	92.4	98.7	105.1	111.4
Central & Eastern Europe[‡]	57.6	69.5	76.0	58.6	77.2	87.0
Total continental Europe	66.7	70.2	81.0	75.0	91.7	98.8

* Includes Portugal
† Denmark, Netherlands, Norway, Spain, Sweden and Switzerland.
‡ Germany, Czechoslovakia, Austria, Bulgaria, Estonia, Finland, Greece, Hungary, Latvia, Poland, Romania and Yugoslavia.
≠ Excludes Netherlands and Norway

Source:　League of Nations (1943b, 9).

The discrepancy between the two regions was less marked in the case of agriculture, but in trade volume Eastern Europe fell short of the prewar level by one-quarter or more. Though detailed and reliable national income statistics are not available for this period, the above evidence, taken in conjunction with the population increases, implies that real per capita income probably deteriorated through the decade following the outbreak of war, despite recovery from the low levels recorded in the immediate postwar years.

The lagging performance of Europe is not difficult to explain. Apart from making good the ravages of war, the economic and political conditions in Europe were anything but conducive to rapid progress in the post-armistice years. Scarcely a year went by without some event or series of events hampering progress. Strikes, political upheavals and border hostilities abounded throughout the continent in the period 1919–22. In 1920–21 most of the Anglo-Saxon countries experienced a sharp contraction in economic activity which cut short the recovery, and for some it spelt the beginning of an intermittent policy of deflation in preparation for a return to the gold standard. At the same time inflationary pressures and currency disorders were building up in many continental countries, culminating in the violent hyperinflations in Germany, Austria, Poland, Hungary and Russia. Early in 1923, at the height of the German inflation, France and Belgium occupied the Ruhr as a consequence of a shortfall in reparation deliveries, which paralysed the industrial region to no one's benefit. Then in 1924 Germany and Poland experienced partial stabilization crises, to be followed by a serious weakening of the French and Belgian currencies in the following year.

Currency disorders and inflation were widespread throughout Europe in these years and were easily the most spectacular events. For some seven years the European exchanges 'danced and jumped with spasmodic and tireless energy' (Loveday 1931, 31). Currency instability was one of the main factors impeding general recovery in Europe, even though some countries gained initially from depreciated currencies and the inflationary financing of investment. Ultimately the adverse consequences probably outweighed the temporary benefits (see below). Some countries allowed inflation to run completely out of control, resulting in a collapse of their currencies, which eventually did more harm than good to their economies and left them in a weaker state than before. More generally, the great uncertainty caused by extremely volatile exchange rates undoubtedly hindered the recovery in European trade and was one reason why most countries were anxious to return to some form of the gold standard or fixed exchange rate system as and when they could. Much time and energy was spent in guessing the movements of exchange rates and in speculative currency deals rather than in real trade transactions (Aliber 1962). If some countries improved their competitive position for a time through currency depreciation there were probably few lasting benefits. The artificial stimulus which it provided often led to the creation of inefficient undertakings which later collapsed or had to be supported by the state once stabilization of the currency was undertaken.

RECONSTRUCTION PROBLEMS OF EASTERN EUROPE

The reconstruction of Western Europe pales into insignificance compared with the problems confronting Central and Eastern Europe. Virtually all the countries of the region were faced with a whole series of almost insuperable problems and with resources very much inferior to those of the West European powers. The list of difficulties is almost endless: physical devastation and resource losses; territorial changes giving rise to integration problems; financial chaos including unbalanced budgets, inflation and currency instability; balance of payments disequilibrium; unemployment and rapidly rising populations; problems arising from agrarian reform; political instability and weak administrative systems; and inefficient tax structures. All these and more at a time when political and social conditions were highly unstable due to poverty and starvation, ethnic conflicts, continued border disputes and inexperienced democratic governments.

Nor did the postwar climate improve matters. Indeed, events conspired to compound many of the problems. The postwar territorial adjustments, as noted in Chapter 1, simply served to complicate the task of reconstruction since the former large internal market of the Austro-Hungarian Empire disappeared and new economic links and trading relationships had to be forged by the successor states. Political and economic unification of the component parts of the new states was a huge task in itself quite apart from the need to repair war damage and replace losses. Adjustment to these new conditions would obviously take time but that was something that these countries did not have on their side as Berend and Ranki (1969, 71) explain:

> Even in normal conditions, a considerable period of time, in fact an entire historical era, would have been required to complete the adjustment to new conditions, the integration into a unified economic whole, the opening up of new development possibilities and the attainment of a steady and sustained rate of economic growth. But history did not allow the problem to be presented in this fashion. The needs of the new order became apparent at a moment when the problems of transition from a war to a peace economy were being added to the already difficult problems faced by an economy crippled by war, and all clamouring for immediate attention. The simultaneous appearance on the scene of all these problems brought about complete economic chaos, almost inextricable confusion, and a state of utter hopelessness.

The new states, Czechoslovakia, Poland and Yugoslavia, but also Romania due to its substantial aggrandizement, faced the most difficult task in terms of economic unification, quite apart from the social and political issues of assimilation. Poland provides an excellent example of the problems involved in integrating diverse economic systems. Landau (1992, 144–55) claims that the economic unification of the territories incorporated into the new Poland was more complex and took longer than political assimilation. Each of the former occupied zones had different economic legislation, different legal, fiscal, monetary and currency systems, different customs regulations, tax structures and railway systems, as well as contrasting commercial laws and practices relating to the establishment and operation of business undertakings. The wide variety of practices in use is readily illustrated by the railways where it was difficult to keep things moving throughout the country because there were 66 types of rails in use, 165 kinds of locomotives and 32 different passenger vehicles.

The task of unification in Poland was complicated, moreover, by the fact that the level of development and the extent of war damage varied considerably from region to region so that separatist economic tendencies emerged in the most favoured provinces. In many cases therefore it was several years before integration could be fully implemented. Fiscal unification, for example, took three to four years to accomplish and even then it was not fully comprehensive, while in the case of currency reform the Polish mark only became the official medium of exchange throughout Poland in November 1923 when it was finally applied to Upper Silesia. Thus it was not until 1924 that economic unification was achieved over a fairly wide area, including transportation, legal and monetary systems, and in the development of uniform markets in capital, labour and internal trade and price levels. Even then many regional differences remained but the main task of economic integration was nearing completion.

Nor could Eastern Europe expect much help from external sources. Relief assistance from the West was limited in amount and duration and was mainly confined to alleviating famine. When assistance dried up the import of capital into continental Europe (other than intergovernmental loans) was relatively small and most of it tended to go to Western and Northern Europe. Thus between 1919 and 1923 bond issues by Central and East European countries amounted to $210 million compared with $575 million for Western and Northern Europe (League of Nations 1943b, 29). Unsettled political and economic conditions meant investors were naturally reluctant to grant long-term loans to these countries and increasing nationalism and policies of nostrification did not help matters either (see below). In the absence of long-term financing they had to rely on short-term credits when and where they could obtain them. But the flow of these was very erratic, they were usually expensive in terms of the rates of interest charged, and they did nothing of course to solve the long-term capital shortage (Hertz 1947, 163–5).

Given the unstable and far from promising conditions in Eastern Europe it is scarcely surprising that international lending on private account was very limited. What was really required at the time was some international cooperative action on the part of the creditor nations to provide impoverished countries with access to supplies of capital at reasonable cost. Instead, the major creditor nations, the United States and Great Britain, supplied loans primarily to reliable borrowers who for the most part could look after themselves. The League of Nations might also have provided a vehicle for such assistance, but unfortunately its resources were very limited partly because of the lack of American backing. Thus apart from one-off loans to those countries where the worst had already happened – for example Austria in 1922, Hungary in

1924 and Bulgaria and Estonia in 1926 – the League rendered very little in the way of aid to the stricken countries of Europe (League of Nations 1926; 1928; 1930a; 1930b; 1945c).

Organized international lending on an adequate scale would certainly have eased the capital shortage of the region and might well have obviated some of the subsequent problems with regard to borrowing of the later 1920s. Capital imports would have facilitated the task of reconstruction and recovery and by so doing could have helped to avoid some of the worst financial and currency disorders. It was not until after 1924, when economic and political conditions became more stable throughout Europe, that the flow of private lending increased markedly. But by that time the damage had been done with the result that the international lending of the latter half of the decade became a blessing in disguise (see Chapter 3).

A further factor complicating the situation was that, at a time when the pressure on land resources was increasing faster than ever, the traditional safety-valve of emigration was fast closing up. In most East European countries population was rising much faster than in the West: in Hungary and the Balkans for example the rate was three times or more that of the UK. After the war overseas emigration from Europe was very much reduced largely due to the more restrictive policy imposed by the United States on new entrants to that country. Much of the reduction in overseas emigration to the New World was in fact borne by Eastern Europe whence large numbers had flowed in the later nineteenth century. Between 1920 and 1924 the annual gross emigration from South-East Europe to non-European countries was but a mere 53 000 compared with 178 000 a year in the period 1906–10 (Royal Institute of International Affairs 1940, 76–9; Kirk 1946, 83–8, 279). The collapse of emigration therefore put further pressure on the already densely populated farm lands which was one reason why the demand for land reform was so strong in the postwar period.

Yet land reform itself could not solve the fundamental problems of the region. Initially it probably made things worse in so far as it led to a fragmentation of holdings and an increase in small-scale farms in place of larger capitalist farms catering for the market both at home and abroad. Moreover, the continued presence of strip farming in some countries coupled with the peasants' lack of equipment, resources and technical knowledge was scarcely conducive to efficiency improvements. The overall effect of land reform is difficult to estimate precisely since the extent of it varied considerably from country to country, while the changes themselves took many years to complete. Initially however it probably had a perverse effect on production and yields by reducing the scope for mechanization and other methods of improving efficiency, and by the general disorganization arising from the reorganization of holdings (Woytinsky and Woytinsky 1953, 498; League of Nations

1943a, 49). Certainly where reform contributed to a further fragmentation of holdings and an extension of strip farming, as in the case of Romania and Bulgaria, yield levels tended to decline (Roberts 1951, 62). The problem of dwarf holdings became worse over time as particle inheritance led to further fragmentation with the result that 'A holding of a few acres may consist of as many as forty small strips, separated from each other by several miles. Large areas of cultivated land were wasted in the form of paths enabling owners to walk from one strip to another. The strips are incapable of efficient production' (Seton-Watson 1946, 81). Not of course that land reform was designed with the express intention of boosting the efficiency of agriculture since, as noted earlier, it was motivated largely by political and social necessity.

The slow recovery of agriculture after the war cannot however be attributed solely to the impact of land reform. Undoubtedly the chief factor initially was the severe deterioration in the whole productive apparatus as a consequence of wartime devastation and loss of livestock and equipment, together with the upheaval caused by the reorganization of boundaries. Hungary, for example, lost much of her livestock and the territories which she ceded under the Treaty of Trianon were among the best for cattle grazing (Morgan 1933, 212–5). Farmers were also desperately short of capital and credit facilities to undertake the reconstruction of their holdings, while the break in primary product prices at the beginning of the decade exacerbated the problem by squeezing profits. An additional burden was the increase in taxation of the agrarian sector to help finance industrialization. In the face of all these problems it is not surprising that agricultural output still remained below the prewar level by the middle of the decade.

It was recognized of course that the recovery of agriculture and an improvement in its efficiency could never provide the solution to the main problem, namely increasing pressure on resources and the widespread underemployment of manpower on the land. The obvious long-term solution inevitably entailed faster industrial development but the prospects of that taking place were anything but good in the uncertain conditions prevailing at the time. Shortages of plant, equipment, raw materials and capital were widespread, and the new states had little means with which to pay for imports of these items. Financial disorders including budgetary deficits and currency depreciation, along with political instability, did not hold out much hope of obtaining assistance from abroad.

Several countries had also lost large parts of their industrial interests, either through wartime destruction or pillage or via the terms of the peace treaty settlements. Hungary and Austria, for example, were forced to give up substantial industrial assets as a result of the treaty provisions. The component parts of the former Austro-Hungarian Empire were deprived of their large internal market, while Poland lost her eastern market in Russia as a result of the new socialist regime (Zweig 1944, 89). The disorganization of infrastructures, especially transport, due to wartime destruction and boundary changes; and the turbulent economic conditions prevailing in the early post-war years, together with the poverty of the mass of the people, were scarcely conducive to rapid industrial advance. Furthermore, the governments of the new regimes were not in a position to provide much assistance initially because of their precarious budgetary positions, inefficient tax systems and the large burden of public debts, both internal and external. Most of the countries were saddled with some external debt, either reparations as in the case of Hungary and Bulgaria, or the former debts of the Ottoman and Austro-Hungarian Empires.

INDUSTRIAL STRATEGIES

In the circumstances abnormal expedients had to be employed to foster reconstruction and industrialization. It was patently clear to most of the statesmen of the new republics that economic modernization was imperative and that this meant giving priority to industry rather than to agriculture. Yet though there was a conscious policy designed to favour industrial develop-ment which was partly driven by the force of nationalism, that policy lacked coherence and rationality with the result that the measures applied were sometimes contradictory in terms of the chief objective. The main policies adopted in this period may be classified as follows: protection and trade regulation; state assistance in various forms; increasing state intervention, including the confiscation of alien property; and the use of inflation and currency depreciation as an instrument of recovery.

All countries used trade regulation extensively both for revenue purposes and as a protective device. In the chaotic conditions following hostilities many of the wartime regulatory measures, including prohibition of imports and exports, were retained. Because of the severe shortage of raw materials and foodstuffs governments were reluctant to abandon export controls, apart from which they were often an important source of revenue. In the fiscal year 1920–21 Bulgaria's receipts from export duties were actually greater than those derived from imports (Condliffe 1941, 179). The need for revenue together with currency fluctuations and the shortage of foreign exchange also meant that it would be unwise to dispense with import controls (League of Nations 1942a, 110). Hence it was not until well into the 1920s that many of the wartime emergency measures were relaxed.

This transition period formed the prelude to the introduction of new tariffs which were much higher and far more extensive than those prevailing before the war (Montias 1966, 47–8). One of the most severe was the Bulgarian tariff where rates of duty were increased by between 100 and 300 per cent over those prevailing before 1914 and highly protective tariffs were imposed on every branch of activity in which Bulgaria had an interest (Berend and Ranki 1974a, 201). The new Hungarian tariff of 1924–25 introduced stiff protection for industrial goods covering over 2000 items, with duties on imports very much higher than the equivalents under the former monarchy. It also included heavy duties on some products used by farmers, for example 200 per cent levied on nails, hoes and agricultural machinery, the proceeds of which were used to subsidize industry (Janos 1982, 219–20; Hanak 1992, 176). Romanian tariff policy also tended to favour industry at the expense of agriculture which faced high import duties on machinery and implements (Roucek 1932, 311). Similarly, the new Czech tariff structure when it was completed in 1925–26 was almost double the old Austro-Hungarian and represented 36.4 per cent of the total value of imports.

Apart from Poland, all the successor states had much higher tariffs than before the war, though, contrary to popular impression, the 1920s were not generally years of increasing tariff protection (Bairoch 1993, 4–5; League of Nations 1927). Clearly therefore the new states were using tariff measures to foster their industrial development, though it is very difficult to determine just how effective they were given the many conflicting influences at work during this period. Certainly there is much evidence to suggest that the number of industrial concerns expanded quite rapidly in the early 1920s throughout the region (Mitrany 1936, 195), but, as we shall see later, much of this growth may have been induced by the inflationary climate of these years. On the other hand, forced industrialization through tariff protection has been criticized on the grounds that it led to inefficient enterprises, that it benefited a few favoured individuals rather than the mass of the population and that rural peasants were crippled because they bore the burden through higher taxes and higher prices (Logio 1932, 180–81; 1936, 132; Hertz 1947, 102–3).

Similar criticisms could be applied to the state's own activities including the assistance given to industry in various forms. State intervention increased generally in this period, both in terms of direct ownership and regulation. In some countries state control of enterprises was quite extensive, as in Poland where 10 per cent of the value of Polish property was in public ownership by the early 1920s, and this share increased slowly during the rest of the decade. The extension of state control was not motivated solely by the demands of reconstruction. The need to provide employment, to develop armament production, and for purposes of increasing budgetary revenues as in the case of state monoplies, were also important considerations (Roszkowski 1989, 124–6).

Nationalism was also another important driving force behind the takeover of foreign assets in the quest to reduce dependence on foreign interests. As Pasvolsky (1928, 75) pointed out:

The notion that political independence was incompatible with economic dependence on foreign countries took deep root in the new Danubian countries. It acted as a powerful stimulus to industrial development in the primarily agricultural countries of the Danubian group, and found its principal expression in the commercial policies of these countries.

The confiscation and nationalization of alien properties under the policy of 'nostrification' was particularly prominent in Yugoslavia and Romania, and to a lesser extent in Czechoslovakia where the sequestration of assets belonging to Austrian, Hungarian and German capitalists was carried out in the case of the banks and many industrial establishments. Nationalistic policies were probably at their most extreme in Romania where a virtual ban was imposed on foreign capital which was not lifted until 1929 (Roucek 1932, 314–5; Turnock 1974, 125).

Industry was also favoured with many privileges and incentives, including exemption from taxes, cheap factory sites, subsidized railway rates, maximum fuel prices, exemption from customs duties on imported raw materials and equipment, and specific subsidies to encourage the development of certain sectors, for example armament production. In so far as state budgets would allow, infrastructure facilities and educational provision were improved, albeit rather slowly.

Though one of the main objectives of all these measures was that of encouraging industrialization and greater self-sufficiency, the new states did not have any coherent and consistent plans for restructuring their economies. Policy measures tended to be rather *ad hoc* and ill-coordinated and often they were contradictory. For example, foreign capital was shunned despite the need to boost investment and capital accumulation, and rural interests were heavily taxed, which inevitably restricted the development of the domestic market for industrial goods. Romania provides a prime example of the way in which the new mercantilist doctrines were used to foster industrialization at the expense of agriculture which left that sector short of machinery and equipment, cheap credit, livestock and technical facilities. Tariff barriers were raised to very high levels which pushed up the price of industrial products used by farmers, and the price of agrarian products was kept low by price control, while the peasants bore the main burden of taxation (Madgearu 1930, vi; Hertz 1947, 102–3).

The lack of coherence in policy can be attributed in part to inexperienced bureaucracies, despite their large numbers, and partly to the bribery, corruption and dishonesty prevalent in official, political and business circles. Such practices were probably most rife in the Balkan countries, especially in Romania where hordes of politicians and officials waxed fat on the Treasury, as did the business intimates and friends of the Bratianus brothers (leaders of the Liberal Party) who dispensed largesse liberally to their supporters.

According to Logio (1932, 128) the state administration was 'annexed by the party bosses and the public budget has been confiscated for the benefit of the clients of these parties'.

INFLATION AS AN AID TO RECONSTRUCTION

Given the limitations of public policy in the reconstruction period and the obvious difficulties under which governments laboured, it was only to be expected that policymakers would take advantage of short-term expedients as a solution to reconstruction and industrialization. Inflation and currency depreciation were the obvious candidates for such purposes since they tended, at least initially, to stimulate investment and exports, while at the same time allowing hard-pressed governments to draw on resources in a relatively painless way. However once they ran out of control they did more harm than good, as many countries found to their cost in the ensuing stabilization period.

All the countries of Eastern Europe, along with much of the rest of Europe, experienced varying degrees of inflation in the postwar years, and in the case of Hungary and Poland hyperinflation eventually took hold, leading to the complete collapse of their currencies. A wide variety of mechanisms contributed to the widespread inflationary phenomenon in Europe during this period. The most important single factor was that of excess demand which was usually associated with the large budgetary deficits caused by the methods used to finance the war – short-term borrowing rather than taxation and funded debt – and the reconstruction needs arising therefrom. In all severe inflations therefore the crucial component was the increase in the nominal money supply which far outstripped the increase in the availability of goods. Theoretically inflation could have been stopped at any time by resolute policies to check the growth in money supply. But in the difficult circumstances of the postwar period, printing money became a convenient way of providing governments with real resources at a time when they lacked the strength or the will to impose adequate taxation systems to provide for their revenue needs. Issuing money was an easy way out since it provided revenue by a special kind of tax on real money balances. The tax base was equivalent to the volume of real cash balances in the hands of the public, while the tax rate was determined by the rate of depreciation in the value of money which in turn was synonymous with the rate at which prices rose. In other words, the revenue collected in real terms was the product of the rate of rise in prices (the tax rate) and real cash balances (the tax base). While politically more acceptable than taxation and easier to administer, the effectiveness tended to diminish over time and hence ever larger doses of money growth and inflation were required to keep the process going. Eventually, of course, when pushed to the limits, the state's ability to generate real revenue diminished sharply as the costs of collection rose and the value of money became almost worthless (Cagan 1956, 77–90; Horsman 1988, 234; Jacobs 1977, 294–8; Brown 1988, 122).

It is doubtful whether East European countries deliberately fostered inflation, at least initially, as a conscious economic policy for the purposes of avoiding social collapse or promoting economic reconstruction. But as Ranki (1983c, 479) notes, governments did eventually recognize that it could be utilized as an instrument of recovery and a source of government revenue provided it was not allowed to get completely out of control. The burden of course fell on those least able to protect themselves from the inflation tax (that is the price level), namely creditors, savers, fixed income recipients, and holders of cash and bonds.

While inflation and associated currency depreciation had obvious drawbacks which became all too apparent in the course of time (see below), they did for a while provide a boost to activity and employment which meant that these countries avoided the sharp postwar contraction in economic activity which occurred in the Anglo-Saxon countries in 1920–21 as a result of the imposition of severe fiscal and monetary retrenchment to contain inflation. The stimulus was most evident in industry which benefited from the boost to exports through currency depreciation, the improvement in real input costs due to wages lagging behind final product prices (a fall in real wages), and cheap loans that could be paid off in worthless money. Furthermore, the fall in the value of money encouraged a flight into fixed assets such as capital equipment and buildings.

Most countries, by all accounts, appear to have gained some benefits from the inflationary process. Physical reconstruction proceeded rapidly in Poland in the early 1920s and was almost complete by the middle of the decade. Industrial employment rose by 135 per cent to 82 per cent of the 1913 level, and unemployment had been virtually eliminated by the time hyperinflation set in during the latter half of 1923. Currency depreciation helped Polish industry to re-establish itself in the domestic market and also to exploit the markets of more stable currencies. The inflation tax was an important source of government income, accounting for two-thirds of budgetary revenues in the period 1918–23. A large part of the proceeds was redistributed by the state mainly to business in the form of subsidies and credits many of which became more or less outright gifts because of the rapid decline in the value of money. The main beneficiaries were businesses and the propertied classes who gained at the expense of the rest of the population (Zweig 1944, 32; Landau 1983, 514–8).

A similar process was evident in Hungary where inflation also occurred on a mammoth scale. Virtually every industry apart from clothing recorded an expansion in capacity and many new enterprises were founded (Pasvolsky 1928, 159–60, 350–52). The sharp decline in real wages, to less than half the prewar level at the height of the inflation, stimulated industrial activity and employment (Ranki 1983b, 527; Berend and Ranki 1974b, 103). The steel, metal and coal industries in particular expanded rapidly and both employment and output in manufacturing rose by about one-third. Even so, at the peak of the inflation total industrial production was still only about 75 per cent of the prewar equivalent (Berend and Ranki 1974a, 199).

Though inflation was less severe in Czechoslovakia and the Balkan countries, nevertheless they all seemed to have derived some gain from it. Industrial investment and exports were stimulated and 'new companies shot out of the ground like mushrooms in these favourable conditions of low labour costs, high prices, and insatiable consumer demand' (Teichova 1983, 556). Between 1918 and 1922 there was feverish enterprise creation in Yugoslavia with more than 500 new factories established and a 38 per cent increase in manpower (Berend and Ranki 1974a, 199). Bulgaria recorded a dramatic jump of 91 per cent in industrial production between 1919 and 1923 so that by the latter year it was over 50 per cent greater than in 1911, though arable farming still remained weak in comparison with former peacetime levels of production (Berov 1983, 491–5). Even in Czechoslovakia, where inflation was brought under control at a fairly early date, investment and industry generally were stimulated for a time so that by 1921 industrial output was back to the prewar level (Berend and Ranki 1974a, 199).

Overall, therefore, the inflation boom, though it varied in timing and extent, does appear to have stimulated industrial activity for a time. Only in Czechoslovakia and Bulgaria, however, did the level of output match or exceed that of prewar. In most other cases industrial output fell short of the prewar equivalent (averaging 75 per cent) even at the peak of inflation. Moreover, in broader perspective the benefits were more apparent than real. While inflation undoubtedly gave an artificial boost to the East European economies, as was true elsewhere, for example in Austria and Germany, once it got out of hand it probably did more harm than good. It may have given the illusion that postwar reconstruction and recovery were taking place, but in the longer term there were few real and lasting gains. In any case, when stabilization was finally effected there was usually a sharp check to economic activity and employment as is normally the case in such circumstances (Gordon 1982). The post-inflation depression was particularly severe in Poland and Hungary with falls of up to 20 per cent in industrial production. Thus many of the gains were lost in the stabilization period so that by the mid-1920s industrial activity in the region as a whole was below that of prewar, in some cases by a substantial margin. The League of Nation's data on manufacturing suggest that Poland fell short by 37 per cent, Hungary by 23 per cent and

Romania by 8 per cent. Trade volumes too remained well below the previous peacetime levels, though the output of primary commodities made a better showing. Only Czechoslovakia, which had inherited the majority of the industrial activities of Austria–Hungary and had been the first to undertake financial and currency reform, achieved real and lasting recovery, with a rise in manufacturing production of more than a third compared with 1913 (League of Nations 1945b, 134–7; Loveday 1931, 30).

Inflation also gave rise to serious resource misallocations since it led to the haphazard creation of enterprises many of which were inefficient, and a flight of savings into physical assets in an effort to maintain real values. Had there been some conscious attempt to direct resources and investment into constructive endeavours, the final outcome might have been more favourable from the point of view of subsequent requirements. But as Einzig (1935, 77– 8) pointed out: 'In the almost complete absence of economic planning, the beneficial effects of unorthodox finance were reduced to a minimum, and its destructive effects were increased to a maximum.' Some of the inflation-inspired enterprises collapsed like a pack of cards once the artificial conditions were removed, leaving a trail of abandoned assets the quality of which left much to be desired (Kavka 1960, 115). Others had to be propped up by state protection once stabilization was imposed (Einzig 1935, 77). The suboptimal nature of many of the investments was an inevitable outcome of the feverish scramble for assets in the inflationary conditions of the time. The real gains from inflation became gradually weaker and eventually negative as resources and savings were diverted from productive capital assets into speculative activities as wealthholders attempted to protect themselves from the ravages of inflation. This involved not only a flight into tangible assets and commodities but also a move into gold and more stable foreign currencies, together with speculation in company shares which were issued in ever larger quantities during the inflationary boom (Berend and Ranki 1974a, 198).

Inflation also had an adverse impact on income distribution and the level of savings. The distribution of income and wealth became less equitable since it was businessmen, landowners, debtors and speculators who gained at the expense of the rest of society. The losers were wage and salary earners, those on fixed incomes, small savers and the lower middle classes generally. Real wages and salaries lagged well behind prewar levels and deteriorated steadily during the course of inflation. In Poland, for example, real wages fell to about half their prewar level in 1922–23, though even this was an improvement compared with the 30 per cent recorded in 1919. Hungarian workers suffered a similar loss, while in Czechoslovakia real wages were only about one-third of the prewar level by 1920. Salary earners also experienced losses of similar magnitude with the added disadvantage that their employment opportunities were less buoyant than those for wage earners. For the peasant community the results were mixed. Inflation wiped out much of the farm indebtedness, but it also destroyed rural savings, while the terms of trade of the agrarian sector deteriorated during inflation. Furthermore, much of the inflationary tax burden was borne by the poorer sections of the community including of course the peasantry. Not surprisingly therefore the inflationary episode gave rise to much social unrest especially in urban areas. Poland, for instance, was subject to waves of revolutionary activity in the latter half of 1923 when inflation was at its height (Landau 1983, 5, 18–19; Berov 1983, 485; Teichova 1983, 535).

Perhaps even more serious from a longer-term point of view was the way inflation affected savings propensities. Inflation effectively wiped out the savings of those unfortunate enough to hold their money in liquid form, either in savings accounts, bonds or other forms of investment which did not maintain their real value. The grim experience of this period inevitably reduced the saving propensity of many of the victims of inflation in the post-stabilization years with the result that there was a shortage of savings for investment. This in turn raised the cost of capital since borrowing and loan rates were well above international levels in the later 1920s, which meant that the rates of return on capital investments had to be that much higher to make them attractive.

Overall, therefore, inflation brought only temporary relief to the hard-pressed countries of the region. It could never solve their fundamental problems of low accumulation and low levels of efficiency. Added to which, the inflationary stimulus had serious negative consequences in its later stages. The real crunch of course came when stabilization policies were implemented since these led to sharp contractions in activity and employment. The episode also conditioned the policy stance to the great depression of the early 1930s since renewed budgetary and trade balance problems gave rise to fears that inflationary pressures might emerge once again. Meanwhile there was an interlude of prosperity in the later 1920s, though even this was based on insecure foundations (see Chapter 3). Before that could take place, however, monetary and financial regimes had to be stabilized and it is to these issues we now turn.

STABILIZATION OF CURRENCIES

Few countries emerged from the war with their monetary and currency systems unscathed. Nearly all currencies, except the dollar, lost their stability and depreciated once the tie with gold was broken or the artificial pegging practised by some countries during wartime was abandoned. By the end of 1920 most European currencies were well below their prewar par values, and in the case of all Central and East European countries these were 25 per cent or less of the former parities (League of Nations 1920, ix; 1943b, 42). Such falls were only to be expected given the very weak state of their economies, the large budgetary deficits and the inflationary pressures arising from the methods used to finance the war (Davis 1920, 10–13).

Restoration of monetary stability was regarded as a matter of some urgency after the war since it was believed that large fluctuations in exchange rates were inimical to the recovery of trade and production. Some form of fixed exchange rate system based on gold had obvious appeal simply because the prewar gold standard was deemed at the time to have been a key factor in ensuring international stability before 1914. Few countries however could hope to achieve their original prewar parities, so that stabilization normally involved a return to a fixed exchange rate well below the prewar level. But initially even this was out of the question since economic conditions in many countries were not propitious for early stabilization, and in any case for some countries inflation and currency depreciation became a convenient way of easing the path of reconstruction.

The stabilization of European currencies was a long-drawn-out affair and there was no coordinated plan to implement stabilization as was the case after the Second World War. Each country stabilized and returned to a fixed exchange rate under a revised gold exchange standard as and when conditions were deemed suitable, which depended on the ability and willingness of the country to bring its financial affairs under control. The consequences of this haphazard process of stabilization were that many exchange rates were in disequilibrium from the start; some were overvalued, such as the pound sterling, the Italian lira and the Swedish krona, while others, notably the Belgian and French francs, were undervalued. Thus the revamped international monetary standard of the postwar period never worked smoothly and when depression hit the world economy at the turn of the decade it became a source of strain. As Yeager (1966, 290) observed, the new gold standard was little more than a facade and gold standard methods for securing balance of payments equilibrium were largely destroyed.

Because of the many competing demands on their limited resources, most East European countries had great difficulty in securing early control over their financial affairs. The stabilization process therefore took the best part of a decade, and as can be seen from Table 2.2 it was accomplished at different dates and levels during the course of the decade. Apart from Germany, Austria and Russia, all of which had to introduce new currencies following hyperinflation, these were the lowest stabilization values in Europe. The methods of achieving stabilization varied considerably depending on the extent of inflation, the degree of external assistance, the relative strengths of the countries concerned and their willingness to restore order to their financial systems.

Table 2.2   Currency stabilization in Eastern Europe

Country	Date of stabilization*	% of prewar value
Bulgaria	1924 (1928)	3.8
Czechoslovakia	1923	14.4
Hungary	1924	new currency introduced
Poland	1926 (1927)[†]	new currency introduced
Romania	1927 (1929)	3.0
Yugoslavia	1925 (1931)	9.2

* Dates of *de jure* stabilization where different from *de facto* stabilization are shown in brackets.
† Poland stabilized the gold value of her currency in 1924 but was forced to abandon it in 1925.

Source: League of Nations (1946a, 92–3).

As might be expected, Czechoslovakia, whose economy was much stronger than those of other countries in the region by virtue of the inheritance of a large part of the former monarchy's industrial base, was the first to succeed. Czechoslovakia was the only successor state to avoid the ravages of a long and severe inflation. A great deal of credit for the achievement must be attributed to Alois Rasin, the first minister of finance of Czechoslovakia, who was a strong advocate of financial prudence. He was determined to ensure that the new republic was given a sound monetary and financial system. First, monetary reform was enacted early in 1919 when a new unit of currency, the Czech crown, replaced the old currency notes of the former empire then still circulating in Czech territory. Second, Rasin reduced the amount of currency in circulation by 20 per cent and set a ceiling on the note issue to prevent excess creation of money. Third, fiscal reform was undertaken promptly so that state finances were put on a secure basis and the budget was balanced in 1920–21. This involved the imposition of new and higher taxes, especially on the increased value of property, which provided support for the monetary reform (Gruber 1924, 200; Pryor 1973, 194–5; Wiskemann 1938, 141–3; Rasin 1923).

The reforms were not met with instant success. Prices continued to rise through to 1921 and the new currency fluctuated quite sharply in the first few years. On fundamental grounds there was no valid basis for weakness in the currency. What appears to have happened is that initially the crown tended to track the movements of the German mark, in the mistaken belief that it was yet another suspect currency. Once this illusion was dispelled the crown appreciated, partly in response to a flight out of the mark but also because of the deflationary policy of 1922 which brought an end to the rise in prices. The new level of the crown was therefore maintained and in 1923 stabilization was finally completed (Gruber 1924, 183–9; Berend and Ranki 1974a, 181–2).

Hungary and Poland provide a very sharp contrast to Czechoslovakia, since both countries experienced hyperinflation which eventually led to the collapse of their currencies and the introduction of new units of account. The Polish inflation was by far the worst, with prices rising 2.5 million times as against 23 000 times in the case of Hungary, though still well short of Russian and German magnitudes. Both countries secured external assistance for purposes of stabilization. Hungary was able to carry out stabilization fairly quickly and effectively, whereas Poland made several attempts before success was achieved.

The Hungarian approach to stabilization was similar to that of Austria two years earlier in that both governments formulated a tripartite reconstruction package which comprised balancing the budget, reorganization of the central banking system and the flotation of a foreign loan. Fiscal reform was not however a prerequisite of monetary stabilization; in fact rather the reverse since the introduction of a new monetary unit became the basis for an effective fiscal policy. In the words of the League of Nations (1946a, 23), 'stabilization of the currency, while simultaneous with a plan for budget reform, preceded its accomplishment'. Much of the credit for the success of the operation however is attributable to the return of confidence as a result of the government's firm intention to bring inflation under control and the intervention of the League of Nations whose reconstruction scheme for Hungary included the raising of an international loan in 1924. The financial reforms were supervised by representatives of the League until 1926. The inflationary spiral was brought to a halt in the middle of 1924 as confidence returned and the exchange rate of the crown was stabilized by linking it to the pound sterling. The monetary reform was completed the following year with the introduction of a new unit of account, the pengö. Once the currency was stabilized fiscal equilibrium was restored in a very short space of time with only a quarter of the international loan being required for this purpose (Horsman 1988, 61–2; Yeager 1981, 52–5; Berend and Ranki 1974b, 99–110; League of Nations 1926, 37–9).

Polish stabilization was a much more complex and long-drawn-out affair. Up to 1921 little effort had been made to halt inflation since the executive machinery was too weak to impose effective fiscal control and an efficient system of tax collection. Political influence was highly fragmented among many competing factions so that administrations were short-lived and often powerless, while the new republic was still engaged in border hostilities with

Russia, Czechoslovakia, Germany and Lithuania (Zweig 1944, 35; Heilperin 1931). Henceforth several abortive attempts were made to stabilize by fiscal reform. The first two occurred between 1921 and 1923 but both failed after temporary success, largely because the fiscal effort was relaxed too soon (Jack 1927, 181–4). Another attempt was made early in 1924 by which time Poland was in the throes of hyperinflation. Following the recommendations of Hilton Young's report on Polish financial conditions (Hilton Young 1924), stringent fiscal measures were introduced, including valorization of taxes on a gold basis, which brought the hyperinflation under control and stabilized the exchange value of the new currency, the zloty, which replaced the Polish mark. Success was short-lived, however, partly because the fiscal measures were again relaxed prematurely, and partly because the parliamentary regime was too weak to carry through the drastic measures which proper financial reform required (Zweig 1944, 40–46). Other factors contributed to the renewed weakness of the currency, including a deterioration in the trade balance, poor harvests, a tariff war with Germany and the virtual absence of aid from abroad with which to bolster confidence (Mlynarski 1926, 27; League of Nations 1946a, 26; Smith 1936, 148–57). Following a further bout of inflation and exchange depreciation, though moderate by past standards, the final attempt was made in 1926–27. This time success was assured by virtue of the fact that General Pilsudski, who assumed control of Poland in May 1926 by military coup, introduced a harsh package of fiscal and financial reforms designed to bring a halt once and for all to the financial disorders of Poland. These measures soon restored confidence in the currency and the new exchange rate was formally legalized in the autumn of the following year with the help of a foreign stabilization loan (Yeager 1981, 53–4; Horsman 1988, 101–3; League of Nations 1946a, 27).

De facto stabilization of the Balkan currencies took place between 1924 and 1927 but the final legal stabilization occurred somewhat later, mostly with the aid of specific international loans. Though the fiscal and monetary problems of these countries were no less acute than elsewhere, all three managed to contain inflation and currency depreciation within manageable proportions thereby avoiding the extreme disasters which befell Hungary and Poland. The timing of the initial stabilization in each case was closely related to movements in world prices for commodities since these accounted for the bulk of their exports: cereals, timber and petroleum products in the case of Romania; cereals, eggs and tobacco in Bulgaria; and cereals, timber and animals products in Yugoslavia. There was little hope of effective stabilization in the early 1920s following the collapse of primary product prices after the postwar boom. But when prices began to firm up in subsequent years, the trade balances of these countries improved and currency depreciation was halted. *De facto* stabilization therefore became possible in the mid-1920s and *de jure* recognition was later achieved with the aid of international loans (League of Nations 1946a, 126–31; Koszul 1932).

CONCLUSION

It is difficult to do full justice to the complexity of problems which confronted the successor states in the several years following the conclusion of hostilities. Here attention has been focused primarily on the main economic issues, but one should constantly bear in mind that for all these states reconstruction was a much broader task involving political, administrative and social integration as well as economic unification. Each of the fledgling states had to fashion a political and administrative system within a parliamentary democracy which took account of the diverse nature and aspirations of the territories and peoples it had inherited. In this respect Yugoslavia, Czechoslovakia, Poland and Romania had a more complex task than Bulgaria and Hungary. Probably one of the most difficult problems was that of creating a uniform and coherent state administrative apparatus and a permanent bureaucratic machinery staffed with competent and corruption-free officials in countries whose experience in such matters was notably lacking.

Despite the tribulations of the early postwar years the process of economic and political unification was nearing completion by the middle of the 1920s, as was the task of physical reconstruction. But levels of economic activity were still some way short of the prewar standard in most cases with the main exception of Czechoslovakia. Moreover, despite various attempts to foster industrialization in the reconstruction period, the results only had a very marginal influence on the structure of economic activity. Agriculture still remained the dominant element, especially in terms of employment, in the Balkan countries, and even in Poland and Hungary it continued to loom large. The relative inefficiency and poverty of the agrarian sector meant that there was little chance of it generating a surplus of savings which could be used to finance industrial expansion. Hence in the later 1920s the region became increasingly dependent on foreign capital which was to render it even more exposed to the influence of events in the international economy as the following chapters will demonstrate.

3. Indebtedness and instability in the later 1920s

Most commentators regard the later 1920s as a period favourable to sustained economic expansion. Though not all the problems arising from the war and its aftermath had been solved by any means, by 1925 the task of European reconstruction and recovery was nearing completion and economic and political conditions were far more stable than they had been a few years earlier. This was despite the fact that Germany purposely refused to recognize her new eastern frontiers with Czechoslovakia and Poland as permanent, which signalled her intention of future revision. Nevertheless, the evacuation of the Ruhr (1923), the revised reparations settlement with Germany in 1924, the negotiated agreements regarding allied war debts, and the signing of the Locarno accord in 1925 between Great Britain, France, Germany and Italy guaranteeing the existing Franco-German frontier, did much to boost international confidence and reduce political tensions and suspicions of future war. Most of the great inflations had run their course and Britain's return to the gold standard at the prewar parity in April 1925 paved the way for the completion of currency stabilization elsewhere. Thus after 1925 currency instability and unsettled international debt issues ceased to dominate the economic landscape. Furthermore, primary commodity prices had firmed considerably after their disastrous drop following the postwar boom. Henceforward, therefore, as Loveday (1931, 47) noted: 'Real progress began to take the place of a painful struggle to regain a plateau of prosperity which had been lost...'. There were, it is true, still signs of tension and weakness in the international system, but these were all but forgotten as the world looked forward to sustained prosperity powered by the boom in the American economy.

THE WORLDWIDE BOOM

The expansion of economic activity in the later 1920s was more rapid and widespread than in the period from the beginning of the war through to 1925, and certainly more securely based than that of the early 1920s. In the four years 1925–29 world industrial production rose by over 20 per cent, which was a slightly larger absolute increase than in the decade or so to 1925. World output of primary commodities was somewhat slower, rising by over 10 per cent or 2.6 per cent a year, but even this was much better than the 1.4 per cent annual increase recorded in 1913–25. Much of the increase was attributable to raw materials, the output of which rose by 27 per cent, whereas the expansion of food production was much more modest, of the order of 6 per cent (1925–29). The volume of world trade expanded by 21 per cent, or nearly 5 per cent a year, which was relatively high by historical standards.

What is perhaps especially noteworthy is that most regions of the world shared in the prosperity and that there was a much greater degree of conformity in rates of advance than in the first half of the 1920s. Data contained in Table 3.1 relating to industrial production show a quite striking similarity in the performance of the major regions of the world in the years 1925–29. The chief exception was the USSR which registered a dramatic increase in industrial production. However, much of this merely represented a recapturing of what had been lost in the war and the early years of the new Bolshevik regime when industrial output had plummeted to a fraction of the former peacetime levels.

Table 3.1   *Indices of industrial production for selected regions 1925–29 (1925=100)*

Region	1925	1926	1927	1928	1929
Industrial Europe*	100	95.6	113.2	116.5	123.1
Agricultural Europe†	100	105.6	112.2	113.3	122.2
United States	100	106.0	105.0	110.0	123.0
Canada	100	113.8	121.5	133.8	143.0
USSR	100	143.8	168.4	205.3	256.1
Rest of world**	100	107.7	108.8	113.2	119.8
World total††	100	102.2	108.7	113.0	120.7

*   Austria, Belgium, UK, Czechoslovakia, Denmark, France, Germany, Luxemburg, Netherlands, Sweden, Switzerland and the Saar
†   Bulgaria, Estonia, Finland, Greece, Hungary, Italy, Latvia, Poland, Portugal, Romania, Spain and Yugoslavia
**   Includes ten countries in Latin America, Africa, Asia and Oceania: Argentina, Australia, Brazil, British India, Chile, Japan, Mexico, New Zealand, Peru and South Africa
††   The world indices are probably slightly on the low side since the League of Nations' estimates for the United States require some upward revision

Sources: League of Nations (1933b, 45, 49; OEEC 1960, 9)

As far as commodity production is concerned, there was again a fairly widespread advance, though in this case there was much greater diversity between regions than for industrial production, while most of the expansion was accounted for by raw materials. Europe as a whole regained some of the ground she had previously lost, while Eastern Europe tended to perform slightly better than Western and Northern Europe. Thus total primary production in Europe excluding the USSR rose by almost 18 per cent in the period 1925–29, as against a world increase of just over 10 per cent, while Eastern Europe's advance was of the order of 20 per cent (League of Nations 1933b, 17; Loveday 1931, 49).

Eastern Europe's progress in manufacturing was particularly impressive in the later 1920s, though one should bear in mind the fragile nature of the data and the fact that for many predominantly agrarian economies expansion was from a fairly low base. All six countries outstripped the European and world averages and there were substantial gains in Poland, Hungary, Bulgaria and Romania in the later 1920s (Table 3.2). By the end of the decade only Poland had failed to get back to the prewar level of output, reflecting the setbacks encountered in the reconstruction and stabilization crises of the period. At the other extreme, Bulgaria experienced an impressive rate of growth in manufacturing output which was the highest in the Danubian region (Lampe 1986, 68–9). After the reconstruction period, the whole area, according to Spulber (1966, 28–30), recorded an expansion of capital formation and a diversification of output, with notable gains in coal, iron and steel, cement, oil production, raw material extraction and food processing. Adaptation was assisted by an influx of foreign capital and the continued encouragement of industry by

Table 3.2   Indices of manufacturing output, 1913–29 (1913=100)

Country	1920/21	1925	1929	% increase 1925–9
Bulgaria	–	–	179.0	–
Czechoslovakia	69.8	136.4	171.8	26.0
Hungary	64.0	76.7	113.9	48.5
Poland	35.1	63.1	85.9	36.1
Romania	47.2	92.2	136.9	48.5
Yugoslavia	–	–	140.0	–
Europe (18 countries)	66.9	89.6	110.7	23.5
World total	93.2	120.7	137.5	13.9

Sources: League of Nations (1945b, 136–7); Berend and Ranki (1974a, 298–300)

state subsidies, tax reliefs, import controls, high tariffs and export bounties. The drive towards self-sufficiency was also accompanied by a further extension of state enterprise and the takeover of foreign assets.

The policy of state-induced industrialization and economic nationalism was not an unqualified success however. It has frequently been criticized on the grounds that it led to a squandering of scarce resources on projects of dubious quality, including arms production, building works and transportation facilities, some of which were designed for prestige purposes. This placed a correspondingly heavy financial burden on agriculture in the form of taxation so that the agrarian sector was starved of resources to improve its efficiency (Hertz 1947, 102–3). Moreover, such changes as there were did not herald a dynamic transformation of the structures of the economies in question. Rates of capital accumulation remained well below the levels achieved before the war, while industrial activities were still concentrated heavily on the development of branches such as textiles and food processing which were redolent of a bygone age. Nor did industry keep pace with the technical changes and methods of production of the modern era. Apart from Czechoslovakia, the region's industry was scarcely affected by Western developments in business organization, rationalization, new methods of production and factory layout, mechanization and mass production, and the use of new forms of energy such as electricity (Berend and Ranki 1974a, 238–40). Even where large-scale enterprise prevailed the techniques of operation and level of efficiency fell way behind those in the major Western economies. In fact, the limited nature of the domestic market and the difficulty of securing export outlets often forced large firms to take measures which were technically and organizationally outmoded. The Hungarian iron and steel and heavy engineering industries, for example, have been described as little more than 'general stores' since their plants produced many varied items in small quantities (Berend and Ranki 1974b, 134–42). The dual nature of production continued to prevail, with a large number of workshops or factories catering largely for the domestic market, alongside a few large concerns of indifferent quality, whose ability to compete in the international market was limited.

Income gains were far less robust than the expansion in production. Although the data for the period are still somewhat tenuous, it nevertheless seems certain that all countries recorded some progress in income per capita from 1924 through 1929, and that all except Poland surpassed prewar levels by at least 10–15 per cent. Progress was of course held back by rapid population growth and the slow recovery of agriculture.

AGRARIAN WEAKNESSES

Despite a more favourable price regime for agricultural commodities in the later 1920s, the agrarian sector, notwithstanding its overwhelming importance in most countries, did not play a dynamic role in the economies of Eastern Europe as it had done for a time at the turn of the century. Production, which had recovered slowly in the first half of the decade, made only modest progress subsequently, so that by 1929 prewar levels of output had been barely surpassed in some cases. Productivity (yields per hectare), on the other hand, actually stagnated or even declined compared with the prewar reference point, since lack of capital, the upheavals arising from land reorganization and the prevalence of extensive methods of production left little room for improved efficiency and modern methods of production. For the Balkan countries productivity levels of the most important crops were some 13 per cent down on prewar, and in other countries by a few per cent. In the case of livestock production, there was again only modest advance, with the Balkan countries recording the best performance (Berend 1985, 168–70, 199).

Given the high agricultural content of most East European economies and their dependence on imported supplies for industrial development, probably the first and most important step was to reform agriculture and improve its efficiency so that it could increase exports to provide much-needed foreign exchange, while at the same time generate surplus savings for use outwith the sector. Where an enlightened agricultural policy was followed, as in the Czech case, it helped to support the prosperity of industry. Here land reform was accompanied by technical and financial assistance to farmers who improved their methods of production and concentrated on the more profitable crops such as sugar-beet. Significantly, Czechoslovakia was the only country which recorded consistent yield improvements over the period 1913–29 (Berend 1985, 169). The Balkan countries also diversified their agrarian base, with a shift away from cereals towards tobacco, fruit and vegetables, animal products and forest products which had a stronger international market. But overall the performance of the main trading sector was disappointing with trade volumes falling short of peacetime levels.

Despite these changes, agriculture continued to remain the chief unsolved problem for most East European countries. The combination of peasant self-sufficiency, small holdings, overpopulation, primitive techniques, low accumulation and high indebtedness inevitably resulted in low levels of efficiency by any standards. The problem moreover defied solution in an environment basically hostile to peasant interests (for example high taxation) and in which the peasantry itself was often opposed to new techniques and mechanization (Fischer-Galati 1970, 40; Rothschild 1974, 331). Generally speaking, the structure and methods of agriculture remained remarkably static; except on some large estates, practices were based on traditional techniques and methods, with many peasant plots lacking even the most basic implements. It is quite possible that the relative backwardness of agriculture compared with Western practice actually increased in some countries during the course of the 1920s (Berend and Ranki 1974b, 126–32). Under such unpromising conditions agriculture could be of little help to industry either in terms of a capital provider or as a market for industrial goods, and whose foreign exchange-earning function was highly erratic (Aldcroft 1988, 597). In fact, as far as capital accumulation is concerned, the agrarian sector may well have acted as a drag on the rest of the economy as Moore (1945, 97) explained:

> The widespread prevalence of high indebtedness relative to assets and income indicates not only that self-capitalization in agriculture is low, but also that far from accumulating capital the peasant is frequently in the position of steadily depleting his resources and of borrowing to postpone the time of complete insolvency. In fact, whether the capital depletion takes the form of soil exhaustion and obsolescence of equipment or the form of growing indebtedness, it is clear that the process may be a spiral escaped only by capital originating outside of the agricultural organization.

Thus, despite the quantitative importance of agriculture in most of the East European countries, it made little contribution to the dynamic transformation of their economies, and in the course of time it became an increasing source of vulnerability. 'Whereas agriculture had been the prime mover of economic dynamism from the sixties to the eighties of the previous century, it became the most vulnerable point in the economy, the main constraint on the growth and the socio-economic transformation which were so crucially needed' (Berend 1985, 209).

Despite the creditable growth performance in Europe and elsewhere during the later 1920s, the foundations of prosperity remained fragile and precarious: 'a period of surface harmony and apparent economic prosperity', according to Marks (1976, 108), or in Beyen's (1951, 3) words, 'years of hope and vigour', which 'ended in despair'. There were certainly signs of underlying weaknesses within particular economies at this time, and the same could also be said more generally for the working of the international economy. These weaknesses of course became all too apparent once the basis of the prosperity was undermined with the collapse of international lending and the downturn of the American economy at the end of the decade.

Along with Latin America, Eastern Europe was probably one of the most vulnerable regions of the world at this time. Its prosperity in the latter half of the 1920s – and ultimately the means of breaking the structural bottlenecks in the longer term – was based on extremely precarious foundations. It was dependent principally on three factors: a favourable market environment for primary products, especially agricultural commodities; trade expansion and the development of new markets; and the import of foreign capital. Each of these in turn can be seen as a source of weakness.

Overcommitment to primary commodities

With the sole exception of Czechoslovakia, the dominating factor in the prosperity of Eastern Europe was the state of agriculture, and that sector in turn was the main determinant of the region's foreign trade potential (Spulber 1966, 27). Agrarian products and raw materials accounted for the bulk of exports. In the case of the Balkan countries and Hungary foodstuffs made up one-half to two-thirds of all exports, and about one-third in Poland (Drabek 1985, 470–74; Svennilson 1954, 87). Cereals and cereal products constituted the largest element, even though dependence on these items had diminished compared with before the war, especially in the Balkans, as alternative crops such as fruit and vegetables, poultry and livestock, tobacco and forest products were developed for the international market (Lampe and Jackson 1982, 368–9). If we also include raw materials, then some three-quarters or more of all exports consisted of primary commodities, whereas in the case of Czechoslovakia the share was only about one-quarter (Drabek 1985, 470–74).

This overwhelming dependence on commodity exports left the region very exposed to the vicissitudes of the international market in commodities. Commodity markets are notoriously volatile, especially in prices, since because of the relatively inelastic nature of both demand and supply, quite small changes in the latter can produce very substantial price responses. There were two main problems facing producers in the 1920s: first, the increasingly hostile market environment as importing countries sought to protect their domestic producers, more especially in agriculture; and second, the tendency for international commodity prices to weaken, resulting in a deterioration of the terms of trade for primary producing countries.

The most difficult market was that for cereals, especially wheat, as a consequence of the enormous expansion of acreage in North America, Australia and Argentina in the war and early postwar years, and the subsequent recovery of European production during the course of the 1920s. By the late 1920s, with bumper crops in Europe and Canada and the re-entry of Russia into the international wheat market, the world was awash with wheat. To make matters worse, the consumption of wheat per head in the more advanced countries (the importers) was declining as a result of dietary changes. Thus for the years 1924–29 world wheat output (excluding the USSR) rose by almost 17 per cent above the 1909–14 average, whereas world consumption was barely 11 per cent greater. Consequently, stocks in all the main producing regions were rising steadily from 1925 onwards and prices began to wilt. By the middle of 1929 total world stocks, at 28 million tons, were twice the average of the early 1920s, equivalent to more than a year's exports by all the main trading countries (Tracey 1964, 118).

Thus the international market for East European grain producers was scarcely an auspicious one. Cereal exports of the region trailed well behind prewar levels and their share of the world market declined. Whereas for the period 1909–13 net exports had averaged 8 million tons per annum, during the years 1925–29 they were only 0.61 million tons, and even in the best year no more than a quarter (2 million tons) of the previous peacetime volume. In the postwar years, 1919–25, the region had been a net importer. Several factors were responsible for this sharp reduction. First, population pressures in the exporting countries increased the amounts required for domestic consumption. Second, by the time the East European producers were in a position to return to the world market on a significant scale, that market had tightened considerably compared with before the war. Western European countries were consuming less cereals and at the same time protecting their own domestic producers, while increased competition from overseas sources undercut the less efficient East European farmers. Third, the increased production and exports of Eastern Europe in this period merely served to exacerbate the oversupply conditions in the international market (Drabek 1985, 403–6).

World markets were somewhat more favourable in newly developed areas, especially fruit and vegetables and animal products – one reason why some countries grasped the opportunity to diversify their production structures after the war. There was also a healthy demand for many of the industrial raw materials of the region, especially Romanian oil and the metal ores of Yugoslavia, the exports of which expanded very rapidly. Even so, the price structure in commodities generally was by no means wholly favourable to primary producers in these years. Despite some firming up of prices after the slump of the early 1920s, the latter half of the decade saw renewed weakness in commodity prices and a reversal of the terms of trade for primary producers. World food prices fell continuously after 1923, apart from 1927, while raw material prices peaked in 1925 and then declined more rapidly than food prices through to 1929. In 1926 tobacco prices also fell substantially, which was a severe blow to Bulgaria since over one-third of her exports now came from this source (Crampton 1987, 104).

Overall, world commodity prices fell by 15.4 per cent in 1925–29, with raw material prices experiencing a fall of 18.8 per cent and food prices 14.1 per cent (1923–29). By contrast, the price of manufactures fell by only 10.7 per cent. In other words, the terms of trade shifted against primary producers by some 5 per cent. Over the longer term from 1913 the terms of trade deterioration was more than twice as large at 11.1 per cent (Drabek 1985, 475). Of course not all producers were affected to the same extent, but there is little doubt that towards the end of the decade the prices of most commodities were coming under pressure and that market prospects were visibly deteriorating. The situation was probably most acute in the chief food products such as cereals. Ranki (1983a, 51–2) estimates that by the third quarter of 1929 world agricultural prices were some 30 per cent lower than the average for 1923–25, while over the same period stocks had risen by 75 per cent. These price changes and the resulting unfavourable shift in the terms of trade were important factors in the trade deficits of the Balkan countries and Hungary in 1928–29.

Counterfactual reasoning might tempt one to speculate that heavy reliance on primary commodity exports was a dead-end for the countries concerned, and that even without the subsequent world depression it would have spelt grief for them. Ellis (1941, 75), for example, argues that for Hungary the writing was already on the wall given the increasing self-sufficiency in its chief markets for grain coupled with the competition from American producers. Weakening markets and prices not only affected external balances adversely, but it also meant that the ability to import much-needed capital equipment and service outstanding debts was correspondingly impaired. Furthermore, the concentration on primary production resulted in few dynamic forward and backward linkages to the rest of the economy, while the agrarian sector, as noted earlier, was not a source of accumulation. Be that as it may, events were soon to intercede in a dramatic fashion so as to leave no question about just how vulnerable East European economies were to the march of external events (see Chapter 4).

Market shifts

The break-up of the Austro-Hungarian Monarchy was a serious blow to the succession states as far as trading relationships were concerned, since it meant the loss of a large free trade area on which several countries had depended heavily. For example, 80 per cent of Hungary's agricultural exports had been sold in the Czech and Austrian areas, while an equally large part of Czechoslovakia's industrial products had been marketed within the monarchy's borders (Berend and Ranki 1969, 174). Overall intra-regional trade accounted for some two-thirds to three-quarters of the total intercourse of the countries of Eastern Europe (Berend 1985, 163). The other main loss was the Russian market which had been of especial importance to Poland.

The new states were therefore forced to develop fresh markets and new trading links after the war in what was an increasingly competitive and hostile trading environment. The loss of the former internal market also meant that these countries became more trade-sensitive and more vulnerable to the vagaries of the international trade cycle as they sought new trading connections outwith its borders. Despite their proximity and historical traditions intercourse among the Danubian countries declined in relative importance, partly because the isolationist and protectionist policies prevalent after the war tended to be most severe against neighbouring states and less so against Western nations. This was no doubt an inevitable result of the national rivalry among the countries of the region, but the need to earn foreign exchange in key currencies to service debts also featured prominently. The shift away from regional trade can also be explained by the fact that most of the countries, apart from Czechoslovakia, had trading structures that were largely competitive rather than complementary. Their exports consisted mainly of agricultural products and raw materials, while import needs were for manufactures and capital equipment.

The most obvious and worthwhile strategy therefore was to cultivate trading links with the Western industrial nations. Throughout the 1920s the Danubian countries drifted further away from one another, while economic relations with Western Europe and the United States were correspondingly strengthened. By 1929 intra-regional trade had declined to about one-third of the total trade turnover of the region. In compensation, stronger trading connections were developed with most of the larger industrial nations including the United States, France, Germany, the UK and Italy. Thus Czechoslovakia's exports to the United States more than doubled in 1924–29, while Hungary and Romania found promising markets in the UK and Italy and also in some of the smaller industrial countries (Svennilson 1954, 197; Drabek 1985, 420).

The diversion of trade away from the Danubian region was not however an unmixed blessing. The market for agricultural products, and especially cereals, became more restricted in the course of time due to stagnating consumption, overseas competition and the protection tendencies in the importing countries. At the same time the ability of East European countries to compete in the market for industrial goods was somewhat limited due to the backward techniques and low levels of productivity of the domestic producers (Berend and Ranki 1974b, 99–110). Even some parts of Czech industry were finding things difficult in international markets. Several branches of Sudeten industry, especially textiles and glass, were particularly sensitive to Japanese competition from the mid-1920s onwards, while many of the luxury and more ephemeral local manufactures, such as toys, musical instruments, clocks, beads and wood artifacts, experienced a precarious existence partly because of the loss of much of the prewar tourist trade, including the absence of the Russian aristocrats (Wiskemann 1938, 163).

All things considered, Eastern Europe probably did remarkably well in compensating for the loss of its former secure market. Though Europe as a whole barely recovered her prewar volume of trade during the 1920s, Eastern Europe managed to do so by a modest margin thanks to strong growth in the latter half of the decade (Svennilson 1954, 220; Loveday 1931, 71). But the composition and structure of that trade was not without its weaknesses. Much of the trade expansion was artificially induced by policy measures such as export bounties, subsidies and tax privileges, while domestic producers were sheltered by high tariff protection. More serious still was the continued heavy reliance on primary product exports which was an increasingly vulnerable element at a time when international commodity markets were weakening. Moreover, the loss of the secure prewar market and the concomitant shift in trade direction westwards meant that Eastern Europe was more vulnerable than ever before to the international business cycle. Such exposure was also magnified by the fact that in the intervening period Eastern Europe was becoming more indebted to Western creditors.

Foreign capital and instability

In the early postwar years the flow of capital into Eastern Europe was relatively limited for obvious reasons. Much of it was designed to help with relief, immediate reconstruction and later stabilization of currencies and little found its way into productive enterprise. A substantial part was distributed through official channels and private capital was confined largely to speculative ventures. Once economic conditions were more stable the floodgates were opened to Western credits and in the later 1920s Eastern European countries borrowed heavily and often unwisely with the result that their external solvency became a matter of some concern. They were by no means unique in this respect. Many Latin American countries, some African ones, as well as the White Dominions (the latter having the highest per capita debt levels in the world), seriously overcommitted themselves and were engaged in an uphill struggle to meet their obligations on past loans (Aldcroft 1991b, 53).

The need for imported capital was not in doubt despite nationalistic protestations to the contrary. The low level of domestic accumulation, which even in the later 1920s remained well below prewar, necessitated recourse to foreign borrowing. In Hungary, for example, domestic accumulation averaged only 5–6 per cent of national income compared with 10–15 per cent before the war, and even in the peak year the proportion was still only 8 per cent (Berend 1974, 184). In the Balkan countries the shortfall was probably even worse. Thus foreign capital was clearly needed to finance the development and structural transformation of these countries. On the surface the requirements were satisfied by a stream of loans and private capital from the United States and the UK who replaced the region's former chief creditors,

France and Germany. The total amounts exceeded the prewar volume of capital on a annual basis. In most countries apart from Czechoslovakia, which for most of the time was a net creditor, foreign capital accounted for 50–70 per cent of the financing of their economies. In Hungary foreign capital was about equal to domestic accumulation, while in Poland the ratio of domestic to foreign capital was 4:6, with nearly 40 per cent of the total capital of joint-stock companies being of foreign origin (Wellisz 1938, 148; Rose 1939, 194). Foreign participation was even higher in Bulgaria and Yugoslavia: in the former case 72.3 per cent of the national debt and 48 per cent of equity capital was owned by foreigners, while for Yugoslavia the respective shares were 82.5 and 44 per cent (Logio 1936, 140; Berend 1974, 186).

It has been suggested (Lethbridge 1985, 557) that foreign capital made a significant contribution to the economies of Eastern Europe in this period. This conclusion must be questioned in the light of what we know about the uses to which it was put and the problems to which it eventually gave rise. Borrowing from abroad was expensive, the proceeds were often used unproductively and it led to a rising burden of debt and servicing costs which proved fatal once the flow of capital was curtailed and economic conditions deteriorated.

One of the main problems with foreign investment in this period, and by no means unique to Eastern Europe either then or later, was that insufficient attention was given to ensuring that the debt burden was self-liquidating. To maintain solvency it behoves countries which borrow for development purposes to ensure that the resources are used in such a way that they generate a stream of exchange earnings so that the debts incurred can be serviced and eventually amortized. This was certainly not the case in Eastern Europe, nor in Latin America for that matter, and since then there have been many examples in the Third World of the inappropriate use of foreign aid.

In the particular case in question, only a small proportion of the overseas borrowing went directly into productive enterprise or into activities that would generate immediate exchange earnings. By far the larger part of the proceeds was used for financing non-essential imports and social infrastructure investment, the accumulation of private balances abroad, and the payment of interest and dividends (Political and Economic Planning 1945, 110). Bandera (1964, 66, 130–32) claims that only 30–50 per cent of public external loans were used directly in productive investment or as a basis for such investment. Further, he argues that private capital, motivated by profit, was not always in the best interests of the debtors and probably only assisted modestly in the pursuit of national economic objectives. The flow of foreign capital was unstable, a significant part of it consisted of short-term funds, and it was generally believed that to attract foreign investors sound deflationary policies were essential to ensure that external balances were adequate for the future transfer of debt services. Such policies were however self-defeating since they had an unfavourable impact on domestic capital formation. This in turn hampered structural diversification and resulted in high comparative costs.

Berend and Ranki (1974a, 213–23; 1974b, 99–110) also regard the inflow of capital as far from an unmixed blessing. Foreign loans failed to exert a really stimulating influence on the economies of the region since only a small proportion found their way into productive schemes such as electrification and the development of transport and industry, or into activities which would generate exchange earnings. A large part of the funds was used to convert old debts, or to promote social investments, finance consumption and even line the pockets of corrupt officials. Not surprisingly, therefore, the burden of interest and amortization was far beyond the capacity of these countries to accommodate.

For illustrative purposes the Hungarian experience is not untypical. In the years 1924–29 foreign capital flows (both long- and short-term) were approximately equivalent to domestic accumulation. However, of the long-term capital, about 40 per cent went to repaying former debts including some dating from before the war, 25 per cent was used for financing consumption, 15 per cent was invested in social infrastructure projects undertaken by municipal governments, including public health, education and housing, and only 20 per cent found its way into productive investment (Berend 1974, 186–7). In the case of agriculture, one-third of the long-term credits raised by the private sector went into that sector but had very little visible effect in development terms since only one-tenth was devoted to productive investment. The remainder was used for land purchases, consumption, building projects and interest payments. Rothschild (1974, 168–9) accuses Hungary's rulers of soliciting credits that were too large relative to the current capacity of the economy to deal with them. On the other hand, the situation may simply have reflected a failure to ensure, for various reasons including waste through graft and corruption and the pursuit of prestige projects, that sufficient resources, either external or domestically generated, were channelled into exchange-earning activities in the first place. Either way, it does not alter the fact that the stream of foreign credits was not always used wisely and that it served to screen the precarious nature of Hungary's development which tended to focus on traditional sectors.

The utilization of capital inflows was probably no better in Poland and the Balkan countries (Berend 1974, 188). One-quarter of Romania's foreign loans, for example, are said to have been absorbed in ostentatious consumption on estates and in the civil service (Rothschild 1974, 168–9). Nötel's (1974, 79) estimates of the end-use balance of payments distribution of capital imports for Hungary, Bulgaria, Yugoslavia and Poland tend to confirm the general pattern. Of the $604.6 million inflow of both long- and short-term capital between 1924 and 1928 ($238 million of which was short-term), he found that one half was used for financing a surplus of goods and services, one-tenth was used for the purchase of gold, while the remaining two-fifths provided for the exchange requirements to meet interest and dividend payments.

Throughout the period of credit expansion the balance of payments position of all East European countries apart from Czechoslovakia was visibly weakening. Capital inflows therefore served to plug the leaks which occurred principally on the trade and interest and dividend accounts, with Hungary and Poland being the most severely affected. The reasons for the deterioration are evident enough as Nötel (1986, 185) explains:

> Export expansion in these overwhelmingly agricultural countries remained extremely irregular and rather modest in most cases. Import expansion, under the pressure of long-repressed import demand, outpaced export expansion whenever not restrained by inflation or currency management. Deficits increased and surpluses vanished, in consequence, not only on trade accounts but also on trade and services accounts. The deficit on interest and dividend payments, with the exception of Romania, also increased considerably in all these countries.

Altruistic motives were not of course the dominant feature of the investing countries. Political factors, including diplomatic influence by creditor nations, often determined official loan policy, while for private capital it was clearly the incentive of the good returns to be made. Borrowing costs were both very high and mostly inflexible. Since only a small fraction of the foreign capital absorbed by Eastern Europe in the later 1920s went directly into equity issues, there was little opportunity for adjusting the financing burden when times were difficult by reducing dividend payouts. Most of the capital went into fixed interest securities at nominal rates of interest of 6–9 per cent, but real rates were usually much greater, averaging 8–12 per cent and in some cases even higher, after allowing for the deep discounts on the sale of new issues (Political and Economic Planning 1945, 110). Consequently, a large proportion of the debt service burden remained fixed when incomes and activity declined.

A further complication was that high interest rates attracted short-term funds which, up to 1929 at least, offset autonomous declines in long-term capital inflows. The snag was that the national credit systems tended to convert these external short-term loans into long-term domestic ones. This proved to be an obvious source of danger once economic conditions deteriorated, since it was then very difficult to attract short-term credits by high interest rates to offset the autonomous decline in long-term lending when short-term funds were scuttling to safer havens. Hungary and Poland, with half or more of their total debt in a short-term form, were the most seriously affected, though the average for the region was around 20 per cent. Furthermore, short-term foreign liabilities constituted 20–40 per cent of commercial bank deposits in most Eastern and Central European countries (Macartney 1937, 466; Williams 1963, 94). In view of the fluctuations in international money markets and the extremely volatile nature of short-term funds, especially after 1929, these large holdings of short-term deposits were to become a serious problem for the countries concerned once international financial conditions deteriorated. With the sharp fall in export earnings short-term indebtedness relative to export receipts rose rapidly, averaging 81 per cent by 1931, and no less than 124 per cent if Czechoslovakia is excluded (Nötel 1986, 229).

But even before the disastrous events of the early 1930s it is clear that the debt burden of the region was becoming increasingly unmanageable. As the data in Table 3.3 indicate, an increasing proportion of export earnings were required to service the transfer of profits, interest and dividends abroad, and this share rose dramatically once export eanings collapsed. Moreover, since the servicing of foreign loans called for 'strong currencies' obtainable from a limited range of exports, the actual strain on the balance of payments was somewhat greater than these figures suggest (United Nations 1949a, 59). At the same time, outpayments for capital services accounted for an ever larger share of net capital inflows – 40 per cent in the case of Hungary and 28 per cent for Poland in 1928. The real crunch came with the sharp curtailment of American lending from the middle of 1928 onwards and a decline in lending by other creditor nations a year later. Net capital outflows from the main creditors fell from $2241 million in 1928 to $1414 million in 1929 and $363 million in 1930 (North 1962, 40). Capital inflows into Bulgaria, Hungary, Poland and Yugoslavia were almost wiped out in this two year period, falling from $245.6 million in 1928 to £116.1 million in 1929 and a mere $8.1

Table 3.3   Debt servicing as a percentage of exports

	1924	1926	1928	1931/32
Bulgaria	9.2	8.5	12.3	22.0
Hungary	2.4	11.1	17.9	48.0
Poland	9.0	7.5	11.3	27.0
Romania	3.5	9.4	14.6	36.0
Yugoslavia	–	11.5	18.1	36.0

Sources: Drabek (1985, 425); Nötel (1986, 223)

million in 1930. Even in 1929 the total inflow of capital only just about matched outgoings on interest and dividends. Thus the former import surplus on goods and services which previously had been financed by means of an inflow of credits was all but eliminated, so that henceforward inward capital movements ceased to contribute to domestic resources (Nötel 1974, 84–5).

The sudden contraction in capital inflows undoubtedly exposed the tenuous nature of the East European economies, and it suggests that the debtors' insolvency was hastened rather than caused by the depression of the early 1930s (Bandera 1964, 110–15). In reality, the maintenance of the fragile equilibrium in both the European and international economy was heavily dependent on the continued flow of funds from creditor to debtor nations. Thus even had conditions in the United States not determined the subsequent course of events, a reaction was bound to have come in time simply by dint of the increasingly insupportable debt burdens of the borrowing countries. Indeed, by early 1928, Benjamin Strong, the governor of the New York Federal Reserve Bank, was said to be sceptical as to the wisdom of making further loans to Europe (Aldcroft 1991b, 53). In that year the debtor countries of the United States and Britain were paying $675 million more in interest, dividends and amortization than they were receiving in new loans, and by the following year this burden had nearly doubled (Royal Institute of International Affairs 1937, 284). Thus equilibrium in external accounts was often only maintained with the help of short-term credits which later became a destabilizing force.

The severity of the situation was of course greatly intensified by the impact of the depression, not least by the massive fall in commodity prices and hence export earnings, and by the further fall in capital inflows in 1930, which meant that the burden of adjustment ultimately fell with a vengeance on the domestic economic structure as desperate remedies were sought to clear the impasse (see Chapter 4). But the seeds of insolvency had been sown well before the worldwide crisis erupted and the day of judgement was only a matter of time (Jaszi 1935). Thus even without a severe international downturn and financial crisis, the East European countries would have found their position increasingly untenable because there was no obvious means of liquidating the growing burden of external debt (Aldcroft 1977, 254).

4. Policies to combat depression

Even before the international collapse of the early 1930s the economic situation in Eastern Europe was becoming increasingly untenable (Bandera 1964, 115; Lee 1969, 141). Weakening markets for agricultural products and mounting external debts in the later 1920s exposed the vulnerability of the economies of Eastern Europe. Thus the crisis of the early 1930s merely hastened the day of reckoning. Effectively it shattered the fragile prosperity of the region and eliminated any hope of reintegration into the international economy. On balance East–Central Europe, and more especially those countries closely associated with the German economy, probably suffered more severely from the depression than many Western countries (Maddison 1973, 20–21; Raupach 1969). The massive fall in primary product prices, the collapse of international lending and the great contraction in international trade had very serious implications for Eastern European countries in terms of their balance of payments, fiscal systems, debt burdens and standards of living.

The severity of the depression not only meant a struggle for economic survival throughout the region, but it also had profound social and political implications. It strengthened the forces of nationalism and statist policies, it exacerbated the already serious ethnic frictions, and it weakened the forces of democracy. One by one, with the sole exception of Czechoslovakia, the weak democratic regimes established after the war succumbed to the power of the Right, and by the end of the decade authoritarian regimes or dictatorships were in place thoughout the region (Zarnowski 1983). Political radicalization was, as Rothschild (1974, 23) notes, a product of economic despair and 'in interaction with the judiciously orchestrated German drive for hegemony in the area, reopened the whole question of East Central Europe's international, domestic, political, and economic order'.

IMPACT OF THE DEPRESSION

Given the region's heavy dependence on agriculture, the massive fall in primary product prices, especially for cereals, was little short of catastrophic. Commodity prices fell more steeply than the prices of industrial goods, with the result that there was a marked deterioration in the terms of trade, except for Czechoslovakia. On average food and raw material prices fell by one half to two-thirds in 1929–32, whereas the price of manufactures declined by just over a third, so that the terms of trade of primary producing countries deteriorated by approximately 27 per cent (Drabek 1985, 475). This was in sharp contrast to the position in Western industrial countries, especially Britain, which benefited from the fall in commodity prices as a result of an improvement in the terms of trade.

In the early stages of depression the problem was exacerbated by the fact that farmers attempted to counteract the loss of revenue through price changes by increasing output and raising the quantities exported (Timoshenko 1933, 92, 96). This policy met with only limited success, however, since external market conditions deteriorated rapidly after 1930 so that export volumes declined. Export receipts therefore dropped sharply through a combination of price and quantity factors. They fell by no less than 73 per cent in Romania, and on average they had declined by 1932/33 to some 40 per cent of their 1929 level. This enormous shrinkage in export earnings entailed a serious loss of international purchasing power and a rising external debt burden. Since international debts remained fixed in nominal terms the debt servicing power of exports fell by between one half and two-thirds in Hungary and the Balkan countries (Nötel 1986, 217–9). Only Czechoslovakia as a creditor country was free of this burden, though her export earnings fell sharply because of the collapse of her former markets for consumer goods.

For the farm producers and peasants the price collapse was devastating (League of Nations 1931). Agrarian incomes declined by up to one-half in Poland and the Balkans and by one-third in Hungary. The price scissors gap, that is the disparity between agricultural and industrial prices, made their plight even worse. The price of goods purchased by the peasants rarely declined by more than one-third whereas the price of the produce they sold often fell by double that amount (Seton-Watson 1946, 82, 122; Roberts 1951, 71, 177). At times the gap became so wide that farm producers had to give up nearly double the prewar amount of grain and cattle to secure the same quantity of manufactured articles (Hertz 1947, 194).

As farm incomes declined debt burdens increased as a proportion of income and by 1932/33 many peasants were on the verge of bankruptcy. In the case of Hungary, for example, the interest paid on agricultural loans was more than 25 per cent of total yearly income and some 60 per cent of the land of smallholders was fully mortgaged. Total debt as a proportion of agrarian income rose from 78 to 133 per cent over the period 1928–33 (Held 1980, 224; Berend and Ranki 1974a, 245). Similarly, in Yugoslavia one-third or more of rural households were heavily in debt and their total indebtedness was equal to 80–90 per cent of their cash incomes (Rothschild 1974, 271). In fact throughout the region agrarian indebtedness was a pervasive problem.

One contemporary observer who had made an extensive tour of the area reckoned that more than 70 per cent of all peasant holdings in Eastern Europe were threatened by debts in the depression and that many peasant households were worse off in terms of purchasing power than before the war (Tiltman 1934, 118–20, 169, 249). The plight of the peasants was made worse by the high interest rates charged by lenders and the heavy burden of taxation. For many life became so difficult that they were forced to sell their land to survive.

The collapse of farm incomes also had serious fiscal implications. At a time when the demand for relief payments and social assistance was increasing governments were faced with dwindling tax revenues. This meant they were forced to curtail expenditure wherever possible and hence there was little scope to implement expansive policies to combat the depression. As Schönfeld (1975, 197–8) rightly notes, 'Der finanzielle Spielraum der Regierungen die Depression durch öffentliche Aufträge und Subventionen zu bekämpfen, wurde immer geringer'.

The final blow came with the breakdown of the international financial system in the crisis of 1930–31 which effectively undermined the solvency of debtor countries. Long-term foreign lending from Western creditors was already faltering in the later 1920s and by 1931 it had virtually dried up. In the meantime gold and foreign exchange reserves had drained away, while short-term liquidity was hastily withdrawn in the panic flight of capital in the 1931 financial crisis (United Nations 1949a, 10). The curtailment of foreign lending not only adversely affected domestic investment and activity, but it also dealt a fatal blow to external equilibrium (League of Nations 1932b). During the later 1920s most of the debtor countries in Eastern Europe and elsewhere had relied heavily on capital imports to plug the gap in their external accounts. Of the total inflow of funds, both long- and short-term, into Hungary, Poland, Bulgaria and Yugoslavia between 1924 and 1928, one half went to cover an import surplus of goods and services, while most of the remainder was earmarked for servicing foreign debt. Even by 1929 the writing was on the wall, for in that year capital inflows were barely sufficient to cover interest and dividends, and thereafter they dwindled rapidly to insignificant proportions. Through the crisis period as a whole, 1929–33, capital imports covered less than half of interest and dividends due on debt, which meant that the former import surplus of goods and services had to be converted into a positive balance (Nötel 1974, 84–5; 1984, 182–3).

Thus the collapse of export purchasing power, the loss of gold and exchange reserves and the end of foreign credits rendered Eastern Europe insolvent. The financial situation was also complicated by the accompanying banking crisis in Central Europe owing to the fact that a substantial proportion of the equity capital of some East European banks was owned by foreigners, including Germans (Cottrell 1983, 309). Nötel (1986 227) has described the sequence as follows:

> The financial crisis of mid-1931, superimposed upon the protracted export crisis in both commodities and manufactures, transformed the haunting spectre of the collapse of national currencies, within a few months or weeks, into an immediately threatening and practically unescapable reality for most east European countries. The sudden shift from continuing, even if irregular, capital imports to fast-spreading capital withdrawal and flight – with the balance-of-payments position already weakened by the sharp and long-lasting fall in export receipts and the rising or at least maintained debt service – in all countries threatened to exhaust, or actually exhausted, the rapidly shrinking proceeds and reserves of foreign exchange.

Czechoslovakia apart, it was the agrarian sector which effectively determined the scale and severity of the depression (Aldcroft 1980, 110–11). For most countries the industrial sector was too small to offer significant relief, but in any case it too suffered a serious setback. Experience varied more widely than in the case of agriculture depending in part on the structure of individual economies. The worst-hit sector was the light end of manufacturing which tended to predominate in the region as a whole (Zauberman 1976, 598). For the Balkan states the decline in industrial output was scarcely of great moment given the insignificant size of this sector in their economies, though as it happens Bulgaria fared quite well in this respect with a modest expansion through the depression. On the other hand, both Poland and Czechoslovakia were very badly hit and for the latter the situation was especially serious given her extensive industrial interests (see Table 4.1).

Table 4.1   *Declines in per capita GNP and manufacturing production,*
           1929–33 (% changes)

	Per capita GNP 1929–33	Industrial production 1929–1932/33
Bulgaria	–11.8	+8.9
Czechoslovakia	–14.5	–41.0
Hungary	–6.6	–19.8
Poland	–5.1	–28.7
Romania	–10.6	–18.3
Yugoslavia	–14.4	–17.1
Europe	–4.9	

Sources: Bairoch (1976, 297); Tomaszewski (1977, 149); Berend and Ranki (1974a, 298–300); League of Nations (1945b, 136–7)

Overall the data for GNP and industrial production, though far from reliable, coupled with the evidence presented above, do suggest that Eastern Europe suffered more severely from the depression as a whole than Western Europe. The prospects by the early 1930s certainly looked very bleak since on top of a long-standing structural problem the countries of this region now had to grapple with the task of recovering from depression. For the rest of the decade they struggled to cope with these twin problems, largely unsucessfully, until overtaken by international events.

POLICY OPTIONS

From the vantage point of the 1990s one can readily appreciate the limited range of policy alternatives available to the statesmen of the early 1930s. After all, the immediate problem was not so much one of recovery but of avoiding economic and financial collapse. Hence if the initial policy response appears to lack coherence and logic one should bear in mind that drastic measures, often *ad hoc*, defensive and taken in haste, were required to shore up tottering economies. Such policies were likely to depress activity and employment but this was the price to be paid when international solvency was seriously in question. They included severe deflationary fiscal and monetary policies together with a battery of restrictions typical of siege economies designed to deal with external imbalance. Among the latter were the temporary closure of banking and financial institutions, rigorous exchange control, limitation on debt payment, the raising of tariffs, and the imposition of quotas and other import restrictions. In view of the spread and intensity of the depression, the defensive measures adopted by most of the major economies, and the limited theoretical guidance and practical experience on how to deal with a large-scale economic downturn, it is difficult to conceive of ready alternatives open to the policymakers of Eastern Europe. Desperate problems called for desperate remedies uninspired by any ideological motives (Kofman 1990, 217). It was only when conditions began to improve towards the middle of the decade that attention was switched to what appeared to be more constructive measures.

The policy reaction was not however quite so indeterminate as one might suspect from a reading of the immediate response to the crisis. Several factors helped to shape the course of policy over the medium term apart from the pressing one of economic salvation. One factor was the almost pathological fear of rekindling the inflationary conditions of the first half of the 1920s which were to contemporaries closely associated with currency depreciation and budgetary deficits. Hence the emphasis on fiscal prudence which ideally meant balanced budgets and currency stabilization, even though such objectives would be detrimental initially to the real economy (League of Nations 1935b; 1938, para. 8; 1944, 167).

Second, in line with this approach, and so as to restore international confidence with a view to encouraging a resumption of foreign lending, debtor nations were reluctant initially to repudiate or to default on their foreign debts. In time default or negotiation of moratoria became unavoidable. For the same reason there was an equal reluctance to depreciate currencies since this would weaken international confidence by raising the spectre of inflation, while it would also entail a rise in the nominal value of debts and debt service costs in domestic currency terms (Bandera 1964, 119).

A third and longer-term factor which helped to shape policy was the growing influence of nationalism. This had already been very much in evidence in the 1920s, manifested in the nostrification measures to reduce the incidence of alien property rights (Pasvolsky 1928, 75). It gathered increasing momentum in the following decade and interacted neatly with the trend towards greater state intervention and the ideology of autarky and self-determination. It also appeared to offer a more promising solution to the problems of the region than any attempt to regain entry into the international economy or any schemes for Danubian federation. The latter would have required a sinking of national differences and the moderation of revisionist tendencies (Condliffe 1941, 303; Schlesinger 1945, 420, 435; League of Nations 1932a). Meantime, liberal capitalism and bourgeois democracy had become discredited and this left the way open for right-wing autocratic administrations to exploit nationalist sentiments in both the economic and political spheres. At the same time, focusing on the nationalist issue facilitated the diversion of social unrest. It was to prove a high-cost strategy, however, since it helped to pave the way for German infiltration into the area with ultimately disastrous consequences (Macartney and Palmer 1962, 285–8).

One final issue which exerted increasing influence on policy in the later 1930s was that of rearmament. Defence expenditure had always been a significant component in the budgets of these countries, but the increasing international tension in the latter half of the decade led to an even greater diversion of resources to military purposes. Indeed, from the mid-1930s onwards many of the state-sponsored industrial projects were based on strategic considerations and the needs of defence (Tomasevich 1949, 179).

Against this background of policy determinants one can also detect some subtle shifts in policy direction during the period. Until the middle of the decade the emphasis was very much on orthodox and defensive measures, understandably so, since the main priority was that of avoiding complete financial collapse, and providing relief for the most distressed sectors of the population to reduce social upheaval. Thereafter there was a definite element of relaxation in the tight policy stance both on the external and domestic fronts and a shift towards more constructive measures of development. These changes were prompted by the recovery in international trade, the pressure of defence needs, the spirit of statism and the growing influence of Germany in the economies of the region. Some of the more ambitious schemes to foster industrial development and structural adaptation were obvious manifestations of these changes.

DEFENDING THE CURRENCY

The immediate task, however, was to tackle the external problem so as to avoid international insolvency. Most European countries took action to defend their external accounts soon after the start of the crisis. Almost every conceivable form of trade and payments restriction barring blockade was employed and by the middle of the decade trade and commercial policy had reached a historical nadir (Friedman 1978, 158). Though commercial policy often achieved its immediate purpose, that of improving the balance of payments, it was of course at the expense of domestic activity since trade restriction was income-destructive and allowed little scope for expansionary policies (Friedman 1974, 413).

But whereas many of the Western countries eventually removed the constraint of the 'golden fetters', that is by coming off gold and letting their currencies depreciate, allowing more room for manoeuvre on the domestic front, this option was not followed in Eastern Europe. In fact external policy was much more orthodox and restrictive in these countries. Tariff levels were raised sharply between 1929 and 1931, followed by extensive import controls and then exchange control (Condliffe 1941, 103; Pollard 1981, 302). Bulgaria, Yugoslavia, Hungary and Czechoslovakia all introduced exchange control in the latter half of 1931 and Romania followed suit in May 1932. Only Poland resisted until the spring of 1936 (League of Nations 1933a, 222–3; 1937, 11; 1942a, 70).

The question is why did Eastern European countries attempt to defend their currencies in the face of depreciation elsewhere? Britain's departure from the gold standard in 1931 signalled a general retreat, which clearly left these countries at a disadvantage with respect to international trade and domestic policy. Several considerations are relevant in this context. Trade balances had generally been unfavourable before 1929 and they were considerably worsened by falling export values and adverse terms of trade thereafter. Rising protection in Western markets, especially on agricultural products, did not help matters either. In addition, the sharp reversal of capital imports and the very limited international reserves meant that import surpluses could no longer be financed and hence imports had to be reduced at all costs.

Protection of domestic industry and agriculture also became an important concern in a world awash with goods. Initially however there were even more pressing motives for the introduction of exchange control and the defence of currencies. One was the desire to check the capital outflow in the financial panic of 1931. A second important factor was the reluctance to relinquish former currency parities, grounded on the belief that depreciating currencies were bad for inflation as the experience of the early 1920s had demonstrated. Currency depreciation also raised the burden of debt service costs and in any case there was a belief that debt servicing should be maintained if at all possible to demonstrate financial soundness, and exchange control would facilitate the collection of foreign exchange for that purpose (League of Nations 1943f, 9–11; 1944, 162–7).

The burden of the debts was considerably relieved during the course of the decade. Partial or complete suspension of servicing was implemented by all countries between 1931 and 1932. Further relief was later secured through negotiated agreements with the major creditors on capital sums and the terms of repayment, while devaluation in Britain and the United States also brought substantial relief. The overall effect was to reduce the total outstanding debt of the six countries from $3.8 to $2.0 billion between 1931 and 1937, while debt servicing costs as a share of export proceeds fell from 25 to less than 10 per cent during the same period (Condliffe 1941, 243–4; Nötel 1974, 89–91).

On the surface trade restriction and exchange control seem to have produced results. The capital outflow was staunched and trade balances generally improved. In aggregate for the six countries an overall trade deficit of $32.5 million in 1929 was converted into a surplus of $141.9 million in 1931, though much of this improvement occurred before the introduction of exchange control (Nötel 1974, 87). In the longer term the costs probably outweighed the benefits. Exchange control tended to raise domestic prices and made exporting more difficult in so far as it maintained fictitious currency values. One estimate suggests that in 1934 East European currencies were overvalued in relation to the pound and dollar by up to 60 per cent (Nötel 1986, 229). Furthermore, protection of the currency limited the scope for relaxation of macroeconomic policy given the need to compress domestic costs and prices. In short, the net effect was a lower level of trade and income than under conditions of depreciation (Heuser 1939, 230). Contemporary studies (Harris 1936, 103; Ellis 1939; 1941, 152) concluded that exchange control countries tended to experience a worse trade and income performance than either gold or paper currency countries. More recently Eichengreen (1992a, 351; 1992b, 233) has confirmed these conclusions by showing that gold bloc and exchange control countries had a much weaker industrial performance in 1929–36 than countries with depreciated currencies.

Recognition of the adverse effects of external controls was manifest in the subsequent efforts to relax or modify them. Late in 1934, for example, Bulgaria eased its exchange control system with considerable benefit to its trade performance in the following year. Eventually most countries apart from Poland introduced a measure of devaluation in a concealed form. This was done principally by the use of export bonuses or currency premia so that exporters received more domestic currency from their export sales that they would have been entitled to under the official rates. The terms of the premia varied a great deal from country to country, ranging between 20 and 50 per cent. However, even with this relief currencies still remained overvalued relative to free market currencies (Lampe and Jackson 1982, 464–5; Ranki 1983a, 90; Royal Institute of International Affairs 1936, 85–9; League of Nations 1938, 5; 1944, 171).

EXCHANGE CONTROL AND GERMAN INFILTRATION

Arising out of the closer affinity among exchange control countries in trade and payments was the spread of clearing agreements. Though only accounting for some 12 per cent of world trade in 1937, over half the trade of Hungary and the Balkan countries including Greece passed through clearing and no less than 80 per cent in the case of Germany (League of Nations 1935a, 15; 1942b, 70–2; 1944, 182–3). Clearing agreements entailed the bilateral balancing of claims between exchange control countries thereby eliminating the need for foreign exchange. In other words, they were an important device for minimizing the need for free foreign exchange.

One drawback as far as Eastern Europe was concerned was that such agreements fostered German penetration of the region, more especially in Hungary and the Balkans (Fisher 1939; Berend and Ranki 1958). It was difficult to resist this encroachment since Germany was one of the few countries prepared to buy agrarian products and other commodities at reasonable prices and supply much-needed capital equipment in return. As can be seen from Table 4.2 Germany secured a strong trade foothold in South-Eastern Europe, even more so following the Anschluss with Austria in March 1938.

There is still some controversy as to the division of benefits from the system. Conventional wisdom asserts that Germany exploited the region for her own purposes to gain access to food and raw materials on favourable terms, and in so doing she piled up large import surpluses with the countries, the Reichsmark balances from which could only be used to purchase German goods. Indirectly therefore one could argue that Germany was rearming at the expense of weaker nations. In turn Germany was accused of dumping large

Table 4.2   Germany's share of East European trade (%)*

	Exports to Germany				Imports from Germany			
	1929	1932	1937	1938	1929	1932	1937	1938
Bulgaria	22.9	26.0	43.1	59.0	22.2	25.9	54.8	52.0
Czech.	22.1[†]	19.6	13.7	20.1	24.9[†]	22.9	15.5	19.1
Hungary	11.7	15.2	24.0	40.0	20.0	22.5	25.9	40.9
Poland	34.2[†]	16.2	14.5	24.1	26.9[†]	29.1	14.5	23.0
Romania	27.4	12.5	22.3	26.5	24.1	23.6	28.9	40.0
Yugoslavia	8.5	11.3	21.7	42.0	15.6	17.7	32.4	39.4

*   Figures for 1938 include Austria
†   Figures refer to 1928

Sources: Hiden (1977, 173); Kaiser (1980, 325–6)

quantities of unwanted goods such as aspirins and cuckoo-clocks on Eastern Europe. Contemporary reports maintain that Yugoslavia received enough aspirins from Germany to last a decade, while Romania did even better with aspirin supplies sufficient to relieve 500 years of headaches! (Einzig 1938, 26; Jones 1937, 76–7).

Apocryphal or not, there was a credit side to the relationship. One has to remember that these countries had few other secure outlets for their products and evidence suggests that they did receive more than ephemeral goods in return. They acquired a large part of their machinery and arms supplies from Germany as well as a variety of consumer goods (Basch 1944, 179; Momtchiloff 1944, 56, Appendices 1–4). Moreover, Germany's apparent monopsonist power was by no means as exploitive as *The Economist* (1938a, 1938b, 1938c, 1939a, 1939b) would have had its readers believe. German purchases helped to raise the export prices and incomes of these countries since they generally paid above world prices, while Germany did not take undue advantage of her position to turn the terms of trade in her favour (Bonnell 1940, 131; Kaiser 1980, 160; Royal Institute of International Affairs 1939, 119). Possibly increasing dependence on the stronger economy slowed down structural diversification and reintegration into the world economy as Basch (1944, 183) suggests, but that was somewhat academic given the conditions of the time and Germany's long-term plans for the region. Rothschild (1974, 22) has little doubt that Eastern Europe gained from the association with Germany:

Contrary to frequent allegations at the time and since, Germany did not flood East Central Europe with cuckoo clocks, aspirin and thermometers in exchange for grains, minerals and timber; rather she supplied capital goods for industry, encouraged the diversification of vulnerable one-crop agriculture, and supplied a steady market at reasonable prices.

Yet in the light of later events it is difficult to agree wholeheartedly with such a sanguine judgement. Trade relationships with Germany could be very unpredictable and the large unrequited balances, though reduced in time, left the countries highly vulnerable to political and economic pressure when market conditions deteriorated as they did later in the decade (Friedman 1976). An illustration is provided by the German decision in September 1939 to refuse purchase of Yugoslavia's bumper plum crop despite previously guaranteed contracts. The incident had a happy ending however. Undaunted by this reversal, the plums were turned into brandy, the Bosnians got drunk and so they 'were able to absorb on a mass scale the aspirin dumped on Yugoslavia by the Germans through clearing agreements' (Hoptner 1962, 103).

More seriously, Germany undoubtedly used her trade connections with South-East Europe to infiltrate Nazi agents and spread political propaganda. Political agents were widely employed, ostensibly under cover of commercial disguise, throughout the region. In one case, the Germans established a soya-bean company in Romania employing no less than 3000 commercial agents to spread the Nazi gospel, while in Bulgaria German military experts dominated the army (Jones 1937, 64, 82). In fact Nazi 'commercial' agents were thick on the ground in South-East Europe by the end of the decade and the countries in question realized only too late in the day that economic dependence was but a prelude to political control (Munk 1940, 151). One by one they were eventually swallowed up in the Third Reich.

As far as trade shares are concerned, Eastern Europe did not have much to gain from the new relationships. The main change was a sharp increase in intercourse among the members of the Reichsmark bloc countries, which raised their share of *intra*-European trade mainly as a result of Germany's increased trade with her satellites. By contrast, Eastern Europe's share of world trade declined between 1928 and the late 1930s, largely because of a contraction in the region's trade in primary products. There was however a small gain in the share of world exports of manufactures, though as with the rest of Europe there had been a deterioration in absolute terms since 1913 (Aldcroft 1989, 32; Yates 1959, 32–3, 47–50; League of Nations 1941).

FISCAL AND MONETARY POLICIES

There was little prospect in the early 1930s of governments adopting expansion programmes to combat the depression even had they been inclined to follow an enlightened approach to economic management. One of the main constraints in this respect was the dire state of public finances as revenues collapsed under the impact of recesssion while expenditure commitments remained sticky in a downward direction. Yields from indirect taxes and dues fell by at least one-third, and those from direct taxes by more than a half during the depression (Schönfeld 1975, 197–8). Consequently governments were more concerned about devising ways of countering recession-induced budgetary deficits by expenditure cuts and tax increases than they were in stimulating activity and employment by fiscal means. Moreover, the classical goals of currency stabilization and budgetary equilibrium were seen as top priorities in re-establishing confidence at home and abroad (Spigler 1986, 141; Rosner 1934). And in any case, internal compression by macroeconomic policy was necessary to maintain international competitiveness given the overvalued exchange rates.

Monetary and fiscal policies were therefore distinctly deflationary in the first half of the decade. The most extreme case was that of Poland where severe deflationary policies were vital in view of the large budgetary deficits and the decision to maintain the stability of the zloty without resorting to exchange controls. Total budgetary expenditure was reduced by one-third in the years 1930 to 1934, while stringent credit controls were imposed by the banks (Landau 1984, 129–30; Gorecki 1935, 109; Taylor 1952, 43). The approach was very much influenced by the example of contemporary France, where the authorities were also forced to compress the whole cost and price structure to offset the overvalued franc (Smith 1936, 168–78; Zweig 1944, 54–6). The deflationary measures certainly helped to intensify and prolong the depression in Poland and it was not until 1936 that the policy stance was reversed (Korbonski 1992, 251).

Similar macro policies were followed in most other countries at this time with varying degrees of intensity. The Hungarian statesmen believed that a rigid deflationary policy was necessary to encourage foreign investment again, while retrenchment policy in Yugoslavia relied heavily on French advice (Polonsky 1975, 56–7). The main exception appears to have been Czechoslovakia where fiscal policy exerted a mildly positive impact in the early 1930s (Pryor 1979, 236–7).

Despite the constraints imposed by adherence to orthodox budgetary policy, governments were obliged to implement some measures of relief such as public works and unemployment assistance to ease the social impact of the crisis, though at the same time they were forced to trim expenditure in other directions to balance the books. Towards the middle of the decade the fierce macro stance began to be modified. Yugoslavia was the first to change course when in 1934–35 cheaper money and reflationary government expenditure through public works loans signalled the end to past orthodoxy (Royal Institute of International Affairs 1936, 128). Other countries soon followed suit: Hungary and Poland for example launched large-scale programmes of investment in 1936–38. This shift in policy was partly predicated on the general improvement in economic conditions and state finances, but increasingly important as time went on was the pressure of defence needs in an increasingly uncertain world. According to Hauner (1986, 50):

> The rising military expenditures and investments thus constituted one of the most effective instruments of state interventionist policies, by means of which the majority of east European states sought after the depression to re-activate a whole range of economic sectors, particularly domestic savings, which in turn were to contribute to the strengthening of the defence potential.

By the end of the 1930s defence accounted for up to one-third of public spending in most countries and one half or more in the case of Poland and Czechoslovakia (Overy 1989, 5). The increasingly hostile international climate of the 1930s and the threat of aggression on the part of totalitarian powers, especially the USSR and Germany, together with the lack of viable alliances with major powers except the French, who could not be trusted to come to the rescue in an emergency, prompted most East European governments to take precautionary measures to secure their safety (Schwartz 1973, 13–14). Poland and Czechoslovakia in particular had a big military build-up in the 1930s. Poland was not only one of the most friendless of the new states and the most disliked but she was also very conscious of the potential threat from Russia and Germany, both of which had scores to settle with her relating to their prewar frontiers. Poland was therefore determined to become an effective military power at whatever cost to the welfare of its citizens. Similarly, the Czechs were acutely aware of their vulnerable position as the only democratic state surrounded by fascism and communism and the claims of Hungary and Germany with respect to frontiers and lost minorities. Czechoslovakia of course had been a leading arms manufacturer in the Austro-Hungarian Empire and her prowess in this field continued unabated in the interwar years with considerable strengthening of her defence capability in the 1930s. In 1937 the Czech armament industry consisted of 76 factories producing a wide variety of weapons and defence equipment. By far the most important was the Skoda works at Pilzen which was among the largest in the world. Czechoslovakia's defence capability was certainly impressive and Hitler was informed by his army staff intelligence that her frontier defence fortifications were formidable (Irving 1978, 98). All to no avail, however, and to the ultimate gain of Hitler since the eventual break-up of the country considerably increased Germany's war potential (Overy 1989, 54).

Whether the concentration on defence activity was ultimately beneficial to the economies concerned is a debatable point. As far as Poland is concerned Overy (1989, 4–5) is very sceptical and argues that the quest for military might weakened an already fragile economy and gave rise to permanent financial insecurity, low living standards and social unrest. This was one reason no doubt why the death of Pilsudski in 1935 was followed by what amounted to military control under the banner of a front organization, the Camp of National Unity. On the other hand, the Czech experience suggests that government-sponsored rearmament spending was an important stimulating force to the economy (Pryor 1979, 236–7). Yet if budgetary spending patterns are analysed closely one is struck by the heavy incidence of certain types of expenditure not all of which could be said to be in the best interests of the economic and social needs of the economies in question. On average defence and civil administration accounted for half or more of government outlays, and if debt service is also included then barely one-third was left for economic and social services including infrastructures. By way of contrast, in contemporary Sweden no less than 60 per cent of state spending was devoted to the latter purposes (Political and Economic Planning 1945, 118–9, 164). This point is reinforced when account is taken of the very poor infrastructure in Eastern Europe. Services such as water, electricity, transport, port facilities, communications, not to mention education and medical services, were far inferior to those in the West, more so in Poland and the Balkans than in Czechoslovakia which was more on par with the West. Moreover, the infrastructure in Eastern Europe deteriorated further relative to that of the West during the interwar period (Ehrlich 1973, 22; 1985, 369; Berend 1974, 191; Wellisz 1938, 252–4; Logio 1936, 213).

The taxation side of the fiscal system was even more anomalous. Taxes were highly regressive and for the most part they lacked equity and economic logic. The administration of the tax system was, it seems, designed more to suit the convenience of officials as Tomasevich (1955, 688) found in the case of Yugoslavia, where indirect taxes accounted for three-quarters of total revenue. The principles of the state's tax system were those 'of charging its citizens as often as possible and as heavily as possible; taking the money where it could find it, and getting it from those who make the least outcry, rather than according to the principle of the ability to pay'.

Regressive fiscal systems are typical of backward countries and in this respect Eastern Europe was no exception. The low income groups tend to be the hardest hit and in this case it was primarily the peasants (Jelavich 1983, 241). In the three Balkan countries for example some 50 per cent of the total cash income of the peasantry disappeared in taxation. In view of their very low incomes at the time this is an incredible imposition and was no doubt one of the main factors responsible for discouraging investment and improvements and in turn for the general backwardness of the sector (Political and Economic Planning 1945, 122; Tomasevich 1955, 702). Yet whereas the peasants were taxed heavily more prosperous groups such as government officials, rent receivers and businessmen escaped with relatively light burdens. Moreover, the distortions of the tax system were legendary. Owners of urban housing in Yugoslavia paid little tax on their rental incomes and enjoyed subsidized interest rates, with the result that some 50–60 per cent of capital formation found its way into residential property, presumably at the expense of more productive sectors of the economy (Tomasevich 1955, 686–7). By any standards of comparison this was a very high proportion but it was by no means unique for similar investment-distorting tax anomalies were widespread, especially in the Balkans. The structure and administration of taxation systems were ripe for reform for, as one survey concluded: 'There are few spheres of public policy in which a constructive approach would yield speedier results' (Political and Economic Planning 1945, 124).

THE AGRARIAN PROBLEM

For most countries of the region agriculture remained a problem without end, no nearer a solution by the eve of the Second World War. Inevitably, given the size of the sector and the severity of the crisis, the government was forced in a number of ways to ease the situation. But intervention proved to be no more than a holding operation: it did little to change the status quo so that by the end of the decade the fundamentals of the agrarian problem remained much as before.

The most serious aspect of the agrarian crisis was the collapse in values rather than volume which held up surprisingly well. For example, Hungarian farm output was little changed between 1929 and 1934 but in value terms it almost halved (Zauberman 1976, 598). Coupled with the adverse shift in trade terms and the rising burden of debt and taxation many farmers and peasants were in dire straits. As the League of Nations demonstrated in its studies on European rural life (1939a, 1939b), at the trough of the depression returns on farm capital were totally inadequate and often non-existent, and recovery when it came was painfully slow. Most studies of the period point to the unhappy lot of the peasantry whose real incomes declined precipitously, often well below the levels prevailing before the First World War (Tiltman 1934, 118–20, 169; Held 1980, 226).

One should of course take account of the fact that those engaged on the land generally consumed much of what they produced so that the real impact

of the crisis was less disastrous than the low returns on capital would appear
to imply. However, even the poorest peasant could not live by bread alone.
Clothing, shelter, farm tools, fuel, repairs and other goods and services had to
be paid for at a time when the farmer's terms of exchange had moved against
him. Peasant families in Hungary for example had 33–49 per cent less to
spend on essential goods and services than before 1927 and they had also lost
real purchasing power since 1913 (Held 1980, 226). The position was not
much better for large commercial producers trading in a glutted world market
and when their customers were bent on protecting their own agrarian interests. Furthermore, East European producers were additionally handicapped
in world markets because of their low level of efficiency and the overvalued
exchange rates.

The exigences of the immediate crisis should not obscure the fact that the
poverty of agriculture also had deep-seated causes. Unyielding agrarian systems, based on traditional ownership patterns and practices despite the postwar reforms, and exacerbated by rapid population growth and a growing
shortage of fertile land, were scarcely the recipe for prosperity even at the
best of times. The Slovenian experience provides a good illustration of the
way in which widespread small-scale ownership, coupled with a shortage of
good land, set limits to improvements in efficiency. Given the adverse man–
land ratio, investment in agriculture only made sense if it could substitute for
labour, but the rate at which this was possible depended on the availability of
employment outwith the agrarian sector. Though the latter increased after
1933 it was never sufficient to cope with the excess labour on the land, and
so, in the absence of positive measures to realize resource reallocation, the
most that could be achieved were marginal improvements in agrarian practices such as better seed selection, improved manuring practices and selective
livestock breeding, none of which did very much to solve the fundamental
problems (Hocevar 1965, 131, 148–54, 166). To a greater or lesser degree
these conditions were replicated throughout the region and it was not until
after the Second World War when a determined effort was made to speed up
the pace of industrial development that the more fundamental problems were
seriously addressed.

Governments did of course attempt to alleviate the immediate consequences
of the crisis by a panoply of different measures including protection, debt and
taxation relief, subsidies and export premia, price support schemes, concessions on rental payments, marketing boards and financial incentives to reduce
costs, improve efficiency and encourage the adoption of new techniques
(League of Nations 1939a, 29, 93–4, 98–9; 1939b, 15–17, 27–30). The list
appears impressive but for the most part the measures were too limited and
incoherent to provide a radical solution to the fundamental agrarian problems
of the region. They no doubt helped to stave off complete disaster, but they

did little to transform the agrarian structure. Consequently investment in agriculture stagnated, incomes remained low, relative efficiency declined further and the surplus agricultural population remained as large as ever.

One of the chief drawbacks of the postwar land reforms, which were piecemeal and variable in their coverage, was that they were based primarily on tenurial rights rather than on economic logic in order to satisfy the long-standing aspirations of the peasantry. While in social and political terms this clearly made good sense, it did little to ensure the viability of small farms, nor did it resolve the antiquated pattern of landholdings in some countries where the scattering of strips still prevailed. Many holdings were therefore inadequate for one reason or another to provide peasant households with a reasonable livelihood and hence under-employment remained a pressing prob-lem. In the Balkans and Poland for example a large part of the agrarian manpower could have been eliminated without detriment to output since the marginal product of labour was close to zero and in some cases negative. In practice this solution was scarcely feasible simply because there was nowhere for the surplus population to go (Zauberman 1976, 594–5; Moore 1945). Yet failing the shift of labour out of agriculture there was very little prospect of raising efficiency and so the agrarian sector could not perform the role it had done previously in the West, that is acting as a source of capital accumulation and a market for industrial goods (Teichova 1989, 900–904). The inherent limitations of the agrarian structure in its then present form, together with the social and political implications of millions of under-employed rural workers, eventually prompted governments to turn their attention towards rapid industri-alization as a way out of the impasse (Aldcroft 1993a, 181).

But such transformation lay in the future; meantime there were more pressing issues to be resolved. The most urgent was the farm debt problem and here governments sought to alleviate the burden by declaring moratoria or negotiating a general scaling down of debts. The Romanian peasant, one of the most heavily indebted in the region, gained relief through a govern-ment moratorium on debt repayment in 1932 and two years later the principal capital sums were halved and interest rates thereon reduced (Lampe and Jackson 1982, 451; Seton-Watson 1946, 83). Some 70 per cent of farm debtors derived benefit from these provisions which also included a pro-gramme of agricultural reconstruction (League of Nations 1939b, 15–16). In 1933 the Bulgarian government followed a similar line and granted a five-year moratorium; it also reduced by 50 per cent the principal capital debts of small farms of less than 10 hectares and lowered interest rates. Yugoslavia implemented even more extensive relief between 1932 and 1936 including reduced taxation and the elimination of the debts of some 654 000 small farms (Berend 1985, 178). Similar relief policies were also promulgated in Poland and Hungary (League of Nations 1939a, 29, 98–9; 1939b, 16).

Another method of providing relief was by the use of subsidies, including direct production subsidies and export incentives. These were employed most extensively in Czechoslovakia, the only importer of agrarian products in Eastern Europe. Import substitution was encouraged by stringent control of imports and generous subsidies which by 1937 accounted for nearly 13 per cent of the value of output. This experiment proved too ambitious and later had to be modified since it resulted in severe overproduction of wheat. It also stimulated a sector in which Czechoslovakia was at a comparative disadvantage in international trade (Pryor and Pryor 1975, 509, 531).

Most other countries concentrated on export subsidies, either direct incentives or special export premia to offset the overvalued exchange rates. By the middle of the decade most countries were using export premia which varied between 20 and 50 per cent (Lampe and Jackson 1982, 465–6; Royal Institute of International Affairs 1939, 145). In addition, state purchasing and marketing boards were established for a variety of products including cereals, sugar and potatoes, which helped to bolster prices and facilitated the sale of produce, especially abroad. The marketing of some agrarian products was virtually monopolized by official agencies and in time they became a useful device in barter trade negotiations with Germany and other countries. One of the more successful was the Czecho-Slovak Cereals Company of 1934 which had powers to purchase all home-grown cereals at a fixed price for resale and which conducted all transactions with foreign countries (League of Nations 1939b, 27–30). Romania and Poland also operated price support schemes with some degree of success (League of Nations 1939a, 93, 98). One drawback of these policies, however, was that in so far as the price support schemes tended to encourage crop production they simply accentuated the problem of overproduction.

Efforts to modernize agriculture through product diversification, technical change, cost reductions and general efficiency improvements were somewhat less extensive. In this respect the Balkans, especially Bulgaria, were in the forefront by encouraging a shift away from cereals (already under way before the crisis) towards stock breeding, industrial crops, dairy and poultry production, fruit farming and market gardening. These innovations met with some degree of success though it should be noted that by the end of the period the proportion of land devoted to cereals still predominated (Lampe and Jackson 1982, 368–9; Crampton 1987, 139). Technical improvements such as crop rotation, new strains of crops, the more widespread use of fertilizers, the stable feeding of livestock and new machinery and implements were also encouraged in all countries, as was the spread of agricultural education and training (League of Nations 1939b, 17). Progress was inevitably slow and spasmodic and in many areas agricultural practices and methods remained woefully backward by Western standards. This was particularly so in the

Balkan countries, one illustration of which must suffice. Bulgaria used minimal amounts of nitrates, phosphates and potash per hectare (0.01 kilo per hectare or less) compared with 4.4, 8.9 and 5.0 respectively in Czechoslovakia and 10.7, 24.1 and 7.9 respectively in Denmark (Crampton 1987, 129).

Government intervention therefore helped to alleviate the worst effects of the depression and brought about a limited measure of improvement in the 1930s. Nevertheless, farm incomes remained depressed, often less in real terms than prewar, while agricultural methods and practices did not change radically. Taxation also remained a source of grievance among the peasantry. Farmers and peasants believed they were unfairly penalized in this regard for the benefit of industry and rearmament, and that exports were subsidized at the expense of domestic consumption (Basch 1944, 101–2; Hertz 1947, 102–3). On both counts they may well have been right, but by then peasant farming in its traditional form was no longer viable.

THE DRIVE TO INDUSTRIALIZE

The 1930s saw a more determined effort to industrialize than ever before. Most political parties recognized the need to develop alternative forms of employment and the depression made this even more imperative (Turnock 1974, 126). The virtual absence of capital inflows also meant that Eastern Europe would have to look to its own resources for development. As it transpired, the shift in prevailing economic and political ideology also prompted a change in direction. With liberal capitalism discredited the forces of nationalism and nostrification gathered strength, while the emergence of autocratic forms of government facilitated the advance of more autarkic methods of control and state ownership and direction of industry, especially in sectors of strategic importance (Turnock 1986, 59). Whether in fact there was sufficient coherence in the state promotion of industry to warrant the term 'planning' being used is open to debate (Ranki and Tomaszewski 1986, 40–41).

Not all the measures taken to foster industry in this period were new by any means. Subsidies, tariffs, tax breaks, public works, export promotion and other incentives to encourage industry and import substitution had all been employed before the 1930s, while state ownership of infrastructure such as railways, communications, ports and forests had a long history. The main difference compared with the past was the much greater intensity with which governments used their powers to encourage industrial development, together with the much enlarged role of the state as consumer and owner of economic enterprise. A whole range of additional regulations, laws and decrees was enacted to control and direct the process of production, while the state further enlarged its own sphere of ownership by taking over enterprises, especially those formerly under foreign control. Many of the controls imposed to protect external accounts and currencies in the early 1930s also gave added dimension to the drive for further state control and self-sufficiency. From the middle of the decade many of the projects for industrial expansion were of course related to defence, often in association with Germany's rearmament plans (Singleton and Carter 1982, 61; Tomasevich 1949, 179).

State ownership varied considerably from country to country. It was most extensive in Poland and Romania, least so in Czechoslovakia, while other countries lay somewhere in between (Spulber 1959, 268). Poland probably had a higher incidence of state ownership than any other European country barring the Soviet Union. In addition to the traditional infrastructure holdings, the Polish state owned some 100 industrial companies with over 1000 establishments by the end of the 1930s, and employed about 1 million persons exclusive of those in the armed forces. Most of the military equipment was supplied by official undertakings, while 80 per cent of the chemical industry, 50 per cent of the metallurgical industry, 40 per cent of iron and steel, 20 per cent of oil refineries and most of the main transport services belonged to the state. In addition, there were five state monopolies in alcohol, matches, tobacco, salt and lotteries (Spulber 1966, 35; Taylor 1952, 93–4). Romania came a close second to Poland in the extent of state involvement in the economy. By 1939 the capital invested in state economic enterprises was actually larger than that invested in private commercial and industrial undertakings, while 70 per cent of the metallurgical output was consumed by the state, mainly for defence purposes (Roberts 1951, 32, 69, 82). Elsewhere state ownership and control were less extensive. In Yugoslavia they accounted for 15 per cent of industrial investment in 1938, chiefly in metals, chemicals and food processing. If cartels, which came under the control of the Ministry of Commerce and Industry in 1935, are included the share rises to 22 per cent (Lampe and Jackson 1982, 500). State-owned enterprises in Bulgaria totalled 169 in 1939 and accounted for 8–9 per cent of industrial production, and 15 per cent if cooperatives are included (Lampe 1986, 100–110). By contrast, the incidence of state ownership was much lower in Hungary, around 5 per cent of industrial investment (Berend 1974, 189).

The increasing role of the state was also accompanied by the spread of cartels which eventually became an instrument of government policy. By the late 1930s they accounted for over 40 per cent of Hungary's industrial production, 66 per cent of the Polish, 23 per cent of the Romanian and most of the Czech (Berend and Ranki 1974b, 141; Spulber 1959, 276; Teichova 1985, 958–9; 1988, 44–6). Cartels were basically restrictive devices for controlling markets. They curtailed competition by fixing prices, allocating production quotas among members, and generally regulating the conditions of trade. In other words, they stifled competitive forces and encouraged industrial collusion and concentration, especially in heavy industry. Many of the cartels were international in scope and during the later 1930s Germany was able to manipulate the cartel system to increase its influence in South-Eastern Europe (Teichova 1989, 960–61).

The most prominent feature of the industrial strategy of this period was the launching of large-scale investment programmes, some of which were associated with public works for the relief of unemployment, but generally based on strategic considerations in the rearmament phase. Whether such programmes can be regarded as manifestations of genuine pump-priming activities as Zauberman (1976, 600) infers, is questionable given the obvious political pressures which motivated the shift in policy direction. That notwithstanding, most countries embarked on large-scale expansion projects from the mid-1930s. Yugoslavia announced a large programme of public works in 1934–35, while in 1936 Poland unveiled its ambitious six year defence expansion plan. This involved the expenditure of 6000 million zloty (later scaled down) on armament plants, military equipment and general defence supplies. In conjunction with this project there were plans to develop the central industrial district of Poland (that is the area bounded by Warsaw, Cracow and Lvov) as a major industrial region, which would concentrate heavy industry and military equipment away from Poland's frontiers (Hauner 1986, 101–2; Taylor 1952, 96–8; Landau and Tomaszewski 1985, 118–9). Two years later Hungary also announced a five-year rearmament programme of 1000 million pengöes with emphasis on public works and defence activities (Berend and Ranki 1985, 91–2; Royal Institute of International Affairs 1939, 118). The Romanian programme also had a distinctly strategic flavour. Two-year monopolies were offered by the government for the establishment of industries considered essential to the national welfare, while the state also contributed part of the capital cost of new arms factories and guaranteed to purchase the output on favourable terms (Royal Institute of International Affairs 1939, 129–30). Finally, Czechoslovakia's ambitious defence drive involved the modernization and mechanization of the armed forces and an extensive programme of fortifications, which by the later 1930s (1936–38) absorbed 50.6 per cent of total public spending (Hauner 1986, 89).

How successful was the policy of forced industrialization? Indices of manufacturing for the years 1929–38 would seem to indicate worthwhile achievement in most cases. The Balkans certainly did very much better than the other three countries (Table 4.3). On the other hand, Czechoslovakia, the most advanced nation, stagnated during the 1930s. Even at the cyclical peak of 1937 manufacturing output was considerably below the level reached in 1929, largely due to the weakness of industries heavily dependent on exports such as glass, porcelain, textiles and metals. It should

Table 4.3   Indices of manufacturing output, 1929–38 (1913=100)

Country	1929	1938	% change
Bulgaria	179	245	36.9
Czechoslovakia	172	146	−15.1
Hungary	114	143	25.4
Poland	86	105	22.1
Romania	137	178	29.9
Yugoslavia	140	190	35.7

Sources: Berend and Ranki (1974a, 298–300); United Nations (1949b, Table 36); League of Nations (1945b, 135–7)

be stressed however that the data for this period are far from robust and estimates of both income and industrial production vary considerably. Nevertheless Jackson and Lampe (1983, 408–9) do lend support to the optimistic interpretation of the industrial record of the Balkans. They argue the case for relatively fast industrial expansion in South-East Europe before the Second World War, with growth rates for the period 1928–38 of 4.8 per cent a year for Bulgaria, 3.4 per cent for Romania and 2.4 per cent for Yugoslavia. They are particularly impressed by some of the structural shifts from artisan activities to modern factory production and also by the pace of import substitution in sectors such as textiles and food processing. However, their conclusion on Yugoslavia is perhaps somewhat excessive: 'Modern, mechanical production had ... become the predominant form of industrial activity by 1939 in a territory where little statistical significance had existed before the turn of the century.'

Further consideration, on the other hand, points to the conclusion that the efforts to foster industrialization were not an unqualified success. Without doubt industry was the most dynamic sector of the economy and in most cases its share of national income increased modestly. But, as Tomaszewski (1977, 150–1) notes, even the rapid industrial advance in the Balkans did not have a very significant effect on the growth of national income. By 1938 industry's share of national income was still one-quarter or less, with only Bulgaria showing a significant gain on 1920. In the case of Hungary and Poland the share was around one-third compared with well over one-half in the highly industrialized nations of the West. Only Czechoslovakia, with just over half of its income generated by industry, could match the latter (Berend and Ranki 1974a, 307–8). Thus for much of the region prosperity was still very dependent on the state of the harvest.

Overall, therefore, the scale and scope of the industrial changes were too limited to bring about a radical transformation of the economic structure. The fundamental problems of the region remained basically unchanged. Surplus manpower on the land could not find employment elsewhere since the numbers employed in industry were still quite modest, especially in the Balkans, and the increase in industrial employment was nowhere near sufficient to absorb the growing agrarian population. To take the Yugoslav case: the number of industrial workers rose by about half a million in 1929–37 but during the same period the total population increased by 1.8 million (Basch 1944, 241).

Furthermore, one might also question some aspects of the industrial promotion policies. State policy tended to foster unproductive and non-economic investments. This is reflected in the large share of investment that went into residential construction, the emphasis on defence-related activities especially later in the period, and the fact that some state enterprises were designed mainly for tax revenue purposes. Despite the declared official line stressing the importance of industry, the proportion of total investment going into this sector was quite modest, and a good part of it was defence-oriented in later years (Political and Economic Planning 1945, 102). Berend (1974, 191–2) has drawn attention to the weakness of industrial investment and also to the lag in infrastructure facilities noted earlier. What is remarkable is the very high proportion absorbed by housing, averaging 40–60 per cent in the Balkans, stimulated largely by the very favourable tax treatment of rental incomes (Political and Economic Planning 1945, 102; Tomasevich 1955, 687).

State control and direction also tended to lead to excessive bureaucratic interference and at times an unfriendly attitude towards private enterprise. Warriner (1940, 16) argues that it was the bureaucrat, rather than the capitalist or large landowner, who exploited the worker in the Balkans. It has also been suggested that attempts to foster industry were at the expense of agriculture which remained short of capital and heavily taxed (Hertz 1947, 102–3).

Since the state's financial resources were limited, it is curious that it adopted a rather ambivalent attitude towards the mobilization of savings both at home and abroad. The state could not hope to replace the role of foreign capital when overseas lending dried up in the early 1930s and the nostrification policy designed to discourage foreign enterprise did not help matters. Indeed, as Turnock (1974, 125) points out, the buying out of foreign interests at competitive prices imposed heavy obligations in strong currencies, and in turn required a mobilization of savings beyond the means of the national economies. It is true that foreign capital still retained a significant presence in Eastern Europe, but the less congenial climate tended to discourage new enterprise and skill formation from abroad, with the exception of that from Germany in later years. Similarly, the mobilization of domestic resources was sometimes adversely affected by inappropriate fiscal policies including high taxation, while the structure of taxation tended to direct savings into less essential activities such as housing.

As far as the industrial sector itself is concerned, there hangs a question mark as to the pattern of development. The main force of the argument here is that the distribution of investment was sub-optimal in terms of growth; that is a large part of industrial investment found its way into textiles, food processing and light industries, to the comparative neglect of modern dynamic sectors such as chemicals, electrical engineering, telecommunications and motor manufacturing (Berend 1974, 192–4). Even by the late 1930s textiles and food and beverages accounted for one half or more of the industrial product in most countries, while the production of raw materials and in some cases their processing accounted for a further significant proportion. What was particularly lacking was the production of highly refined industrial goods, especially in metalworking, chemicals, and the electrical and mechanized transportation industries, which would have acted as a spur to 'autocentric industrialization' (Ambrosius and Hubbard 1989, 198). The motor vehicle, for example, did not replace the railways as an engine of growth as it did in some western countries (Wellisz 1938, 225). There were of course some notable exceptions as in the case of Hungary, and especially Czechoslovakia which fits better into the western model of development, but generally speaking industrial structures were unbalanced and uni-dimensional. 'Low quality, unsophisticated consumer goods dominated industrial production; higher quality capital goods were just beginning to appear' (Ambrosius and Hubbard 1989, 198).

Given the emphasis on traditional branches of industry it is scarcely surprising that the industrial structure remained fairly static. Textiles recorded the main gain in employment share, except in Poland and Czechoslovakia, with little advance in producer durables (Teichova 1981, 183–4). Import substitution was of course much easier in traditional activities especially textiles, given the low domestic purchasing power and the shortage of capital and skilled labour. Protection of the domestic market therefore tended to favour substitution in the least cost sectors. Thus in Yugoslavia the number of textile factories rose from 30 in 1929 to 363 in 1936. Despite the greater encouragement to heavy industry due to rearmament, the market for the products of heavy industry (exclusive of government procurement, which was often considerable) was limited by the depth of demand at home and the lack of comparative advantage in foreign markets. Moreover, cartelization, by firming up product prices, helped to compress domestic demand.

Eastern Europe, like Southern Europe, also retained its traditional dual industrial structure, with many small-scale inefficient firms competing with a few modern large-scale enterprises. Small business remained as viable as ever partly because of the abundance of cheap labour, the weakness of big business and the predominance of those activities in which small firms flourished. Large firms were relatively inefficient by Western standards and they failed to make much progress in modern production and management practices. Indeed, Western-style mass-production methods were conspicuous by their absence and the typical large concern has been described as little more than a 'general store' supplying a multiplicity of articles in small batches to limited markets within a protectionist framework. Again there were exceptions to the general rule and of course Czechoslovakia's firm structure does not fit the East European pattern.

The irrational features of some of the official industrial policies are well documented in the case of Czechoslovakia, the country with the largest and most advanced industrial sector in the region. Czech industry suffered badly in international markets during the depression and recovery was slow and chequered. This was partly the result of its uncoordinated domestic and foreign trade policies which led to relative expansion in sectors with a comparative disadvantage in world markets, notably agriculture where subsidized import substitution was vigorously pursued, and a loss of share in those industries having a comparative trade advantage. The Czechs failed to capitalize on their previous industrial success in overseas markets with the result that exports and production in industries enjoying comparative advantage stagnated, while those sectors at a comparative disadvantage managed to regain or exceed former peak levels of activity recorded in the later 1920s (Pryor 1973, 201; Pryor and Pryor 1975, 509, 520).

More generally, though a policy of industrialization was continued in the 1930s, it was often difficult to make headway given the conflicting forces at work. Foreign capital was discouraged by the continued policy of 'nostrification' and the takeover by the state of foreign enterprises, despite the fact that domestic capital accumulation was limited both by the low level of savings and the restrictive capital and money markets. Nor was there much prospect of public finance filling the gap for private enterprise given the increasing emphasis on defence later in the period. There was, moreover, no unambiguous consensus on industrialization. Traditional elements in society, for example the landed élites, financial interests, and some of the state bureaucracies, still remained quite powerful and they were often opposed to modernization. At the same time, the increasing influence of Germany's demands on the region has also been seen as a retardative factor as far as industrialization is concerned (Ambrosius and Hubbard 1989, 280).

THE INTERWAR YEARS IN PERSPECTIVE

A summing up of the progress and achievements in this difficult period is not easy. On the one hand, against a very unfavourable international background the countries of Eastern Europe made some solid progress, especially in industry. On the other hand, most of the absolute gains in growth were swamped out by population changes so that the net gains in per capita terms were quite modest. Furthermore, such changes as did occur were insufficient to alter the conventional picture of an absence of fundamental change in economic structures. Apart from Czechoslovakia, they remained for the most part low-income, agrarian-dependent economies where farm and family dominated the way of life (Lodge 1941, 97, 111; Sanders 1949, 42, 49). Such conditions were not conducive to rapid economic development. Berend and Ranki (1974a, 318) conclude as follows: 'East–Central Europe became an area struggling with permanent crisis and fraught with inner contradictions in a tense explosive atmosphere where everything called for change.'

In absolute terms most countries managed to surpass their previous cyclical peaks of 1929 and 1913 by a reasonable margin. Unfortunately much of the increase was offset by population growth – up to three times the average for Western and Northern Europe (League of Nations 1941, 50) – so that the income per capita changes were quite small, especially in the 1930s. Over the years 1929–38 income per head stagnated or fell in Yugoslavia and Czechoslovakia, and rose modestly in other countries with the exception of Bulgaria which recorded a significant advance. Taking the region as a whole, average income per capita advanced by no more than a few per cent, that is well below the European average (Bairoch 1976, 297; Lethbridge 1985, 528; Spulber 1966, 58). Comparison with 1913 suggests a slightly better relative performance *vis-à-vis* Europe as a whole (see Table 4.4).

On balance therefore the gap in income levels between Eastern and Western Europe did not diminish during the interwar years; indeed it widened slightly. By the end of the period Czech GNP per head was about half that of the major Western nations which represented a distinct slippage since 1913. For most other countries income per head ranged between 30 and 40 per cent of that of the West, and in all cases apart from Bulgaria there had been a relative deterioration since 1913. In fact by every conceivable standard of measurement Eastern Europe was less productive, less healthy and less literate than Western Europe.

No doubt the region had the potential to do better as later experience was to demonstrate. But before the Second World War the cards were stacked against it. Weak states carved out of former empires, buffeted by crises and an uncongenial international environment and riven with internal divisions, they had little chance of success. Unstable parliamentary democracies of the

*Table 4.4   GNP per capita levels (1960 US dollars) and percentage
           changes, 1913–38*

	GNP per capita level			Percentage changes		
	1913	1929	1938	1913–38	1913–29	1929–38
Bulgaria	263	306	420	59.7	16.4	37.3
Czech.	524	586	548	4.6	11.8	–6.5
Hungary	372	424	451	21.2	14.0	6.4
Poland	301	350	372	23.6	16.3	6.3
Romania	320	331	343	7.2	3.4	3.6
Yugoslavia	284	341	339	19.4	20.0	–0.6
Europe	534	571	671	25.7	6.9	17.5
Belgium	894	1098	1015	13.5	22.8	–7.6
Denmark	862	945	1045	21.2	9.6	10.6
France	695	982	936	34.7	41.3	–4.7
Germany	757	770	1126	48.8	1.7	46.2
Netherland	754	1008	920	22.0	33.7	–8.7
Sweden	680	897	1097	61.3	31.9	22.3
UK	996	1038	1181	18.6	4.2	13.8

Source: Bairoch (1976, 297)

postwar years degenerated into totalitarian or personal regimes which made
them a sitting target for a disgruntled predator (Roucek 1939, 8). The Germans had always regarded the new states as transient phenomena destined to
become part of the greater Reich once Germany was in a position to enforce
its claims to the territories of the former Austro-Hungarian Empire. Their
inherent weakness and isolation left them highly exposed to the ambitions of
a revisionist nation. Nothing materialized by way of federation to strengthen
the power of the Danubian states, largely because the states themselves were
not willing to make the sacrifices that cooperation entailed (Tennenbaum
1944, 149–61; League of Nations 1932a). In turn, the Western powers, principally Britain and France, were not prepared to defend a system which they
had originally created. Neither of them could be said to have had a true
European policy aimed at restoring harmony and balance in the new Europe.
Britain adopted an ambivalent attitude towards Europe, intervening only
when its own interests were threatened, and in later years more concerned

with her imperial connections. France, on the other hand, played a more active role but only in so far as it suited her own notions of security. Hence, by way of default, a revived Germany had more or less a free hand in Europe to turn the states into vassals of her empire. As Butler (1941, 163) saw it: 'Standing tightly together they might possibly have survived. In isolation they were foredoomed to perish as soon as European security collapsed with the failure of the League, the decay of France, and the indifference of Britain.'

5. War and the emergence of new regimes

Within the space of less than a decade Eastern Europe suffered a devastating war, exchanged one lot of masters for another and underwent a radical change in political regime. For a time these events left the East European states in a weaker position than had been the case in the later 1930s. However, out of the turmoil of the 1940s the geographical and political map of Europe was considerably strengthened compared with the fragmented position prevailing before the war. Now two strong power blocs, ideologically opposed, dominated the continent. This removed the power vacuum arising from the peace treaty settlements following the First World War and improved international stability. Whether the citizens of the new East European republics, including East Germany, stood to gain from the new configuration which placed them within the orbit of the Soviet Union, is another matter.

GERMAN DOMINATION OF EUROPE

Within less than two years following the outbreak of war in September 1939, the map of Europe had been radically transformed. Hitler's march across the continent, already begun in a preliminary way before hostilities started with the annexation of Austria and Czechoslovakia, proceeded unchecked and by the beginning of 1942 the new German Empire was virtually synonymous with that of continental Europe. The majority of countries were either occupied by, allied to, or in some way controlled by Germany, ruled by Nazi-appointed governors or by puppet dictators (Lee 1987, xiv). The new regime stretched from Brittany in the west to the mountains of the Caucasus in the east, and from the Arctic tip of Norway to the shores of the Mediterranean. Independent states and territories disappeared almost overnight under Hitler's onward drive to dominate Europe and only a few states managed to maintain their autonomy, and even then it was not very secure. These comprised the neutral states of Portugal, Spain, Eire, Switzerland, Sweden and Turkey.

All the East European states came within the orbit of the axis powers. Hungary, Romania and Bulgaria slipped from initial neutrality into a quasi-alliance with Germany. They retained a semblance of sovereignty by joining

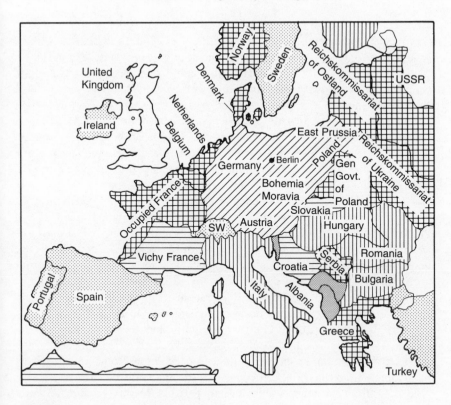

Extent of the Third Reich

States under German occupation or administration

Puppet regimes under German influence

Germany's allies, including Italy

Italian acquisitions

Neutral states

States at war with Germany and her allies

Source: J. Lee, *The European Dictatorships*, London: Methuen, 1987.

Map 2   Germany at war 1939–45

Hitler ostensibly as military allies, but in practice they became very much satellite dependencies of the German Reich. The fate of Czechoslovakia, Poland and Yugoslavia, countries with the strongest pro-West leanings, was very much worse. All three were invaded and dismembered between 1938 and 1941. Czechoslovakia was first on the list when in October 1938 she lost the Sudeten lands which were occupied by Germany. The following March Germany invaded the rest of Czechoslovakia and dissected it as follows: southern Slovakia, western Ruthenia and the sub-Carpathian Ukraine went to Hungary, Bohemia-Moravia became a protectorate of the Reich, while the rest of Slovakia was set up as a nominally independent state. Poland received similar treatment in September 1939. Western Poland, including the Free City of Danzig, was incorporated into Germany, central Poland became a protectorate under the General Government of Poland, while much of the remainder of Poland was absorbed by Russia. Following the invasion of the latter in the summer of 1941 the Russian Polish territories were then occupied by Germany. Finally the turn of Yugoslavia came in April 1941. Northern Slovenia and the major part of Serbia were incorporated into Germany, southern Slovenia and most of the Dalmatian coast went to Italy, which additionally acquired Montenegro as a protectorate. Other parts of Yugoslavia were distributed among Hungary, Bulgaria and Italian Albania, while Croatia (including Bosnia and Herzegovina) became an independent state under German and Italian military influence. In addition, Romania, one of the main gainers from the treaty settlements following the First World War, lost a large proportion of her new territory to Russia (Bessarabia and northern Bukovina), to Hungary (the northern part of Transylvania) and to Bulgaria (southern Dobrogea). These territorial arrangements remained firm until the latter half of the war when Germany's hegemony began to wane.

It is difficult to detect a consistent and logical strategy in Hitler's territorial ambitions. In some respects the changes harked back to the nineteenth century in so far as the territorial incorporations into Germany and Hungary reflected the former German and Magyar spheres of influence in Europe (Radice 1986, 312). On the other hand, there is certainly little evidence of a concerted attempt to rectify the imperfections of the fragmented units arising from the peace settlements after 1918 since the new arrangements tended to multiply the number of administrative units, currencies, fiscal systems and legal frameworks.

In fact the new Nazi empire consisted of a rather motley collection of territories acquired in a very unsystematic manner and ruled in different ways. As each piece of new territory was acquired Hitler assigned to it, in a rather *ad hoc* manner, that type of governance which seemed least likely to pose a threat to the Reich's military plans. There was probably also some attempt, at least initially, to allot a form of administration suitable to its final place in the Nazi conception of the New Order for Europe. This envisaged the formation of a single economic community for the whole of the continent working under German direction, with the Reich as the industrial hub of the system and the outer areas servicing the German industrial machine. Thus the central industrial core of Europe was brought under direct control by incorporating into the German Reich such areas as Alsace-Lorraine, Luxembourg, Polish Upper Silesia and the Czech and Austrian industrial areas. Much of the rest of Western Europe and the less highly industrialized eastern agrarian regions were subject to more indirect control. On the other hand, some of the regions designated as 'colonial territories' such as the occupied parts of Russia and the General Government of Poland, though kept apart from the Reich itself, were nevertheless controlled from Germany and allowed virtually no hand in their own administration. The result was that the scope for economic integration proved very limited. In fact apart from the centralization of financial dealings in Berlin and the use of the Reichsmark as the main unit of settlement within the German dominated territories, little progress was made towards a new order despite considerable propaganda on the subject in 1940. Indeed, by 1942 the German media had lapsed into silence on the subject even though the new German empire was far from being a coherent and efficient economic machine.

The failure to consolidate the hegemony achieved during the years 1938–41 and to recognize the independent aspirations of the different nations was undoubtedly a factor which eventually helped to undermine the credibility of the regime, as the Soviet Union was also to find to its cost in Eastern Europe many years later. The question is why so little was done to realize the wider ambitions for a more united and integrated Europe.

One reason must surely be that Hitler and the Nazi Party never had any very clear conception of what was involved in setting up a new order. No complete and comprehensive plan for the restructuring of Europe was ever published, with the result that the concept remained vague and confused, being based largely on the somewhat conflicting statements made by Reich ministers from time to time. Second, while the new order may never have been explicitly defined, it no doubt provided a useful concept for 'legitimizing' the more extreme ideological beliefs of the Nazi regime, possibly to its own ultimate detriment. As Rothschild (1989, 26) points out:

> Had Hitler's 'new order' not been such a blatantly transparent screen for racial imperialism, exploitation, and genocide, had he instead offered a dignified status and role to the East Central European peoples under his hegemony, he might have averted their resistance movements, harnessed sustained local support, and possibly consolidated East Central European conquests as a rampart against the Soviet Union.

This certainly accords with the Nazi concept of the supremacy of the Ayrian race and the belief that peoples of inferior stock, for example those in Eastern Europe, should be subjugated for the benefit of the master race. A third possible reason is the speed of conquest. In the first two years of hostilities the rapid military victories outran the regime's planning for a new empire. The success of Hitler's campaigns exceeded even the most optimistic expectations and as a result of the rapid acquisition of new territories the Nazi regime was heavily occupied with the immediate task of administering them. Then just at the time when the Reich should have been in a position to give more attention to the idea of a new Europe, that is when it was master of much of the continent, things began to go wrong and the conglomerate empire began to crumble. In particular, the Russian giant refused to 'collapse on schedule', the coalescence of the allied powers under American leadership significantly altered the balance of power, while the cohesion of the axis powers began to weaken with the capitulation of Italy in the summer of 1943. This meant that Hitler was faced with a long campaign of attrition requiring the assistance of all European nations. The war therefore turned into a struggle for survival involving a shift towards immediate objectives and the abandonment of long-term planning for the future of Europe.

The failure to devise an efficient and humane system of harnessing the resources of Europe undoubtedly played a part in the eventual downfall of the Nazi regime, as it also helped to determine the future structure and political complexion of Eastern Europe. Be that as it may, Germany managed nevertheless to draw upon considerable resources from the rest of Europe to service its war machine, often at considerable cost to the countries concerned. 'Like a gigantic pump, the German Reich sucked in Europe's resources and working population' (Kulischer 1948). In fact after 1939 much of the increase in the product available to Germany came from foreign contributions, including foreign labour in Germany which accounted for over a fifth of the civilian labour force in the later stages of war. Such contributions helped to maintain German living standards at the expense of the exploited territories.

Initially the eastern states of Europe were seen mainly as a source of food and raw materials and supplies of labour. The close relationship between Germany and her eastern neighbours, already apparent before 1939, is demonstrated clearly by the data for trade shares. In 1940 some 44 per cent of Romania's exports went to Germany, 59 per cent in the case of Bulgaria, 49 per cent for Hungary and 36 per cent for Yugoslavia (Milward 1977, 87). Subsequently the main objective of German policy was to extract the maximum benefit from the occupied territories regardless of the cost to the populations in question. This inevitably involved harsh measures, including the imposition of heavy levies, looting, the removal of plant, equipment, food and raw materials, the transfer of labour resources, the elimination of the most undesirable elements of the population, and the exploitation of labour under atrocious working conditions. Pillage and exploitation were probably carried to the most extreme in the case of Romania (Constantinescu 1964). Initially the policy paid off in the form of increased output and resources available to Germany, but in time it yielded diminishing returns. The combination of a deterioration in physical assets, general destruction following military operations, and increasing resistance on the part of the exploited populations eventually led to a fall in output and decline in living standards in the occupied territories during the later stages of war. This trend became even more pronounced once the liberation armies got under way.

Despite the emphasis on primary commodities, Germany's military needs dictated the mobilization of industrial resources wherever possible. The most obvious areas to tap within the East were the industrially more developed regions such as the Czech lands, western Poland and parts of Hungary, though in time even the much less industrialized Slovakia and the Balkan countries were to receive a boost to industrial output from German demands. In the case of Slovakia, for example, industrial production for military purposes more than doubled during the war (Selucky 1991, 159). Apart from the Czech lands incorporated into Germany, probably one of the chief beneficiaries was Hungary, where industrial output rose by more than a third at the peak of 1943 compared with prewar, with up to one-half of munitions output destined for German sources (Milward 1977, 89). Despite the stimulus to output in many of the basically agrarian countries it is unlikely that there was much permanent net addition to industrial capacity. In fact, up to the end of the war the region as a whole must have sustained quite considerable losses in this respect, especially when one takes into account the damage through military conflict and the severe depletion of industrial capacity in occupied Poland and Yugoslavia.

DEVASTATION AND DESTRUCTION

Whatever temporary gains may have arisen from servicing the German war machine, ultimately Eastern Europe bore a heavy cost. The scale of the losses and destruction was generally greater than during the First World War and Eastern Europe suffered more than the West. Apart from the millions of people killed, murdered, tortured, wounded, displaced or simply reported missing, there was widespread destruction to property and equipment, severe devastation of agricultural land, and total disorganization of transport and financial systems. By the end of the war normal economic life had ground almost to a standstill in many areas and output levels in both industry and agriculture were extremely depressed, in some cases to less than half those of prewar.

This is not the place to recount in detail the extent of the loss and destruction but a few examples will put the problem in perspective. Of the six countries Yugoslavia and Poland undoubtedly fared the worst. The bitter partisan and inter-ethnic fighting in the former case resulted in massive losses in assets and lives. About one-tenth of the population perished, around half of the country's transport equipment including roads was destroyed, as was half the livestock, one-fifth of the housing stock, and a third or more of industrial capacity including 70 per cent of ironmaking facilities (Pollard 1981, 311; Rothschild 1989, 57–8). Yugoslavia experienced one of the worst falls in standards of living in Europe and by the end of the war a large part of the population was on the verge of starvation.

Poland fared little better. Bitter resistance fighting took its toll on the population – 6 million people perished, half of them Jewish. Property and equipment suffered extensive damage: one-third of the housing stock, two-thirds of the industrial properties, one-third of the railway lines and 80 per cent of the rolling stock were destroyed. In the agrarian sector about 60 per cent of the livestock, 25 per cent of the forests and 15 per cent of the agricultural buildings were lost or destroyed (Pollard 1981, 311; Rothschild 1989, 28). Damage to the land through wanton 'laying waste' by the armies of occupation and liberation and lack of fertilization rendered much land temporarily infertile. In the short term perhaps the most serious problems were the shortages of working capital and livestock. For Eastern Europe as a whole over half of the prewar livestock was lost during the war.

The losses suffered by Hungary were of a similar order of magnitude though generally speaking she probably fared a little better than Yugoslavia and Poland. More than half the industrial capacity and two-thirds of the transport equipment were destroyed or rendered obsolete, the livestock population was reduced by nearly half and one-fifth of the housing stock was eliminated (Nötel 1986, 522).

War damage in the rest of Eastern Europe, though still serious, was far less extensive. Romania, Bulgaria and Czechoslovakia managed to avoid the worst of the direct conflict and hence they emerged from the war with their production structures in somewhat better shape. The comparative position is shown by the figures quoted by Pollard (1981, 311) for capital losses relative to respective national incomes in 1938:

Romania 29%	Hungary 194%
Bulgaria 33%	Poland 350%
Czechoslovakia 115%	Yugoslavia 274%

It is difficult to give precise estimates of the income and production losses overall since in the later years of war the position was so fluid and disorganized that any figures are at best subject to considerable error. There can be no doubt however that they fell very far short of prewar levels. Tentative estimates of national income in real terms through 1938–46 suggest quite steep falls even though some recovery had taken place from the low point of 1944–45. The declines range from 50 per cent or more in the case of Yugoslavia and Poland, 40 per cent in Hungary and 25 per cent in Czechoslovakia. These figures may be compared with declines of between 10 and 20 per cent for France, the Netherlands and Belgium. The level of industrial production relative to prewar was even lower, and in some cases almost at a standstill in 1945.

The overall reduction in productive activity was somewhat greater in some cases than the actual physical losses of assets and population would appear to indicate. This can be explained by the chaotic conditions prevailing at the end of the war. The loss of capital stock was perhaps the least of the immediate worries in 1945. Far more telling from the point of view of immediate production was the sheer scale of the dislocation and disruption to economic systems arising from six years of mobilization and warfare and reflected in the severe shortage of working capital, of essential raw materials, components and repair facilities, the scarcity of technical skills, bottlenecks in communications, the problems involved in converting from war to peacetime production and, above all, the utter exhaustion of generally undernourished populations. After many years of struggle and severe privation workers were in no fit state to exert themselves. Acute food shortages meant that per capita food intake was well below peacetime levels, especially in the urban areas. This shortfall stemmed from the sharp deterioration in agricultural production, especially in basic filler foods such as bread grains and potatoes in many of the occupied areas. Poland, for example, suffered a 60 per cent drop in bread and coarse grains output, while meat production was only 14 per cent of prewar. The shortage of fats and animal products was even more acute due to livestock losses and low yields through lack of fodder. In some countries the production of fats was but a fraction of prewar: 13 per cent in the case of Poland, 25 per cent in Yugoslavia and less than 50 per cent in Czechoslovakia.

The shortage of basic commodities was of course part of a worldwide problem at the end of the war. Even by 1947–48 world production of food was still some 7 per cent less than prewar and in the intervening period there had been a net addition to global population. Moreover, shortages of shipping space and dislocation of inland transport facilities impeded the movement and distribution of supplies. These problems apart, Europe's position was exacerbated by the fact that she had little means to pay for imports of essential commodities, especially from the dollar area which was virtually the only source of supply. The export trade of Europe had been diminished during the war so that her capacity to import was very restricted. In the immediate post-liberation period the volume of imports into Europe as a whole rarely exceeded 50 per cent of the 1937 level and in some Eastern countries it was almost negligible. Thus while physical shortages and transportation constituted immediate problems, it soon became apparent that the main difficulty was going to be that of earning sufficient foreign exchange to pay for essential imports. In the final analysis, therefore, the ability to carry out reconstruction would depend very much on the assistance of the United States, the only country in a position to supply both goods and financial aid on a large scale (United Nations 1947; 1948).

Thus by the latter half of 1945 the economic outlook throughout Europe was indeed grim. The immediate problem was not that of a shortage of assets, despite the heavy losses and destruction, but a severe scarcity of essential supplies, and especially food, to revive a weakened and undernourished population. Imports of essential materials were also urgently required to bring about a recovery of production but because of the low export potential Europe had not the means to pay for them. Europe's position was aggravated by many other factors including large public debts, new waves of inflation especially in former ex-enemy countries, loss of markets and unfavourable terms of trade, and by social and political upheavals. It soon became apparent therefore that Europe would not be able to undertake the task of reconstruction unaided, and that the task would be immeasurably more difficult and protracted if the postwar peace settlement followed the pattern of the previous war. Fortunately, the policies of the allied governments and of the American in particular proved to be more constructive than those after 1918. Unfortunately for Eastern Europe the situation was less promising since the emerging ideological split between the two superpowers meant that the countries of this region derived only limited benefit from the more positive Western policies.

THE DIVISION OF EUROPE

Much has been written on the issue of how and why the Western allies won the war but seemingly lost the peace to the Soviet Union. The implication is that the West let slip the opportunity to shape the configuration of Europe and allowed the Soviet Union to exert its hegemony in Eastern Europe and East Germany. There is an obvious element of tendentiousness in this argument, no doubt a reflection of Anglo-Saxon attitudes on the matter. In fairness, one should point out that the Soviet Union was the main liberating force in the

East and hence it no doubt felt that it had some justification to determine the fate of that part of Europe, as did the Americans in the West. Second, the Soviet Union, like France on more than one occasion, had an interest in strengthening the eastern sector of the continent to ensure that the German menace did not resurface. Third, The Soviet Union was recognized, albeit reluctantly in some cases, as the saviour of Eastern Europe and it was therefore only natural that Eastern countries should gravitate in this direction. Fourth, the USSR had territorial interests, legitimate or otherwise, of long standing in some of the Eastern countries, especially Poland and Romania. Finally, the territorial arrangements following the First World War were generally recognized to be unsatisfactory, not least by the Americans who up to a point were prepared to let the Russians have a free hand in the East provided they kept out of the West. In fact the United States displayed relatively little interest in the fate of Eastern Europe apart from Poland since the region was regarded as somewhat peripheral to its own military, political and economic interests. It was not therefore prepared to take any positive action to forestall the spread of communist regimes in Eastern Europe (Jelavich 1983, 303–4).

Whatever one's own point of view on the matter, the fact remains that the postwar settlement after 1945 was a distinct improvement on that following the First World War. Despite initial attempts to burden the vanquished, the reparations bill was much lighter and the territorial changes were much more modest. Hence there was no repetition of the prewar power vacuum in Central–East Europe. Furthermore, the scale of postwar assistance was far superior to that after 1918. However, one must bear in mind that Eastern Europe under Soviet tutelage fared badly compared with Western Europe.

The most striking feature of the settlement after 1945 was not so much the change in the configuration of Europe but the emergence of spheres of influence between the two superpowers. The victors in 1945 did not rush into formal peace treaty negotiations but instead arranged informally among themselves what boundary adjustments should be made and the terms of demarcation within Europe. Because of strong political differences between the Western powers and the Soviet Union this inevitably resulted in the marking out of spheres of influence in Europe which eventually gave rise to the East–West split. The Soviet Union, because of her role in the liberation of the East, felt she had a right to exercise hegemony in this region.

Nowhere was this more evident than in the case of Germany whose dissection was paramount to Soviet security. Discussions regarding the future of this country had been taking place well before the end of the war. Spheres of influence were worked out by the European Consultative Commission, a body set up following a conference in Moscow in October 1943 of the foreign ministers of the United States, the United Kingdom and the Soviet

Union. This commission fixed the boundary limits of the zones of occupation in Germany: the three western zones which subsequently became the Federal Republic of Germany, and the Soviet zone which was later to form the German Democratic Republic. The division of Germany centred on Berlin which effectively became the dividing line of the East–West split between the major powers. Russia was thereby placed in a strong position to control the region east of the western line of her occupation zone, and her hand was considerably strengthened in this respect after the Yalta and Potsdam conferences of February and July 1945. Russia was allowed to increase her territory appreciably, mainly at the expense of Poland, while the western boundary of her empire was determined by a line running from the Bay of Danzig north to Braunsberg to a point on the frontiers of Lithuania and Poland. This gave Russia an additional 274 000 square miles of territory and 25 millions of population. Poland, by contrast, emerged somewhat smaller than before 1939 as a result of losses in the east, with an area 20 per cent less and a population two-thirds the former size, though the extermination of some 3 million jews by the Nazis accounted for around one-third of the population loss. However she did secure somewhat better western frontiers than after the First World War and also more fertile land than that lost in the east even though it was temporarily devasted (Halecki 1978, 330).

Subsequent peace negotiations with ex-enemy countries further strengthened the Soviet Union's position in the East and restored some of the German conquests. Romania was forced to give up Bessarabia and northern Bukovina to Russia, and Hungary was reduced approximately to her prewar size, losing southern Slovakia to Czechoslovakia and northern Transylvania to Romania. Bulgaria surrendered land formerly acquired from Yugoslavia with Nazi support, while the latter acquired Italian conquests including most of the Istrian peninsula and the Dalmatian Islands.

Though the territorial changes were relatively modest compared with those after 1918, they were significant in terms of later political events and they also involved considerable movements of population. The main losers were Germany and Poland, while the principal beneficiary was the Soviet Union, not simply in terms of territory and population, but also because she was left in a strong position to exert her influence in Eastern Europe. However, in contrast to Western Europe which benefited from the East–West rivalry in the form of United States aid and support, Eastern Europe only received limited reconstruction assistance and the Soviet Union subsequently exacted retribution from the ex-enemy countries in the form of reparations (see below).

THE ROAD TO SOCIALISM

Though by the end of the war the Soviet Union was already a predominant force in Eastern Europe, only Yugoslavia had succumbed to the socialist challenge with the establishment in November 1945 of the Socialist Federal Republic of Yugoslavia. Here the work of Tito and the partisan cause in creating new political institutions and mobilizing the disparate ethnic elements under the banner of nationalism was instrumental in achieving a change in regime (Irvine 1993, 250, 289). Elsewhere, interim coalition governments, with communists as just one element, were the general rule in the immediate postwar years and sovietization was achieved in a process of stages (Seton-Watson 1950, 169–71).

Yet within the space of some three years all the countries in the region had acquired full socialist regimes, adopting the Soviet model as their yardstick. In view of the fact that the majority of the populations in these countries had no strong leaning to the communist cause, the sudden transformation requires a word of explanation. Halecki (1978, 337) reckons that in Poland barely 5 per cent of the population were really committed to the communist cause. It is of course tempting to see the role of the Soviet Union as the main force of change in view of its already powerful position in the East and, like Germany in the 1930s, it had been for many years infiltrating its agents into these countries in order to spread the communist gospel. However, though communist parties gained some ground they were far from being a dominating force at the time in question.

Rothschild (1989, 26, 122–3), in attempting to explain the conundrum, sees a certain degree of continuity between German conquest and control and the shift to communist rule, which marked a break with what went before. The great depression and the Second World War seriously weakened the power of the old political guard at a time when there was growing demand among the population for change. The communists exploited these opportunities to the full, and in many respects their methods of gaining control bore a striking resemblance to those of the former national socialists in Germany (Newman 1970, 369). Within the large multiparty coalitions of the early postwar years the communists, with assistance from the Soviet Union, were able to subvert the normal political processes and emerge as the dominant force by the means of fraudulent electoral practices and terrorist tactics (Jelavich 1983, 303). Non-communist elements were steadily ousted from power by subversive means including beatings, jailing and threats of death. As the element of terror increased many either capitulated or fled abroad leaving the communists to assume a commanding position. By the end of 1948 communist administrations were fully in control in all these countries, under new rulers who owed their position to the Soviet Union: Bierut and

Berman in Poland, Gottwald and Slansky in Czechoslovakia, Rákosi in Hungary, Dimitrov in Bulgaria, Ana Pauker in Romania, and of course the veteran communist leader Walter Ulbricht in East Germany (Schwartz 1973, 25, 28). Having achieved power they set about preventing any reversal by an intensive campaign of Russification, adopting the Soviet model of a one-party state and centralized control which in the course of time led to the abuse of their position and the subjugation of the population to the dictates of authoritarian regimes. Herein were sown the seeds of their own destruction for below the surface 'dangerous tensions and enormous tides of dissatisfaction were building up' (Schwartz 1973, 29).

For all the East European countries, therefore, the later 1940s were a period of violent political and social upheaval involving a complete change in the system of property relationships and the emergence of the state as the main agent of economic activity.

During the reconstruction phase between 1946 and 1949 all countries made rapid strides in the transition from capitalism to socialism. In many cases a start had been made by the coalition governments but once the communists assumed full political control the process was greatly accelerated. Land reform was first on the agenda followed by the expropriation of industry, finance and banking, trade and finally distribution. By 1949 most major branches of economic activity, including banking and finance, were owned and operated by the state. Foreign trade also became a state monopoly and the countries of this region were encouraged by the Soviet Union to draw closer together economically to the exclusion of contacts with the West. Early in 1949 the Council for Mutual Economic Assistance (CMEA or Comecon) was established for the purpose of fostering closer economic relationships and more integrated development among the countries of the socialist camp. It was also seen as an antidote to the Marshall Aid programme in the West, though Comecon's role in this capacity was very limited by comparison.

Progress towards the socialization of agriculture was more protracted. The first main task had been that of land reform in order to satisfy the strong demands of the peasantry for greater equality in landownership. The land reforms of the interwar years, though a step in the right direction, had not solved the land problem. There were still many large estates and many peasants without land or an adequate means of livelihood. Except in Bulgaria, therefore, which already had a very equitable system of landownership, extensive and radical land reforms were promulgated in all countries. At this stage land was not nationalized, but instead redistributed to small and landless peasants. In the process the large capitalist landowners were more or less wiped out. Not until the early 1950s, with the decision to collectivize against promises to the contrary by the communist leaders, was the transition to socialized agriculture finally made.

It is difficult to assess precisely the impact of land reform since it was so soon overtaken by collectivization. No doubt it provided many former landless peasants with a reasonable means of livelihood for the first time and helped to ease the long-standing problem of land hunger, but at the same time it fragmented many large commercial estates into tiny plots not all of which were efficiently farmed. The changeover therefore retarded the postwar recovery of agricultural production. Nor could agrarian reform solve the basic problem of overpopulation on the land which could only be achieved by more rapid industrialization and structural change (Jedruszczak 1972, 210). On the other hand, Brus (1986, 596) maintains that since there were enough viable holdings for economic efficiency the subsequent decision to collectivize was political rather than economic.

The full development of socialist planning took somewhat longer to achieve since until private enterprise was finally eliminated it was difficult, if not impossible, to implement rigorous planning exercises. Given the long historical tradition of state intervention and the urgent need to foster industrialization, there was fairly widespread support for the introduction of some form of economic planning. In fact even in the immediate postwar years when the task of reconstruction was the main priority, tentative steps were already being taken towards planning. Short-term reconstruction plans were launched in this period which focused attention on large-scale industry and set output targets for other sectors. Towards the end of the decade, when the reconstruction phase was drawing to a close and the policy of nationalization was nearing completion, attention was turned to longer-term and more comprehensive planning using the Soviet model (Kemeny 1952; Krejci 1977). Yugoslavia, the first country to set up a socialist state, was also the first to introduce long-term planning with the inauguration of a five-year plan in 1947. Subsequently, however, it was Yugoslavia which departed radically from the Soviet camp and adopted an independent line following its expulsion in the summer of 1948 from the Communist Information Bureau (Cominform), which had been set up late the previous year to facilitate Moscow's control over international communism (Dyker 1990, 19–21). Other countries followed suit as their recovery plans drew to a close. Both Bulgaria and Czechoslovakia launched five-year plans in 1949, Hungary followed in 1950 as did Poland with a six-year plan, while Romania brought up the rear with a five-year plan in 1951 (Seton-Watson 1950, 246–53).

The main objective of the new planning initiative was to build up powerful economies by means of central planning and direction of economic activity to the almost total exclusion of the private entrepreneur and market forces. This therefore involved the final offensive against private enterprise especially in the retail sectors, together with the extension of socialized means of production to agriculture. By the early 1950s there were very few traces of private enterprise left other than in agriculture. A second feature was the shift in the system of taxation towards the Soviet model, namely the adoption of the turnover tax which became the chief source of state revenue. However, the most important element in the new programmes was the implementation of centrally drawn-up plans setting out in some detail the targets to be met in different sectors of the economy. For illustrative purposes the Czech five-year plan of 1949 may be used, though bearing in mind that it was the revised format which represented the ideal of Eastern bloc planning. This set targets for all branches of economic activity and 'norms' for labour productivity, while conversion ratios between resource inputs and final output were specified in detail. Wage rates and material allocations were to be related to these norms. The plan also laid heavy emphasis on the need to maximize growth by boosting investment with priority being given to heavy capital goods and military equipment at the expense of consumer products. The original intention had been far different, however. It had been one of balanced economic development between major sectors which allowed a certain degree of freedom in planning and decision-making at the enterprise level. But pressure from the Soviet Union and other Eastern bloc countries, as a consequence of the perceived military advantages in Europe following the Korean War, soon forced the Czechs to undertake drastic revisions and fall into line with the methods and institutions of Soviet command planning (Selucky 1991, 163–5; Bernasek 1970). As we shall see in a later chapter, the planning exercises produced some remarkable results in terms of the sheer growth in output but in time they inevitably gave rise to a crop of problems.

RECONSTRUCTION AND RECOVERY

Though reconstruction was initially slower in Eastern Europe than in the West, the extent of the recovery in output, especially in industrial production, was by the end of the decade quite remarkable given the daunting circumstances facing the countries of the region at the close of the war. In relative terms the loss and destruction was much more severe than in Western countries and by the end of hostilities levels of activity, both in industry and agriculture, were but a mere fraction of those obtaining before the war. Above all, there was an acute shortage of almost all goods, especially food, such that many people were on the brink of starvation (League of Nations 1946b). Had it not been for the relief supplies dispensed under the aegis of the United Nations Relief and Rehabilitation Administration (UNRRA) the loss of life through destitution would no doubt have been very serious. Relief supplies from this agency were of particular importance to the allied sympathizers; in the period 1945–48 the amount received by Czechoslovakia totalled $261 million, that by Poland $473 million while Yugoslavia got $416 million. Although much of the UNRRA aid was in the form of food, clothing and medical supplies there was also some assistance for the rehabilitation of industry and agriculture. Probably the chief beneficiary was Poland where UNRRA supplies in the eighteen months through to the end of 1946 amounted to 10 per cent of the total supply of goods and services available to that country and as much as 16 per cent at the peak in the second quarter of 1946 (Nötel 1986, 523–4, 577).

This temporary assistance undoubtedly provided a welcome lifeline to these countries, especially since most of the aid was free of charge, though Western experience under Marshall Aid was to demonstrate that much more was required. Most of the UNRRA aid went to fulfil short-term needs and was heavily concentrated in the two years 1945 and 1946. Moreover, the assistance was only available to allied partisan countries so that Bulgaria, Romania and Hungary received virtually nothing. The same was true regarding the distribution of Western credits from commercial sources most of which went to Poland ($251 million) and Czechoslovakia ($168 million). Nor of course was there any follow-up aid for mainstream reconstruction as in the West, since the emergence of the cold war precluded Eastern Europe from participating in Marshall Aid.

Furthermore, the Soviet Union did little to help its socialist brethren. Instead, it subsequently demanded from the ex-enemy countries substantial reparations with only Bulgaria escaping lightly. Eastern Europe was denuded of much of its machinery and other assets which were shipped back to the Soviet Union to help reconstruct the latter's devastated economy (Schwartz 1973, 21). Thus in 1945–46 Hungary's reparation deliveries to the USSR amounted to 17 per cent of an already very depressed national income, and even in subsequent years the share ranged from 7–10 per cent. In the case of Romania the proportion of national income surrendered in this way accounted for some 14–15 per cent of income in 1947–48, over half the deliveries being in oil (Brus 1986, 573). But the severest exactions were those imposed on East Germany. In fact the German Democratic Republic had the double burden of reparation payments and meeting much of the cost of Soviet troops stationed on its territory. At the peak in 1950–51 Soviet takings accounted for over 17 per cent of the GDR's national income, and the impositions continued, though at a declining rate, well into the 1950s until the riots of 1953 forced the Soviet Union to modify its claims (Cairncross 1986, 211–8). Most of the burden fell on personal consumption which remained very depressed compared with prewar.

In sum, therefore, Eastern Europe was probably treated even more harshly than after the First World War. The scale and scope of the short-term relief was of similar magnitude but it was confined largely to three countries, while in both cases there was no long-term assistance for rehabilitation. Reparations penalties, on the other hand, were undoubtedly much more severe than was the case after 1918 when, apart from Germany, most of the smaller ex-enemy countries ended up paying very little.

Several other factors, apart from those already mentioned, helped to complicate or retard the process of recovery. Frontier changes and population movements posed considerable problems for Czechoslovakia, Poland and East Germany, especially the movement of German nationals to the West. Inflation and currency disorders were also a common feature, especially in former occupied countries, and most countries had to carry out extensive monetary and currency reform. In some cases, notably Hungary and Romania, the upward price spiral was allowed to assume hyperinflationary dimensions – the Hungarian experience being the worst in all recorded history – before being brought under control by the introduction of new currencies (Falush 1976a, 1976b; Syklos 1991). Poland also suffered a very sharp rise in prices in the first two years after the war, but Czechoslovakia and Bulgaria took early steps to suppress inflation and stabilize their finances. By 1948, when the German currency was reformed, most countries had managed to achieve stabilization of their monetary and currency systems.

Finally, one should mention the upheaval in the political and social systems of the countries in question, involving the transition from coalition governments with mixed economic systems to socialist regimes and state ownership of the means of production, which in the interim period were to cause some dislocation.

However, judging by the strength of the recovery some of these factors, especially the last, were possibly not as damaging as one might imagine. By 1949 the general level of activity in the group of countries as a whole had already exceeded the prewar level, the main exceptions being Romania and East Germany. This was largely due to the very striking recovery in industrial production and productivity which were accorded priority in the reconstruction plans. Apart from the special case of East Germany, where the repressive policy of the Soviet Union retarded recovery and delayed the introduction of a reconstruction plan until 1949, all countries had surpassed their prewar levels of industrial production by the end of the decade, and in some cases, for example Bulgaria and Poland, by a large margin, whereas two years earlier output levels still fell well short of the earlier peacetime levels. Agriculture, on the other hand, lagged well behind. In 1948–49 agricultural production in the six countries was still only about 80 per cent of the average level of 1934–38 (Zagoroff 1955). Because of the relatively low priority accorded to agriculture in the planning mechanism and the dislocations caused by the subsequent collectivization programme it was to be some years before agriculture fully recovered from the ravages of war. In the case of Czechoslovakia, for example, it was not until 1965 that the output of this sector matched the prewar level (Selucky 1991, 159).

The slow recovery in agriculture and services had the effect of moderating the gains in national income, while per capita changes varied considerably from country to country partly because of differing population experiences. Thus in East Germany and Romania per capita income levels remained below those of prewar because of population movements and lower rates of recovery than elsewhere. Poland and Czechoslovakia, on the other hand, recorded significant increases in income per head due to population losses and strong industrial recovery. The figures in Table 5.1 give some indication of the comparative strength of the recovery though one should bear in mind the somewhat fragile nature of the estimates for these years.

Table 5.1   *Per capita levels of national income, industrial production and agricultural production in 1949 (1934–38 = 100)*

	National income	Industrial production	Agricultural production
Bulgaria	108	210	86
Czechoslovakia	138	146	107
Hungary	115	144	93
Poland	166	230	122
Romania	88	113	88
Yugoslavia	–	155–265	83

Source: Brus (1986, 626)

Improvements in consumption did not match those of national income changes, however. Though the distribution of income was certainly more equitable than before the war due to land reform, increasing employment opportunities, the steady elimination of capitalist producers and the narrowing of occupational income differentials, the amount consumed by the population was deliberately restricted by the planning authorities in the interests of pushing up the rate of investment and the emphasis on producer durables. Food consumption was particularly depressed due to the slow recovery of agriculture and only in Czechoslovakia did it approach prewar dimensions by the end of the reconstruction period. For most non-food products per capita consumption also fell well short of former levels. In this respect East Germany was undoubtedly the most seriously affected. The individual consumer bore the brunt of the reparation policy of the Soviet Union with the result that consumption levels remained very depressed for several years. Even after 1950 the share of national income going to personal consumption was still only around 50 per cent as against more than 60 per cent before the war. As Cairncross (1986, 217–8) notes: 'The East German consumer was the main contributor to reparations through forgoing an exceptionally large share of what he produced.'

Taking all things into consideration, the reconstruction and recovery of the East European economies was quite spectacular. After a slow start the overall performance stands comparison with that of most of the nations of Western Europe. It is perhaps all the more remarkable given the severity of the losses and scale of destruction, the political and social upheavals in the immediate postwar years, and the limited assistance from the region's mentor, the Soviet Union. It speaks much for the determination and achievements of the reconstruction planners in their quest to place their economies on a firm footing. By the end of the decade all the countries had institutionalized their planning mechanisms under communist rule, the transition from capitalism to socialism had all but been completed except for agriculture, and connections with the international market economy had been largely severed. Planning by the state had in fact become a way of life for these countries. Whether the new order was capable of continuing to deliver the needs of society in the postwar period is another matter. For, as Zauberman (1976, 604) points out, the political and social tensions which later arose in most of the satellite countries of the Eastern bloc suggest that their populations were not prepared to pay the heavy price in welfare terms that fast growth and structural change entailed.

6. A new start under socialism in the 1950s and 1960s

By the beginning of the 1950s there was no easy turning back from the socialist road for the countries of Eastern Europe. Politically they had all embraced communism and the climate was right for a radical departure from prewar norms with rapid industrialization seen as the engine of growth. The creation of an industrial working class (with the exception of Czechoslovakia, the peasantry remained in the majority) was viewed as a political prerequisite so that the authoritarian regimes could look towards building a bedrock of support. At least that was the theory! In varying degrees, the countries of Eastern Europe were now to adopt the main features of the Soviet command economy.

The USSR's experience in the 1930s, when rapid growth was achieved (albeit at enormous social cost) while market economies floundered, suggested this was a logical step. A centrally planned system was perceived as the ideal means to eliminate the fluctuations of capitalist economies in favour of steady growth and full employment. The exception was Yugoslavia, whose political ostracism from Moscow forced it to seek better trading relations with the West and eschew central planning. The deviant Yugoslavs introduced workers' self-management, the economic pariah of the Soviet system. Other East European states, falling as they did more firmly within the Soviet sphere of influence and isolated from the West, were compelled to dance to Moscow's tune with little variation being allowed until after Stalin's departure.

Following the postwar reconstruction phase, policies were initiated which sought to accelerate industrialization (1949–53). Stalin's death in March 1953 introduced some degree of moderation and rethinking (1954–70) but without altering the fundamental goals. By the end of the 1960s the East European economies had recorded impressive growths in output. The nature and distortions inherent in pursuing a Soviet-style economic programme were however to throw up increasingly intractable problems whose destabilizing influences would take firmer roots in the succeeding two decades.

THE FIRST FIVE-YEAR PLANS

There were several key features of the Soviet command economy which were to be mirrored in Eastern Europe (Bialer 1986, 6–8). First, the state (meaning the communist party) owned and directed the economy. This meant, in effect, that political objectives dictated which sectors received the lion's portion of the nation's resources. The inevitable result was selective and unbalanced development. Economic growth became dependent on a fix of ever greater inputs of labour and capital. Such extensive growth was the opposite to the intensive growth paths pursued by Western economies which were based on the platform of rising labour productivity, intense innovation and the diffusion of new technology. Enterprises were given targets and became accountable to industrial ministries and their offshoots. Second, land, mineral resources, banks, commerce and foreign trade were nationalized, each of them overseen by a state monopoly. Soviet-type 'single channel' banking replaced competitive commercial banks, with each bank undertaking a specified role such as foreign trade, investment and saving. Third, in stark contrast to Western market economies, the management of the economy was such that primary units of production and services exercised very little autonomy. Fourth, quantity was emphasized over quality. Managers were rewarded for increased output even though this was usually achieved at the expense of quality and with no consideration of costs. Fifth, whereas in the West money supply, the price mechanism and credit acted to reduce costs and bolster productivity, in the command economy these influences were either absent or ineffective. Last, the consumer was asked to endure innumerable deprivations which would have been intolerable in the West and which ultimately sparked revolution in Eastern Europe.

The communist pattern of industrialization dictates that producer goods will expand at the expense of consumer goods. As a consequence, there was inevitably little or no consumer choice in the command economy as it developed in the USSR and Eastern Europe. What the state could offer its citizens was not very much beyond basic essentials. The consumer and agricultural sectors were the sacrificial lambs on the communist altar from the start. And, despite various changes in emphasis over the next four decades, they remained the Achilles heel of the command economy.

Under the East European version of the Stalinist model, the State Planning Office conceived a comprehensive and detailed plan for the entire economy which embraced quantitative targets for the production and distribution of goods and services. Economic ministries then disseminated instructions to branch directorates or directly to enterprises for implementation. Once a plan was adopted, legally binding instructions (plan directives) were issued to economic agents. In industry and agriculture there were compulsory delivery quotas which were so demanding that little could be sold outside the state system. Moreover, production and distribution were separated with state monopolies being created to direct finished goods internally and externally. Lest malpractices should occur, there was a host of correcting bodies, from local officials of the communist party to the state security apparatus (the ultimate deterrent), charged with stamping them out. Because it owned the means of production, the state could and did influence wage rates in favour of particular sectors. Thus in Czechoslovakia, for instance, relatively high wages were paid outside the consumer goods and services sector (Johnson 1989, 11–16). Similarly, the state authorities determined the distribution of resources to fulfil plan targets.

The initiation of the first five-year plans (in the Polish case a further year was added) all started close together – Czechoslovakia and Bulgaria in 1949, Hungary the following year, Poland, Romania and East Germany during 1951. The plans (Table 6.1) emphasized the rapid development of heavy industry (sector A) which enjoyed priority over lighter consumer industries (sector B). Stalin had defined industrialization as the development of heavy industry, especially mining, metallurgy and engineering. Around 75 per cent of industrial investment in the first Soviet five-year plan (1928–32) had been consumed by heavy industry's requirements.

Table 6.1   *First five-year plans of the East European countries (pre-plan output = 100)*

	Bulgaria	Hungary	Poland	Romania	Czechoslovakia
All industry	219	310	258	244	198
Sector A	320	380	254	260–270	233
Sector B	175	245	211	225–210	173
Steel		275	230	357	179
Machinery	680	na	360	216	352
Metal working	266	490	300	220	231
Agriculture	159	154	150	188	137

Source: Smith (1983, 32)

The Czech version sought to raise industrial production by 57 per cent with the metal industry designated to play a crucial expansionary role. The Bulgarian plan directed most investment to industry (40 per cent) and the least to agriculture (17.8 per cent). Similarly, the Hungarian plan (1950–54) allocated 42 per cent of investment to industrial development, a figure achieved through paring down agriculture's share to a miserly 16 per cent. One party leader suggested that Hungary was to be 'transformed into a country of iron and steel', an ambition which ignored Hungary's heavy dependence on imported raw materials – 80 per cent of its iron ore and more than 90 per cent of its coking coal (Tampke 1983, 48).

In Russia during the 1930s there had existed an enormous pool of unemployed or under-employed peasants who could be exploited to form an urban working class provided the factories were built. Apart from Czechoslovakia and the GDR, the countries of Eastern Europe could likewise draw upon a large labour surplus from their agricultural sectors to provide the workforce for rapid industrialization. Official statistics placed three-quarters of the Romanian working population on the land in 1950, while 40 per cent of the 1 million industrial employees were engaged in the related food, textiles and extractive industries (Jeffries 1992, 203). In Hungary over half the labour force was engaged in agriculture as late as 1949. As might be expected, industrial employment and labour productivity increased fastest in the least developed countries, that is Bulgaria, Romania, Yugoslavia and Poland. This was due to their ability to utilize agricultural labour surpluses and absorb the technology available from more advanced countries in the Soviet bloc (Gomulka 1986, 173).

Although Yugoslavia eschewed a Soviet-style economy in 1948, the same year that relations with Moscow were irreparably ruptured, the country broadly followed East European patterns of development until 1955 even if it did not follow the Soviet socialist bible in detail. Heavy industry received precedence over light industry, with factories producing machines and equipment being accorded top priority. In view of the Soviet threat, defence requirements were considered paramount. There was a greater concentration of industrial enterprises as nationalization proceeded apace – by 1963 only 335 industrial enterprises employed less than 60 workers compared with 1654 in 1936. As elsewhere, there was also great emphasis on improving the economic infrastructure, especially in the transport and energy sectors, with unskilled labour from the villages undertaking the building work (Bicanic 1973, 74–5).

Where Yugoslavia differed fundamentally from the typical socialist economy was in its policy of 'factories to the workers'. Even so, the great majority of industrial output was still confined to the 'social sector'; the law restricted private industry to a very junior role. After 1952 all enterprises of any significance were deemed to be 'socially' owned. The doctrine of self-management was born of the need to survive the economic chill imposed by the Soviet bloc. To escape from this refrigerated state also demanded non-alignment in foreign policy. The successful courting of the West was paramount to the survival of Marshal Tito's regime. Between 1951 and 1960 the United States extended to Yugoslavia $2.7 billion of military and economic aid, in return for which Tito gladly stopped supporting the Greek communists, repaired relations with Greece and Turkey, and settled the dispute over Trieste with Italy.

WEAKNESSES OF THE STALINIST COMMAND ECONOMY

Soviet-style central planning engendered four areas of shortage: first, from its emphasis on investment over consumption; second, from the overconcentration on heavy industry; third, because of the tendency of enterprises to produce only a limited range of manufactured goods; and lastly, through wasted potential because cost and efficiency did not matter (Swain and Swain 1993, 112).

The first approach resulted in a deteriorating standard of living. As Table 6.2 indicates, industry took the lion's share of investment resources, thereby depriving agriculture which struggled to feed the population. Thus Poland and Yugoslavia failed to match their prewar levels of grain production until 1957; Czechoslovakia took another three years to achieve the same. Indeed, all three suffered falls in grain output per capita in the early 1950s (Warriner 1964, xv).

Table 6.2   Share of investment by branch, 1953–55

| | Industry* | | Agriculture | |
	1953	1955	1953	1955
Bulgaria	40	39	14	20
Czechoslovakia	42	39	14	20
GDR	50	52	17	15
Hungary	48	41	6	11
Poland	52	43	10	15
Romania	57	57	7	14
Yugoslavia	45	34	5	9

*   In Yugoslavia 'manufacturing and mining'. Comecon countries gross investment; Yugoslavia net investment in fixed assets.

Source: Swain and Swain (1993, 113)

The command economy compelled its enterprises to introduce production methods which were highly resource-intensive. The 'heavy industry at all costs' approach quickly encountered severe problems which compelled a rethink. In essence, the burden the citizen was asked to bear was too great, provoking social unrest which governments could not ignore. The Hungarian regime under Mátyás Rákosi, which conspicuously adopted the most radical heavy industry programme, succeeded only in reducing the standard of living and increasing unemployment. Industrial growth was not fast enough to absorb the loss of jobs resulting from the choking of the handicraft trades. By the summer of 1953 some 2000 villages were bereft of cartwrights, blacksmiths, shoemakers, barbers and tailors. Moreover, there was a food crisis arising from the elimination of the kulaks (peasants with over 13 hectares of land), a mass exodus from the land which left large areas uncultivated, and under-investment in agriculture (Tampke 1983, 49). These problems were duplicated to a lesser or greater extent across Eastern Europe. Czechoslovakia suffered a severe winter in 1952–53 when a shortage of heating fuel arose from heavy industry's excessive requirements. In East Germany the heavy industry programme ran into trouble through a dearth of materials.

The third weakness – a lack of choice – can be seen through one telling example. Before 1939 the Hungarian shoe industry offered the consumer a range of 80 different types to choose from. By the early 1950s that figure had crumpled to just 16. Following Stalin's death, there was a brief respite under the more liberal regime of Imre Nagy whose 'new course', commencing 4 July 1953, placed greater emphasis on agriculture, food processing and consumer goods in an effort to raise the standard of living. But the old guard resumed control in March 1955 when the A sector once more took precedence over the B sector. Industrialization and agricultural collectivization returned with a vengeance, leading to the famous uprising of the autumn of 1956 (Berend and Ranki 1985, 220–25). The same year there was a revolt in Poland. These followed on the popular uprising in East Germany of 17–18 June 1953 which in turn was preceded by riots in Plzen, Czechoslovakia, provoked by the drastic devaluation of the currency and the ending of the rationed supply system. Cumulatively, in conjunction with the de-Stalinization drive in Moscow, the protests forced a rethink of priorities by the various governments of Eastern Europe.

The final weakness of the command economy – wasted potential and inefficiency – was, like the persistent flies annoying grazing cattle in high summer, not to go away. The planning mechanism did not function as smoothly as had been anticipated. The gigantic bureaucracy spawned a veritable mountain of paperwork which militated against expeditious decision taking. While there were target productivity rates, the physical output plan de-emphasized their importance to enterprise managers. The greater the resources that were available to an enterprise the easier it was to achieve plan fulfilment. Consequently enterprise managers tended to exaggerate their raw material and labour requirements and to hoard these in anticipation of higher targets. Similarly, there was a propensity to over-order capital equipment, a defect which the system encouraged because capital charges were either non-existent or derisively low. Such inefficiencies abounded because the system generally rewarded rather than penalized violations. Personnel in ministries and agencies responsible for plan compliance were lax in their application not least because their bonuses depended on the perceived performance of firms for whom they were responsible. As a consequence, exaggerated reports of efficiency deluded the central authorities into believing that the results were as required, if not better, when the opposite was often true.

A CHANGE OF EMPHASIS

The death of Stalin, the end of the Korean War in July 1953, and the relaxation of international tensions which followed, allowed the USSR and its East European satellites to remould their economic policies. It was now recognized that achieving industrialization in one fell swoop over a single five-year plan period could not be done. The industrialization drive of the early 1950s had partly been impelled by the fear of a third world war. The receding of this harrowing prospect, and the need to avoid further serious protest movements from developing, dictated that some consideration now be given to the needs of the population. In the Soviet Union, the 'new course' (political relaxation) followed Stalin's departure as his less dictatorial successor, Nikita Khrushchev, conceded in 1956 that there were 'different roads to socialism', implying the Soviet pattern did not have to be slavishly emulated. Although this message was primarily aimed at winning Yugoslavia back to the fold (in which intention it patently failed), its ripple effects were soon in evidence across Eastern Europe.

In East Germany, the ruling Social Unity Party (SED) announced its own 'new course' involving less emphasis on heavy industry and greater attention to consumer goods, a stance assisted by Moscow which prudently ended reparations. The second five-year plan (1956–60) embraced further concessions to the consumer. While several of the aims of the first plan were continued, not least the intensified development of capital goods industries, greater nationalization of industry and collectivization, improving the lot of the consumer, received almost as much emphasis. Food rationing was to cease as soon as possible, a better supply of durable consumer goods was promised, working hours were to be cut in some industries, and investment in housing was to increase. In May 1958 food rationing was finally abolished (prematurely as it turned out, for this triggered a rapid rise in meat and butter sales, causing shortages). Just as the USSR declared it would overtake the United States so East Germany committed itself to beating its rival West Germany in per capita consumption in all main food products and consumer goods by 1961 (Childs 1987, 7). This was a quite unachievable objective, but its very existence symbolized just how much the emphasis had changed. The need to stem the continued outflow of citizens to the West, which was depriving the economy of skilled and unskilled labour, was a major influence – though ultimately, in 1961, it was the newly erected Berlin Wall rather than an improved standard of living which finally stemmed the tide.

Hungary considered a more radical change of course after the catharsis of its uprising, with around 200 economists and experts charged with developing a 'new economic mechanism'. The Varga Commission, as it was known, suggested that compulsory plan directives should be replaced by a controlled market mechanism, with real prices and a profit motive. The ruling élite saw its proposals as too revisionist and instead adopted partial reforms. The need to assuage the peasantry saw the temporary ending of rapid collectivization, and a planned market economy in agriculture was allowed to flourish. Tax breaks and price incentives replaced compulsory delivery quotas as the means to influence what was grown. The forced collectivization of the first five-year plan was replaced by an extended transitory phase lasting until 1965 (Berend and Ranki 1985, 228). A further measure of appeasement was evident when the new Kádár government increased wages by up to a third of 1955 incomes. With GNP growth still sluggish (rising by only 5 per cent in 1957), this concession was financed through aid from other members of the Council for Mutual Economic Assistance (CMEA) (see Chapter 7). A loan of 1.2 billion roubles from Moscow provided the means to offer a greater selection of consumer goods. The second three-year plan (1958–60) and the second five-year plan (1961–65) were characterized by their flexibility. Unrealistic targets were avoided with heavy industry's goals reflecting available resources. These changes paid off. Living standards rose by around a third over 1957–60 as more consumer goods became available. Televisions, washing machines and refrigerators became commonplace and from the early 1960s private motor cars made their appearance (Tampke 1983, 54).

Similarly, the new Polish five-year plan (1956–60) emphasized the acceleration in the development of the consumer goods sector as a means to improve the standard of living. At the same time, there was no fundamental alteration of the original goals of the first plan. Indeed, during the course of the second, investment in sector A was increased. In Czechoslovakia limited decentralization was enacted in 1958–59. New economic production units were created, consisting of large enterprises or groups of smaller enterprises with shared characteristics. Where there were more than 1400 national enterprises before 1958, the reform reduced these to less than 400 production units. This system was however intended not to replace the existing planning process, but to make it more efficient. Hence, while the size of enterprises increased and their management could take decisions on technical advancement and expansion, the leading players remained directly subordinated to ministries. Again, the old faults remained. Though many of the production units increased their output targets, labour productivity targets remained modest. Moreover, it still paid managers not to reveal excess capacity and to exceed the requirements of a slack plan rather than to increase the planning targets and chance underfulfilment (Stevens 1985, 74, 80–81).

THE REFORMS OF THE 1960s

Although economic reforms started to infiltrate the East European command economies in the later 1950s, it was not until the following decade that a definite and widespread reform movement became apparent. There were several factors involved. One was continued ideological relaxation from Moscow. In October 1961 the Khrushchev regime forcefully and openly denounced Stalin and his methods. The Soviet leader, in seeking 'better plan fulfilment', suggested that enterprises be given greater freedom 'to mobilize internal reserves and make more effective the use of capital investments, production facilities and funds' (Johnson 1989, 41–2). Moscow was no longer certain of the way forward, encouraging more independent and innovative policies across Eastern Europe. The green light for reform is often attributed to an article by Professor Yevsai Liberman, entitled 'Plan, Profit, Premium', published in *Pravda* on 9 September 1962. It suggested that enterprises should be given greater freedom of decisionmaking in the microeconomic sphere. In the crucial determinant period 1962–64 Czechoslovakia, East Germany, Hungary and Bulgaria all experienced a change of leadership with their reform movements finding advocates at the lower echelons of economic policy making. As Czechoslovakia would discover to its cost (see Chapter 7), there was a limit to the deviance that Russia would tolerate, but at least it was able to experiment until 1968. Second, growth rates had generally declined across Eastern Europe in the late 1950s and early 1960s with productivity performance also decelerating (Table 6.3). Applying ever bigger doses of Stalinist medicine, such as the completion of agricultural collectivization (see below), had failed to do the trick. Resources were becoming scarcer. Plentiful labour, which had given an impetus to economic growth earlier, could no longer be counted on.

By the early 1960s there was generally no rural labour reservoir to draw upon while plant and machinery had become technologically backward and

Table 6.3   *National income, 1956–65 (% annual rates of growth of net
material product)*

Country	1956–60	1961–65
Bulgaria	7.0	5.8
Czechoslovakia	7.0	1.9
GDR	7.1	3.4
Hungary	6.0	4.1
Poland	6.5	6.2
Romania	6.6	9.1
Yugoslavia	8.0	6.9

Source: Kaser (1986, 95)

unreliable, impacting adversely on productivity levels. Poland and Romania, still possessing substantial rural populations, were less afflicted by this problem – though it was bound to hit them at some stage. The more advanced countries of Eastern Europe, led by East Germany and Czechoslovakia, were compelled to consider increasing the role of intensive factors of growth to utilize inputs more efficiently. Improving production methods through technological innovation, higher quality management and organization to minimize waste and the division of labour in foreign trade were at the heart of the debate.

Reformist economists in various countries emphasized that the centralized planning system was too inflexible and wasteful. As early as December 1954 Gyorgy Peter of the Hungarian Central Statistical Office had produced a draft model of market socialism which incorporated several ingredients eventually adopted in 1968. There was the recognition that extensive growth needed to be supplanted by intensive growth. High growth rates had been achieved in the immediate postwar period and beyond through major extensive factors involving the creation of the basic infrastructure of a command economy and the concomitant industrial labour force. The impetus given by reconstruction, when the restoration of plant and infrastructure gave disproportionately large returns on investment, fed into the first five year plans, with the movement from the land into factories sustaining growth.

A consensus began to emerge among the economics profession (with the exception of Romania and Poland) about the way forward. First, 'plan' and 'market' were no longer deemed to be two irreconcilable extremes, but could now be fused to the benefit of the socialist economy. Second, a balance needed to be maintained between 'administrative' and 'economic' (financial inducements) levers, with the emphasis switching to the latter over time. Third, financial accounting had to be improved as the economy became more complex so that investment decisions were rationally calculated. Fourth, the interests of workers and plan targets needed to be harmonized and waste made unprofitable to an enterprise. Fifth, greater efficiency would accrue if enterprise managers were allowed a liberal dose of autonomy. They should be permitted to put to advantage their knowledge of local conditions to reduce costs and improve efficiency and be rewarded accordingly. Last, a means had to be found to avoid the overcentralized distribution of machinery, materials and semi-finished goods to enterprises, which caused delays in production and encouraged over-ordering and hoarding (Johnson 1989, 54–8).

In many instances, officials who were tarnished by their association with the failures of past planning were replaced by more reform-minded individuals, often with a formal training in economics. They were encouraged to go outside formal administrative channels in their quest for the Holy Grail of sustained economic growth. In East Germany Erich Apel quickly rose through the ranks. Joining the party in 1957, he was appointed the Central Committee secretary for economic affairs, became a candidate member of the Politburo in 1961, assuming the chairmanship of the Planning Commission a year later. His previous post was occupied by protégé Gunter Mittag and together they drew up the blueprints for a 'new economic system' closely assisted by various research institutes. Hungary's Planning Commission went through a similar metamorphosis with Rezso Nyers, a holder of a degree from the country's most revered school of economics, becoming secretary for economic affairs. He persuaded the Politburo to establish eleven committees of economic experts to compose the draft for the New Economic Model. In Czechoslovakia change came more slowly, but it materialized nonetheless. By late 1964, when the Central Committee approved an economic reform package, the reformers were very much in the ascendant. In Bulgaria the purging of hardline Stalinists was undertaken in close consultation with Khrushchev. Before the reforms were finalized 50 enterprises were subjected to experiments.

Romania and Poland were the laggards. Reformers did not win the ears of Romanian policymakers in the early 1960s. In Poland the reformist movement which showed its head above the parapet in the late 1950s was snuffed out when several Stalinist hardliners returned to dominate the economic decisionmaking process. Reformists soon found themselves demoted. With some slack still to be taken up *vis-à-vis* the movement of people from the land to factories, the Poles could afford for a time to take a dim view of reformists. Indeed, they managed not only to maintain former growth rates, but even to exceed them slightly. Employment increases remained an impor-

tant factor in economic development where in other socialist countries manpower shortages were being encountered (Landau and Tomaszewski 1985,
257–9). Yugoslavia, already more liberal, did not see the need to introduce
economic reform until 1965 and then this essentially amounted to a correc-
tion of the anomaly of the existing system which failed sufficiently to reward
workers' self-management. Accordingly, after 1965 enterprises were exempted
from taxes on net income and profits so that they had more money to distrib-
ute. Also personal incomes were to increase in line with improvements in
labour productivity (Bicanic 1973, 214).

THE IMPLEMENTATION OF THE REFORMS

As Moscow's staunchest allies, it is not surprising that East Germany and
Bulgaria adopted reform programmes which most closely matched Russian
practice. At the other extreme, as might be expected, was non-aligned Yugoslavia. In between Czechoslovakia and Hungary diverged most emphatically
from Soviet experience. It requires emphasis that in the period 1961–67 the
East Europeans themselves formulated their reforms which were not prescribed by Moscow. Indeed in the mid-1960s the officially controlled Soviet
media published favourable accounts of the reform process in Eastern Europe
(Johnson 1989, 79–80). This is not surprising in view of the fact that not one
of Moscow's satellites abandoned socialism. In essence the basic structure of
the communist economy remained intact – the state was still overwhelmingly
in control of economic activity. The liberal phase was only perceived by
ideologists as a transitional interlude before pure communism was attained,
akin to the New Economic Policy pursued by the USSR in the 1920s (Aldcroft
1993b, 190).

The reforms sought to introduce incentives which would so stimulate
enterprises that the result would be a coalescence of their interests and those
of the central planners. 'Trusts' or 'associations' were created, consisting of
several enterprises, which became a middle layer of management sandwiched
between the ministry and enterprise. These assumed different acronyms –
DSO (Bulgaria), VHJ (Czechoslovakia), VVB (GDR), WOG (Poland) and
Industrial Centrals (Romania); Hungary continued to employ the term 'enterprise' for larger units (Smith 1983, 77). Their actual organization varied from
country to country with Romania's predictably the most centralized, but a
common thread was the issue of less specific directives which allowed the
new organizations greater flexibility in drawing up their own plans. Generally the number of compulsory indicators was reduced, enterprises enjoyed a
greater say in microeconomic decisionmaking, profitability inducements were
introduced and, notably in Poland, workers' committees in enterprises were

entertained. Although central controls remained, there was some relaxation. In some instances, prices were allowed to move, albeit within a fixed range. Again, though some flexibility was allowed in the number of employees and their wage levels in any given enterprise, the wage fund was still determined centrally. There was, then, some devolution of decisionmaking and the introduction, in much diluted form, of the market mechanism. Prices, taxes and subsidies were the financial instruments which were used to influence the decisions of enterprise managers.

Within the CMEA (see Chapter 7) the two extremes of the 1960s reforms were epitomized by the GDR and Hungary. In the East German case, their economic experiment, the so-called 'New Economic System' (NES), did not last for long and was never very adventurous. During its short duration (1964–69), the requirements of fulfilling the state output plan remained omnipresent. By 1967 the NES had become the 'Economic System of Socialism', signalling the regime's unease at its tinkering with the purities of the command system. After a more protracted debate on the way forward, Hungary unveiled its New Economic Mechanism (NEM) on 1 January 1968. The main planks of Stalinist planning were cast aside with planning reduced to managing financial instruments and taxes. The profit motive was dangled in front of enterprises as their prime incentive. At the same time, this was a much convoluted version of the capitalist market. The hand of the state remained highly visible. For instance, only a selection of prices was entirely free-floating; the other two categories were fixed or restricted in movement. Similarly, there were three types of enterprise fund and as many taxes applied to them. What singled out the Hungarian version of economic reform was the seriousness of its application which led, for a time, to a society that favoured the consumer, whose problem was no longer a lack of goods but a finite cash pile to take advantage of their availability (Swain and Swain 1993, 134–6).

Outside the Soviet bloc, Yugoslavia had gone furthest on the reformist road. In the early 1950s the command economy was largely dismantled with most prices freed in 1952 and enterprises permitted to engage in foreign trade, egged on by a sixfold devaluation of the dinar. Even so, a true market economy was not permitted. The state remained in control of the banking system and state agencies still carried a lot of weight since much enterprise revenue was received by territorial and federal authorities. By the same token, foreign trade carried the state's firm imprint through tariffs, licences, the manipulation of exchange rates and the distribution of foreign currency. As inflation and unemployment began to raise their ugly heads and the trade deficit worsened so their influence drove the Yugoslavs to greater reforms in the mid-1960s. These gave the self-managed enterprise far more autonomy as tax changes increased retained income. The banking system was also freed up, with banks now able to invest beyond territorial zones. A retail sales tax, more liberalized prices, tariff reductions and the lifting of import restrictions were the other key ingredients of a system which approached Western practices more closely than any other East European experience.

At the other extreme, the Poles and Romanians did little more than tinker with their command economies. In Poland there was much talk but little action and the Romanians were not inclined to stray very much from the rigid Stalinist model. Some changes were belatedly discussed in the late 1960s (when growth rates decelerated), but were not to be implemented until 1978. The system of 'workers' participation', introduced in 1968, was ephemeral and meaningless. Again, while the number of categories of centrally controlled consumer goods was reduced, no less than 170 remained under state direction (Swain and Swain 1993, 139–40).

AGRICULTURE'S PERFORMANCE

Agriculture was the quintessential building block of the communist command economy. Before 1939 agricultural exports to the West had been traded for manufactured goods and technology; in some instances, foreign capital had facilitated the process through constructing the requisite railway lines. Up to the 1970s postwar Eastern Europe sought to achieve economic growth without recourse to foreign capital. Agricultural performance had to improve sufficiently to continue to feed the growing urban population – and thus obviate any need to import food supplies – in spite of the mass exodus from the land occasioned by intensified industrialization. Ideally, food surpluses would be available for export to help pay for imported industrial plant, especially in the period when industry was finding its feet and could not contribute greatly to exports. There was, too, a political objective – the desire of the ruling regimes to gain control over the peasant communities. By introducing socialism to the countryside, it was hoped to eliminate the power of the rural bourgeoisie. The imperative need was 'to obtain control of those areas capable of producing the largest surpluses with the least diversion of state resources' (Sokolovsky 1990, 17).

As it had been in Russia in the 1930s, the collectivization of agriculture was originally envisaged as the ideal vehicle to achieve these objectives. The large-scale cultivation entailed by collectivization was seen by the state as a way to improve the total productivity of the agricultural sector. The collectivization drive in the USSR initiated in 1929 was motivated by a grain crisis which brought food rationing to the cities, thereby threatening the industrialization programme. Similarly, the decisionmakers in Eastern Europe wished to ensure a plentiful supply of cheap food for the rising urban population. In turn this would help to keep the lid on wages.

The problem was that throughout the 1950s agriculture was a low priority area in the economies of Eastern Europe. Capital investment in agricultural machinery and equipment was inadequate because of heavy industry's requirements. Another drawback was that some agricultural products were more suited to collectivization than others. Wheat headed the list of amenable commodities; corn was less compliant while fruit, vegetables and animal products exhibited a definite aversion to collectivization.

The collectivization drive in Eastern Europe began in the wake of Russia's denunciation of Yugoslavia and its deviance from accepted communist practice which included the failure to collectivize agriculture. Yugoslavia had in fact rushed headlong into collectivization after the war, but was deemed to have failed to lay down the appropriate political and economic framework (Wadekin 1982, 35). The Moscow-inspired Cominform resolution of 1 July 1948 condemned Yugoslavia for treating the peasantry as a single entity, for ignoring the fact that small individual holdings gave rise to capitalism, and for failing to nationalize the land. Following this declaration, all the East European governments moved officially towards collectivization, despite their earlier promises to the contrary.

Although the repression meted out in pursuit of collectivization did not match the Soviet experience, nevertheless class warfare was declared on 'kulaks' – rich peasants – who might face any number of punishments, including imprisonment and deportation. Even so, peasants were permitted to join lower types of collectives with only the higher forms emulating the Soviet *kolkhoz*. In strictly legal terms a difference with the Soviet model lay in the failure to nationalize the land. But while in theory a peasant might own the plot he brought into the collective farm, in practice he could only sell or bequeath it to the state or the collective. The public sector therefore effectively acquired most of the farming land. Such differences were more apparent than real and often derived from the lessons drawn from Soviet practice.

Under Nazi-controlled or dominated territory a system of delivery quotas was established that compelled each peasant household to provide specified amounts of farm produce to the state. Especially effective in Czechoslovakia, Hungary and Poland, after the war the East European regimes manipulated this inherited system to their advantage: excessive quotas were imposed on the more affluent peasants while collective farms were treated very lightly, with frequent exemptions. Any failure to meet quotas led to an instigated propaganda campaign which asked the village poor to find the 'concealed' surpluses of their better-off neighbours (Sokolovsky 1990, 27). This was the big stick which was wielded to lubricate collectivization.

The state could and did manipulate the peasantry in other ways. Taxes were levied at their greatest extent on affluent peasants and most leniently on collective farms. Machinery, fertilizer, quality seed and other inputs were in short supply and their distribution was controlled by the state. Naturally state and collective farms received a greater proportion of what was available from supply cooperatives and machinery stations. The latter were based on the Soviet model and pooled available agricultural machinery, both that confiscated from former estates and larger peasant farms and newly produced. Individual peasants were also denied the right to purchase from state production.

Seeking political stability, Hungary and Poland ended the hated machine and tractor stations (MTS) in 1956, preceding the Soviet Union by some two years; East Germany, Czechoslovakia and Bulgaria then followed suit; Romania kept hers but integrated them into the larger collective farms. When the Hungarian collectivization drive started anew, collective farms were permitted to own machinery, obviating the need for MTS. Poland transformed her MTS into servicing and repair stations serving individual peasants as well as collective farms. Yugoslavia had been first in dissolving the MTS system in 1951–52, with the general agricultural cooperatives taking over their functions.

THE EXPERIENCE OF INDIVIDUAL COUNTRIES

As Table 6.4 indicates, collectivization proceeded at different speeds across Eastern Europe during the 1950s. In Yugoslavia the process came to a virtual standstill, with only a few collectives in evidence after 1954. The political situation in Poland and Hungary in 1956 led the former to abandon collectivization altogether while the latter did not resume its campaign until 1958. And then the emphasis was different, with the class struggle model being rejected in favour of recruiting the kulaks. By 1960 Czechoslovakia and East Germany were fully collectivized; Hungary joined them in 1961 and Romania the following year.

Bulgaria led the way in the collectivization drive which it began on a voluntary basis between 1945 and 1947. By 1950, 2038 collective farms had been created and two summers later the first collectivization campaign was complete, with cooperatives now dominant. This achievement reflected the leadership's close adherence to the earlier Soviet model and its associated intimidation. Bulgaria was also the first East European country to introduce 'agro-industrial' cooperation (1968). The communist system intended state farms to be substantial production units with their activities confined to a few selected types of crops or animals. Bulgaria went for the 'bigger is better' approach and in the late 1950s embarked on a programme to amalgamate collective farms into massive units of 4000 hectares, larger even than the *kolkhozes* in Soviet regions.

Table 6.4   The socialist sector in Eastern Europe

Country	Year	Number of cooperatives	% of agricultural area socialized
Bulgaria	1947	549	–
	1953	2744	57
	1956	3100	78
Czech.	1950	3760	24
	1952	7835	44
	1962	8165	90
Hungary	1949	1500	7
	1952	5315	34
	1962	4018	97
Poland	1950	635	10
	1955	9076	23
	1961	1783	13
Romania	1949	1952	5
	1955	2152	13
	1962	5398	74
Yugoslavia	1950	15605	22
	1960	150	8

Source: Dovring (1965, 200)

As one of the most advanced countries, Czechoslovakia's agricultural sector already played a secondary role within the economy when collectivization began, comprising only 17.6 per cent of GNP in 1948 (United Nations 1952, 26). Moreover, the communist party could already count on a mass base of support among the peasantry. Indeed, collectivization was welcomed in parts of the Czech lands because it provided much-needed agricultural machinery and buildings as well as enticing state subsidies. Czechoslovakia was unique in Eastern Europe in not having any surplus labour. But where other countries in the Soviet bloc lacked the resources to support agricultural modernization, Czechoslovakia was blessed with the facility to do so, with industry able to provide machinery, chemical fertilizers and capital construction.

The Polish leadership, with a large peasant population to consider, had prudently concentrated its collectivization efforts in the frontier area extracted from Germany in the peace settlement. In 1949, when the drive began, only 3 per cent of arable land was collectivized, a figure which rose to a high point of 8.5 per cent in December 1954, involving around 173 900 peasant households (Sokolovsky 1990, 61). As early as 1948 guerilla fighters made their appearance in the countryside, ready to challenge collectivization. The resistance was such that in 1956 the campaign was abandoned. After reaching 10 200 that year, by the close of 1957 just 1700 cooperative farms remained. Even so, peasant farms still had to make compulsory deliveries to ensure that the government could count on a minimum reserve of basic foodstuffs. This requirement tended to negate specialization, with some farmers even having to purchase certain farm products to meet their obligations. In 1966 a government resolution restricted the takeover of arable land for non-agricultural purposes and dictated farming methods: farmers were required to use a minimum amount of fertilizers, a system known as *agrominimum*. The state was also entitled to take land from declining farms. This hostile regulatory framework engendered an odour of mistrust and uncertainty between peasants and government bureaucrats which was not conducive to efficiency. Unlike Yugoslavia, the Polish system continued to be weighted in favour of the socialized sector which included cooperatives and state farms. While organizational adjustments diminished their number in the late 1960s, in terms of area and employment they continued to grow, reflecting state favouritism. In the 1960s the state farms and cooperatives outperformed private farms, increasing their contribution to final agricultural output from 11.3 per cent in 1960 to 16.3 per cent by the end of the decade – though their production costs were higher (Landau and Tomaszewski 1985, 270).

The Hungarian collectivization drive provides an interesting case study of the shifts in government policy which were required to make it work. The campaign focused on the grain-producing areas and in its early phases assumed Stalinesque proportions, reflecting the view that agriculture was holding back socialist development. Between 1950 and 1953, 23 per cent of working Hungarian peasants were compelled to join cooperatives. A flexible definition of a 'kulak' was employed which enabled administrators to subdue any local resistance. Indeed, a list of 70 000 'kulaks' was compiled which included a motley collection of 50 000 peasants, 10 000 village store owners and 1600 tradespeople (Sokolovsky 1990, 98). Special internment camps were established for dissident kulaks and the officially controlled media waged a relentless campaign which catalogued their 'crimes' – among them supplying infected grain to the state, faking planting and hiding crops. Absurd quota levels found 800 000 Hungarian peasants in 1952 without sufficient grain to make bread or plant a new crop, with half as many again receiving sentences for defaulting on cultivation and delivery requirements or secreting their produce. It was no wonder that many of them offered parts or all of their land to the state, from which state farms were formed (Revenz 1990, 36).

The liberal Nagy regime perceived forced collectivization and the lack of economic incentives to individual peasants to be an ill-conceived strategy which had merely succeeded in alienating the middle peasants whose allegiance Lenin had seen as the key to socializing agriculture. Accordingly it reversed the policy, allowing peasants to leave cooperatives, a move which resulted in the dissolution of 60 per cent of all cooperatives between June and December 1956. The more conformist Kádár administration at first hesitated to interfere with agriculture on the old scale, but its gradualist approach to collectivization was finally abandoned in 1958.

Later that year, it was decided to resume collectivization but without the element of class struggle that was the centrepiece of the Stalinist variant. Instead, concerted efforts were made to win over middle peasants; where it worked this strategy saw the rest of the village follow their leaders. Should the middle peasants decline to join an existing cooperative, they were encouraged to form their own and allowed to assume assertive positions within them. Moreover, kulaks were now permitted to join cooperatives and after two years to seek a leadership role. The carrot emphatically supplanted the stick: if peasants contributed land to cooperatives, the latter would pay the land rent. Cooperative members also enjoyed welfare benefits such as pensions and health insurance. Much more generous state subsidies to purchase machinery, livestock and equipment underpinned the economic viability of the cooperatives as never before. In essence the divisive policy of the past was replaced with one which won over whole villages, whatever their inhabitants' individual status. This approach enabled collectivization to be completed by 1961 with 95.6 per cent of arable land then falling within the socialist sector (Sokolovsky 1990, 147–8). The New Economic Mechanism went a stage further, ending direct central control over the agricultural cooperatives and confining state intervention to pricing, credits and subsidies. Further, provided agriculture remained their prime activity, the cooperatives were permitted to seek supplementary work outside the sector.

In East Germany collectivization was achieved within the period 1952–60. By the latter date under 8 per cent of the agricultural area was privately farmed, with cooperatives constituting 84.2 per cent of the total. The regime then concentrated on superimposing industrial forms on to agriculture with the aim of achieving self-sufficiency in agricultural products. This process saw the amalgamation of agricultural production cooperatives, whose number fell from 19 313 in 1960 to 3946 by 1980. The amount of farm equipment also increased significantly. In 1960 there were 70 865 tractors and 6409 combine harvesters. By 1970 the figures read 148 865 and 27 186 respectively (Childs 1987, 7, 44).

Romania was a laggard economy with agriculture continuing to be the largest employer until as late as 1978. Indeed, the agricultural labour force actually increased during the 1950s, a trend which was only reversed the following decade through the more extensive use of machinery, fertilizers and pesticides. Although a high proportion of land was devoted to agricultural use, rainfall was poor in the most fertile soils, creating a huge drag on potential performance, especially as the authorities were remarkably slow to increase the amount of irrigated land, which did not appreciate significantly until the 1980s (Turnock 1986, 178, 187–90).

Yugoslavia's collectivization drive was halted dramatically by the disastrous harvest of 1952, the worst in living memory. The communist party then came up with 'the breakthrough on a narrow front' strategy which concentrated state investment in the fertile Voivodina. Although the compulsory sale of foodstuffs to the state at fixed prices was ended and the emphasis was increasingly placed on market-determined prices, the state continued to control the prices of politically sensitive agricultural products such as meat, wheat and rice.

Whatever solution was adopted, the stark fact remained that all states continued to struggle to provide cheap food for the urban masses. In the second half of the 1950s, with the exception of Bulgaria, agricultural growth slowed across Eastern Europe. While overall there had been considerable improvements by the end of the 1960s, especially in mechanization and the use of fertilizers, there were nevertheless some alarming signals, not least a 'mounting strain on food supplies ... in some countries of the area', reflecting the wild fluctuations in the size of annual crops (United Nations 1971, 75). In 1962 Bulgaria, for example, was compelled to import wheat from Canada to quell disturbances in several towns arising from food shortages. Admittedly, inclement weather played a part but the full potential of what was harvested or slaughtered simply was not realized, resulting in exorbitant losses. Throughout the region storage and freezing facilities were inadequate as were processing capacity and transport. Indeed, this lack of a proper infrastructure was said to have resulted in the loss of as much as a quarter of gross harvest output (Brown 1988, 133–4). Statistically, the extent of mechanization in some countries might have been impressive, but behind the illusory comfort of figures lay the reality of extensive inefficiency. Tractors, for example, were not replaced frequently enough and many stood idle through a lack of spare parts.

To the political consternation of the regimes, rising incomes were making the population more discriminating in their eating habits. By the mid-1960s the rise in meat production had decidedly slowed down. Meat output in

Bulgaria and Poland was especially worrying, the growth rate having fallen to 1.1 and 1.6 per cent a year respectively over the period 1965–70. Although elsewhere the figure was above 2 per cent, the trend was still worryingly downward. By 1970 East Germany and Poland, in particular, were finding it difficult to meet the demand for livestock products. The GDR was compelled to import more fodder than it intended and to appeal to small producers to raise their output. Poland's problems were compounded by the emphasis on grain production during 1966–70 at the expense of animal products. Moreover, the switched emphasis from pork to beef and veal proved disastrous – the output of the latter failed to improve in the late 1960s when pork production stagnated after rising by 11 per cent during the early 1960s. Grain imports were only marginally reduced over the period, falling from an average of 2.5 million tons over 1961–65 to 2 million tons during 1966–70.

THE GROWTH RECORD

After two decades of socialism the countries of Eastern Europe could boast of impressive growth rates. Including the USSR, by 1970 the socialist countries of Europe were responsible for some 30 per cent of world industrial output, a substantial improvement on the 18 per cent evident in the early 1950s. Between 1950 and 1970 industrial production increased five times in Czechoslovakia, sevenfold in East Germany, sixfold in Yugoslavia and eleven times in Bulgaria and Romania. As might be expected in economies modelled on the Soviet example, engineering became the leading sector, accounting for between one-fifth and one-third of total industrial output by 1970. Again reflecting rapid industrialization, the region's agricultural labour force declined by a fifth over the period. In Bulgaria the percentage of the working population engaged in agriculture and forestry fell from 64 to 38 per cent. The decline was less marked elsewhere, for instance in Poland and Hungary, reflecting the fact that there was already some under-employment in the sector at the start of the period (Cipolla 1976, 606–9).

The period was dominated by extensive growth, for which reason – even allowing for the massaging of official statistics which was endemic across the region, not least in Romania – Eastern Europe returned faster rates of input growth than Western Europe. This was particularly true of employment. While employment in the West only grew at an annual rate of 0.6 per cent over the 1950s and 1960s, the East returned a much more impressive 1.7 per cent. Even so, factors unique to Eastern Europe need to be taken into account. The movement of population out of agriculture, the extensive development of heavy industry and the overriding emphasis on output over efficiency and quality combined to create, at times, labour shortages. Indeed, such was the need to maximize labour potential that women were extensively re-cruited, constituting a greater proportion of the labour force than in Western Europe.

What is apparent from a later vantage point is that, notwithstanding the reforms of the 1960s, the socialist system remained flawed. Much of the economic growth was accounted for by greatly increased capital inputs, especially in industry while, despite some adjustments, services and agricul-ture remained the poor relations. While fixed capital stock in industry rose by an annual average of 8.3 per cent over the two decades, for services and agriculture the figure was only a little more than 5 per cent (Aldcroft 1993b, 179–83).

The reforms of the 1960s sought to improve economic efficiency by ra-tionalizing the system of planning and management. The results were mixed and did not produce the expected results. As one commentator (Johnson 1989, 49–50) notes, by the close of the decade policymakers were growing increasingly concerned at

> the widespread and expensive waste of labour and physical productive resources due to excessive absenteeism, job-hopping, hoarding, and bad planning in the distribution system; the presence of severe shortages of certain goods simultane-ously with the rapid expansion of unsaleable inventories, due to failures of quality control and simple lack of responsiveness to consumers' preferences; and pro-nounced sectoral imbalances in the distribution of manpower and capital that were adversely affecting agriculture, construction, transportation and light industry, in the process creating costly bottlenecks for future industrial development.

Herein lay the seeds of the black market which would take an even firmer grip in the 1970s and 1980s.

What was transparent by the end of the 1960s was that a more marked shift to intensive growth was required if the East was ever to hope to match the West in the technological and scientific spheres of production. Despite all the reforms, there remained a development lag between East and West which could only be bridged by greatly improving productivity and product quality, which in turn meant replacing antiquated plant with the latest state-of-the-art manufacturing equipment only available from the capitalist West. In the 1960s East Germany alone managed to keep pace with the West, while it was only against the poorer performing market economies, such as Britain and Portugal, that Eastern Europe did not fall behind. In the 1960s East Germany and Czechoslovakia, the two most developed countries, shifted the emphasis to high-tech industries as they ended the growth phase built on a rapid increase of factor inputs (Griffith 1989, 50–52). Soon the rest of the pack would be compelled to follow suit.

At the end of the day, with the exception of Yugoslavia, the reforms were inhibited by the need to placate the Soviet Union which would not tolerate the usurpation of socialism in favour of a pure market economy and the associated introduction of democratic government, as Czechoslovakia found to its cost in 1968. Hungarian reformers became noticeably more cautious after the traumatic crushing of the 'Prague Spring'. The requirements of membership of the Soviet bloc, a subject to which we now turn, were such as to ensure that the extent of any economic reforms, especially when they were loaded with political ramifications, were fettered by the onerous demands of the Kremlin.

7. Eastern Europe within the Soviet orbit

Ascendancy over Eastern Europe was to serve the USSR's interests in a composite mixture of ideological, political, economic and military ways. At the close of the Second World War, with the British and French Empires reduced to shaky edifices of their former selves and the axis powers no more, the United States and the USSR emerged as the only superpowers strutting the world stage. Their diametrically opposed ideologies of capitalism and communism set them on a collision course and for the next four decades and more there would be times when the military stand-off between them caused by each side's possession of formidable nuclear arsenals threatened to turn the cold war into a hot one. When the Communist Information Bureau, or Cominform, was founded in September 1947 Josef Stalin's acolyte, Andrei Zhdanov, developed the theory of the two camps – the 'imperialist', 'anti-democratic' camp led by the United States and the 'socialist', 'anti-imperialist', 'democratic' camp championed by the USSR (Sword 1990, 16). Not through choice, but through circumstances beyond its control, Eastern Europe was placed firmly in the latter camp. Somewhat ironically, it was Josef Goebbels, the Nazi propaganda minister, who had first warned of an iron curtain descending on Eastern Europe. The phrase was given greater meaning when in 1946 Winston Churchill's flowery rhetoric encapsulated the description – 'From Stettin in the Baltic to Trieste in the Adriatic, an iron curtain has descended across the Continent' (Balfour 1981, 33). Eastern Europe, liberated from one form of oppression, was plunged headlong into another dark age.

Much of the USSR's influence and its global power status rested on maintaining its dominance over Eastern Europe, a region which the Red Army had simultaneously liberated and claimed as it drove German forces back remorselessly across their borders. The heavy casualties which were sustained in this final phase of the European conflict provided the Soviet government and people with an emotional attachment to the region. Eastern Europe soon became a potent symbol of Soviet power, confirming to the Russian people that the communist creed of Marxism–Leninism had successfully penetrated far beyond their borders and that there remained the possibility of a world communist revolution.

The changing relationship between the Soviet Union and Eastern Europe revolved around the need of the former to stamp its authority on the region.

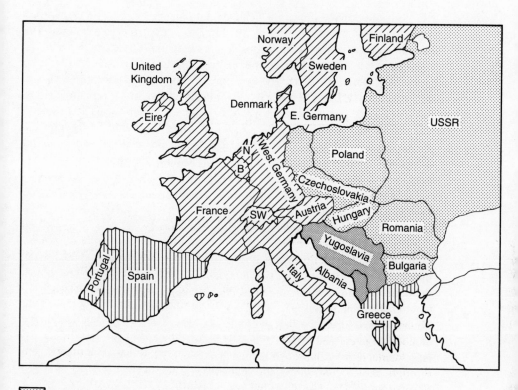

Communist states under the influence of the USSR

Communist states eventually outside the Soviet bloc

States experiencing right-wing regimes but eventually establishing parliamentary democracies

Parliamentary democracies

Source: J. Lee, *The European Dictatorships*, London: Methuen, 1987.

Map 3   The political division of Europe after 1945

The USSR's postwar security considerations dictated that most of the nations of Eastern Europe must be favourably disposed towards it. The means by which the region's 'friendship' was achieved took a variety of forms. The first was military coercion. While many of the regimes enjoyed little mass support, the backing of the Red Army ensured that they remained in power.

Moscow laid down a limit to which national independence could be asserted which came to be epitomized by the Brezhnev Doctrine (see below). The second was the economic relationships between the Soviet Union and her satellites as represented by the umbilical cord of the Council for Mutual Economic Assistance (CMEA). The economic exploitation of Eastern Europe in the immediate postwar period gave way after Stalin to Soviet economic aid to the East European members of CMEA, the extent of which varied according to their importance and loyalty. The willingness of Moscow to be the gigantic dustbin for the inferior goods offered by its Eastern satellites, which would have been unsaleable on the world market, sustained poor economic performance in the East far beyond its natural shelf life and perpetuated inefficiency.

HIGH STALINISM IN EASTERN EUROPE

Stalin's final years, from 1948 to his welcome death in March 1953, have come to be known as the period of 'high Stalinism' in Eastern Europe. The Soviet bloc was essentially his creation, born of the need to avert a repetition of a life and death military struggle with Germany which had cost over 20 million Soviet lives. Whereas before the Second World War 'socialism in one country' had been the rallying cry, after it the ripple effects of the conflict and Russia's overwhelming desire to prevent a resurgent militarist Germany from invading it for a third time in the twentieth century dictated that 'socialism in one region' was now a paramount requirement.

'Eastern Europe' as a political term belongs firmly to the postwar period – prewar geographers had placed Eastern Germany, Poland, Czechoslovakia and Hungary in Central Europe while Romania, Bulgaria and Yugoslavia were clustered in South-Eastern Europe (or the Balkans). Above all, Eastern Europe represented a geopolitical bloc centred on Moscow. The Soviet superglue began to be applied to all states bar Yugoslavia when the other six were referred to by Soviet spokesmen as the 'people's democracies' of Eastern Europe – although very quickly their regimes became the antithesis of democracy. In fact, with the exception of Czechoslovakia, all the communist parties lacked popular support. It has been estimated that in the immediate postwar period the Soviet Union could count on only about 50 000 true supporters out of a total population in the five other countries of around 75 million (Gati 1990, 15). To bolster support, the parties opened their membership lists, offering powerful positions to many. Even former fascists were not excluded provided they obeyed orders. In Poland Soviet citizens with Polish ancestry were recruited to make up the numbers. Most of the leaders who came to prominence as a result of such machinations 'needed little urging to obey Stalin's dictates' (Schwartz 1973, 28).

Yugoslavia was unique in that it was not overrun by the Red Army. The Tito regime accordingly did not owe anything to Russian military might and quickly asserted its independence. In March 1948 all Soviet military and civilian 'advisers' were ordered to leave the country, leading three months later to Cominform's expulsion of Yugoslavia. Soviet efforts to undermine Belgrade included the deployment of Cominform agents, the waging of economic warfare, a virulent propaganda campaign, menacing troop movements and border incidents, but fell short of actual military invasion, a move which would have threatened to turn the developing cold war into a poker-hot East–West conflict. Stalin's efforts to bring down the impudent ideological pariah – 'I will shake my little finger and there will be no more Tito' – therefore proved a dismal failure. During Stalin's final years and afterwards 'Titoism' would represent an alternative form of socialism with greater freedoms, but one which most East European countries were understandably reluctant to embrace. Lest they did so, Stalin initiated a purge of communist parties in the region designed to eliminate potential Titos. In Hungary, Bulgaria, Czechoslovakia and Poland leading politicians under suspicion were subjected to rigged show trials on the Stalinist model, following which came execution or imprisonment. In Czechoslovakia alone almost 200 people were executed between 1948 and 1952, the most notable being the communist party's general secretary, Rudolf Slansky (Schwartz 1973, 32, 35; Brown 1988, 37).

Although all the countries of Eastern Europe were important to the Soviet Union, some were unquestionably more important than others. In the Kremlin's eyes, there was a pecking order. At the top stood East Germany which, as long as it remained an entity, would emasculate German power and maintain the postwar status quo. Next came Eastern Europe's largest country, Poland, the route used by the Nazis to invade the Soviet Union which also now assumed a double importance as a lifeline to the GDR. To allow Poland to tumble out of the Soviet orbit was tantamount to saying goodbye to East Germany, which could not long survive cut off from the oxygen of Soviet economic sustenance, hemmed in as it was by two democratic states on either flank.

Eastern Europe was conveniently divided into northern and southern tiers. Moscow viewed the northern tier, embracing East Germany, Poland and Czechoslovakia, as by far the most important. Bismarck had said that whoever controlled Bohemia was master of Central Europe, a lesson which was not lost on Hitler or Stalin. In economic terms, the trio were also the most significant. East Germany and Czechoslovakia were the more advanced industrial powers while Poland, blessed with an abundance of raw materials and a young population, possessed the potential to outperform most countries in the region (Brown 1988, 33–5).

By comparison, South-Eastern Europe never assumed the same significance in Soviet eyes because the threat posed by this tier to their security was marginal. Yugoslavia, Albania and Romania all defected from the bloc in 1948, 1961 and 1964 respectively without suffering military consequences. On the other hand, these powers were beaten with the Soviet economic stick whereas Bulgaria, which stayed loyal, enjoyed considerable economic favours (see below). Soviet military tolerance of events in this region was in stark contrast to the northern tier where the GDR (1953) and Czechoslovakia (1968) experienced direct Soviet armed intervention and Poland (1981) indirect. Hungary, while strictly speaking a southern tier country, was perceived as a linking bridge between the two tiers of Eastern Europe and consequently also encountered Soviet military repression in 1956.

Up to Stalin's death the states of Eastern Europe were treated by Moscow as little more than Soviet colonies to be plundered for economic gain to assist postwar recovery. The extent to which the achievements of the fourth Soviet five-year plan, which surpassed most of its targets, was attributable to the reparations imposed on Eastern Europe is debatable; the harshness of them is not. East Germany, Hungary and Romania, tainted with the Nazi brush, lost considerable transport resources and industrial equipment, even entire factories such as the Zeiss works at Jena. But nor were the USSR's allies, Czechoslovakia, Poland and Yugoslavia (until 1948), treated much differently. The eastern part of Germany was exploited most of all and to an extent which so alarmed the Western powers that they refused to sanction the transfer of reparations from their respective German zones. As well as reparations, the USSR also imported raw materials from the East, paying much below world market prices. There were, too, unfavourable trade treaties imposed by the Russians in territories they occupied and so-called mixed companies, established by them to reap their profits (Bullock 1991, 1044–5).

Yugoslavia apart, there was no escape from this economic pillaging. In the summer of 1947 Czechoslovakia, Poland and Hungary all expressed interest in the Marshall Plan, but the idea was quashed by Stalin who feared their defection to the West. Czechoslovakia actually participated in the negotiations, but Soviet pressure soon forced its delegation to withdraw. One authority (Griffith 1989, 53) calculates that in the first postwar decade the Soviets plundered around $14 billion from the six East European countries, which was roughly equivalent to the amount spent by the United States on reviving Western Europe under the auspices of the Marshall Plan.

At the same time, it should be recognized that the Soviet Union gradually came to concede that if it was to continue to occupy the void in trade links with Eastern Europe left by the defeated Germans then it had to offer the juicy carrot as well as the hefty stick. Moscow therefore made loans of grain and other foodstuffs to relieve food shortages and provided some raw materials and consumer goods, accepting anything the East Europeans could offer in return. In 1947 the Soviets renegotiated credit agreements with Bulgaria,

Czechoslovakia and Yugoslavia and wrote off half the Hungarian and Romanian reparations burden (van Brabant 1989, 14). Herein lay the seeds of the future economic relationship between Russia and its satellites.

In January 1949 the CMEA, or Comecon, was formed in Moscow, comprising the Soviet Union, Bulgaria, Hungary, Poland, Romania and Czechoslovakia. East Germany joined its ranks in 1950. It has been suggested that the Russians created the CMEA as an antidote to the Marshall Plan (Smith 1983, 174). This interpretation is supported by the communiqué from the conference which stated that 'broader economic co-operation between the peoples of the people's democracies and the Soviet Union' was intended because the founder members 'do not consider it possible to subordinate themselves to the dictates of the Marshall Plan, as this plan infringes on the sovereignty of countries and the interests of their national economies' (Sword 1990, 18). Alternatively, the move has been seen (van Brabant 1989, 11–12, 14) as a wrecking manoeuvre to nip in the bud emerging efforts towards regional economic integration among the East European states. Indeed, the growing trading links between the Central–East European states was such that by 1948 the Soviet share in their trade was down to 10–20 per cent. This trend was equally apparent in the Balkans where Bulgarian and Romanian trade with East European countries reached 75 per cent and 50 per cent respectively. There were several Balkan federation schemes as well as a Czechoslovak–Polish trade agreement which were designed to promote closer economic links among the member countries.

As Smith (1983, 151) suggests, left to their own devices the East Europeans could have developed complementary and interlinking economic systems. The president of the Hungarian Planning Office disclosed that the overall aim was 'to adjust the development of industrial branches ...[so that] a more or less coherent economic system should be developed by the Eastern European People's Democracies', a pronouncement which so worried Stalin that he personally vetoed the plans. The Bulgarian–Yugoslav plan had especially alarmed the Kremlin which was anxious to isolate Yugoslavia economically and stamp out its alternative socialist economic vision.

Then, too, Moscow was anxious to offset Eastern Europe's rapidly growing trading links with the imperialist West. This was effectively achieved by the cold war's escalation which led the Americans to impose bans and restrictions on East European goods, with Czechoslovakia, Hungary and Poland especially feeling the icy chill. America's embargo on exports of strategic and technological products, which made up around half the international traded goods to Eastern Europe, was soon extended to preclude all recipients of Marshall Aid from engaging in trade with the Soviet bloc (Smith 1983, 150). Subsequent moves towards integrating West European economies further isolated Eastern Europe and drove it headlong into Soviet embraces.

Czech growth was hindered by the strategic embargo, Poland was impeded by the development of the European Coal and Steel Community, while later still the European Economic Community's (EEC) agricultural policy was to dampen the export potential for Romania, Bulgaria and Hungary's agricultural sectors.

Whatever its origins, the CMEA was moribund in its early years and the opportunity, if it existed, of properly integrating the member economies was lost as individual governments drew up their early five-year plans in isolation, ensuring that there was much product duplication. There was an attempt to browbeat the Czechs into becoming the main supplier of investment goods for the Soviet bloc, but this fell through when it was realized that other CMEA members lacked sufficient goods to barter exchange for Czech exports whereupon, under Soviet pressure, the emphasis of Czechoslovakia's initial five-year plan switched from consumer goods to heavy industries (Skilling 1991, 164). Thus, when Stalin spoke of 'two parallel world markets', this description only applied in broad terms to the amount of intra-bloc trade, with the percentage of Soviet imports emanating from Eastern Europe increasing dramatically from between the late 1930s and 1953 (Holzman 1987, 19).

Table 7.1 indicates that trade between East European countries virtually doubled in relative importance as the Soviet bloc was created. Depending on which base year is selected, East European trade with the USSR increased in relative importance between ten- to twentyfold, a much more dramatic figure than was achieved by the EEC which began with an intra-trade percentage of approximately 35 in 1959 and only reached around 70 in the 1970s, notwithstanding the elimination of many trade barriers. At the same time, it should be recognized that the EEC was launched from a firmer economic base. Indeed, the percentage of intra-CMEA trade peaked in 1953, falling off in subsequent years while remaining considerably higher than the prewar norms.

Table 7.1   Soviet and East European imports, various years (% of total imports)

	1928	1938	1950	1953
E. European imports from E. Europe	18.7	15.7	31.1	30.7
E. European imports from USSR	2.1	1.6	33.9	41.2
Total E. European imports from CMEA countries	20.8	17.3	65.0	71.9
Soviet imports from E. Europe	11.8	5.5	59.1	61.0

Source: Holzman (1987, 180)

Much of the rapid growth of intra-CMEA trade in its early years can be explained not by trade creation but rather by the diversion from trade with the West. One estimate suggested that the socialist nations' trade with the capitalist world declined precipitously from 73.8 per cent of its total trade in 1938 to just 14 per cent by 1953 (Holzman 1987, 180).

The economies of the Soviet bloc were far more intertwined in the defence field. On 21 June 1950 the Korean War broke out and would just outlast Stalin, ending on 27 July 1953. Six months into the conflict the Soviet leader addressed his military commanders and representatives from each satellite country. He identified three key weaknesses in the American war effort – the nullification of their technological supremacy by the swarms of North Korean and Chinese troops, a reluctance to use nuclear weaponry, and a slowness to attack. From this Stalin deduced that the Soviet bloc could overwhelm Western Europe before the lumbering American military machine had got out of first gear. Time was of the essence if the bloc's absolute dominance in conventional forces was to be telling (Skilling 1991, 164–5).

It was fortunate that Stalin died before putting his megalomaniac ambitions into practice. Even so the requirements of the Soviet arms build-up further distorted the economic orientation of the economies of its satellites, especially those of Czechoslovakia and Poland, towards a heavy industry emphasis. Indeed, their economies might be described as epitomizing the warfare state, the antithesis of the welfare state. In the Czech case the output of key machinery products to oil the civilian economy declined as the defence industries absorbed half the total industrial investment over 1949–53. The totally unrealizable requirements of the Soviet militarization programme led the fearful Czechs to invite Soviet advisers to arrange their command planning system so that they could be blamed for failing to meet them (Skilling 1991, 164–5). The influx of Soviet technicians was such that new housing had to be built to accommodate them at Brno and Plzen, the main centres of arms production. The prewar Polish arms industry was also rejuvenated under the stimulus of the Korean War with factories being re-equipped and staffed by Soviet technicians (Holloway and Sharp 1984, 65–6).

Soviet support for the CMEA lapsed with the outbreak of the war, as each member was required to develop their industrialization programmes autonomously and contribute to the arms build-up. Any chance there might have been of achieving true regional economic integration was lost. Instead, individual countries duplicated the emphasis on heavy industry and shared a similar economic structure characterized by inefficiency and waste. Nationalism also played its part with East European leaders preferring to operate in isolation. Hence Hungary opted to develop its own poorly endowed coal deposits rather than assist in the expansion of Polish coal mining despite its greater potential (Smith 1983, 31, 175).

THE TRANSFORMATION OF THE CMEA

Stalin's death, the revolts in East Germany (1953), Hungary and Poland (both during 1956) and Khrushchev's denunciation of Stalinist methods combined to produce a reassessment of the Soviet Union's trading links with its East European partners, leading to the CMEA assuming greater prominence in their economic relations. As a result intra-bloc trade was remarkably steady for many years (Table 7.2).

Table 7.2   Eastern Europe: trade with the USSR as a percentage of total trade, 1960–78 (current prices)

	Exports	Imports
1960	36.9	38.1
1965	39.8	38.2
1970	36.4	36.7
1973	34.6	30.9
1975	34.5	31.9
1978	35.4	35.1

Source: Dawisha and Hanson (1981, 92)

For much of the 1950s the CMEA had been virtually a dead letter with the first full economic summit not taking place until May 1958. In the late 1950s and early 1960s, in response to the EEC's creation, Khrushchev tried to develop multilateral economic ties and encourage the socialist division of labour through looking to persuade each member to specialize in its strongest areas. For instance, Romania was asked to concentrate on agriculture and food processing while East Germany and Czechoslovakia would further develop their heavy industrial bases. But this would have widened the performance gap between the northern and southern tiers and Bucharest vetoed the proposal. In fact continuous disagreements between the East European members were an ever-present barrier to regional integration and the frequent communiqués referring to greater cohesion were no more than hot air. A brief attempt by the Soviets to introduce supranationalism was soon dropped in the face of vehement Romanian opposition.

Several efforts were made to break this deadlock during the CMEA's existence. In 1971 the Soviet leader Leonid Brezhnev wished to develop joint investments generally and Soviet energy resources in particular. To elicit support he introduced the 'interested party' rule: only member states with an interest in a joint project could participate and those who refused to join could not exercise a crippling veto, as had happened all too often before. Brezhnev's clumsily titled 'Comprehensive Programme for the Further Extension and Improvement of Co-operation and the Development of Socialist Integration by CMEA Member Countries' was adopted but only about ten joint projects actually materialized.

The largest was the building of the Orenburg natural gas complex in Siberia and a linking pipeline to the Soviet–Czech border. The project cost around $6 billion with all member states making a contribution (Romania least of all). For East European members the windfall was a guaranteed supply of natural gas, though the facilities belonged to the Soviets who also retained the profits. The CMEA additionally created a few joint companies in Eastern Europe which included the production of cotton yarns, electric power transmission and computer programming. But only about a dozen companies were created, all of them were small, and usually only two member states participated in each project (Gati 1990, 125–6).

As the dominant economic and military power, the Soviet Union was unquestionably the moving force within the CMEA. It was no accident that the headquarters and sprawling bureaucracy were located in Moscow. Generally any long-term proposals were initiated by the Soviets. Over time the Soviet Union's CMEA role was transformed from that of an exploiter – paying below world market prices for East European exports and extracting higher prices for its exports – to one of a sugar daddy, prepared to sacrifice and run down its raw materials' reservoir, and stoically accepting shoddy goods in return. The trade war with the West precluded Eastern Europe from earning the hard currency required to import basic fuels and raw materials and the Soviet Union, with its vast energy and raw material resources, readily stepped in. With the exception of Poland and Romania, the CMEA six suffered from a narrow raw materials base on which to build their modern economies. This weakness was Moscow's ace card for addiction to the fix of Soviet energy and raw materials bound the Soviet bloc more tightly together economically. The leaders of the various communist regimes, which relied on the backing of Moscow to remain in power, were generally happy to inhale. They were more than eager to conclude a series of long-term bilateral agreements with the USSR to ensure the delivery of raw materials.

The later history of the CMEA will be dealt with in subsequent chapters. What is relevant here is the way in which the Soviet Union manipulated the CMEA to support the communist governments of Eastern Europe. Two American economists (Marrese and Vanous 1983) caused considerable controversy when they suggested that Moscow provided large hidden economic subsidies to its allies in exchange for their political and military loyalty. The authors looked through a mass of data on Soviet and East European trade. They posed the question of whether the Soviet Union would have gained more from trade with the West, paid for in dollars, than it did from trading with Eastern Europe using transferable rubles. To calculate the difference between the Soviets' opportunity cost (foregone potential trade with the West) and the losses incurred from the decision instead to favour Eastern Europe, the latter trade was revalued at hypothetical dollar prices. Because the data were incomplete, Marrese and Vanous injected a series of presumptions and estimates into their methodology. They concluded that for the period 1960–80 implicit Soviet trade subsidies to Eastern Europe were around $87 billion. Most economists considered that the Marrese–Vanous estimates were too high (Brada 1985; Holloway and Sharp 1984, 220–31). What is not in doubt is that Soviet subsidization was extensive and considerable.

As might be expected, the main beneficiaries of this generosity were the GDR, Czechoslovakia and Poland; Hungary and Bulgaria received gratuitous treatment (though subsidies to Bulgaria increased in the later part of the period); Romania predictably hardly benefited at all. At the heart of the Soviet–East European trading relationship was the Soviet willingness to provide 'hard goods' (that is with a relatively high value on the world market), especially energy and raw materials, and accept low quality East European products (primarily 'soft goods' with a low value on the world market). Marrese and Vanous (1983, 8) suggested that Moscow's laxity was attributable to the 'unconventional gains from trade' received in return. For example, Soviet security and defence benefited from bases, transportation facilities, military manpower and defence industries across Eastern Europe.

East Germany, the top dog, permitted 20 Soviet divisions to be stationed on its territory and, through its economic links with West Germany, acted as a conduit for Western expertise and technology and was the Soviet Union's principal supplier of technologically advanced goods. Equally, the Soviets were always conscious of the GDR's vulnerable strategic position and it was no accident that it became the Soviet Union's most important trading partner. Czechoslovakia, after the hiccup of 1968 (see below) became a loyal satellite, housing five Soviet divisions and, with the GDR, offered the unique advantage of a border with West Germany, the main focus point of East–West tension. Moscow's assistance to Poland was considerable; for instance, in November 1976 it bolstered the tottering Gierek regime with credits of over $1 billion. Hungary and Bulgaria were less strategically important and with economic performances above the CMEA average their regimes were less threatened. Romania, with its maverick foreign policy and obstructive attitude within the CMEA, was hardly likely to have been the apple of Moscow's eye, which explains its low standing in Soviet calculations. Reduced Soviet interest in the country is illustrated by the fact that in 1958 Moscow readily complied with Bucharest's request to withdraw its armed forces. Russia's contempt for Romania was eloquently expressed by Khrushchev himself in June 1962 when visiting a Bucharest factory. To the astonishment of his Romanian hosts, he pulled off the table cloth and its decorative flower vases to expose a shabby table top. 'For me', he exclaimed, 'there are all these pretty things but for the workers there is only this trash!' (Schwartz 1973, 56). This episode was symptomatic of the deterioration in Soviet–Romanian diplomatic relations which was reflected in the economic field. Indeed, Marrese and Vanous (1983, 8–12) concluded that during the period 1964–80 Romania actually paid trade taxes and did not profit from Soviet subsidies. Seen in these terms, the Soviet Union's actions were perfectly explicable – it rewarded supporters and punished detractors.

THE DEFENCE QUESTION

In the period of 'high Stalinism' Eastern Europe's defence forces were transformed into a mirror image of the Red Army, with uniforms virtually indistinguishable from those worn by Soviet forces. Several thousand Soviet military officers became 'advisers' to East European militaries and in some instances, such as the Polish case, actually became regular officers in the national armies. By 1949, with the exception of the GDR, military conscription had been introduced throughout the bloc and to the extent that within four years the East European armies totalled 1.5 million men (65 divisions). Soviet weaponry also began to be deployed to replace Eastern Europe's antiquated armoury – though Stalin's distrustful mind dictated that it too was obsolete.

There was some relaxation following Stalin's death – individual national uniforms reappeared and status of forces agreements were concluded, first with Poland in 1956, then the following year Hungary, Romania and East Germany were added. Soviet advisers were recalled and replaced with native communist officers. On 14 May 1955 the Warsaw Pact was established which comprised the Soviet Union, the CMEA six (Bulgaria, Czechoslovakia, East Germany, Hungary, Poland, Romania) and Albania (which left in 1968). The move just preceded West Germany joining NATO and it was in direct response to this perceived threat that the powers had convened in Warsaw. With memories of the Second World War still vivid, West Germany's eastern neighbours were understandably perturbed at the prospect of German rearmament. The Poles in particular were concerned that West Germany might seek to reclaim the eastern territories lost to them in the 1945 peace settlement. The pact had three key objectives: first, to defend the Soviet Union's buffer zone in Eastern Europe against internal and external threats; second, to uphold orthodox (meaning pro-Soviet) communist regimes in the region; and last, in the event of war, to move quickly westwards to destroy NATO forces and occupy their territory.

The Warsaw Pact (or, to give it its proper title, the Warsaw Treaty Organization) was the military counterpart of the CMEA. Likewise the pact's early years were empty ones. It has been suggested that the pact was originally formed to provide the Soviets with an ace card to play to secure the withdrawal of American troops from Western Europe. In 1955 at Geneva the USSR offered to dismantle the pact if NATO also pressed the self-destruct button but went away empty handed (Sword 1990, 19). The pact's first multilateral military manoeuvres did not take place until 1961 (as the cold war threatened to turn hot), after which they were held on a fairly regular basis (nineteen times between 1960 and 1968). As with the CMEA, the pact was dominated by the Soviet Union which shaped its structure, issued foreign policy statements and provided the headquarters organization, located in the Soviet Ministry of Defence. Indeed, four-fifths of the pact's forces were Soviet so Russian was appositely the pact's operational language. The so-called 'joint command' was staffed entirely by Soviet officers and only Soviet marshals were to become commanders-in-chief with East European officers being denied any operationally significant posts. Romania was the greatest critic of Soviet dominance but its pleas for changes, including a rotating commander-in-chief and a greater voice in nuclear weapons deployment, fell on deaf ears. From the mid-1960s Romania drew back from the pact, refusing to allow troop manoeuvres on its territory and not partaking in joint exercises elsewhere (Holloway and Sharp 1984, 41–5; Gati 1990, 143–9).

Behind the facade of unity and massed strength all was not sweetness and light. While the Soviets were overwhelmingly concerned with the perceived threats emanating from the United States and West Germany, their smaller allies worried more about traditional enemies. In the case of Bulgaria, its concerns centred on Turkey and Yugoslavia; for Hungary it was Romania and vice versa; Poland was suspicious of East Germany. And, collectively they feared their giant eastern neighbour much more than the West.

This atmosphere of distrust was reflected in weapons provision from the Soviet arsenal. In the 1970s, for instance, while Soviet air forces boasted modern variants like the MIG-23, the East European air forces retained outdated aircraft. It was the same story with tanks – the antiquated T-54/55 continued to be the mainstay of non-Soviet forces (Griffith 1989, 139). The East European military establishments resented the inferior equipment they were landed with compared with that of Soviet forces. Again, a pecking list influenced by the northern–southern tier scenario is evident with the more up-to-date (or less out-of-date) weapons going to East Germany, Czechoslovakia and Poland and the least useful to Bulgaria, Hungary and Romania.

The upshot was that standardization was decidedly lacking. By the late 1970s there were no less than five types of battle tank serving with the pact, a range of gun calibres which demanded different ammunition, and eight makes of personnel carrier, creating a maintenance nightmare (Dawisha and Hanson 1981, 163). Several reasons coalesced to explain the denial of state-of-the-art Soviet military equipment to Warsaw Pact members. Most important, if it came to war with NATO, there was no firm belief that the East Europeans would use the weaponry as intended – indeed they might even turn it against Soviet forces.

Although the rhetoric of the Warsaw Pact declared its members' willingness 'to defend the gains of socialism', in practice the burden of defence was unevenly shared. The secrecy surrounding individual members' defence expenditure renders exact quantification impossible. On the other hand, the veil of secrecy was not such as to shroud the issue in complete mystery and some broad trends are apparent.

From the early 1960s the Soviet Union sought to obtain a margin of advantage over NATO and its Warsaw Pact allies were inevitably drawn in. In 1965, orchestrated by Moscow, the Political Consultative Commission of the Warsaw Pact began to coordinate defence burden sharing. Czechoslovakia, as one of the more industrially advanced members, could be expected to take a greater share. But public criticism during the momentous year of 1968 led the Czech minister of defence to impose a moratorium on increases in defence spending. Hungary proved reluctant to divert resources from sector B to defence, while Romania also failed to comply with Soviet wishes. The defence burden fell most heavily on East Germany, which came to assume the role of the USSR's chief ally, though all of the six countries' economies suffered to some extent from the opportunity cost arising from diverted skilled manpower and displaced resources (Table 7.3).

Generally, East European governments devoted greater resources to defence than their Western counterparts. Yugoslavia's heavy emphasis on defence to the 1970s, when relations with Moscow improved, reflected its fear of Soviet invasion. The East European defence industry which developed in response to Soviet demands was a varied patchwork. Continuing its tradition as a major weapons supplier, Czechoslovakia built up a considerable arms production capability. Indeed, between 1950 and 1968 the Czech defence industry benefited from a minimum input of 35 per cent of total annual capital investment. The Slovak republic had the largest factories and by 1987 was responsible for almost 61 per cent of total national defence production and 60 per cent of the defence industry workforce (Cupitt 1993, 92). This lop-sided concentration would hit hard once the cold war thawed out. The Polish defence sector was also substantial, though a small R & D base meant great reliance was placed on Soviet designs. East Germany's

Table 7.3   Military expenditure as a share of net material product (percentages)

	1952	1955	1960	1965	1970	1975	1980	1985	1989
Bulgaria	n.a.	6.2	4.0	3.5	3.1	3.0	3.0	3.4	n.a.
Czech.	n.a.	7.8	5.4	5.9	4.8	3.2	3.1	3.3	3.7
GDR	n.a.	n.a.	2.7[a]	3.4	6.1	4.0	4.2	4.6	n.a.
Hungary	n.a.	n.a.	2.0[b]	2.9	3.6	2.5	2.5	3.6	2.8
Poland	3.2	5.6	4.0	4.4	4.8	2.8	3.0	3.6	1.8
Romania	n.a.	n.a.	n.a.	n.a.	n.a.	2.2	1.7	1.3	1.9
Yugoslavia	19.3	10.3	7.2	5.4	5.0	5.7	4.9	3.8	2.9
USSR	39.1	33.1	18.6	18.1	16.5	n.a.	n.a.	n.a.	n.a.

[a]   1958
[b]   1959

Source: Kaldor (1992, 15)

defence production was small; aircraft manufacturing soon ended, reducing its role to computers, chemical warfare and logistics vehicles. Hungary produced light military vehicles and computer equipment but, no doubt because of 1956, was precluded from producing tanks. Romania was the only pact member to go outside the Soviet bloc to aid its defence production which was geared towards self-defence after the Soviet-led invasion of Czechoslovakia (Dawisha and Hanson 1981, 162–3).

Soviet dominance of the East European defence industries was inherent in the fact that the latter produced Soviet designs under licence for use by the Warsaw Pact. It was not until 1976 that this monopoly was broken when a Czech design was adopted as standard for the pact. But as this was only the harmless L-29 AERO trainer the deviation was more apparent than real. The Soviet monopoly sometimes caused great disruption. In 1959 Khrushchev decided to close down the Poles' jet fighter programme and withdrew the licences, forcing Warsaw to turn to basic jet trainers to keep the sector going. East Germany also suffered when its aero-engine industry was repressed, leading to the loss of 20 000 jobs. In 1969–70 the Joint Technical Committee was established as part of an overhaul of the Warsaw Pact. The Soviets used this forum to press their allies into specialist arms production. So Poland and Czechoslovakia became the only significant producers of tanks and armoured fighting vehicles, each being favoured with licences for the manufacture of the T-72 tank in 1980. Still, the Soviets remained concerned at what they regarded as the over-comprehensive weapons production of many of their allies who, to their chagrin, also developed their own designs for export to the Third World and Middle East. Czechoslovakia and Poland, the biggest arms producers, resisted further Soviet efforts in this direction, ensuring that the campaign was only a partial success (Holloway and Sharp 1984, 65–77).

KEEPING THE LID ON THE BOILING KETTLE

It would have suited the Kremlin very well if all the countries of the Soviet bloc were as poodle-obedient as Bulgaria. On two occasions under Todor Zhivkov this ultra-loyal ally actually proposed that it should be officially incorporated into the Soviet Union, only to be prevented by embarrassed Soviet leaders (Held 1992, 105). Unfortunately such steadfast allegiance was atypical of the bloc as a whole and Moscow was to face two types of challenge. First of these was popular rebellions. These erupted with varying degrees of threat in Pilsen and East Berlin (1953), Poznan and Budapest (1956), Warsaw (1968), various Polish cities (1970 and 1976) and Poland (1980–81). Second was the demand for autonomy from orthodox ruling communist parties such as occurred in Albania (1961) and Romania (1964). Of these, the first type was by far the more serious and emboldened the Soviet Union to respond with the use of military force, either directly or indirectly. The second type did not demand military intervention, especially as the socialist nature of the regime was not being questioned; it could be satisfactorily dealt with by politically ostracizing the rulers and imposing economic hardship as further evidence of disapproval.

Stalin's death was certain to spark rumblings of unrest across the Soviet camp. His body had barely been interned when a small-scale revolt erupted in Pilsen, the location of the famous Skoda Works, when the rioters trampled on pictures of the hated Stalin and violated the Soviet flag. The local Czech police forces were able to quell the disturbances unaided, but they were a symptom of the restiveness which pervaded Eastern Europe and a sign of things to come – only on a bigger scale. The East Berlin rising of 16–17 June 1953, occurring barely a fortnight after the Czech mini-explosion, marked the first occasion when photographs appeared in the world's free press showing unarmed workers hurling stones at Soviet tanks. The brief-lived uprising was sparked off when the GDR raised work norms in an effort to bolster economic performance. East Berlin construction workers took umbrage at their reduced wages and went on strike, other trades joined in and the domino effect quickly spread the strike wave to other cities. Soon the strikes became anti-regime riots – pictures of Stalin and the East German leader Walter Ulbricht were torn down, and secret police and communist officials were attacked. Economic grievances were transformed into a demand for the end of the Soviet occupation and the reunification of Germany. The worried government felt compelled to request Soviet assistance. Since there were 20 Soviet divisions surrounding Berlin the response was swift. The demonstrators suffered double figure fatalities with a further seven ring-leaders later executed (Roskin 1991, 97–8).

The Hungarian Revolution of 1956 provided the first main challenge to Soviet domination after Stalin. It was fanned by events in Poland the same year. As with the disturbances in Czechoslovakia and East Germany three years before, there was an interaction between the two uprisings which fed off each other. A new ingredient was Khruschev's February 1956 speech to the Twentieth Congress of the Soviet Communist Party in which he had denounced Stalin as an insane dictator who needlessly murdered thousands of loyal supporters. The diatribe was intended to be secret, but American intelligence sources obtained a copy and the State Department mischievously published the text. 'Throughout Eastern Europe the speech stirred contempt for a system that had permitted itself to be run for so long by a monster' (Schwartz 1973, 46).

In Poland there had been a reaction against the extremes demanded by the Stalinist economy and the belief that the ditching of collectivization and a stronger emphasis on consumer goods was required. After intellectuals spoke out workers responded by demonstrating for 'bread and freedom'. Fifty thousand workers took to the streets in Poznan, an industrial city west of Warsaw, denouncing higher prices and work quotas. As had happened in East Berlin, the movement quickly mushroomed and became anti-communist in tone. The government panicked and called out the Polish Army and 54 demonstrators were killed with hundreds wounded.

It was recognized that there was a limit to Soviet tolerance and for this reason a former disgraced communist leader, Wladyslaw Gomulka, was installed in office in October 1956 as the next best thing to a Stalinist. An alleged Titoist and nationalist, he had been removed from office in the 1948 purges. In the end, he was to prove an inspired choice. But one of his first actions was to sack the Soviet marshal who for years had acted as the Polish minister of defence and chief of the army.

Moscow soon took fright. Khrushchev and other leading lights from the Kremlin made an unannounced flying visit to Warsaw on 19 October 1956. Their threats were given added credence by the Soviet troops which moved up to the capital from their outside barracks and took up defensive positions around the city. The situation was only defused when Gomulka persuaded the Soviet Party that his reforms were intended to stabilize Poland and provide a more loyal ally who would stay inside the Warsaw Pact. The 'Polish October' led to the end of forced collectivization and the expulsion of Soviet officials from major government posts. Over time Gomulka would introduce some reforms, but was careful not to offend Moscow unduly and 'did little to change the economy, which stayed centralized, state-run, corrupt, and inefficient' (Roskin 1991, 100).

Khrushchev's anti-Stalin speech had rehabilitated one of Stalin's victims, Bela Kun, leader of the brief-lived first Hungarian communist government, who was executed in 1937. By this action the Soviet leader inadvertently helped to stir the embers of discontent in Hungary which threatened to flame up into an inferno of revolt. In the summer of 1956 the Kremlin tried to dampen the fires when it installed Ernö Gerö as Hungarian leader. But very quickly his policy of forced industrialization resulted in a precipitous decline in the standard of living. The disenchanted population was encouraged by the seeming success of the workers' demonstrations in Poland. In Hungary too the economic symptoms for reform were much the same – resentment at food shortages, disdain for collectivization and a desire for more consumer goods. The Hungarian Revolution of 1956 started on 23 October when in Bucharest a gigantic statue of Stalin was pulled down and the epithet 'WC' (water closet) daubed on its head. On 24 October 1956, after demonstrating the previous day in support of the Poles, students occupied the principal radio building in Budapest and broadcast their radical demands. Among them were free elections, the removal of Soviet troops and a new government under the liberal Imre Nagy who had been ousted from power in 1955 by hard-line Stalinists. The Hungarian secret police fired on the demonstrators, causing fatalities and leading to the storming of their headquarters where several security police were beaten to death. Soviet forces moved into Budapest but took no action. With the Hungarian army defecting to the rebels, the panicked politburo, with Moscow's blessing, asked Nagy to become premier in order to diffuse the situation (Schwartz 1973, 50).

Had Nagy heeded developments in Poland, he might have remained in power. But any caution he had was swept aside by the expectations his appointment aroused. After being removed from power, Nagy had reinterpreted Marx's writings and been struck by a passage in which a call was made to defend 'basic laws of morals and justice' both between individuals and nations. From this Nagy developed policies to retard the use of force in domestic policy and internationally to adopt a position of neutrality. He now put these beliefs into practice. A multi-party political system was announced, a coalition government formed which included non-communists, and the hated political police force was disbanded.

As long as communism remained in the ascendant, Moscow might conceivably have tolerated some domestic reforms. For a brief period it seemed as if Nagy's gamble had paid off as Moscow appeared to accept developments benignly. The Kremlin even announced that 'the principles of full equality, respect for territorial integrity, state independence and sovereignty and non-interference in each other's domestic affairs' were required between members of the 'great commonwealth of socialist nations'. (Balfour 1981, 172). Giving credence to this message, the few Soviet troops in Hungary were withdrawn to their bases. In reality, the Kremlin could not long tolerate a threat to communist rule which would jeopardize its influence over the whole bloc. Accordingly, in the early hours of 31 October massive Soviet reinforcements were poured into Hungary, prompting a defiant Nagy to announce his country's withdrawal from the Warsaw Pact and to appeal to the West for assistance. No outside help was forthcoming and on 4 November Soviet forces reached Budapest. Although ten days of street fighting followed, the poorly armed Hungarian soldiers and citizens were no match for Soviet tanks and 32 000 were slaughtered. At the same time a more fortunate 250 000 plus citizens fled to the West via the still open border with Austria. Nagy and his close supporters took refuge in the Yugoslav embassy but were persuaded to leave by a false promise of safe conduct abroad from the successor government under the Soviet stooge János Kádár. In the event, they were arrested by Soviet forces, removed to Romania and most, including Nagy, were executed in 1958 (Roskin 1991, 102). Even Tito recognized that Nagy had gone too far too fast. Nonetheless, this martyr's achievements were not entirely crushed by Soviet tanks. The international outcry which greeted Soviet actions led the Kremlin to pursue a more hands-off policy towards Hungary which allowed its leaders to introduce considerable reforms albeit within a communist framework.

THE PRAGUE SPRING: 'SOCIALISM WITH A HUMAN FACE'

To the mid-1960s Czechoslovakia was among the USSR's leading allies. Under the leadership of its president and first secretary, Antonin Novotny, an atmosphere of fear was created. Western visitors found even taxi drivers unwilling to talk about the situation. Then the rumblings of reform began to be felt as growing dissatisfaction with the falling standard of living became increasingly vocal. Prague's food shops could readily be picked out by the queues of people which stretched way outside. Indeed, over 40 per cent of the average diet consisted of cereals, a reflection of the limited supplies of meat, milk, eggs, fruits and vegetables (Stevens 1985, 103). By the end of 1967 a coalition of forces was building up – workers demanding better living standards, managers wanting meaningful reform, intellectuals and students seeking the end of repression and censorship – against the government.

The Czech Communist Party sensed the dangers and in January 1968 replaced Novotny as first secretary with the little known Alexander Dubček.

Somewhat ironically, in view of subsequent developments, Dubček, the leader of the Slovakian Communist Party since 1963, was regarded as a safe choice unlikely to upset the Kremlin. But he already had a reputation for espousing a cause – in this case that of the poorer part of Czechoslovakia. Dubček has however been incorrectly portrayed as a liberal in the tradition of John Stuart Mill. In fact he was a devout communist who was amazed at the Soviet-led military intervention which his economic experiment aroused. As he put it after Russian tanks had smashed his dream: 'They have done this to *me*, who has devoted his entire life to co-operation with the Soviet Union.' Rather Dubček tried to introduce a degree of liberalization which he dubbed 'socialism with a human face'.

Dubček's accession to power provoked the appearance of a mass movement of Czechs and Slovaks from all walks of life demanding economic and social reforms. The people resented the emphasis on heavy industry which deprived them of consumer goods. Faced with an angry population Dubček, at first cautious, was impelled towards more radical reform which carried its own momentum. Dubček's early efforts to appease the population fell on deaf ears and he was quickly swept along on the tide of more fundamental change.

The 'Prague Spring' began on 22 March 1968 when Novotny was stripped of the presidency in favour of a popular moderate. Dubček pledged: 'There is only one path and that is forward.' He promised 'the widest possible democratization' with the hand of government to be less in evidence in the affairs of business, courts and trade unions. In response to ethnic tension, there was some devolution of power between Czechs and Slovaks. The following month the Central Committee issued a document called *Czechoslovakia's Road to Socialism* which quickly gained notoriety. Its promises included granting federal status to Slovakia, the introduction of a limited form of private enterprise, freedom of speech and religion and the curbing of police activities. The central direction of the economy was denounced and blamed for the 'slow increase of wages ... stagnation of the living standard ... the catastrophic state of housing ... the precarious state of the transport system, poor quality goods and public services' (Schwartz 1973, 74–5). Freedom of choice – for enterprises, consumers and workers – was at the heart of what became known as the 'action programme'.

The Prague Spring was certainly less radical than the later *perestroika* and *glasnost*. 'The major reforms were not intended to terminate the Communist system but to change it substantially and to create a more democratic type of socialism' (Griffith 1991, 247). Indeed, the Communist Party was still to retain its 'leading role'. The movement was less important for what it actually achieved than for what it threatened to do. Enjoying its new-found freedom resulting from Dubček's abolition of censorship, the Czech press had a field day exaggerating the scope of future developments and enjoyed speculating about the prospect of massive Western financial aid and the severing of Comecon links.

Such a heady atmosphere undoubtedly sent the Kremlin decisionmakers' hearts into palpitations. With West Germany developing *Ostpolitik*, which was designed to improve relations with the East so that it became less a potential enemy and more a prospective friend, Moscow was worried about the continued cohesion of the Soviet bloc. Already in 1967 Romania had established diplomatic relations with the FRG to be followed by Czechoslovakia at a consular level. The new Soviet leadership was also concerned at the Czech-inspired signs of unrest which were appearing in its own backyard, especially in the Ukraine and the Baltic republics (Holloway and Sharp 1984, 121). Uncensored Czech press articles were being disseminated across the bloc and having an unsettling effect. Moreover, the Czechs' willingness to consider negotiating a loan from the West Germans and the World Bank raised the unwelcome prospect of Czech trade being reoriented to the West which would deprive the Soviet Union and other CMEA members of its technology supplies (Dawisha and Hanson 1981, 16–17).

All these factors combined to make the Soviet leadership willing to pay a high cost to retain Czechoslovakia within the bloc. Dubček later revealed (Dubček 1993, 135) that the Soviets started lobbying against his reforms behind the scenes. In January 1968 Dubček had been summoned to Moscow to elaborate his plans to Brezhnev and the politburo. Later he was to write a harrowing account of the meeting.

> I tried to explain what it meant to introduce socialism into a country such as Czechoslovakia, already so industrialised, at least in its western parts. Also, our society had long been accustomed to modern political culture. The existing system did not fit our circumstances, I said, and had led to the growing tensions and conflicts which were at the root of the stagnation and current crisis. Changes were essential if the socialist system was to function effectively.
>
> I carefully avoided all terms that would trigger hostility from these dogmatic Marxist–Leninists – such as 'reform' or 'revision'. Instead, I spoke of 'renewal' and 'revival', which I knew they could not connect to any 'sinful' episode from the past. Nevertheless, as I watched the impassive and sombre faces before me, I realised I wasn't really getting through to them (Dubček 1993, 134).

Over the next few months Dubček tried to elicit the sympathy of his Hungarian and Polish counterparts but his efforts were in vain. No doubt they could see more clearly than he what was to come.

On 23 March 1968 Brezhnev, by now firmly in control of the Kremlin after Khrushchev's ousting in October 1964, convened a meeting of Soviet and East European communist leaders at Dresden, ostensibly to discuss economic affairs. Ulbricht gave the gathering an altogether different complexion when his opening address spelled out that the situation in Czechoslovakia was the main talking point. Dubček was tempted to walk out but stayed to hear the criticisms (Dubček 1993, 140–42). The hostile atmosphere, which continued with a one-to-one meeting with Brezhnev in Moscow on 4 May failed to deflect the brave Czech from his reforms.

Gentle persuasion having failed, more strong-arm tactics were then decided on. Four days after the Brezhnev–Dubček summit a Warsaw Pact meeting opted for 'military training' exercises on the Czech border which took place in May and June. To ram home the message the Soviets pressed for and received permission to hold joint military 'manoeuvres' with the Czechs on their territory. These exercises started in June and had the dual function of bullying the Czech leadership and, if this did not work, to prepare for invasion.

Although he denied any intention of wanting to leave the Warsaw Pact, Dubček declined an invitation to a meeting on 14 July in Warsaw. From this gathering came the 'Warsaw Letter' to the Czech Central Committee which condemned the reforms and requested that the press be muzzled again. The threat was made to 'sever Czechoslovakia from the socialist community' (Holloway and Sharp 1984, 123). Still, the Czechs refused to move, leading Brezhnev to arrange a bilateral meeting which took place at Cierna railway station on the Slovak–Soviet border. The entire Soviet politburo showed up at the railwaymen's clubhouse for what was to prove a last ditch effort to find a political solution. Dubček was conscious of the thousands of letters, telegrams and resolutions of support he had received, a revelation which failed to move Brezhnev – 'If I gave instructions, I too could have a ton of letters like that here in no time' (Dubček 1993, 168). By the third day Brezhnev was feigning 'illness' and all that resulted was a meaningless joint declaration which suggested that each government 'would creatively solve the problems of further socialist development' and enunciated the principle of 'equality, preservation of sovereignty, national independence [and] territorial inviolability' (Dubček 1993, 170). Here was a latter-day equivalent of the Munich Agreement and, like Neville Chamberlain, Dubček was deceived into believing that the other signatory would respect the accord. Dubček refused to consider the possibility of a Soviet invasion or an appeal to either the West or the United Nations (Griffith 1991, 247–8). Indeed, the Czech leader was immensely pleased with himself because he had managed to fend off Brezhnev's customary farewell kisses through using a huge bouquet of flowers as a shield (Dubček 1993, 169)!

Any glibness on Dubček's part was quickly dispelled. Without warning on the night of 20–21 August Warsaw Pact forces invaded Czechoslovakia. Soviet troops made up the bulk of the invasion force of around 500 000 with Bulgaria, East Germany, Hungary and Poland providing token contingents.

Of these East Germany and Poland were decidedly for intervention; Hungary was more lukewarm, fearing that snuffing out the Prague Spring would adversely affect its own reforms (Gati 1990, 46). At their government's request, the Czech people wisely did not fight and there was no mass resistance. Some efforts were made to confuse the invaders by altering signposts and railroad workers impeded the movement of military trains. Slogans and graffiti, many in Russian, greeted the foreign forces, such as 'This is not Vietnam' and 'The Russian National State Circus has arrived, complete with performing gorillas' (Schwartz 1973, 79). Dubček and his cohorts were arrested at gunpoint by the KGB and taken to the Ukraine. In October they were coerced into signing a fifteen-point 'friendship' treaty which met Soviet requirements, including the 'temporary' stationing of Soviet forces in Czechoslovakia (Sword 1990, 60). Any prospect of taking radical action which did not please Moscow had gone. The following August the first anniversary of the invasion was marked by demonstrations. On this occasion the Czech army was used to crush the protesters in Prague, Brno and Gottwaldov with over 19 000 troops, 300 tanks and 200 armoured vehicles being deployed.

The transformation of the situation in Czechoslovakia within a year reflected the iron grip which the Soviets now exercised following their crushing of the Prague Spring. Lest there were any doubts about what the Soviet Union would tolerate the parameters were spelled out in *Pravda* two months after the event. In an article entitled 'Sovereignty and the International Obligations of Socialist Countries' the key paragraph read:

> There is no doubt that the peoples of the socialist countries and the communist parties have and must have freedom to determine their country's path of development. However, any decision of theirs must damage neither socialism in their own country nor the fundamental interest of the other socialist countries nor the worldwide workers' movement, which is waging a struggle for socialism. This means that every communist party is responsible not only to its own people but also to all the socialist countries and to the entire communist movement. Whoever forgets this by placing sole emphasis on the autonomy and independence of communist parties lapses into one sidedness, shirking his international obligations (Gati 1990, 47).

Known as the Brezhnev Doctrine, for the next 20 years or more its existence exercised a chilling and chastening effect on the Soviet bloc.

Across Eastern Europe the example of Czechoslovakia imposed a straitjacket on the extent and nature of any political and economic reforms. In Czechoslovakia there was a complete reversal of the attempts to create the conditions for market socialism. In April 1969, following Soviet pressure, Dubček was deposed and sent into internal exile in Bratislava where he became a part-time forestry clerk. Thousands of his supporters were also rooted out of the party. The process of 'normalization' was ironically assigned to another Slovak, Gustav Husák. A hard-line communist, he quickly condemned as tantamount to 'complete anarchy' attempts 'to separate and create two independent spheres – the enterprise sphere and the central sphere – thus basically violating the principles of democratic centralism in the national economic management' (Stevens 1985, 190). Price controls returned and in 1971–72 material balances were reintroduced for 450 basic products, representing around 60 per cent of industrial output. All the main levers of central planning reared their ugly heads once more, including the centralized deployment of basic resources and materials. The extent of plan fulfilment again became the main consideration in management performance. Husák's repressive regime, with the Soviet garrison to back him up, was to remain in power for over 20 years (Griffith 1989, 249).

THE WORKERS' REVOLT IN POLAND

The Prague Spring had touched off simmerings of discontent in Poland, Gomulka's leadership having proved an immense disappointment to the population: he remained wedded to the concept of the leading role of the party and central planning; worse still, he lacked administrative and economic expertise (Brown 1988, 161). In spring 1968 a Warsaw theatre staged a nineteenth century play which depicted Poland's earlier plight under Russian oppression. The event attracted capacity audiences eager to hear and applaud such lines as: 'Polish history is conducted in a prison cell' and 'Everyone sent here from Moscow is either a jackass, a fool or a spy'. The embarrassed Gomulka regime closed down the play, provoking student demonstrations which were suppressed with extreme police brutality (Schwartz 1973, 82–3).

Moscow had considered getting rid of Gomulka, but Brezhnev was distracted by events in Czechoslovakia. Just over two years later, in December 1970, the Polish leader was not to be so fortunate. After West Germany had finally recognized the disputed Oder–Neisse boundary as Poland's western border, Gomulka felt secure enough to tackle the serious deterioration in the economy. Agriculture had performed disastrously in 1969 and 1970 resulting in a considerable shortfall in grain and meat supplies. Gomulka rationalized that by altering the pattern of consumption all could be put right. Two weeks before Christmas he rashly imposed steep price rises on basic foods, clothing and other scarce essential items in an effort to reduce their consumption while simultaneously reducing the prices of tape recorders, television sets and other consumer durables which were readily available. This strange concoction was to prove his downfall.

There was a spontaneous reaction of revolutionary proportions among the workers of such Baltic coastal cities as Gdansk, Gdynia and Szczecin. The military had to be called in and the fatalities were greater than were recorded for any uprising since Hungary in 1956. Gomulka was replaced by Edward Gierek, whose reputation as a reformer made him acceptable to the workers. He immediately cancelled the price increases and pushed more investment towards the food and consumer goods industries. From 1971 to 1975 the rate of real growth showed an annual rise of around 10 per cent and real wages also rose appreciably. Western credits (see Chapter 8) were used to increase the standard of living and for a time all was well (Brown 1988, 174–6).

By June 1976 the government was spending more on food subsidies than in 1970, a situation which could not go on indefinitely. Gierek calculated that the improved living standards which he had engineered would make the population more amenable to price hikes. As in December 1970, the subsidies were suddenly removed with prices rising by 60 per cent on average. Nationwide strikes persuaded Gierek to remove the price increases as suddenly as he had introduced them. But his days were now numbered and the strikes were a manifestation of what was to come four years later. The Baltic coastline was becoming a hotbed of worker unrest and growing worker cohesion was symbolized by the formation of the Workers' Defence Committee. Indeed, by the late 1970s there existed a plethora of action groups, among them committees for free trade unions, farmers' self-defence committees, the Young Poland Movement and the Confederation for an Independent Poland. There was, too, a growing affinity between the workers and the Roman Catholic Church which was intensified when the archbishop of Cracow became pope and visited his native land in June 1979 as John Paul II (Griffith 1989, 185–6; Brown 1988, 183–4).

In July 1980 the Gierek regime, by now economically desperate, once more imposed price increases. With the subsidy for meat alone now running at around $3.3 billion annually, the decision could not be put off any longer (Black 1992, 271). The move provoked strikes in Lublin and other industrial centres across the country involving over 800 000 workers. Against this background the workers of the Lenin Shipyard in Gdansk downed tools ostensibly over the dismissal of a female crane driver. But if this was the spark, the flame was ignited by the pent-up grievances the workers harboured towards their hated government. On 16 August a strike committee was established under the leadership of Lech Walesa, a shipyard electrician, which drew up a list of 21 demands, the most important being the establishment of free trade unions unfettered by either state or employer controls (Sword 1990, 113–14).

Solidarity, as the union was called, quickly became a national union with around a third of the population joining. It also had a countryside equivalent, 'Rural Solidarity', which similarly enjoyed a large membership. The Church also gave the movement its tacit support. The government was forced to hold direct talks and felt compelled to concede to Solidarity the status it desired and the right to strike – an unprecedented move in postwar Eastern European history. Gierek suddenly became 'ill' and was replaced by a Polish army general, Wojciech Jaruzelski. Soon the cry went up for a democratic Poland. In July 1981 the Polish Communist Party felt compelled to hold an emergency congress which elected a new politburo; only four of the existing fifteen members survived (Gati 1990, 50).

Moscow watched these events unfold with increasing unease. In December 1980 the Warsaw Pact declared that Poland 'was, is, and will remain a socialist country' but, unlike in Czechoslovakia, direct military intervention did not follow. The chastening effect of the misguided Soviet invasion of Afghanistan the previous year and the fact that the United States was not similarly distracted as it had been in 1968 over its deep involvement in South-East Asia were probably reasons enough for caution. Instead, the Kremlin preferred to exert pressure on the Jaruzelski regime to put its own house in order. Threatening military manoeuvres were conducted periodically and in June 1981 a letter was sent to the Polish leadership promising its 'liquidation' if it did not deal with the 'counter-revolution' (Holloway and Sharp 1984, 131). Although it seems that preparations for a crackdown were first put in hand in October 1980, it was not until a year later that any urgency was injected into them. Moscow cranked up the pressure on Jaruzelski after Solidarity sent a message to the whole Soviet bloc urging its populations to follow their example. The official Soviet news agency, TASS, spoke of the 'extremist circles' in Solidarity and accused its congress of 'anti-Soviet bacchanalia' (Gati 1990, 51).

The Jaruzelski regime finally imposed martial law on 13 December 1981 when several hundred leading Solidarity activists were arrested and interned. A wave of demonstrations and strikes erupted in protest; they were brutally crushed. Solidarity was outlawed in October 1982 though martial law was to last another nine months. The international community made Poland an economic pariah, with the United States imposing sanctions which lasted until 1983 and further damaged the already weakened economy. Although for the moment some measure of stability was restored to Poland, the spirit of Solidarity would not die and by the end of the decade it would return with a vengeance to complete its unfinished business.

THE ROAD AHEAD

The Soviet grip on Eastern Europe undoubtedly influenced both the political complexion of its governments and their economic policies. Above all they were not allowed to introduce anything that smacked of a Western-style market economy which brought the associated danger of democracy. East Germany, Hungary and Czechoslovakia all experienced direct Soviet military intervention when the Kremlin perceived that its interests were under threat.

There was another side of the coin. The Soviet Union conceded that it needed to establish strong bilateral trading links with the more important satellites. In turn, financial and economic aid could make a regime more loyal and possibly prevent its collapse. There was a recognition that economic difficulties generated political instability. For this reason, the Soviets were happy to import sub-standard East European goods which could not find a home on the world market and to export cheap energy and raw materials. For the Kremlin the arrangement created the happy political situation of locking East European economies into the Soviet bloc. In the 1960s and 1970s the construction of crude oil and natural gas pipelines enhanced the ability of the · USSR to export energy to its informal empire. Eastern Europe came to rely on Moscow for virtually all of its natural gas, 80 per cent of the crude oil and petroleum products required and over 70 per cent of its hard coal. Such imports were necessary pump-primers for the command economies which were built on energy-guzzling industries such as steel, chemicals and mining. But for both parties there was a negative side – the Soviets ran down their indigenous resources which East European industry was happy to consume in ever larger doses, exacerbating its inherent inefficiency. One estimate suggests that the bloc's industries consumed 30 to 50 per cent more energy to produce the same units of national income as those of the capitalist West (Kramer 1991, 86). In time the huge clouds of smoke which billowed daily out of East European factories created a serious pollution effect and reinforced the picture of a dull, grey and barren existence which was the lot of the typical citizen of Eastern Europe.

The Soviet Union could not, however, meet all the requirements of its satellites once their economies reached a more advanced stage. Only the West could supply advanced technology which both the Soviet Union and Eastern Europe's economies sorely needed by the start of the 1970s. As Holzman (1987, 114) wrote:

> The flow of technology runs primarily from West to East. The West has an advantage in technology, partly because it represents a larger pool of industrially more advanced nations. But the underlying reason for the West's advantage is that the organization and systems of incentives in the centrally planned Eastern economies are less suited to invention, innovation, and the diffusion of technology than their private enterprise counterparts. Typically, central planning is preoccupied with quantity rather than quality or cost targets; enterprise managers tend to avoid the disruptions and risks associated with introducing new production methods; lack of competitive pressure and poor communication and co-operation between research and development organizations and the users of technology also hinder change. The result is a lag in both the development and the spread of technology.

Without belittling the often impressive achievements of central planning, it can be said that this lag is perhaps its weakest feature.

This shortcoming was to prove an Achilles heel. The onset of *détente*, which for a time thawed the frosty East–West relationship, made it possible for the East to obtain access to Western high-tech imports. But the ramifications of this strategy were to be profound and would lead ultimately to the unravelling of the Soviet bloc.

8. Economic slowdown and renewed pressure for reform

By the early 1970s it was apparent that the socialist goods train was in danger of running out of steam if it did not stop to take on board Western high-tech products and know-how. In 1971 the Soviet Union led the way when it embarked on an import-led growth strategy and most of its satellites followed in its wake. Fortunately this coincided with a warming of the East–West relationship which entered into a cooperative phase represented by *détente*. But the rerouting also brought its own dangers of derailment. A tug of war was set in motion with the East European economies being pulled in two opposite directions. As Table 8.1 demonstrates, to varying degrees, the CMEA six flirted with the West: Poland's entanglement was most pronounced; Bulgaria's was the least involved. In the honeymoon period, 1970–75, Eastern Europe's share of total imports from the West increased from 25.7 to 35.6 per cent (Joseph 1987, 295). This was to have profound implications (see below)

Table 8.1   *Distribution of the CMEA region's trade with the West by countries (total exports and imports of the CMEA region = 100)*

Country	1965 exp.	1965 imp.	1970 exp.	1970 imp.	1975 exp.	1975 imp.	1980 exp.	1980 imp.
USSR	39.8	32.2	41.0	37.0	44.8	45.4	53.9	47.7
Bulgaria	4.0	6.3	3.4	4.7	2.0	4.0	2.1	3.6
Czech.	10.8	12.8	10.4	11.1	8.3	6.8	7.0	6.5
Poland	16.2	13.9	15.4	12.5	16.1	19.9	12.2	14.4
Hungary	7.1	8.4	7.8	8.9	8.3	6.7	6.1	7.3
GDR	14.7	17.2	13.9	15.6	12.1	9.9	11.2	11.9
Romania	7.3	9.2	8.1	10.0	8.4	7.2	7.5	8.6

Note: The columns do not always add up to 100 because of rounding

Source: Koves (1985, 66)

because the socialist economies were now exposed to fluctuations in world market prices and just at a time when inflation was rearing its ugly head.

Hitherto the Soviet piper had played the tune, but from the late 1970s, because of the hard currency debts they had incurred, East European governments also needed increasingly to heed the alternative demands of Western creditors. Indeed, the covert strategy of West Germany since the 1960s had been to ensnare the GDR in a debt trap, making it more amenable to Bonn's whims and ultimately bringing about the possibility of reunification (Roskin 1991, 128). For Eastern Europe as a whole the diversion westwards necessitated a much greater interaction with the world economy than before, for if Western hard currency imports were to be paid for then eventually a corresponding amount of exports in the opposite direction needed to be achieved. As it turned out, Western technology was not to be properly integrated into socialist manufacturing processes so that, by and large, Eastern Europe's 'quality' goods remained uncompetitive on the world market. For example, the CMEA's share of the American import total remained below 1 per cent between 1971 and 1983 whereas newly industrializing countries (NICs) managed to almost double their penetration from 10 to nearly 20 per cent (Joseph 1987, 316). In any event, Western markets were to prove unreceptive to the East's export needs as they were devastated by rocketing oil prices, which led to high inflation and recession.

The result was that by the later 1970s Eastern Europe faced mounting balance of payments problems which first compelled the import-led growth strategies to be reined in and then abandoned altogether. The Soviet Union initially proved willing to shield its eastern satellites from the ravages of the oil-price inflation but increasingly, as it too faced the problem of countering slower economic growth, this benign attitude proved ever more difficult to sustain. Moreover, the difficulty across Eastern Europe was compounded by the continued poor performance of the agricultural sector, which necessitated the region taking ever greater food imports from the West, thereby aggravating balance of payments difficulties. Declining standards of living were the inevitable result and with them came renewed pressure for reform.

FROM CONFRONTATION TO COOPERATION: THE ONSET OF *DÉTENTE*

There were several factors involved in the outbreak of *détente* – political, strategic, economic and cultural. The key to the East–West *rapprochement* resided principally in the defence field. Quite simply the superpower arms race was becoming increasingly difficult to sustain and justify both for the main protagonists and their allies. Some estimates suggested that the United

States was bearing as much as 60 per cent of the cost of NATO defences, while the USSR's contribution to Warsaw Pact expenses was put even higher at 90 per cent (Black 1992, 125). Moreover, there was stiff resistance from the junior partners on both sides against increasing their share of the defence burden. Governments on both sides of Europe contended that to do so would adversely affect standards of living, which in the Western case carried political implications and in the Eastern sector threatened to provoke destabilizing social unrest as it had done in the past.

For the time being, therefore, the military and rhetorical posturing which had symbolized the cold war was toned down and a period of peaceful coexistence was ushered in. During 1972 the United States and the Soviet Union held historic strategic arms limitation talks (SALT I) which resulted in a strict limitation on anti-ballistic missiles entering the nuclear weapons arena. Two years later came further superpower meetings aimed at concluding a SALT II agreement. West Germany led the way in forging *détente* with its *Ostpolitik* which sought to improve relations with the East. Developed in the late 1960s, it blossomed fully in the 1970s. Hitherto, Bonn's only formal diplomatic relations at the highest level with Eastern Europe were with Moscow. East Germany was acknowledged only as 'the Soviet occupation zone' and Poland's new postwar frontier on the Oder–Neisse line was a source of contention. In 1969, the more liberal and accommodating Willy Brandt became chancellor after three years as foreign minister and things really began to happen. In 1970 Bonn concluded a treaty of reconciliation with Moscow. There followed normalization treaties with Poland, Bulgaria and Czechoslovakia and, most significantly, with East Germany. The Basic Treaty of 1972 formalized relations between the two Germanies resulting, the following year, in both being admitted to the United Nations. A stream of official recognitions by non-communist powers of East Germany's separate existence culminated, in April 1974, in the establishment of diplomatic relations with Washington (Brown 1988, 87; Swain and Swain 1993, 173–4).

In the summer of 1975 *détente* reached its apogee when the Helsinki accords were concluded involving 33 European nations plus the United States and Canada. A number of principles were thrashed out behind closed doors and subsequently enunciated in three categories. Basket I in essence confirmed the postwar division of Europe and sought improved relations on this basis; Basket II specifically envisaged economic cooperation, including in the crucial field of science and technology, and the reduction of trade barriers; and Basket III was concerned with human rights, a sensitive area for the East. The Soviets made it clear they would brook no interference in their internal affairs and no member of the Eastern bloc had any intention of introducing the press freedom envisaged. Even so, the non-implementation of Basket III was later to have a significant influence on emerging East European reform movements.

At least while it lasted *détente* did, in some instances, lead generally to less repression because of the perception that harsh measures against the population could adversely affect the flow of Western credits. The GDR, for example, allowed visitors from the other Germany (the figure peaked at 3.5 million visits in 1980), although it was careful to restrict trips in the other direction (Brown 1988, 90). Poland, which set the greatest store on import-led growth, was particularly keen to court international respectability, as was Hungary. Romania, under the increasing dominance of the authoritarian Ceausescu family, was not prepared to alter its ways and abuses of human rights continued. Instead, it craftily declared itself a 'socialist developing nation', a move which led to membership of the General Agreement on Tariffs and Trade (GATT) in 1971 and admittance to the International Monetary Fund (IMF) the following year. Furthermore, Romania's new status allowed it to exploit developing countries' systems of preferences especially with the European Community (Swain and Swain 1993, 162).

There were underlying motives for the pursuit of *détente* on either side. The West hoped that its support would lead to positive reforms – as epitomized by West Germany's *Wandel durch Annäherung* – while the East saw Western assistance as a means to avert reforms ('reform substitution') by improving living standards. The revolt of Polish workers in December 1970 (see Chapter 7) provided a jolting reminder to East European leaders of the potential consequences if the needs of the population were neglected. It became paramount therefore to ensure that there were sufficient supplies of consumer goods for which there was a growing demand, reflecting an increasing reluctance on the part of the populations to accept austerity. The 1971–75 Soviet five-year plan set the tone when, for the first time in the series, consumer goods were accorded a higher growth target than producer goods (Hutchings 1983, 117). By and large, the East European CMEA members followed suit, not least the USSR's most loyal allies, East Germany and Bulgaria. Thus the GDR's plan had as it's 'primary task' improving the 'material and cultural living standard' of the population (Aldcroft 1993, 254). In similar vein Bulgaria's leader confessed to being converted to 'care for the man' and thereby to the 'fuller satisfaction of the growing material and spiritual needs of the people'. Accordingly, the Bulgarian plan envisaged a 50 per cent rise in consumer goods output, an increase in the minimum wage and promised measures to eradicate shortages in 'certain basic merchandise groups'. Poland, scene of the recent disturbances, felt compelled to go one better, leading the new Gierek government to pledge itself to achieving 'a constant increase in consumption and a continuous improvement in the living, social and cultural conditions of the population' (Hutchings 1983, 118–20). It was also hoped that the greater availability of consumer goods would persuade workers to improve their productivity.

For the Soviet Union, the relaxation of East–West tensions provided welcome access to Western technology and expertise both directly and through the conduit of Eastern Europe, especially East Germany. Moscow actively encouraged its satellites to develop Western trading links, seeing these as a means by which they could raise the quality of their goods exported for Soviet consumption (Stevens 1985, 249). Particularly close economic ties were forged with West Germany. Eastern Europe was seen by the Federal Republic as a conjoining market to exploit. For instance, by the mid-1970s this area accounted for almost a quarter of the West German iron and steel industry's exports which helped to offset the effects of recession in Western markets. Indeed, 'by the mid-1980s West Germany had more trade with the Soviet Union and Eastern Europe than any other Western power: three times more than the United States or Japan in 1985, and nearly four times more if one included trade with the GDR' (Ash 1993, 246).

For its part, the United States had never accepted the Soviet domination of Eastern Europe and American postwar policies sought to promote self-determination in the region. To achieve this by military means however carried the unacceptable risk of the mutually assured destruction of both superpowers and their minions through a nuclear holocaust. So instead Washington elected to adopt a policy of stealth, of gradually seeking to prise apart the Soviet's vice-like grip on Eastern Europe by favouring any power in the bloc which promoted more liberal domestic policies and/or adopted a less than lap-dog attitude in its foreign policy posture towards Moscow. In the former category came Hungary and Poland, in the latter Romania. The Americans used the weapon of most favoured nation status to implement their policy of differentiation in the economic sphere. Poland was the first East European country to be accorded this honour in 1960 (only to have it removed in 1982 after the imposition of martial law); Romania followed in 1975 and Hungary three years later. The 1969 Export Administration Act ended the prohibition of the export of goods to socialist countries which might give them an economic advantage. Thereafter, Washington used the Export–Import Bank to proffer credits to allow selected East European governments to purchase American industrial goods and the Commodity Credit Corporation in like manner for agricultural products. Romania, for example, was favoured with 1 billion dollars of credits (Rady 1992, 47). At the same time, American administrations were not prepared to allow unrestricted access to their technology, especially of the military kind (Koves 1985, 58; Brown 1988, 100–108; Griffith 1989, 83–6). This strategy of 'change through trade' did not bear much fruit in the short run but over time it was to contribute to the collapse of socialism in Eastern Europe.

Because East European currencies were non-convertible, payments in these denominations were not acceptable to Western exporters who demanded hard

Table 8.2   *East European indebtedness in the 1970s: gross debt in billions of current US dollars*

Country	1971	1972	1973	1974	1975	1976	1977	1978	1979
Bulgaria	0.7	1.0	1.0	1.7	2.6	3.2	3.7	4.3	4.5
Czech.	0.5	0.6	0.8	1.0	1.1	1.9	2.6	3.2	4.0
GDR	1.4	1.6	2.1	3.1	5.2	5.9	7.1	8.9	10.1
Hungary	1.1	1.4	1.4	2.1	3.1	4.0	5.7	7.5	7.8
Poland	1.1	1.6	2.8	4.6	8.0	11.5	14.0	17.8	20.5
Romania	1.2	1.2	1.6	2.7	2.9	2.9	3.6	5.2	6.9
Yugoslavia	3.2	3.9	4.7	5.4	6.6	7.9	9.5	11.8	15.0
Total	9.3	11.3	14.4	20.8	29.6	37.4	46.2	58.7	68.7

Source: Hutchings (1983, 197)

currency. This prerequisite meant that East European governments were compelled to seek credits from Western countries, banks and sometimes the suppliers themselves. These sources all proved more than willing to proffer liberal doses of credit to Eastern Europe. This was despite the fact that East European governments were notorious for their lack of candour and creative accounting. As a result, over the 1970s the region's debt rose (Table 8.2) appreciably. Moreover, this misguided generosity was further fuelled by the lenders' desire to dispose of OPEC-generated surpluses after the 1973–74 oil price explosion when liquidity was plentiful but Western borrowers were in short supply owing to depressed conditions. Again, as Western suppliers suffered from recession in their home markets, they became more willing to grant export credits to Eastern Europe. On the other side of the fence, borrowers were encouraged to spend prodigiously because the inflation which gripped the West meant that for a considerable period real rates of interest were negative (Koves 1985, 131). The two German central banks established a bilateral clearing system with the *Verrechnungseinheit*, based on the Deutschmark, the clearing unit of account. Furthermore, Bonn guaranteed West German bank credits to East Germany (Jeffries 1993, 273). The Bulgarian and Czech levels of indebtedness were less pronounced than the rest because they did not participate as actively in the import-led growth strategy but rather intensified their trade with the socialist bloc and the Third World. Czechoslovakia also used import restrictions in the early 1980s to bring her debt with the West under control.

A number of false assumptions were made by Western financial institutions. Among them was the belief that at the first whiff of a balance of payments problem, imports would be restricted and exports boosted; that if trouble developed the CMEA countries would obligingly assist one another and specifically, that the Soviet Union would act as a guarantor of last resort (the umbrella theory). Moscow did indeed come to the aid of Bulgaria, but its debts were a molehill compared to the Polish case. For several years Poland had access to virtually unlimited credit (mainly from West German banks) which ensured that it dug itself into a deeper hole. When the dénouement finally came in 1981, Poland's balance of payments crisis was on such a scale that the Soviets' politically motivated financial support proved to be no more than a drop in an ocean of debt (Koves 1985, 128–9).

LOOKING TO BRIDGE THE TECHNOLOGY GAP

The compelling need of Eastern Europe to import advanced Western technologies was based on a number of factors. First, as an economy modernizes so new industries will emerge which require increasingly sophisticated technology if they are to operate efficiently. By the 1970s the extensive sources which hitherto had driven economic growth were petering out across the region. A slow-down could only be averted through dynamic new industries playing a more important role in the economy. Second, the prospective importer lacks the skilled labour and infrastructure to provide the requisite machinery. Last, such imports represent a means to catch up with advanced industrial economies. The late industrializer needs to import the most modern machinery and equipment available or else the technological gap will widen and, instead of improving, competitiveness will deteriorate (Gerschenkron 1966).

In *détente*'s honeymoon period, 1970–75, Eastern Europe's imports of Western technology doubled (Griffith 1989, 97). As Table 8.3 suggests, at the start of the 1970s Yugoslavia was the leading East European country receiving high-tech imports from the West, reflecting its already open economy. In March 1970 Yugoslavia concluded a wide-ranging commercial agreement with the European Economic Community (EEC) whereby it won non-discrimination in trade and most favoured nation status. By the middle of the decade Poland, the most enthusiastic new convert to import-led growth in Eastern Europe, had almost caught up. Inevitably machinery imports from Western sources increased as a proportion of total imports. For the CMEA six this group accounted for 37 per cent of imports by 1977 compared with 29 per cent in 1965 (Koves 1985, 84). Typically, there was no coordinated CMEA strategy on technology imports. The commodity composition of imports from the West was shaped by several factors including economic strategy, the relative shortage of labour, the projected size of an industry and its

Table 8.3 *Destination by country of communist high-tech imports from the industrial West (%)*

	1970	1975	1981	1982
USSR	34	35	31	40
China	9	13	19	15
Bulgaria	2	3	4	4
Czechoslovakia	8	6	6	6
GDR	4	2	4	4
Hungary	5	4	6	6
Poland	7	13	6	6
Romania	9	7	4	3
Yugoslavia	19	14	17	15
Other	3	3	3	2

Source: Joint Committee Report (1986)

modernization needs, the scarcity of certain capital goods, and the specialist needs of the domestic, CMEA and world markets. Agricultural equipment played only a small role except in Hungary where the emphasis on exporting food demanded high quality machinery imports including food processing equipment. In the 1971–75 period, textile and leather products dominated, representing 8 to 11 per cent of all Western capital goods imported by the CMEA six, with the GDR, Poland and Romania placing particular store on this category. As for transport equipment, in the early 1970s the GDR, Bulgaria and Poland imported the most, while Romania, Czechoslovakia and Hungary considered this less important. Electric power and distribution equipment were given priority, reflecting a shortfall in this crucial development area. In several countries, especially Poland, industrial growth exceeded electrical generating capacity. Even when other imports were cut back, the emphasis on providing a modernized electrical energy infrastructure remained except in Romania (Fallenbuchl 1986, 142–4). The extent of foreign participation also varied. For instance, while Romania permitted joint ventures between domestic and foreign firms and Hungary allowed the latter to participate in management and profits, Bulgaria and Poland's conditions were more circumscribed (Stevens 1985, 249).

There can be no question that Western technology imports were abused. Estimates of Yugoslav misuse ranged from a third to half their total debts by the 1980s. This was despite the fact that in 1972 the World Bank had turned down no less than 85 per cent of the prospective projects as wildly optimistic either on cost grounds and/or their potential impact in world markets (Swain and Swain 1993, 168). Poland was undoubtedly the worst case. The Gierek regime failed lamentably to develop a coherent investment strategy with the result that resources were woefully dispersed, economies of scale did not materialize and there was no multiplier effect. The decision to proceed into uncharted waters produced a disaster of Titanic proportions as the Polish economy careered into the iceberg formed by an accumulated mountain of debts which then sank its import-led growth strategy.

Over the period 1971–80 Poland purchased 416 import licences of which the great majority were from the West. Not all of the substantial number of projects begun in the early 1970s were completed. Indeed, by 1980 a colossal 821 billion zlotys were tied up in unfinished projects, reflecting increased gestation periods (Drewnowski 1982, 32). And of the projects that were finished many turned out to be white elephants. The Katowice steel plant, started in 1974, was a classic case of misdirected investment. It produced lower quality steels, for which there was no great demand, and ignored higher grade steels which needed to be imported. By 1980 the cost overrun amounted to 50 per cent with 8.8 billion zlotys sunk into the project's idle machinery, at which point further development was abandoned. At least the Massey-Ferguson-Perkins Ursus tractor and diesel engine plant, also initiated in 1974, went into production in 1980. But instead of the anticipated annual output of 25 000 tractors it managed to produce only 2000, with each unit requiring $4000 of imported parts. The production of the Berliet bus plant was similarly disappointing: 1000 units in 1980 compared to the projected 5000. Moreover, the import content was $2000 more than the tractors required. All this to produce a product which proved to be unsuited to the Polish weather and roads! (Smith 1983, 34–5).

Several other countries in Eastern Europe experienced the 'Polish disease' of exposure to imports of Western technology and mounting hard currency debt. By the later 1970s Hungary's Western imports were growing at a faster rate than CMEA imports (Koves 1985, 101). As a consequence, from 1974 Hungary began to exhibit a substantial convertible currency trade deficit, which amounted to over $3 billion by 1978 (Swain 1992, 131). In 1971 Romania became the first CMEA country to unveil a joint equity venture law *vis-à-vis* Western companies – though the attached strings were so constraining that only half a dozen were in operation by the late 1980s (Jeffries 1993, 315). Romanian imports of machinery and equipment accelerated, not least because Romania's membership of the IMF and World Bank encouraged her borrowing habit (Smith 1983, 220). Romania attempted to lessen dependence on Comecon and to control her growing balance of payments problem by targeting the less developed countries both as a source of raw materials and as a dumping ground for poor quality exports with no sales potential in the

West. This strategy was not to succeed (Swain and Swain 1993, 162–3). Yugoslavia had been a long-standing member of the IMF and was a full member of GATT from 1966 and this status encouraged her to borrow heavily in the 1970s. East Germany's addiction to Western imports was encouraged by West Germany which assumed the status of its most important trading partner after the USSR. The special relationship was epitomized by the Federal Republic designating its exports to its other half as 'deliveries' and GDR imports as 'purchases'. The latter were allowed in without being subject to tariffs and levies – although selective quotas were imposed to prevent dumping (Jeffries 1993, 272–3).

There was an array of complications and contradictions in the import-led growth strategy which ensured failure. To begin with, the implication was one of greater integration with the world economy, yet this was anathema to communist doctrine. When inflation surged in the West from 1973 onwards socialist regimes generally tried to avoid the consequences with the result that internal price distortions and subsidies increased. A related problem was that without fundamental reforms imported technology could not be utilized effectively. The centrally planned system was simply unable to cope. Socialist bureaucracy slowed down technology transfer which meant that Eastern Europe was always trailing behind Western best practice techniques (Wallace and Clarke 1986, 128). Central planners were often ignorant about foreign opportunities and their marketing was woefully inadequate. For instance, Poland produced heavy leather luggage for Western markets which evidenced its failure to recognize that Western consumers now preferred light plastic and soft luggage (Roskin 1991, 117). Even worse, the corruption which was endemic in the system also played a part. Data relating to the production capacity of export firms was generally either incomplete or fabricated. As a result, many enterprises which were expanded and modernized (absorbing expensive imports of components and specialist materials) because of their alleged export potential failed to match expectations. Nor did the frequent failure to meet delivery deadlines help, with many a window of opportunity closing because of dilatory management. Moreover, the absence of effective quality control served only to worsen the comparative backwardness of East European goods *vis-à-vis* Western product lines (Fallenbuchl 1986, 130–1). Then, too, the heavy industry lobby, which had naturally developed out of the earlier emphasis on sector A industries, managed to redirect a significant proportion of foreign lending to meet its own needs (Schopflin 1993, 165–6).

THE ENERGY SHOCKS AND EASTERN EUROPE

For Western Europe the results of the Organization for Petroleum Exporting Countries' (OPEC) severe oil price increases in the wake of the Yom Kippur War were devastating: double-digit inflation for most countries and growing balance of payments problems, leading to a recession. Whereas the first oil shock of 1973 halted Western economies in their tracks, the same was not true of Eastern Europe, with the exception of Yugoslavia which also experienced rocketing inflation and high unemployment (officially recorded at 833 000 by 1981). The more open Yugoslav economy had in fact been plagued by inflation since the early 1960s and the problem was especially acute in the periods 1973–75 and 1978–79. In the 1970s the rest of Eastern Europe enjoyed comparative price stability – although inflationary pressures did

Table 8.4   Comparative inflation in selected countries, 1971–77 (retail prices)

	% annual increase (average)
Italy	13.6
France	9.2
Germany	5.6
Switzerland	5.9
Britain	14.0
Sweden	8.4
Japan	11.2
USA	6.7
Spain	14.9
Portugal	17.5[a]
Turkey	18.6[a]
Greece	13.8[a]
Yugoslavia	18.1
Bulgaria	0.5
Czechoslovakia	0.2
GDR	0.0
Hungary	3.3
Poland	3.2
Romania	0.6

[a]   1972–78

Source: Tyson (1980, 76)

occasionally manifest themselves, especially in Poland and Hungary. There was also undoubtedly an element of hidden inflation which official figures did not disclose. Even taking this into account, Yugoslavia's inflation rate was easily the region's worst (Table 8.4) and in fact exceeded the West European average. It did not help that in July 1973, just before the Yom Kippur War, the dinar had been officially floated and several devaluations were to follow. By 1975 the Yugoslav government was proclaiming that 'inflation is enemy number one in our socialist society and the struggle against it is a major political problem' (Tyson 1980, 74). At the same time, Eastern Europe as a whole could not entirely escape from being contaminated by capitalist inflation which greatly increased the cost of imported Western technology. As Ascherson (1987, 190) puts it, 'Poland was now importing inflation with every machine tool or fertiliser plant bought in the West'. The sheer scale of Polish imports sent its hard currency foreign debt rocketing skywards after the first oil price inflation of 1973–74.

The principal reason why most East European countries could largely ignore the first oil shock was that the majority of their energy requirements were met by the Soviet Union at extremely advantageous prices. The Bucharest formula fixed Soviet oil prices for the duration of a five-year plan. These were based on average world market prices for the preceding five years. Thus for the period 1971–75 CMEA countries were paying prices which reflected earlier stable world market conditions rather than the prevailing situation. In fact Hungarian economists were to estimate that Eastern Europe enjoyed a 60 per cent discount because of its Soviet connections (Kramer 1991, 86). Czechoslovakia did even better because in 1966 it had agreed to provide around $500 million worth of machinery, equipment and steel pipes to the USSR which in return promised to supply 60 million metric tons of oil at a fixed price throughout the 1970s (Stevens 1985, 247). Bulgaria, which had almost all of its energy import requirements met by the USSR, took advantage by recycling Soviet oil to the West. This cosy price situation was not without its problems in the longer term. While Yugoslavia was compelled by spiralling petrol pump prices to develop belatedly her indigenous coal and hydroelectric resources, the rest of Eastern Europe was not deflected from shifting from coal to oil burning, and there continued to be an immense gap in energy efficiency between East and West. Accordingly, the CMEA six increased their dependence on energy imports (ratio of net energy imports to primary energy consumption) from 11 per cent in 1970 to 24.4 per cent by 1980 (Aldcroft 1993b, 258; United Nations 1987, 202).

There was also an environmental consequence. Because of the emphasis over several decades on energy-guzzling heavy industries Eastern Europe became lumbered with the reputation for being the most polluted region in the world. Industrial managers had no environmental regulations to worry about, unlike their counterparts in the West. To quote Keegan (1993, 92): 'Under the communist system ... crude production targets prevailed over environmental considerations.' The extent of pollution was reckoned to be around double the OECD norm. Consequently chemical factories and power plants lacked stack scrubbers and the management had no inhibitions about dumping waste products which contaminated drinking water. As several of the countries shared common borders pollutants produced by one inevitably drifted into another. Cheap brown coal, or lignite, was a particular irritant, emitting sulphur dioxide and leaving the cities with a pall of barely breathable air. Indeed, by the 1980s the more industrialized regions of Poland, Czechoslovakia and Romania were recording abnormal levels of death from lung cancer. The situation was so bad in Katowice in southern Poland that people regularly beat a retreat to deep salt mines to clear their lungs. Similarly, northern Bohemia in Czechoslovakia was another area with excessive pollution (Roskin 1991, 126; Stevens 1985, 286).

Initially, therefore, it was the Soviet Union which bore the cost of higher energy prices in terms of the profits that were foregone. But by 1974 these lost opportunity costs were of such magnitude that the rankled Soviet leadership ended the old system in favour of a rolling average formula. From January 1975 the cost of oil and other commodities was to be subject to annual revision based on the world average of the past three years. Not only did this mean that the revised price of oil was to be determined by 1972–74 world averages, thus incorporating the effect of the first oil shock, but Moscow now demanded that a proportion of the goods provided as repayment should consist of products made from imported materials or manufactured under foreign licence (Hutchings 1983, 193). Hungary, East Germany and Bulgaria were especially affected. Even Czechoslovakia, despite its favourable arrangement with Moscow, found that the energy demands of its heavy industries were such that not all its requirements were met outside CMEA arrangements. All these countries were compelled to increase their exports to the USSR by around 10 per cent which for all bar Czechoslovakia represented approximately 1 per cent of GNP. An indication of the changed mood was captured by Hungary whose prime minister resigned as the New Economic Mechanism of 1974 and 1975 was amended to reflect the new situation.

In the long run, Eastern Europe's increased exposure to international commodity prices, in combination with the Soviet hike in the cost of its oil, was to prove a lethal cocktail. From the mid-1970s, without exception, the East European countries found their terms of trade declining alarmingly, not just with the West but also with the Soviet Union. Czechoslovakia saw the price of Soviet raw materials and fuels rise much faster than that of its own machinery and equipment, while by 1983 East Germany's trade deficit with

Moscow was equivalent to \$4.2 billion. The upshot was to squeeze domestic consumers as exports of goods had to be increased to try to maintain the same volume of imports. The inevitable result was an increased shortage of consumer goods – most apparent in Poland and Romania – just at a time when domestic consumer demand had been rising (Joseph 1987, 75, 125, 295).

The Romanian example illustrates this trend most vividly. Romania was a net oil exporter but its reserves were running out, leading to a wildly optimistic exploration expedition in the Black Sea. The situation was not helped by an earthquake in March 1977 whose epicentre was in the oilfields, which accelerated the fall in crude oil output. To make matters worse, domestic refining capacity was significantly increased during the 1976–80 plan with a view to boosting Western-bound exports of refined oil. This perverse decision occurred at a time when Western demand for oil products was declining and only served to heighten the country's increasing dependence on imported crude oil. From 1977 Romania became a net oil importer. Estranged relations with Moscow led Bucharest to seek salvation in a bilateral trade deal with Iran by which Romania would have received 4 million tons of crude oil annually in exchange for machinery and equipment. But this favourable arrangement was abruptly cancelled following the fall of the Shah in 1979, coincidentally the year of the second oil shock. The Soviet Union would only grudgingly supply part of Romania's revised oil requirements (and then only at world market prices) so that Romania was fully exposed to the inflationary effects of the second price hike. Its import bill for 16 million tonnes of crude oil in 1980 amounted to a staggering \$3.8 billion which produced a deficit on the oil account amounting to \$1.6 billion. Put another way, Romania's failure to benefit from the intra-CMEA price subsidy forced the regime to import most of its crude oil from the gluttonous Middle East, thereby depriving her of \$3.6 billion in the period 1976–80 alone. Like Yugoslavia, Romania in desperation began to develop coal and hydroelectric resources with a view to reducing her dependence on oil (Joseph 1987, 256; Aldcroft 1993b, 258; Smith 1983, 230). Only belatedly did increasing oil prices begin to exert a more pronounced influence over the rest of Eastern Europe. In the early 1980s energy consumption levelled off in Czechoslovakia, Hungary, Poland and Romania and increased only modestly in Bulgaria and East Germany (United Nations 1987, 200).

SLOWDOWN

As the 1970s drew to a close it was apparent that Eastern Europe's attempt to achieve higher growth and better standards of living through its 'Western strategy' had failed dismally. Instead many countries were left with substantial hard currency foreign debt hangovers which were a new and unwanted development. Indeed, by the start of the 1980s the situation was considerably worse in many ways than a decade earlier. The CMEA six could afford to ignore a net foreign debt of under $4 billion in 1970 but they could no longer do so by 1980 when the total read $58 billion (United Nations 1987, 211).

At the height of its import-led growth strategy, Poland's growth of Western imports reached 74 per cent in 1973, but by 1976 the rate had slowed to a mere 10 per cent (Joseph 1987, 295). Yugoslavia too was in great difficulties: by 1977–78 almost a third of its export earnings were being absorbed on importing capital goods and equipment (Singleton and Carter 1982, 239). Something had to give. Most of Eastern Europe's economies had plunged head-first into the swimming pool of Western capitalism and instead of emerging refreshed and revitalized had surfaced gasping for air and saddled with unsustainable debt. Moreover, as *détente* was terminated by the Soviet invasion of Afghanistan in December 1979 and subsequent events in Poland (see Chapter 7), the chill of a new cold war was soon felt in financial markets. Together with the serious concern of Western banks at the prospect of East European defaults, this made it problematic for Eastern Europe to procure credit simply to sustain the import levels required just to run the machinery already brought in. Accordingly, the volume of Western exports to Eastern Europe fell, with manufactured goods declining steeply at an annual average of 12 per cent over 1980–82, leading to shortages in selected consumer goods and what was to become a familiar sight in Eastern Europe: long queues of disconsolate citizens (Joseph 1987, 315–16).

Not surprisingly, Poland represented the most extreme case. By 1977 its cumulative balance of payments deficit stood at $12.8 billion, which then equated to three-and-a-half years of hard currency earnings (Joseph 1987, 294–5). To make matters worse, there was no immediate prospect of future export earnings making any significant inroads into this debt mountain. In 1981–82 Poland's net material product (NMP) went into reverse, recording a 9 per cent average annual fall (United Nations 1987, 218). Towards the end of 1981 Romania followed Poland in seeking a rescheduling of its hard currency debt, at which point the debt–service ratio stood at 35 per cent, with over $4 billion falling due in 1982. Any hopes that the scale of debt could be reduced by inflation were hit by the rise in international interest rates. For instance, Yugoslavia had become dangerously vulnerable to variable-interest 'roll-over' loans from the private sector and by 1981 was paying an average rate of interest of no less than 18.7 per cent on its debts, a far cry from the 7.3 per cent of 1972 (Jeffries 1993, 315; Smith 1983, 236; Dyker 1990, 121–2). East Germany was unique in that it enjoyed an interest-free overdraft facility with the FRG which, in July 1985, was further increased from 600 to 800 Deutschmarks. The West German connection proved a lifeline (in the short term) for while Western sources of credit generally dried up, inter-German trade was not affected and indeed increased in the early 1980s. This was a main reason why East German growth rates remained relatively buoyant. Bulgaria was alone in announcing a hard currency balance of payments in surplus in 1981. Indeed, in the first part of the 1980s she was able to handle total annual debt maturities predominantly from current earnings (Jeffries 1993, 273; Joseph 1987, 59–60, 315).

Romania's debts were rescheduled in June 1982 and the Ceausescu regime decided to adopt a policy of rapid repayment. This reduced gross indebtedness from $9.6 billion to $6 billion by the end of 1985, a feat accomplished primarily through slashing imports and boosting exports. The latter was achieved through curbing domestic supplies of foodstuffs and energy, thereby reducing standards of living to their lowest level since the Second World War. Steep rises in food prices were introduced and the rationing of bread, sugar and cooking oil came into force. By the summer of 1983 long queues for food were a common sight. The typical Romanian consumer was also deprived of meat (apart from poultry). Measures to reduce energy consumption in households and public places were imposed in 1979 and were stepped up subsequently. In November 1983 the government sought a 50 per cent reduction in non-productive energy consumption (heating oil, natural gas and electricity). The draconian policy involved total bans on the employment of refrigerators, vacuum cleaners and electric heaters and lighting in the entrance halls to apartment blocks as well as much reduced public lighting provision. The crusade reached further heights of indifference in the autumns of 1984 and 1985. If any of the population did not realize the full implications they were made acutely aware of them during the terrible winter of 1984–85. Then many indoor temperatures reportedly came close to freezing point as communal heating systems were often deprived of power in the day and gas pressures proved inadequate for cooking or heating. Moreover, households were restricted to a solitary low-power light bulb. Nor could solace and comfort be sought elsewhere for bars and cafes were compelled to close by 9.00 pm. Furthermore, the driving of private vehicles was prohibited for more than two months, compelling workers to find their way to work on foot as best they could (Joseph 1987, 265–6). For the moment the Ceausescu regime's military-style grip on power was firm enough to ensure compliance, but its days were numbered as a crescendo of hatred built up which only awaited the opportunity to be unleashed.

Yugoslavia, exposed to both oil shocks, had seen its deficit on current account break all records in 1974 and again in 1977. By 1979 the figure stood at $3.7 billion and three years later came the predictable debt-service crisis. Yugoslavia had come to rely on the remittances from migrant workers who found jobs abroad, but this source of revenue was severely curtailed by the

Western recession after the first oil shock. By 1977 exports were only meeting 53.7 per cent of the cost of imports, reflecting the fact that trade with the EC was declining. Indeed, EC tariffs forced Yugoslavia to trade more with the CMEA which warmer (or less cold) relations with Moscow made possible. The efficiency of the Yugoslav economy was increasingly compromised by historic nationality disputes which had lurked just beneath the surface but now increasingly showed themselves. There was a clear distinction between less developed regions (LDRs) – Bosnia-Herzegovina, Montenegro, Macedonia and Kosovo – and the more developed ones (MDRs) – Croatia, Slovenia, Serbia proper and Vojvodina. Regional variations were aggravated by the growing inability of the Yugoslav economy to absorb the available labour supply. The unemployment problem was such that in 1978 the government felt compelled to introduce a comprehensive unemployment benefits programme. Inevitably there were more job seekers in the less developed areas – in 1977 unemployment ranged from as high as 26 per cent in Kosovo to as little as 1.6 per cent in Slovenia. Increasingly, each republic and province saw itself as an island which impeded the free circulation of goods across the country and sometimes made it impossible to obtain a product in short supply (Singleton and Carter 1982, 186).

In the early 1970s there was growing disenchantment at the disappointing results of the market forces introduced in the 1965 economic reforms following the MDRs' disenchantment at state investment funds being channelled to the LDRs. Now the latter grew increasingly vocal at the widening regional income differentials. The aging President Tito was anxious to resolve the growing difficulties so that his succession was secure. During the 1970s institutional reforms switched the emphasis in decisionmaking from the federation to the six republics and two provinces. A system of social compacts was unveiled to replace state laws and foster inter-republican agreements on planning, income distribution, prices, employment and foreign trade and a new system of self-management agreements was introduced. These reforms proved ineffectual. Long-standing enmities between republics and provinces slowed the conclusion of social compacts to a snail's pace. For instance there was over a year's delay in implementing the 1976–80 plan occasioned by the lack of consensus on fifteen social compacts for priority sector development. More seriously, divisions delayed the introduction of deflationary measures in the late 1970s and stifled efforts to cut Yugoslavia's addiction to hefty oil imports. In June 1978 an exasperated Tito criticized the creation of protected markets by different republics and provinces (Tyson 1980, 3–10, 52–62).

Tito's death in 1980 only made matters worse. The following year Kosovo sought full republican status and revolted. The situation was only restored by the imposition of martial law. Also in 1981 Yugoslavia secured the IMF's biggest ever loan, a three-year credit of $2.2 million. The attached strings, such as an insistence on cutting public expenditure, adversely affected the standard of living. Inflation roared away once more, reaching 50 per cent in the first half of 1981. In an effort to dampen consumer demand the cash deposits required on many consumer goods were increased to record levels and, looking to conserve energy and reduce imports, the full effects of petrol price increases were passed on to the consumer. Despite such measures in 1982 Yugoslavia found herself unable to meet her debt service. Her predicament was epitomized by nine state ships waiting outside the Suez Canal unable to pay the dues. The World Bank came to the rescue with a rescheduling agreement in April 1983 which involved no less than fifteen countries and 583 creditor banks (Dyker 1990, 122–5).

There was another price Eastern Europe had to pay for the import-led growth mania of the 1970s – the neglect of agriculture. Throughout the decade agricultural production generally left much to be desired. A worrying trend for the region was its increasing resort to grain imports to make up for shortfalls in its own agricultural production. Hitherto the USSR had been a prime source but as its grain output fell, so the West increasingly became the provider, which inevitably worsened the balance of payments position throughout the region. The actual import levels depended on individual harvests but this trend became a permanent one. During the 1970s Poland and East Germany were compelled to provide for continuous grain imports. By 1978 food comprised 23 per cent of Polish imports, reflecting the agricultural sector's inability to meet the population's growing meat consumption (Fowkes 1993, 152). The position might have been worse had the CMEA countries not managed to purchase several food items, including coffee and cocoa, from the Third World (Koves 1985, 91–2). Exports in the other direction declined over the period with the exception of Hungary, which managed to increase marginally its share of the OECD market – though the lukewarm reception given to its processed agricultural products did not justify the emphasis on investment accorded to this sector.

Over the period 1970–85 several countries managed to lift the levels of food consumption per capita. But this was not true of Poland after 1980 nor of Romania where, despite lack of published data, the trend was transparently downwards. East Germany and Czechoslovakia also experienced declines but this was because their consumption levels started higher. The Bulgarian and Romanian populations suffered from the most basic diets which lacked protein. During the 1970s, in line with the general aim to raise living standards, respectable rates of gross agricultural output had been returned in Eastern Europe but, with the exception of Czechoslovakia, these were not maintained in the early 1980s. Livestock output fell everywhere, a trend which can be attributed to declining feedstuff imports, especially oilseeds, during 1981–85. The problem was that modern livestock rearing demanded quality high protein feeds, normally oilseed-based, such as soya beans, which the temperate climates of Eastern Europe could not easily produce.

Another worrying feature, when comparing the early 1970s with the early 1980s, was the general halt to the decline in the agricultural labour force, with East Germany, Poland and Hungary actually recording increases. Again this was a sign of agriculture failing to perform. There are no easy explanations. For instance, if we take machinery supplies, although the tractor-arable land ratio was much lower than in West Europe, conversely the number of combine harvesters per 100 hectares of grain land equalled or surpassed the Western European average. Again, tractors were more plentiful in Poland than in Hungary yet the latter's agricultural performance was far superior.

Land was a scarce commodity across Eastern Europe, which prompted governments to introduce financial constraints on the use of agricultural land by non-farm users. There were also large-scale campaigns in Bulgaria, Poland, East Germany and Romania to extend the area of irrigated land to try to improve productivity. Indeed, by 1980 Poland had increased the area of drained land to 25 per cent of the total while East Germany managed 32 per cent by 1985. Irrigation and drainage were a costly business, however, and with the slowdown in economic growth the investment drives inevitably lost their momentum and thus their effectiveness was limited (United Nations 1987, 182–96).

In the 1970s socialist consumerism had succeeded in diverting the population from political issues. Televisions, fridges and washing machines became more generally available. But the distraction could only be short-term because it was based on the continued flow of Western credits. Once they were dried up, shortages of consumer goods of varying degrees began to manifest themselves across Eastern Europe in the early 1980s, with Hungary providing the best (but still inadequate) level of supplies and austerity-driven Romania the worst. This was an inevitable consequence of the belt-tightening environment which followed the failure of import-led growth. It also reflected the growing importance of the second economy or black market. The legitimate first economy was intimately connected with the second: corrupt officials and workers in the former used their connections to channel resources into the latter. Moreover, the one had repercussions on the other for those who operated in the second economy were naturally determined to do as little work as possible in the first. Of course, the second economy had always existed but its influence was not as pervasive as it became in the 1980s. Hungary was a leader in the field and its second economy became increasingly sophisticated: a moonlighter might not only steal supplies and materials from his workplace but could even charge the unsuspecting state enterprise for the dearest items, thereby increasing his profits (Schopflin 1993, 189–90; Swain 1992, 173–4).

CONCLUSION

During the 1970s total East European exports to the West rose 3.6 times in real terms, with the exports of manufactures and machinery achieving four- and fivefold increases. These figures might appear to be exemplary, but the reality is that they reflect low initial starting points (Smith 1983, 235). What is indisputable is that the price paid for achieving even this modest degree of success was far too high.

As one decade gave way to another most East European countries were experiencing their lowest growth rates since 1945 and with international interest rates at historically high levels they were compelled to be more realistic. Consequently the growth rates envisaged in the 1981–85 five year plans were generally lower than in the preceding quinquennium despite the latter's disappointing results (United Nations 1987, 207). Notwithstanding the unusually modest objectives, the actual average rate of growth was only two-thirds of the projected aggregate growth rate (2.2 against 3.3 per cent). Because of their heavy foreign debt burden, the CMEA six looked to achieve a better export performance. They succeeded in producing a cumulative surplus of $20 billion on their trade balance – although foreign debt remained a serious problem in Poland and Hungary. But while the situation *vis-à-vis* the developed market economies improved somewhat, the CMEA six's trade deficit with the Soviet Union increased largely because of the revised energy pricing formula and Moscow's escalating extraction costs. Measured in current prices, by 1984 the Soviet Union was a net importer of East European machinery and equipment, foodstuffs and industrial consumer goods to the tune of 18.7 billion roubles compared with only 3.4 billion roubles ten years earlier. The Soviets were net exporters of energy to the region whose value had risen from 1.4 billion roubles to 17.4 billion roubles over ten years (Pravda 1992, 84). For example, Hungary's terms of exchange reflected this altered relationship. In 1974 Hungary could trade 800 Ikarus buses for 1 million tons of Soviet oil, but by 1981 2300 buses were required for the same quantity of oil (Gadi 1990, 118).

Soviet statistics suggest that whereas there was a pronounced increase in Soviet energy prices to Eastern Europe from the mid-1970s, the increase in the prices of the USSR's imported East European manufactured goods was much more gradual, giving rise to an improvement of the order of 43 per cent in the USSR's terms of trade with the CMEA six over the period 1974–83. By 1983 the Soviet surplus with Eastern Europe for the previous nine years amounted to 12.8 billion roubles (8 per cent of total Soviet exports during this time). Moscow agreed to consolidate credits over a ten-year period to cover the debt, an unsatisfactory arrangment as it turned out given the depreciation in the value of the transferable rouble (Brada 1988, 165).

Actual labour productivity fell across Eastern Europe with the exception of East Germany. Poland suffered worst of all but there were also alarming falls in Bulgaria, Czechoslovakia, Hungary and Romania. Net material product in 1985 still remained at the 1980 level and through the plan period had averaged a rate below the 1976–80 performance. Though real incomes generally rose (Poland was an exception), combined investment volume actually contracted by 1 per cent compared with the previous quinquennium. This, combined with ridiculously long development periods, ensured that efforts to wean East European economies away from their addiction to excessive doses of Soviet energy and raw materials were not successful. In this period energy intensity levels of output generally increased, ranging from 5 per cent in Czechoslovakia to 13 per cent in Romania (United Nations 1987, 207–19).

Although the five-year plans for 1986–90 repeated the aims of old – improved foreign trade balances, better foreign trade structure, greater output and improved labour productivity – there was an increasing sense that without fundamental economic reform such objectives were unattainable. The traditional system of central planning and management needed to become more flexible and efficient. But because any tinkerings would inevitably arouse the ire of vested interest groups the reforms needed to go deeper than they had ever done before if socialism was to stand any chance of long-term survival. In short, democracy was now required to take a bow. The way forward was to be shown by an unexpected trail blazer: the Soviet Union.

9.   The road to revolution

1989 was to be a remarkable year, one of those rare turning points in world history. Falling exactly two centuries after the French Revolution, it was to match and surpass the traumatic events in France as communism collapsed like a pack of cards across Eastern Europe and the Soviet bloc was no more. One event potently symbolized the transformation. At the start of 1989 the dissident Czech poet, Václav Havel, was languishing in prison. By the end of it he was his country's president! Of the French Revolution, Alexis de Tocqueville was to write: 'The most perilous moment for a bad government is when it seeks to mend its ways' (Gati 1990, 161). Once a totalitarian regime starts to criticize itself and becomes open to censure, its days are clearly numbered. On this occasion, a reformist wave originated in the Soviet Union and surged outwards to engulf the whole of Eastern Europe.

Other points might be identified when the communist systems of Eastern Europe were palpably threatened, in particular during 1956 and 1968. But on those occasions when one country strove to break free from Soviet domination, Moscow brutally smothered the uprising and not surprisingly its other satellites swung obediently into line rather than suffer the same fate as Hungary and Czechoslovakia. 1989 was fundamentally different: the Soviets cheered on from the sidelines as one East European country after another lost its authoritarian regime.

REFORM COMMUNISM

Somewhat ironically, in view of its recent tainted history, the USSR took the lead in implementing reforms. These now had a political as well as an economic dimension and represented a last gasp attempt to sustain the quintessential socialist command economy. A new and dynamic Soviet leader, Mikhail Gorbachev, assumed office in March 1985, determined to undertake fundamental reforms. He redefined the socialist ideal as the attainment of 'free labour and free thought in a free country' (Selbourne 1990, 2). The urgency with which Gorbachev set about his task was born of the realization that while the Soviet Union might be a military superpower, economic stagnation had set in. To the mid-1980s high oil prices sustained the faltering

Soviet economy, but now with world energy prices falling and extraction costs rising this cushion disappeared. Gorbachev was also acutely aware of what he termed the 'absurd situation' represented by the paradox that while his country was fêted as the world's leading producer of steel, raw materials and energy, its malfunctioning economy ensured that shortages were commonplace (Crawshaw 1992, 21). Moreover, the technology gap with the United States remained as wide as ever and this was particularly worrying at a time when a new cold war had begun. Confident of its supremacy, the Reagan administration deliberately engaged the Soviet Union in an arms race. Symbolizing the United States' technological superiority was the 'Star Wars' programme which promised to neutralize any Soviet nuclear strike through a space-based defence arsenal. As part of the renewed antagonism, the Americans gave priority to the installation of nuclear missiles in Western Europe whence they could more easily target the Soviet Union which President Reagan denounced as 'the evil empire' (Black 1992, 141).

It was against this background that Gorbachev launched an unprecedented attack on the Brezhnev era (1964–82) whose philosophy he characterized as 'how to improve things without changing anything'. Gorbachev wanted dramatically to improve worker productivity to which end he attempted to curb alcoholism. He also sought to attack the root causes of the second economy. At the same time, Gorbachev introduced some semblance of market forces such as cost accounting, unemployment benefits and bankruptcy. He also wished to restore the wage differential between skilled and unskilled workers and denounced the current situation whereby 'many people even now receive wages for just showing up at work and hold their posts without having their actual labour contribution taken into account'. The State Quality Commission (*Gospriomka*) was established to improve the output of enterprises – though it had a chequered existence and was abolished in 1990. The emphasis was placed firmly on intensive growth with modernization of the existing capital stock heading the agenda; strategic sectors such as machine tools, instrument making, electronics and electrical engineering stood to benefit (Jeffries 1993, 46, 48).

The sweeping nature of Gorbachev's reforms (when viewed in the context of what went before) was symbolized by two Russian words which would become familiar across Eastern Europe and beyond: *glasnost*, meaning 'openness' or 'publicity', and *perestroika*, which translates as 'restructuring' or 'reformation'. The former had a political dimension and involved both a criticism of past policies and of current government practices. The latter referred to the reform of the economy and embraced such measures as efforts to stamp out corruption at management level and more stringent labour discipline (Black 1992, 232–3).

It requires emphasis that in the beginning Gorbachev did not envisage either the collapse of the Soviet Union or the fall of communist regimes in Eastern Europe. Rather he wished to purify socialism and free it from the excesses and impediments which had come to plague its existence before it destroyed itself. The situation was encapsulated in an early warning which Gorbachev delivered to East European officials during his first year in office (Gati 1990, 105):

> Many of you see the solution to your problems in resorting to market mechanisms in place of direct planning. Some of you look at the market as a lifesaver for your economies. But, comrades, you should not think of lifesavers but about the ship, and the ship is socialism.

Herein lay the dilemma which Gorbachev found it difficult to recognize or resolve: it was impossible to reform communism effectively without actually replacing it. His expressed wish to introduce a 'regulated market economy' betrayed his muddled thinking. In the event, reform communism was to come to nothing, vindicating the view of the Polish philosopher, Leszek Kolakowski, that the two words amounted to an incompatible mix equivalent to 'fried snowballs'! (Roskin 1991, 138).

While Gorbachev's criticisms of the Soviet command economy were equally applicable across Eastern Europe, his policies and overtures met with a generally muted response from the entrenched leaderships of the region. Brown (1990, 121) has characterized their reactions through the use of alpine metaphors: Romania and East Germany moved as slowly as a 'glacier', Bulgaria and Czechoslovakia experienced a slight 'thaw' while Hungary and Poland replied with an 'avalanche'. Gorbachev began a series of visits to East European capitals in 1987 which were designed to further the reform process. In a keynote speech in Prague the Soviet leader emphasized 'the sharply growing importance of exchanges of experience in socialist construction and its *generalization*' (Mason 1992, 51). The hope of several regimes was that Gorbachev would not long survive in power and might conveniently be ignored. As new blood, Gorbachev could afford to attack past policies to score political points but, with the exception of Poland, the long-standing East European leaderships could scarcely admit or condemn past mistakes in which they were heavily implicated.

Gorbachev was considerably younger than any of his East European counterparts, who were in their 60s or 70s with ages ranging from 64 to 75 in June 1987. As old dogs they were not anxious to learn new tricks. In Bulgaria, Todor Zhivkov had occupied the post of general secretary since 1954; in Hungary, János Kádár assumed power in 1956; in Romania, Nicolae Ceausescu had been at the helm since 1965; in Czechoslovakia, Gustav Husák took office in 1969; in East Germany Erich Honecker's extended reign began in 1971, ten years after he had orchestrated the erection of the Berlin Wall and given orders for anyone attempting to cross it to be shot. Even when Kádár left office in December 1987 the transition was more apparent than real. He was merely replaced by another of the old guard, Milos Jakes, who had been part of the leadership since 1969 and as such was held to be responsible for the widespread purges associated with the 'normalization' which followed the Prague Spring (Simpson 1992, 45, 48).

East Germany and Romania were the most resistant to Gorbachev's policies. So, for example, while the 1986 party congress in the USSR assailed the 'years of stagnation' of Brezhnev's final years, the East German equivalent was full of praise for developments since 1971 and Honecker complacently proclaimed that the economy was 'no field for experimentation'. The *raison d'être* for the existence of East Germany was its status as the socialist counterpart to capitalist West Germany. Should East Germany simply become a mirror image of its other half then the justification for its continuance disappeared. Acutely conscious of this, the GDR leadership contrived in a number of ways to resist change. Honecker by turns suggested that *glasnost* and *perestroika* were applicable only to the Soviet case, then that the East German version of *perestroika* had already appeared in the late 1970s and early 1980s when the *Kombinate* took centre stage and intensive economic growth became the goal. One leading member of the government even compared *perestroika* with redecorating and asked disingenuously: 'Would you feel duty-bound to repaper your flat when your neighbour repapers his?' (Pravda 1992, 155–6).

The regime's complacent view was that the East German economy was performing well enough without the need for such unorthodox interference. The stark truth behind the distorted statistics on economic performance, however, was that too much reliance was being placed on combines. In 1979 the combine decree established *Kombinate* as the main unit of production and within two years 133 were operating in industry and construction with an average workforce of 25 000. Combine activity included research and development, production and marketing, with economies of scale trumpeted as their great advantage. But each enjoyed a monopoly, thereby greatly impairing efficiency.

There was little room for the small firm in the East German economy, which by 1987 accounted for only 4.4 per cent of manufacturers employing less than 100 people compared with 35.9 per cent in booming West Germany. At the time, East Germany was paraded as Eastern Europe's most dynamic economy when in reality it was suffering from low productivity and the highest labour costs in the Soviet bloc. The manufacturing sector was still too dominant. It contributed around 70 per cent of GDP while over three-quarters of the GDR's exports went to CMEA markets, a dangerous dependence which subsequent events were to expose with devastating effects on the economy. As for *glasnost*, in April 1987 Honecker spuriously claimed that democratic and free debate was already present so that East Germany had no need to adopt Soviet reforms. The many political prisoners languishing in East German prison would certainly have dissented (Jeffries 1993, 264–5; Wright 1989, 47).

Romania's reaction to Soviet developments was predictably the most hostile of all. The Ceausescu regime was trapped in a time warp and responded as Stalin might have done. The ideological basis of *perestroika* and *glasnost* was challenged with the leading role of the party trumpeted as the only possible route to true socialism. Nor did the situation improve after a visit by Gorbachev to Bucharest in May 1987, when the Soviet leader rebuked Ceausescu for his complacent attitude towards living standards and looked in vain for signs of Romanian *glasnost*. Gorbachev's walkabouts in Bucharest convinced him that the official picture of a problem-free economy was wide of the mark. A full version of Gorbachev's critical speech did not appear in the Romanian press whereas Ceausescu's address, which proclaimed 'the right of each country to decide its own development, path and forms', did (Wright 1989, 47–8).

The Stalinist ways of the regime were intensified with a seven-day working week being introduced later that year. What Ceausescu did not recognize was that Gorbachev had stolen his thunder by pursuing foreign policy objectives which Romania had hitherto called for in isolation: withdrawal from Afghanistan, depleting nuclear stockpiles and removing short-range nuclear weapons from Europe. This Soviet transformation made Romania much less important to the West. While the American vice-president could describe Ceausescu as 'one of Europe's good communists' in 1983, once Gorbachev's policies of accommodation with the West became apparent, then an unfavourable spotlight was shone on Romania's repressive domestic policies. The United States expressed its disapproval by withdrawing Romania's most favoured nation trading status and the European Community similarly shunned trade with the dictatorship. Just how much of a pariah Ceausescu had become was indicated in December 1989 when the Americans encouraged Soviet intimations that they might intervene militarily to ensure victory for the anti-Ceausescu revolutionary forces (Gati 1990, 100; Rady 1992, 65; Pravda 1992, 196; Sword 1990, 130–31; Cipkowski 1991, 127; Gitz 1992, 147).

Czechoslovakia and Bulgaria paid lip-service to Russian policies without pursuing meaningful reforms. A visit by the Soviet leader to Czechoslovakia in April 1987 failed to shake the regime's orthodoxy despite his underscoring its 'responsibility to its people' (de Nevers 1990, 17). Though in that year Czechoslovakia introduced its own programme of economic restructuring, *prestavba*, the leadership was at pains to deny any lineage with the Prague Spring (Wright 1989, 46–7). True, the new Jakes regime in Prague did allow some younger party members to assume leading positions, but despite rhetoric in favour of Gorbachev's reforms little changed in practice. Bulgaria even went so far as to provide daily commentaries on the progress of Soviet reforms. It too introduced its own equivalent to *perestroika* – *preustroistvo* – which Zhivkov suggested had been specifically formulated to meet his country's needs. Bulgarian rhetoric, which turned out to be no more than hot air, spoke of economic restructuring, decentralization and the closure of inefficient plants. A series of decrees was issued which ostensibly looked to introduce market forces into the economy. But there were so many checks and constraints that little flowed from them. For instance, the 56th decree of January 1989 allowed that self-governing enterprises 'might' become firms, but no transforming process was developed. The so-called 'July Concept', unveiled in the summer of 1987, promised much but delivered little. To quote Brown (1990, 125): 'Had even a fraction of the July Concept's provisions become a reality, Bulgaria would have become a Proudhonist Mecca for every political hippy on the five continents rather than the Balkan outpost of millenary Marxism.' The government's ambiguous stance was epitomized by Zhivkov's comment: 'We can and must transform our already transformed Bulgaria' (Gati 1990, 92).

The warmer reception accorded to *perestroika* and *glasnost* in Poland and Hungary reflected their deeper economic ills. Also, events in Poland in the early 1980s (see Chapter 7) and Hungary's recent history of economic experimentation prepared the ground. In Poland, the Jaruzelski regime, acutely conscious of its tenuous legitimacy, went even further than Gorbachev in 1986 when it conceded that 'class contradictions' existed. Looking to court international favour, Jaruzelski gave an amnesty to political prisoners in September 1986 and even allowed the Roman Catholic Church and former Solidarity members to sit with party members on a new government advisory council. Following Gorbachev's visit to Poland in July 1987, the regime held a public referendum on the political and economic reforms that were required. But the old ways continued. Though the government did not elicit the required result, the reforms it wanted went ahead regardless, including painful price increases, albeit tempered by wage rises. Again, the 'privatization' measures introduced in 1988 were entirely spurious and 'resulted simply in senior managers of state enterprises feathering their own nests by selling to one another portions of the firms they managed. Privatisation became cynically regarded by many as yet another *nomenklatura* privilege' (Jeffries 1992, 197). Although Jaruzelski's concessions increased as the economic situation deteriorated further, his personal standing did not improve as he was perceived to be a reluctant reformer driven by events. As Brown (1990, 122) notes, 'Rather than embrace systematic reform like a politician, as Gorbachev did, Jaruzelski accepted its inevitability like a soldier'.

When Gorbachev assumed power, Hungary had the worst growth rate in the Soviet bloc, but until Kádár was replaced as general secretary by Karoly Grosz on 22 May 1988, the reform programme was skin-deep. With the latter's appointment, radical reformers came into the politburo and an open debate ensued as to the best ways of introducing market forces into a communist state (de Nevers 1990, 29–30, 34–5). Gorbachev had a less direct impact on Yugoslavia, for so long the outcast of the Soviet bloc. But he did contribute to the unravelling of the peculiar Yugoslav political system (see below) through his questioning of the authority of the communist party to manage the economy. In a visit to Yugoslavia in March 1988 Gorbachev also downplayed the ogre of Soviet intervention when he promised 'unconditional respect' for the domestic policies of socialist states (Black 1992, 281; Gitz 1992, 134).

ECONOMIC DECLINE

Gradually Gorbachev redefined the traditional Soviet–East European relationship away from that of a dominant superpower crying foul whenever its satellites acted out of turn, to one of a paternal uncle benignly looking after his grandchildren. In essence, the message went out that the East Europeans were free to do as they pleased provided that the one-party state was maintained and membership of the Warsaw Pact continued. Ultimately, even these conditions were to be waived as the situation in the Soviet Union deteriorated and Gorbachev became more radical. An example of the new liberal Soviet outlook occurred when Honecker was allowed to pay a state visit to Bonn in September 1987, an outing which would never have been tolerated by Moscow in Brezhnev's day. Six months earlier, in Prague, Gorbachev announced that his government regarded 'the independence of every party, its responsibility to the people of its own country, and its right to decide the questions of the country's development to be unconditional principles' (Gati 1990, 74).

There was also an ongoing reappraisal by Moscow of the continued value and relevance of the old relationship with Eastern Europe which accounted for a large share of the latter's trade (Table 9.1). In April 1988 the longstanding Soviet Department for Liaison with the Communist and Workers' Parties of Socialist Countries was abolished, to be replaced by a Commission on International Policy which considered Eastern Europe only as part of world foreign policy. In economic terms, the relationship was now perceived by Moscow to be hamstrung by the over-reliance of Eastern Europe (apart from Yugoslavia) on supplies of Soviet energy and raw materials and the

Table 9.1   Eastern Europe and the Soviet Union: share of CMEA countries in total trade, 1988 (percentages)

Country	Exports	Imports
Bulgaria	80.8	73.8
Czechoslovakia	73.1	72.6
East Germany	60.9	62.0
Hungary	44.6	43.8
Poland	40.7	40.6
Romania	40.9	58.4
Soviet Union	48.9	54.1

Source: Collins and Rodrik (1992, 30)

Soviet willingness to accept inferior goods in return which would be unsaleable in the West. Between 1960 and 1988 the USSR assumed the mantle of the world's greatest exporter of oil products and gas and was second only to Saudi Arabia as an exporter of oil. Over the period, oil sales increased dramatically from 18 to 144 million tonnes, yet much of this potential hard currency bonanza was foregone since approximately half Soviet oil went to Eastern Europe (Pravda 1992, 224). The USSR was also dissatisfied with late deliveries by East Europeans and their habit of holding back better quality products for hard currency trade.

Changes began to be orchestrated by Moscow in the wake of Western sanctions over Poland, which led to the long-term goal of so improving technology that dependence on the West could be ended. In 1984, following a summit meeting of CMEA leaders in Moscow, a communiqué announced that

> the CMEA countries will ... develop their structure of production and exports, reconstruct and rationalize their industry with the aim of supplying the Soviet Union with the products it needs ... in particular foodstuffs and industrial consumer goods, some types of construction materials and machinery and equipment of a high quality and reaching world technical levels (Pravda 1992, 75).

The statement made it apparent that there was now a price to be paid for the continued provision of Soviet energy and raw materials: the modernization of East European economies up to Western standards. A series of bilateral agreements with the Soviet Union repeated these demands. In addition, the December 1985 'Comprehensive Programme for Scientific and Technical Progress until the Year 2000' envisaged cooperation in those areas outlined in the 1984 communiqué. Specifically, Gorbachev demanded East European progress in five key fields: nuclear energy, electronics, robots, new technologies and biotechnology (de Nevers 1990, 15; Brada 1988, 167; Gati 1990, 128).

The plain truth was that East European economies were too orientated towards heavy industry and were too inefficient to meet the new Soviet demands. An array of complications ensured failure. First, as in the 1970s, the heavy industry lobby, referred to in Poland as 'the coal and steel community', was not going to lie down and allow a fundamental change in the structure of the economy. It was no accident that several East European countries participated most enthusiastically in the quest to maintain the energy sector in the USSR, which implied a reluctance to reduce their dependence on Soviet energy supplies to sustain their heavy industry sectors. Second, because of events in the 1970s, the East Europeans lacked the hard currency necessary to import the Western technology required to comply with Soviet wishes. For instance, in July 1988 Moscow suddenly demanded supplies of food, food processing equipment, light consumer goods and high-tech products at below world market prices. At that date Hungary and Poland's hard currency debts required them to generate annually a surplus of around $1 billion and $2 billion respectively from hard currency trade simply to pay the interest on their outstanding debt. Inevitably this dictated that neither country could import sufficient technology and consumer goods from the West (Gati 1990, 107). By 1988 Western exports to the Soviet bloc had declined to $50.5 billion, under 2 per cent of total world exports. By way of comparison, Japan, acknowledged as one of the most difficult markets for exporters to infiltrate, imported more than three times this figure. In several countries, such as Czechoslovakia, Hungary and Poland, there was some attempt to gain access to Western technology through joint ventures. But the foreign partner was so constrained that Western firms lacked sufficient incentive to participate in large numbers and several that did seized the opportunity to palm off unwanted and outmoded technology.

Third, there was a conspicuous lack of innovation. As Table 9.2 indicates, without exception the East European countries were laggards in generating new ideas, on a par only with the poorer regions of Europe, the chasm being most vividly illustrated by the respective patent records of the two Germanies. During the 1980s, American inhibitions on the transfer of high technology to Eastern Europe compelled the GDR to devote considerable resources to developing its microelectronics sector, but the effort was not cost-effective because the resultant products were much inferior to Western output (Davy 1992, 157). As long as communism and central planning prevailed, there was little incentive to innovate. For example, in Czechoslovakia licences for contact lenses and textile machinery were readily sold to the West because

Table 9.2   European patents by country of origin

Country	1981	1982	1983	1984	1986	1987	1988	1989
Austria	47	72	144	158	220	196	259	270
Bulgaria	0	0	1	2	4	10	10	16
Czech.	0	0	0	1	4	4	1	6
France	438	662	1243	1720	2020	1958	2280	2297
FRG	1464	1927	2953	3502	4504	4116	4960	5610
GDR	0	1	6	9	16	8	12	16
Greece	–	–	–	–	1	4	2	0
Hungary	1	5	18	32	66	55	67	59
Italy	19	40	133	238	396	405	503	652
Japan	75	251	724	1419	2585	2570	3027	3666
Poland	1	1	9	8	6	13	7	11
Portugal	–	–	–	–	–	1	–	1
Romania	0	0	0	1	3	1	–	1
Spain	4	4	8	15	36	34	27	50
Switz.	242	403	565	753	974	968	1108	1119
UK	217	407	740	983	1196	1059	1176	1320
USA	579	1145	2191	3123	4611	4046	4431	5226
USSR	0	0	0	2	1	–	1	4
Yug.	1	0	1	5	2	–	–	1

Source: Bentley (1992, 189)

plan managers were only concerned with meeting output targets (Myant 1993, 160, 28).

Last, the CMEA was not a common market like the EC. Only Hungary and Poland could lay claim to having established comparatively satisfactory domestic wholesale markets. Generally the lack of realistic prices and widespread use of subsidies acted as a barrier to free trade. In July 1988 the CMEA Council (with the exception of Romania) agreed to work towards the 'gradual formation of conditions for the free movement of goods, services and other production factors, with a view towards forming a unified market in the future' (Gati 1990, 130). A year earlier it had been concluded that convertible currencies needed to be introduced, but disputes remained over how to bring this about. The Hungarians wanted the transferable rouble to be made convertible into Western currencies, whereas the Soviets favoured intra-CMEA convertibility as the initial step. The fact that the July 1988 communiqué contained an important rider – 'the improvement in the cooperation mechanism should be effected gradually, as domestic and external conditions mature' – was symptomatic of the general lack of enthusiasm for currency convertibility (Pravda 1992, 77–8).

Since the mid-1980s East European exports had failed to match the spectacular growth in world trade. The newly industrializing countries (NICs) consistently beat the region's countries in penetrating Western European markets, while the expansion of the EC to include Southern Europe, with Portugal and Spain joining Greece as members in 1986, was also detrimental to East European export prospects. For instance, in the second half of the 1980s Bulgarian exports to the West stagnated, but the Zhivkov government persisted in increasing its imports, sustained by Western borrowing. In effect, where Bulgaria had managed to avoid the excesses of import-led growth in the 1970s (see Chapter 8), it now too became ensnared in external debt, which was to reach crisis proportions by 1989–90 (United Nations 1989, 73–4; 1991a, 100–101).

During the late 1980s the East European economies failed to deliver sufficient growth with the result that the scene was set for revolution. The shortage economy became the norm and acted as the catalyst for political change. Somewhat paradoxically, in the 1980s the region's standard of living was about a third higher than that of the USSR with Czechoslovakia, East Germany and Hungary enjoying greater margins, reflecting their better distribution of food and consumer goods. Czechoslovakia's annual average meat consumption per head of 91 kg in 1988 compared favourably with Austria's 90 kg. Best placed of all was Hungary where the affluent could thrive and live well (Selbourne 1990, 17):

> In the fashionable streets of Budapest – Vaci Utca, for example – the shops are full of silks and Sonys. At prices far beyond the reach of the Hungarian proletariat, there are Lacoste shirts, Wrangler jeans and tools by Black & Decker; Aiwa 'music centers', Yves St Laurent perfumes and bottles of Martini. The stout owner of the Nina Ricci couture shop wears a skull-cap; you can pay for his merchandise with American Express, Visa or Soviet roubles.

However, the essential point is that East Europeans did not judge their situation in relation to the USSR but against Western standards, especially their neighbours Austria and West Germany, compared to whom shortcomings were abundantly apparent. For instance, even in 1988 the level of car ownership per household in Czechoslovakia was still barely over half that of West Germany while for Poland it was under one-third. Nor was this the full story for the choice of available models did not even begin to compare with the West, there was a world of difference in quality and East European cars were much older. Most East German car owners had to be content with the outdated Trabant, first produced in the early 1960s, whose spluttering two-stroke engine failed to meet West German exhaust emission standards (Gati 1990, 107; Myant 1993, 11; Simpson 1992, 147).

The younger generation, which had not experienced the deprivations of war, was increasingly vocal in its criticisms and could not be placated with arguments that the situation was better than an earlier period of hardship which it could not relate to. Across the region the workers' creed echoed the Polish saying: 'They pretend to pay us and we pretend to work.' Although official Polish statistics suggested that between 1982 and 1988 real household disposable incomes rose by 29 per cent, this was no stimulus because desirable consumer goods were mostly unobtainable. In East Germany, there were special *exquisit* and *delikat* shops which sold quality goods at high prices. The regime did try to remedy the shortage of consumer goods in 1988 when manufacturers producing those goods in short supply were permitted a 20 per cent mark-up on the usual wholesale price, with an additional 10 per cent allowed for deliveries on time. Although some sensitive prices were kept down (bus and train fares were still at 1949 levels and rent took only 3 per cent of urban household income), the more desirable, better quality consumer goods, such as cars, cameras, televisions and washing machines, were allowed to rise in price, being subject to extortionate taxes, thus putting them out of reach of the majority of the population (*Financial Times* 1990, 13; Jeffries 1993, 268–9).

Hungary, with its tradition of change, went furthest along the reformist road, though in the end it too did not go far enough. In January 1985 a managerial reform was introduced which sought to remove selected enterprises from state direction with hiring and firing delegated to enterprise councils or, in cases where the workforce numbered below 500, the employees themselves. Three years earlier private work partnerships were introduced, which allowed participants to work after normal hours to fulfil contracts within and outside their enterprises, a move designed to regulate the second economy and to placate workers' dissatisfaction with their falling real wages. In 1986 Hungary became the first East European state to establish a bankruptcy law, during which year unemployment benefit was also introduced. Later value added tax was brought in.

Promising as they were, these measures were symptomatic of the incompatibility of communism and market forces which could not coexist without one impeding the other. Thus around a third of the workforce was excluded from the managerial reforms – those involved in the biggest enterprises such as electricity, oil, defence and transport. Similarly, the numbers participating in private work partnerships were restricted to a maximum of 30. So by 1986 only 14.8 per cent of all state industry employees were taking part, causing resentment among those excluded. Efficiency during normal working hours was also impaired because participants were saving their best efforts until later. Again, the number of companies which actually went bankrupt was minimal (in 1986 state funding for unprofitable enterprises still required 30 per cent of the budget), while the ranks of the unemployed were swelled by, at most, 20 000 per annum, a mere 0.3 per cent of the total labour force (Jeffries 1993, 280–82).

THE PRE-REVOLUTIONARY PHASE

With hindsight, it is apparent that in the late 1980s Eastern Europe was experiencing a pre-revolutionary phase. Zbigniew Brzezinski, formerly the security adviser in the Carter presidency (1976–80), wrote prophetically (1988, 70):

> ... change is in fact inevitable. The only question ... is whether change will be deliberately facilitated by the powers that are in a position to enhance this process, or whether it will be inhibited and obstructed, and therefore take place through revolutionary upheavals.

What no regime could do was to insulate its populations from the changes and debates that were raging in the Soviet Union. 'Gorby mania', as the Americans labelled the phenomenal popularity of Gorbachev abroad, could not be kept out of Eastern Europe. To begin with, repressive regimes experienced problems with the long-standing distribution of official Soviet literature. Hitherto, this had simply churned out orthodox socialist dogma, but now it contained the latest developments in *glasnost* and *perestroika*. The Bulgarian authorities, who had happily broadcast Soviet television programmes, now found themselves in the invidious position of seemingly endorsing the questioning of official policies. In November 1988 the Honecker regime felt compelled to ban the liberal Soviet journal *Sputnik* and five Soviet films. In Czechoslovakia, a keynote Gorbachev speech to the Moscow plenum on 27 January 1987 was eagerly followed in Czechoslovakia, with newspapers which carried it the next day quickly selling out (Selbourne 1990, 6).

Public opinion, so long repressed, now began to assert itself more and more and the regimes found it increasingly difficult to keep a lid on the situation. Hoffman (1993) identifies three distinct periods of East European political control. First, the Stalinist era when opponents could expect long prison sentences, labour camps and even execution. Second, a time of tight control when a few people risked the wrath of the regime (such as those involved in Charter 77 in Czechoslovakia) and were subjected to intimidation and imprisonment. Third, the relaxation of government controls to the extent that the large-scale printing and secret distribution of dissident material became possible, as it did in Hungary and Poland in the 1980s. Of course, not all East European countries were to experience these phases. Romania and East Germany, in particular, remained stuck in the first period. The GDR's secret police, the *Staatssicherheit*, better known as the Stasi, had an extensive network of informants and a mountain of files on the activities of dissidents. Indeed, by 1989 it boasted 100 000 full-time workers and around 150 000 freelance assistants. What the Stasi could not prevent was the reception by most of the population of West German television programmes which hammered home the constant message that there was a much better quality of life being experienced on the other side of the Berlin Wall.

There were several warning shots across the bows of the entrenched leaderships. In January 1988 the Jaruzelski regime in Poland raised food prices by 140 per cent, but as in the past the industrial workers showed no understanding of the government's position and once more Solidarity became a major force for change with 55 000 participating in strikes that year. Although the statistics suggest that wages were actually rising faster than prices in Poland, the general perception was that standards of living were falling sharply and the growing shortages did nothing to allay this suspicion (Myant 1993, 65). In August 1988 there occurred the largest demonstration that Czechoslovakia had experienced in 20 years on the anniversary of the Soviet-led invasion. The protest was brutally suppressed with Dubček, the hero of 1968, being officially condemned as a traitor to Marxist–Leninism who had brought the country 'to the verge of catastrophe'. But the warm memories of the hopes engendered by the Prague Spring could not be erased (de Nevers 1990, 45). Early in 1987 around 3000 of the democratic opposition in Hungary marched through the streets of Budapest chanting *The Marseillaise* and calling for democracy. They were inspired by the anniversary of the 1848 uprising against the Habsburgs. Here was an instance, which would soon be multiplied across Eastern Europe, of nationalist tendencies forcing their way to the surface as the authority of the government came into question.

At the end of 1987, 10 000 Romanian citizens rioted in the Transylvanian city of Brasov calling for bread, meat and milk, the shortages of which reflected Ceausescu's determination to use the export of basic foodstuffs to help repay Romania's foreign debt. Three were killed as the army suppressed the rising and emergency foodstuffs were brought in to calm the situation. By this time around 90 per cent of food produce was being exported, and with rationing at levels even worse than during the Second World War queues for food started to form before dawn. Eggs were of such rarity value that they were used as a form of currency! One authority (Richardson 1990) concludes that 'It was hours of queuing for the weekly meat ration and the distinct possibility that there would be none for tail-enders that ultimately led to the dictator's downfall. His personal excesses and the corruption of his government were of only secondary importance'. While there is much to commend this view, it also needs to be recognized that the two elements were not mutually exclusive for they tended to feed on each other to create a combustible mixture. The disturbance was also symptomatic of the unease felt at Ceausescu's megalomaniacal systematization programme which sought to intensify collectivization and augment the proletariat by destroying villages and private plots. This was despite the fact that they produced over a third of meat output, a quarter of fruit production and 40 per cent of milk and eggs. In March 1988 the heartless Ceausescu announced that the number of rural villages was to be reduced by about half to 'at the most 5,000 to 6,000' by the year 2000. Several villages were bulldozed out of existence to make way for agro-industrial complexes, creating widespread anxiety as to which were the next intended targets on the government's secret hit list. Many villages were inhabited by the ethnic Hungarian minority ensuring that the policy caused relations with Budapest to deteriorate (Rady 1992, 68–70; de Nevers 1990, 53).

Small illegal demonstrations became more commonplace in East Germany in the late 1980s despite the police brutality they invited, with Leipzig the favoured place of protest. Many demanded the right to emigrate and to some extent the Honecker regime addressed the issue. The range of relatives whom citizens could visit in West Germany was extended to include not only parents, children, uncles and aunts but also cousins, even distant ones. Where, in 1985, only 66 000 visits by GDR citizens of below pensionable age to the West had been allowed, by 1988 7 million trips were being made, involving around 10–15 per cent of the population. However, this move only created resentment on the part of those who were not eligible, while those who went and returned helped to reinforce the impression that life was emphatically much rosier on the other side of the Berlin Wall. The authorities therefore became increasingly finicky about who could travel with many of the birth certificates required being rejected on dubious grounds, such as illegible signatures or the use of a common name (Davy 1992, 160; Simpson 1992, 143–4).

REVOLUTION

The economic backdrop to the revolutions which engulfed most of Eastern Europe during 1989 was provided by faltering economic performance with recession looming on the horizon. Aggregate net material product (NMP) for the CMEA six in this dramatic year was to grow by under 2 per cent, less than half the figure recorded in the previous year. In fact economic performance was at its lowest ebb since the immediate postwar period. For East Germany, experiencing its third consecutive year of slower growth, 1989 was the worst year since 1961; for Hungary, 1989 represented the second year of reduced growth; Bulgaria suffered an absolute decline in NMP for the first time since the war, which led the leadership at the end of the year of revolutions to concede that the economy was 'on the verge of cardiac arrest' (Sword 1990, 51). Inflation, so long repressed, now became increasingly open across Eastern Europe, encouraged by fiscal deficits. The most indebted countries were worst affected with Bulgaria, Hungary and Poland registering inflation rates of 9 per cent, 17 per cent and 240 per cent respectively over 1989. Moreover, large internal budgetary deficits were also evident. Hungary was one of the worst cases. In 1989 its budget deficit amounted to 55 billion forints (3–4 per cent of national income), with the total domestic national debt as high as 65 per cent of national income. Poland was similarly afflicted with a state budget deficit equivalent to 3.4 per cent of NMP by 1989, a reflection of yet another attempt by the government to keep down food prices in the shops in an effort to appease the population (United Nations 1990, 2–7; Myant 1993, 67).

Making matters worse were the strikes in the USSR which, when added to internal transport difficulties and the increasing reorientation of Soviet trade priorities towards the West, ensured that the CMEA six suffered through an interrupted flow of raw materials and energy supplies. By 1989 the CMEA was no longer the force it had once been in Soviet–East European economic relations. In August Hungary complained to Moscow about late deliveries of crude oil, electricity, various raw materials and Lada cars. The Czechs felt themselves to have been similarly short-changed. While it was true that Soviet crude oil production was some 3 per cent adrift of the plan target for 1989, the suspicion in some East European capitals was that the USSR was deliberately orienting its oil exports to the West to counter escalating hard currency trade deficits (Pravda 1992, 79). The need to repay external debt (Table 9.3) was a common constraint. Although Romania had virtually eliminated its liability by 1989, the political fallout was to cost the Ceausescu regime dearly. Of the other countries, all except Czechoslovakia were held back by the extent of their external debt. Despite their reformist outlook, during 1989 the Hungarian and Polish economies were constrained by debt servicing which amounted to 42 per cent and 56 per cent respectively of hard currency export earnings (United Nations 1990, 86–90).

It was the changed attitude of the Soviet Union which made revolution in Eastern Europe possible. Where before (see Chapter 7) the latter's status as a *cordon sanitaire* was enshrined in Soviet military doctrine, now it was increasingly judged by Gorbachev and his reformers as an unnecessary burden on the Soviet economy. Moreover, with the exception of East Germany, none

Table 9.3   Eastern Europe and the Soviet Union: external debt, 1989

Country	Billions of dollars
Bulgaria	9.0
Czechoslovakia	6.5
East Germany	20.0
Hungary	18.5
Poland	40.0
Romania	1.0
Soviet Union	46.0
Yugoslavia	17.7

Source: Collins and Rodrik (1991, 10)

of the Warsaw Pact countries had honoured the 1978 commitment to increase substantially defence spending, which in real terms had fallen considerably throughout the 1980s. The result was that while NATO modernized its forces, outside the Soviet Union the Warsaw Pact members' military equipment stocks carried weaponry which was at least one generation removed from NATO's. The reliability of the East European members of the Warsaw Pact came increasingly into question and in 1987 Gorbachev shifted its emphasis to defence which served to 'undermine the historic rationale for close Soviet–East European military integration' (Gitz 1992, 127, 129, 137).

There were a number of trailers which hinted at a liberal non-interventionist policy replacing the Brezhnev Doctrine. Perhaps most significant of all was Gorbachev's announcement at the United Nations in December 1988 that, irrespective of NATO policy, by the end of 1990, 240 000 troops, 10 000 tanks, 8500 guns and 820 combat aircraft would be unilaterally withdrawn from Eastern Europe and the western military districts of the USSR. This unexpected development acted as a curtain-raiser to the dramatic events which were about to unfold. Without Soviet support, the security of the dictatorial East European regimes was now perilously reduced to their own army and security forces. The same month, at the Malta summit, Gorbachev informed the American president, George Bush, that the cold war was over. The withdrawal of Soviet troops from Afghanistan in February 1989 gave an indication of Soviet goodwill. These moves were symptomatic of the Soviet desire to become part again of what Gorbachev called 'the common European home', an aim which drew impetus from the proximity of the introduction of a single market in Western Europe in 1993. The Soviets were by now desperate to secure Western aid and, in the final analysis, were prepared to let go of their burdensome empire in Eastern Europe to procure it (Simpson 1992, 45).

The first signs of change in Eastern Europe came soon into the new year of 1989. In Poland, the Jaruzelski government, which had once dismissed Solidarity as a relic, initiated dialogue with its representatives in order to end a wave of strikes, which culminated on 5 April in agreement not only to relegalize the movement but also to hold semi-free elections in June. The remarkable outcome was influenced by the continuing deterioration in the state of the economy: a government report issued in January disclosed that inflation was running at 60 per cent and that per capita GNP was 13 per cent below the level of ten years before (Cipkowski 1991, 25). The upper house, or Senate, disbanded after the war, was restored and its 100 seats were to be freely contested. The communists reserved for themselves 65 per cent of the 460 seats in the lower house, the Sejm. Both houses of Parliament would elect a president with wide-ranging powers.

The election results were stunning: Solidarity claimed all but one of the seats it contested and where there was competition the communists failed to gain a single seat. Even when they stood unopposed, the communists often lost because of the requirement to attract at least half of the votes cast; mischievous voters crossed out communist candidates' names from the ballot paper. Any hope that Moscow might save the situation was dispelled by Gorbachev who, in an historic address, informed the Council of Europe at Strasbourg on 7 July 1989:

> Social and political orders in one or another country changed in the past and may change in the future. But this change is the exclusive affair of the people of that country and is their choice. Any interference in domestic affairs and any attempts to restrict the sovereignty of states, both friends and allies or any others, is inadmissible (Gati 1990, 169).

If there was any doubt that the Brezhnev Doctrine was still operational it was now dispelled. The following month came final confirmation when a Solidarity-led government was allowed to take office in Poland and Ceausescu's hysterical cries for armed intervention to remove it fell on deaf ears. Indeed, Gorbachev had endorsed the transition in a telephone call to cajole the anti-Solidarity prime minister into acceptance. As one authority observed (Davy 1992, 39), 'without the support of the Kremlin the struggle for the "protection of socialism" was merely pathetic'.

Hungary followed a similar path. In February its government became the first in the bloc to renounce the leading role of the party when it approved the concept of a multi-party system; the Opposition Round Table which quickly materialized was soon locked in negotiations with the ruling communists about the future. In contrast to Poland, the pressure for change in Hungary came mainly from reformists within the government and not from the external opposition, such as the Hungarian Democratic Forum, which did not yet enjoy the kind of mass support Solidarity attracted. It was thus a palace revolution. During March 1989 over 75 000 marched through Budapest demanding the withdrawal of Soviet troops and free elections. The government clearly decided to jump before it was pushed. In May Kádár, having already been ousted as prime minister, was removed as head of state. The party congress in October saw the organization's name changed to the Hungarian Socialist Party and the country's status altered symbolically from a people's republic to a republic. By that time there had been a ceremonial state reburial of Imre Nagy, the heroic leader of the failed 1956 revolution, which attracted huge crowds. The convenient death, soon afterwards, of Kádár in July 1989 provided the ruling party with the opportunity to blame him for the country's economic and social ills, but this tactic was not to save it from subsequent defeat in the free elections which were held in March 1990 when the Democratic Forum swept to power.

But if Poland and Hungary welcomed democracy through 'refolution' (a combination of reform and revolution), the other four members of the Soviet bloc needed to be dragged screaming and kicking across the new frontier. Try as they might, these regimes, sometimes referred to darkly as 'the Gang of Four', could not remain isolated from events elsewhere which quickly became common knowledge through foreign radio and television broadcasts and other sources.

The first breach of the Berlin Wall occurred when, on 19 March 1989, Hungary belatedly signed the 1951 United Nations Convention on refugees. As such it was the first Eastern bloc country to do so which meant that refugees would not be returned against their wishes to a country where their life or freedom was in danger. Although the move was prompted by the desire to retain the several thousand ethnic Hungarians who had fled from Romanian repression, the effect was to tear up the Hungarian–German treaty dating from the 1970s which was designed to prevent East Germans from fleeing to the West via Hungary. The barbed wire and watch-towers along the border with Austria began to be dismantled, leading to an enterprising engineering company making trophies from the remnants to sell as souvenirs of the Iron Curtain! A trickle of East German 'tourists' visiting Hungary started to steal across the border into Austria. The effect was not lost on Honecker who protested: 'The Hungarian people are bound by treaty and socialism to the people of East Germany' (Cipkowski 1991, 72–3). The Hungarians responded by enforcing exit visas, but this did not stop several thousand East Germans from flocking to the frontier area awaiting the rescindment of this decision.

As Bismarck had said, any *Dummkopf* could rule with a state of emergency. This is effectively what East German governments had done since

August 1961 following the erection of the 96-mile-long Berlin Wall. Once the restraints on travel were removed, however, it was only a matter of time before the regime collapsed. That day came on 13 September 1989 when Hungary renounced its bilateral agreement with East Germany. As with the circumvention of the Maginot Line, a way had now been found around another famous but equally flawed defensive line. No less than 30 000 citizens left within the first three days. Honecker tried to stem the tide by closing East German borders and promising any refugees who returned the legitimate right to emigrate. It was all in vain and the exodus continued, 400 000 having moved to the other side of the crumbled wall by the spring of 1990.

Many more stayed behind to seek change from within, with dissidents creating *Neues Forum* to organize the people through leaflets and word of mouth. The fortieth anniversary of the founding of the GDR on 7 October 1989 was celebrated by the regime in East Berlin with Gorbachev as guest of honour. The event was marred by demonstrators chanting 'Gorby! Gorby!' and '*Perestroika*!' Nor was this an isolated incident for other major cities such as Dresden, Leipzig and Plauen experienced similar anti-government protests on this historic day. Afterwards, Gorbachev warned Honecker: 'Life punishes those who delay'. But the East German leader chose to deride the unrest as 'nothing more than Don Quixote's futile charge against the steadily turning sails of a windmill' (Selbourne 1990, 211).

On 9 October a massive crowd of demonstrators in Leipzig bravely faced the prospect of being killed by the government's security forces but, for reasons which remain obscure, no shots were fired and thereafter the protests mounted in size and number to such an extent that on 18 October Honecker was forced out of office, to be replaced by the moderate Egon Krenz. Events now moved quickly. Exactly one month after the Leipzig episode, the Berlin Wall was opened, with many hacking at the detested structure using hammers and chisels, political prisoners were released, and all travel restrictions were lifted. But this hollow attempt to win popularity fell flat when the full extent of the extravagant (by Eastern standards) lifestyles of Honecker and other party leaders, past and present, became apparent, revealing a litany of luxuries including swimming pools, tennis courts, cinemas, beauty parlours, and shops brimming with goods, all of which were funded through money embezzled from state industries. Krenz, who was among those implicated, was forced to resign only six weeks after taking office, along with the entire politburo and central committee. The way was now clear for the reunification of the two Germanies which both populations were now clamouring for. The elections of March 1990 were won by the Christian Democrats, who stood for reunification and four months later the Deutschmark replaced the GDR mark. In September 1990 Britain, France, the Soviet Union and the United States relinquished their occupation rights, paving the way for the official reunification of Germany on 3 October 1990, one year after the 'October revolution'. Having for so long been a focal point of Eastern Europe, the eastern part of Germany was now once more a part of the West (Cipkowski 1991, 88–91; Black 1992, 204–7).

By 1989 all the Bulgarian regime's rhetoric about emulating Soviet reforms had created such expectation among the population that some genuine reforms became inevitable. On 2 February 1989 Zhivkov, the oldest and longest surviving leader in the Soviet bloc, finally admitted the 'stagnation of the previous period' which had damaged 'the vital interests of the workers'. He also conceded that the 'so-called Marxist political economy' was 'in a state of crisis'. The solution was 'revolutionary restructuring', meaning that 'everything, absolutely everything, must pass through the purgatory of revolutionary renewal'. Yet Zhivkov continued to hold that socialist property and the leading role of the party were sacrosanct, directly contradicting his assertion that 'We are advancing towards a new type of democracy' (Selbourne 1990, 143–4). His contradictory leadership was increasingly challenged. Apart from Zhivkov's inept handling of the economy, unease was also created through his clumsy and racist attempts to 'Bulgarianize' the Muslim part of the population which prompted a mass exodus into Turkey, leading to labour shortages. Emerging opposition movements drew encouragement from events elsewhere and on 3 November Eco-Glasnost, an environmental group, held a pro-democracy rally in Sofia. Only 9000 attended but the signs were clear and a week later, following the collapse of the Berlin Wall, Zhivkov was ousted by his party after Moscow indicated its support for events in East Germany. The demand for more fundamental change was not assuaged with cosmetic changes in the country's leadership failing to stem the increasing groundswell of support for democracy. By the end of 1989 the government and the Union of Democratic Forces, representing opposition groups, had agreed to enter discussions as a preliminary to free elections. The result was a narrow victory for the reformed Bulgarian Socialist Party, though by November 1990 its inability to resolve the country's economic problems led to the installation of a coalition which favoured non-communist forces (Dawisha 1990, 186–7; Gati 1990, 182; Mason 1992, 60–2).

For a time it appeared that Czechoslovakia might escape from the revolutionary turmoil. One month after the collapse of the Berlin Wall Czech citizens were still being denied the right to a passport. Indeed, the repressive leadership was intent on subduing any demonstrations by force with Jakes announcing on 12 November that protests would not be entertained. In a complete reversal of events in 1968, diplomatic and military pressure from Moscow ensured that this decision was not carried through (although police brutality was not lacking), and so instead Czechoslovakia experienced a 'velvet revolution' rather than a bloody one. Many East German refugees passed through Czechoslovakia carrying word of the dramatic events in their country and soon copycat demonstrations in Prague were a daily occurrence. Perhaps the defining moment in the Czech revolution came on 23 November when a member of the politburo addressed a group of workers at the huge CKD enterprise near Prague. He informed them that the authorities would not submit to the wishes of '15-year-old children', which outburst only elicited a chant that would soon resonate throughout the nation: 'We're not children. We're not children.' The incident coincided with the takeover of Czech television by its staff who gleefully reported the details to the nation. The next day the crowd in Wenceslas Square swelled to 350 000 and significantly included the inspirational figure of Dubček. Faced by such pressure, the existing party leadership was persuaded to resign, but the communists managed to hang on to power and promised reforms in a reshaped government. Civic Forum, which represented the opposition, was still not satisfied and the pressure on the authorities mounted when a general strike brought the country to a standstill. Within a week the cowed government agreed to hold free elections and permit free travel. On 29 December 1989 Havel, leader of Charter 77, became president, remarking that while it had taken ten years for Poland to experience revolution, ten months for Hungary and ten weeks in East Germany, in the Czech case the feat had been achieved in ten days. 'It has been a revolution against violence, dirt, intrigue, lawlessness, mafia, privilege and persecution', he declared triumphantly (Mason 1992, 62–4; Selbourne 1990, 236).

The focus of world attention shifted to Romania at the end of 1989 as it experienced a revolution whose brutality (there were over 10 000 fatalities) most closely paralleled events in France two centuries earlier. By the late 1980s Ceausescu had become a cruel parody of a dictator. In his quest to revel in a glorious national past, he had appropriately chosen Vlad the Impaler, sometimes known as Count Dracula, as a symbolic figure, even commissioning an epic film of his hero which involved battalions from the Romanian Army. Fatally, Ceausescu came to believe in his own propaganda which portrayed him as 'the saviour of the nation', 'the hero of peace' and the 'most brilliant revolutionary thinker of all times' (Cipkowski 1991, 124–5). The extravagance of Ceausescu, his wife Elena and their extensive family, who occupied various important positions in government and were mocked as 'socialism in one family', was at odds with the austerity demanded of the population at large. Ceausescu was intent on constructing a boulevard through Bucharest which would surpass even the Champs-Elysées with its centrepiece a grand presidential palace, the House of the Republic, featuring 1000 rooms. The dictator also wanted to link the capital with the Danube by canal despite their being 50 miles apart. The army was used as manual labour, a fact which, together with the military being denied funding for weaponry and the officers not receiving promised bonus payments, fostered resentment and ultimately sealed the Ceausescus' fate (Simpson 1992, 225; Burke 1993, 31).

The writing was on the wall when in March 1989 six former party and government colleagues of Ceausescu, including an ex-foreign minister and the founder of the Romanian Communist Party, sent him an open critical letter whose indictments included violating the constitution, the Helsinki accords on human rights, wrecking the economy and agriculture, and favouring 'hairbrained schemes'. Although the letter was couched as a request for 'constructive dialogue that might save the system', its authors were soon arrested and suffered internal exile (Cipkowski 1991, 126). In the autumn a new underground group, the National Salvation Front, emerged, proclaimed that the country was 'on the brink of ruin' and decried Ceausescu's 'disgusting and noxious personality cult' (Selbourne 1990, 241).

Despite outward signs to the contrary, Ceausescu remained convinced that his position was secure. On 14 November the 14th Party Congress elected Ceausescu unanimously for a further five-year term and his long speech received 60 standing ovations. That month he confidently informed West German television that 'At the turn of the century Romania will have achieved communism. The Romanians know that they have to make sacrifices and they do so gladly' (Rady 1992, 91). The tyrant convinced himself that revolutions elsewhere were the result of foreign agents orchestrated by Moscow and Washington, an explanation he also applied to account for the unrest in the town of Timisoara. The authorities there decided to exile an ethnic Hungarian pastor who was preaching against the regime. At first there was only a small protest from local parishioners, but soon disgruntled Romanians joined ranks with outraged ethnic Hungarians and a serious anti-government protest erupted which required the combined intervention of the police, *Securitate* troops and the army to suppress. Around 700 people were killed but the fatalities did not stop the unrest, with an estimated 100 000 taking to the streets of Timisoara on 20 December, when significantly most army troops took their side. That day, having just returned from Iran, Ceausescu denounced the Timisoara demonstrators as 'a few groups of hooligan elements' whose 'terrorist actions' could be explained by their 'close connection with reactionary, imperialist, irredentist, chauvinist circles, and foreign espionage services in various foreign countries' (Rady 1992, 97).

Ceausescu felt compelled to stage a mass rally in Bucharest to demonstrate support for the government which, as events turned out, only confirmed how lacking it was. Ceausescu's rambling speech was interrupted by hecklers who screamed out 'Murderer' and 'Timisoara'. Losing his nerve, the dictator retreated from the balcony of the central committee building, but not before live television pictures had demonstrated his fallibility. After some reflection he returned, offering improvements in wages, pensions and allowances, but the crowd would not be stilled. It refused to disperse and quickly the situation turned ugly as *Securitate* forces fired on demonstrators. Next day, with battles raging throughout the capital and elsewhere, Ceausescu and his wife attempted to escape by helicopter, after high-ranking military officers refused to apply martial law. As they did so, the National Salvation Front broke cover to declare itself the new government and crucially attracted the support of the army, whose troops quickly captured the dethroned rulers. On Christmas Day, following a summary trial by military tribunal at which they were accused of destroying the Romanian people and the economy, Nicolae and Elena Ceausescu were executed by firing squad.

The new government acted swiftly to reverse its predecessor's worst follies: food intended for export was diverted to domestic shops, heating and hot water were restored, even some luxury goods, like coffee, chocolate and oranges, became widely available; what were termed 'megalomaniac' construction projects such as the House of the Republic and the Danube–Bucharest canal were scrapped, with the money saved being switched to repairing buildings damaged during the revolution. In retrospect, the Romanian revolution takes on more of the character of a *coup*, for old communists soon came to dominate the National Salvation Front which, after becoming a political party, swept to victory in the spurious elections of May 1990. Ion Iliescu, who as state secretary of the National Water Council, had been instrumental in constructing the ill-considered Danube–Black Sea canal, after which he had fortuitously lost favour with Ceausescu, was elected president (Cipkowski 1991, 135–8; Rady 1992, 122–9, 170–3).

YUGOSLAVIA'S DISINTEGRATION

The historical roots of the Yugoslav nationalities' conundrum were deep and require some elucidation to comprehend why Yugoslavia's fragile federation was finally shattered in 1990–91. Ethnic hatreds and suspicions went back a long way, with previous violent conflicts over borders and between groups creating indelible scars. Ethnic cleansing, a grotesque feature of the Yugoslav civil war which began in 1991, in fact first made its appearance in the Balkan Wars when an international commission reported 'Houses and whole villages reduced to ashes, unarmed and innocent populations massacred *en masse*, incredible acts of violence, pillage and brutality of every kind' (Job 1993, 61). Similarly, during the First World War there were atrocities committed by Serbs, Croats, Albanians and Bosnians. Even the king was not immune, falling victim to Croat and Macedonian assassins in 1934. The horrors continued in the Second World War when Hitler established a puppet Croatian state led by Ante Pavelic, leader of the Ustashi, the Croatian brand of fascism. These Croats resented what they saw as Serbian domination of the country in the interwar years when the king and the army leadership were Serb, and Belgrade, situated in Serbia, was the favoured capital. Pavelic's regime inflicted genocide on a mixture of Serbs, Jews and Gypsies which prompted the Serb nationalists, known as Chetniks, to massacre Croats and Bosnian Muslims (the allies of the Ustashi) in retaliation. According to the nationality involved, each rewrote their own history, downplaying any wrong-doing by them and highlighting the atrocities of the other side. For instance, the Serbs portrayed themselves as the knights in shining armour during the fight against Hitler, claiming to have tied down 30 German divisions, while Croats massacred all around. The true picture is more convoluted. In 1943 there were only four German divisions in Yugoslavia and not all Croats were fascist collaborators – of Tito's 125 000 strong resistance force that year three-quarters were actually Croats (Stone 1992).

The idea that a viable multinational state could be created against such a background of innate hostility was certainly flawed. What became Yugoslavia did not meet Seton-Watson's definition of a nation as 'a community of people whose members are bound together by a sense of solidarity, a common culture, a national consciousness' (1977, 1). A leading Croat politician who absented himself from the December 1918 unification ceremonies considered his colleagues' actions to be akin to the behaviour of 'drunken geese in a fog'. In view of later developments, it might have been better if President Roosevelt had had his way in 1945 when he proposed that Yugoslavia should be dismembered. As it was, an ethnic jigsaw puzzle was forced together at the insistence of Britain and the Soviet Union which later events proved could only remain firmly in place as long as the dictatorial Tito was at the helm (Doder 1993, 9–10).

During the Second World War Tito, in setting the agenda for the creation of a multinational socialist state, had sought to deflect Serbia and Croatia's historical claims on Bosnia-Herzegovina by stating that its future must be 'neither Serbian and Croatian nor Muslim but rather Serbian and Croatian and Muslim' (Doder 1993, 11). But in creating a federation of six republics on the lines of the USSR (see Chapter 8), he denied the Serbs what they considered to be their rightful domination. Half Croat and half Slovene, Tito earned the rancour of both Serbs and Croats, the two largest ethnic groups which coexisted uneasily. Although they spoke the same language, Serbo-Croat, their different dialects continued to distinguish one group from the other. There were two further official languages (Slovenian and Macedonian) and two alphabets (Cyrillic and Latin), which again underlined ethnic divisions. Nor was there any common religion, with Slovenia and Croatia being mainly Catholic and most of the rest of the country either Eastern Orthodox or Muslim. Under Tito's iron rule, all unofficial expressions of nationalism were banned. The menace posed by the USSR also created a unifying factor which disappeared with the appearance of Gorbachev and the end of the cold war. So too did the willingness of the more prosperous republics to assist the less developed ones, especially Kosovo, the poorest region. Tito proved irreplaceable, with the country being ruled by committee after his death in 1980 and the presidency reduced to an eight-person collective representing the six republics and two regions which could only agree to disagree. Major reform plans were accordingly constantly stalled throughout the 1980s.

By the late 1980s all the signs were that Yugoslavia's frail economy and poorly coordinated market-oriented reforms could not hold back the swelling tide of nationalism: the country was gripped by roaring inflation which shot up from around 72 per cent in 1985 to 1256 per cent by 1989, rising unemployment as demand declined, strikes in protest at wage cuts, and fraud trials concerning state-owned enterprises, all which added to the growing instability. Nationalism was the final ingredient which would set off the touch paper making it impossible for the federal government to function. Despite Tito's territorial adjustments, which had shorn Serbia of Vojvodina and Kosovo, a third of Yugoslavian territory was still Serbian and about 35 per cent of the population was Serb. When Slobodan Milošević became the Serbian Communist Party leader in 1986, he exploited the nationalist card for all it was worth as economic conditions deteriorated. Increasingly Muslims were portrayed as occupiers, a perception which drew on history. In June 1989 the Serbs commemorated the 600th anniversary of the Battle of Kosovo, when an ancient Serbian army had been defeated by Muslim Turkish invaders and Kosovo was not reclaimed from the Ottoman Empire until 1912.

1988 was the year when Yugoslavia's troubles began to come to the world's attention. In October 1988 Novi Sad, capital of Vojvodina, was the scene for 100 000 Serbian demonstrators to chant 'Serbia is one!', 'Give us arms!' and 'Kosovo is ours' (Selbourne 1990, 98–9). The episode followed on from Milošević's refusal to abide by the wishes of the ruling League of Communists of Yugoslavia to cease nationalist demonstrations. The same month there was a huge demonstration of workers in the Montenegrin capital, Titograd. In 1987 Montenegro, Macedonia and Kosovo had declared themselves bankrupt. The Montenegrin government then proceeded to close down several unprofitable enterprises, but had failed to create new jobs to reduce the growing ranks of the unemployed and destitute. The demonstrators called for Serbian leadership and the baying crowd was only dispersed with the use of batons and tear gas. Fearing that Montenegro was on the verge of being absorbed by Serbia, Bosnia-Herzegovina, Croatia and Slovenia rallied in support, although the Montenegrin government still felt compelled to resign to calm the situation. Here, in microcosm, was a portent of the break-up of Yugoslavia which was just over the horizon (Magas 1993, 170–72).

As Yugoslavia was affected by developments elsewhere, so the ruling party felt obliged to concede the freedoms of speech and press which only served to fuel inter-ethnic tensions. These increasingly had their effect on political and economic reforms, such as the intended transformation of state enterprises into joint-stock companies, which measures were continually frustrated by the resistance of various republics. The democracy wave which was sweeping across Eastern Europe hit home in Slovenia in January 1989 when the region's first independent political party since the communist takeovers was created. The 14th Party Congress of the Yugoslav Communist Party convened in Belgrade in January 1990 for what turned out to be the last time. Slovenia pushed for a loosening of the federal structure in vain, with its delegates being laughed and jeered at by the Serbs. Multi-party elections in the republics during 1990 saw Slovenia, Croatia, Bosnia-Herzegovina and Macedonia cease to be socialist republics, but Serbia and Montenegro's resulted in substantial communist victories, once more emphasizing the growing divisions over Yugoslavia's future.

By October 1990, with the support of Croatia, another northern republic, Slovenia, was advocating a solution to unlock the impasse on the lines of the Benelux countries and the EC which were seen as the best arrangement for the implementation of market reforms. But months of negotiations aimed at creating a confederation fell foul of Serbian and Montenegrin opposition. As Yugoslavia's most Westernized republic, Slovenia was best placed to pursue independence. Its frustration at paying federal taxes to support the less developed regions was compounded in December 1990 when, unknown to the federal parliament, the Serbs printed $1.8 billion worth of dinars to fulfil election pledges made by Milošević. Slovenia now took matters into its own hands. On 2 July 1990 the Slovene parliament made a declaration of sovereignty which was followed at the end of the year by a plebiscite when an overwhelming majority (88.5 per cent) of those voting endorsed independence. This decision was officially ratified on 25 June 1991, prompting the Serb-controlled Yugoslav National Army (YNA) to intervene to try to prevent the secession. It failed and within a month Slovenia had been allowed to break free. However Croatia, which also declared its independence at the same time, was not so lucky, containing as it did a substantial Serb minority of 600 000 and a part of territory known as Krajina which formerly belonged to Serbia. The Serb minority, fearing they might suffer a repeat of events during the Second World War, began fighting over Krajina, prompting Milošević to send the YNA into Croatia to assist. A bloody ethnically driven civil war was under way. Once more the Balkans powder keg had exploded (Magas 1993, 301; Black 1992, 288–9; Mason 1992; 1936).

THE DÉNOUEMENT

It only remained for the two main pillars of the postwar relationship between the USSR and most of Eastern Europe, the Warsaw Pact and CMEA, to be formally removed to complete the pile of rubble that had once been the Soviet bloc. The sweeping aside of the communist regimes in the revolutionary ferment of 1989 finally put paid to any prospect of military cooperation between East European countries and the Soviet Union. Reflecting the lessened importance of defence, over the period 1988 to mid-1991 the strength of the Polish armed forces fell from almost 400 000 to 250 000; in Czechoslovakia and Hungary the declines were less pronounced, but still significant. Only Romania bucked the trend, not least because its quasi-communist government needed the support of the army. Aiding this process was Moscow's willingness to agree to withdraw all its forces from Czechoslovakia, Hungary and Poland. There was admittedly some Soviet prevarication, although the process was largely completed by the end of 1991. For instance, Moscow sought compensation for the 2795 military installations in Czechoslovakia and 40 billion forints from Hungary for investments made in roads, airfields and buildings. Despite the rejection of these claims, the Soviet withdrawals went ahead. At the same time, the Warsaw Pact began to disintegrate with Hungary leading the charge out of the organization. Poland followed once the new Germany had guaranteed the sanctity of the Polish–German border and was soon joined by Czechoslovakia whose president declared that the pact had 'outlived its day'. The official end of the military alliance came on 31 March 1991, though in reality it had ceased to exist except on paper some time before that termination date (Gitz 1992, 154–6).

The CMEA held its 45th meeting in Sofia in January 1990 immediately following the demise of communism in Eastern Europe. Frustrated by its earlier unsuccessful attempts to mould the organization to its requirements, the Soviet Union moved to end the organization, a proposal which found unanimous approval. At this time, the CMEA six all expressed the hope that they could eventually join the EC. Henceforth, Soviet–East European trade relations were to be conducted on the basis of hard currency denominations. In August the Soviet Union announced that this decision would take effect from January 1991. Romania and Bulgaria requested a transitional period, but their pleas were in vain. Indeed, the Soviets dismantled the complex system of bilateral and multilateral trade treaties with relish, spurred on by the conviction that they would save considerable amounts of money. In February 1991 the CMEA was formally wound up and although it was replaced by a looser regional organization, the Organization for International Economic Cooperation, its functions were purely consultative and the arrangement seemed unlikely to assume any importance. Eastern Europe had at last broken free from Soviet shackles but, as events would soon prove, their removal did not guarantee economic progress or prosperity (Pravda 1992, 222–7).

10. An uncertain fate

A new era beckoned in the aftermath of the 1989 revolutions in Eastern Europe and the collapse of the Soviet Union which followed in their wake. There was a brief moment when a stable 'New World Order' based on free markets and democracy appeared possible. It seemed that the European continent need no longer be divided into east and west on ideological and economic grounds, but could become fully integrated. Indeed, the Paris Charter of November 1990 found the 34 member states of the Conference on Security and Cooperation in Europe pledging their allegiance to four universal principles – democracy, the rule of law, values of freedom, and the market economy. The new mood was also given expression by the West's notion of being afforded an opportunity, through the end of the cold war, to cash in a hefty 'peace dividend' and free resources devoted to defence for other uses.

Such optimism might be compared with the international situation early in 1914 when Lloyd George struck a false note when he assured the banking world that 'Never has the sky been more perfectly blue'. Soon it was clear, as then, that ominous storm clouds were looming on the horizon and, within a short space of time, the euphoria of 1989–90 had similarly given way to grim realism. There were undoubtedly some worrying developments in Eastern Europe. Far from all communists going down with the socialist ship, they began to stage a come-back and in some cases, such as Romania and Bulgaria, they never really went away. Right-wing parties also emerged which fed off rising nationalism. The trend away from conservative democracy was assisted by disappointment at the West's response to Eastern Europe's requirements, not least its resistance to receiving Eastern exports unchecked, together with delays in hastening the region's full assimilation into the European Community (known as the European Union from November 1993) and NATO.

The seeming utopia of freedom, democracy and Western-style consumerism, so long denied the peoples of Eastern Europe, proved to be the elixir which spurred on the revolutionary movements. They were to learn the hard way that while the complexion and personalities of their governments might be changed overnight, the economy was not so amenable to easy revision. A long hard road lay ahead which was rendered all the more hazardous because there was no established route map to follow. There were simply no precedents to consult on how to transform successfully a mature but decaying centrally planned system into a thriving Western-style market economy. Galbraith identified 'three stages in the development of socialism, the first two successful, the third a compelling failure'. Stage one saw the redistribution of power and income; stage two established the economic infrastructure for modern industry to function with the input–output model 'both stable and comprehensible'; stage three, however, found the socialist economies unable to cope with the demands of the consumer society:

> Specifically, in the modern consumers' goods economy there are a large, even incomprehensible, number of desired goods, many of different styles and designs, these latter changing with consumer tastes, and some ... requiring a variety of supporting services. Services in general also become more important. To meet this dismaying diversity and instability of demand the old planning and command structure does not and cannot serve. There must be some means of communication from consumer to producer and some reward for responding effectively to that message, and the only institution which so serves is the market (Galbraith 1989).

Inevitably, as command economies began to be dismantled, some countries succeeded better than others in introducing market reforms, with the prospective leaders and laggards becoming apparent by 1994. The introduction of capitalism also brought its own problems, not least inflation, unemployment, social inequalities and rising crime, which inevitably hindered the reforms. For some sections of the population the days of communism, when full employment and the price of bread were guaranteed, did not seem so bad after all. Moreover, while communism had largely succeeded in suppressing nationalist tendencies, they now re-emerged with a vengeance, ripping Yugoslavia apart in a horror-laden civil war and, in more civilized fashion, leading to the break-up of Czechoslovakia.

THE FALL IN OUTPUT

All the countries experienced a dramatic and pronounced fall in output in the years immediately following the collapse of communism (Table 10.1). Industrial production also plummeted, unemployment rose sharply, real wages fell and inflation soared. In some cases the fall in output exceeded the precipitate decline experienced by the United States during the great depression and in all instances matched the dismal performance records of Britain and Germany during that convulsive period (Robinson 1993a; Parker 1993, 9; Williamson 1993, 26).

A number of explanations have been advanced to account for the decline in output. Eastern Europe was already heading into recession as the revolu-

Table 10.1   Real growth of GDP in Eastern Europe (%)

Country	1990	1991	1992	1993
Bulgaria	–9.1	–11.8	–11.0	–4.6
Czech Republic	–1.2	–14.2	–7.1	–1.6
Hungary	–3.3	–10.2	–5.0	1.7
Poland	–11.6	–7.6	1.2	5.0
Romania	–7.3	–13.7	–15.4	–5.1
Slovakia	–2.5	–15.8	–6.0	–7.1
Slovenia	–4.7	–9.3	–6.8	1.5

Note: 1993=estimate

Source: Robinson (1993f)

tions took place, a situation that was exacerbated by the collapse of CMEA markets and especially the withdrawal of Soviet demand. The USSR had easily been the biggest trading partner of the CMEA six and for innumerable East European enterprises was their principal customer for finished goods. It has been estimated that in 1991 the fall in Soviet orders represented 1.6 per cent of Polish GDP, 2.2 per cent of Czechoslovakia's and 4.5 per cent in the case of Hungary (Williamson 1993, 28). The worst sufferer was Bulgaria which had been most dependent on Comecon trade. In economic terms it would have been far better if the end of Comecon had happened less precipitately, but political considerations necessitated a speedy divorce, especially Eastern Europe's desire to be rid once-and-for-all of the Soviet connection. The reorientation of the region's trading links Westwards would inevitably take time – in 1989 the trade of Eastern Europe and the Soviet Union with OECD countries accounted for only 3 per cent of the latter's trade (Mason 1992, 163).

Another argument put forward to account for the reduced output is a shift in the pattern of demand. The removal of the Soviet Union from the scene left East European firms vulnerable until they could produce goods which were saleable in Western markets. In the interim period the producer's output naturally declined until resources could be redeployed. The demise of the CMEA left an array of unwanted products which the Polish finance minister, Leszek Balcerowicz, characterized as 'pure socialist production' because they could only exist under central planning. For example, several products, such as Ikarus buses from Hungary and broad gauge railway locomotives from Czechoslovakia, had been designed specifically for the Soviet market. The obsolete product lines represented between 10 and 20 per cent of a typical socialist economy's GDP. In effect, the East European economies were caught betwixt and between: they were no longer centrally planned systems but neither were they yet sufficiently market-oriented. Without exception, the output losses emanated from the state sector with the secondary economy, or private sector, not yet large enough to compensate sufficiently for the decline (Kolodko 1993, 128).

A related consideration in explaining the decline in output is the fact that with the removal of implicit Soviet and explicit state subsidies, the production of some goods was rendered uneconomic because the value of the inputs (at world prices) became greater than the value of the output (negative value-added). Hughes and Hare (1991) estimated that between 19 and 24 per cent of industrial production of Czechoslovakia, Hungary and Poland was affected in this way. Another cause of the fall in output was the widespread policy which looked to attain world prices without a transitional period. Williamson (1993, 36) suggests that this was an avoidable policy mistake. While there is some substance in this view, it does not fully take into account the immediate context: the collapse of many of the socialist economies and the lack of a successful pioneering example to follow forced the new post-communist governments to take a leap in the dark. In any event, Romania opted for price liberalization in stages, but actually fared worse than most other countries in the long run.

At the end of 1991 the United Nations Economic Commission for Europe (1991b, 7–9) opined that 'The declines in output in Eastern Europe and the Soviet Union are now so large that it would be appropriate to speak of a depression'. From a later vantage point, this view appears somewhat premature and at the very least is in need of qualification. There are special circumstances to be taken into account. What requires emphasis is that the fall in output, since it consisted largely of unwanted goods, did not produce a depression in the accepted sense. To quote Kramer (1992, 135):

> Official data showing a precipitous drop in living standards and a sharp rise in unemployment are misleading ... These figures do not adequately reflect qualitative improvements in people's lives, such as the disappearance of lines and the improved quality of consumer goods and services. Nor do the figures take into account money people earn in the private sector but fail to report in order to avoid paying taxes. The statistics also exaggerate unemployment, counting as unemployed those who actually work in the 'second', or unofficial, economy. The unemployment figures also include people who in previous years had been paid wages for work they never performed. The disguised unemployment in the communist era has now been simply acknowledged.

This explanation helps to resolve the seeming paradox in some of the figures: for example, in the year when Czech GDP fell by more than 10 per cent retail sales rose by some 16 per cent; similarly, in Warsaw the number of cars doubled in two consecutive years. The Polish Research Institute calculates that when all things are considered the falls in output in 1990-92 were actually much less than the official figures suggest (Parker 1993, 9). As Kolodko (1993, 129) suggests, the logic of this line of approach is that 'the recession is not a negative phenomenon but, above all, an "economy-clearing" process, improving the overall economic structure of the country in question'. It nevertheless remains true that public perceptions of a faltering economy were not without their political consequences (see below), which no doubt explains why politicians provided misleading forecasts of future economic growth. Just when individual economies emerged from this period of slump was dependent on the success of market reform programmes and in particular the nurturing of the private sector.

In March 1993 Hungary, Poland, Slovakia and the Czech Republic concluded the Central European Free Trade Agreement (Cefta) following a meeting in the Hungarian town of Visegrad. While Cefta was hardly a successor to the CMEA, it did much to halt the decline in trade between its member states who became known collectively as 'the Visegrad Four'. In the first year, around 7 per cent of Poland's trade turnover took place within Cefta while Slovakian trade with Hungary actually produced a surplus, a rarity for this struggling economy (see below). The original aim of Cefta was free trade among its members by the year 2001, but such was its initial success (duty was removed from 2200 items in the first year) that this date was subsequently advanced to 1998 (Butler 1994).

THE TASKS AHEAD

A number of common problems confronted the post-communist regimes in Eastern Europe in their efforts to create free market economies. Broadly, the measures required may be divided into three categories: macroeconomic stabilization, price reforms, and other reforms. The establishment of macroeconomic stability made it necessary for domestic demand and production to be matched and external borrowing related to future capacity to service the debt. As part of this process, the money supply had to be controlled and the budget brought into balance, or nearly so, which required the elimination of most of the price subsidies characteristic of socialist economies. The wages mountain paid out by governments to sustain loss-making state-owned enterprises also needed to be considerably reduced and tax reforms carried out over the medium term. In the socialist system, no formal method of corporate taxation was required because, as the owner of enterprises, the state could extract profits as it saw fit, which gave managers no incentives. Now, business taxes had to be sufficiently liberal to improve efficiency. Price reforms needed to ensure that scarcity and demand was properly reflected as in Western economies. The other reforms required included the elimination of government subsidies to firms, which inevitably meant some bankruptcies, but on the positive side it did help to reduce price distortions; the encouragement of the private sector through incentives and the ending of bureaucratic red tape, with the ultimate aim that it would eventually surpass the public sector; the privatization of state-owned enterprises, which sometimes raised the thorny issue of the exact influence of workers, managers and local authorities; the establishment of a financial sector that could serve the needs of industry; the setting up a legal framework, not least laws to protect private property; and the introduction of an appropriate exchange rate together with currency convertibility (Collins and Rodrik 1992, 10–13; Somogyi 1993, 4).

The privatization of state-owned enterprises and assets is inevitably a long-term process. It takes time to instil management and workers with the behaviour associated with a market economy. In contrast to the situation under a command economy, where enterprises simply fulfilled state orders, firms now needed to find out what sold and what did not, a learning process which contained many potential wrong turns. Economic policy also has political consequences and for a market economy to emerge effectively the government must retain a reformist outlook or else political stability may be jeopardized and with it the enthusiasm of foreign investors. Over time there is the promise of the creation of a property-owning middle class which will support democracy. But there are dangers in the interim period. As Woodward notes (IMF Survey 1993, 11):

> Political considerations do matter in a transition ... Economic change is profoundly political – it is a redistribution of resources, and therefore of power. And although much of the transformation process is directed at the state, and at statism in economics, the government must provide leadership for much of this reform process. It must write the new laws, extend guarantees, adjudicate contracts, define property rights, and negotiate trade agreements.

The Czech prime minister, for one, came to recognize that privatization by itself was not sufficient to guarantee a smooth running market economy and that state intervention was necessary to ensure a level playing field in the interim period (Greenberg 1993). Reform also meant the population enduring the pain of increased inflation and unemployment during the transition, generating political pressures which in some instances (see below) led to trade-offs and compromises that diluted the impact of regenerative economic programmes. Often there arose a conflict between the president, sensitive to the social consequences of particular policies, and the prime minister, who was anxious to press on with change, usually under the influence of outside organizations such as the IMF and World Bank. Such disputes were to hold back the drafting of constitutions in Bulgaria, Poland and Romania. Similarly, the effectiveness of Bulgaria's short-lived anti-communist government of the Union of Democratic Forces was stifled because the president harboured grave misgivings about the pain demanded by the economic policies favoured by the prime minister (Robinson 1993c). A politically charged decision facing all regimes was how and when to streamline the generous social welfare benefits systems which had been inherited from the days of communism, such as transport and the housing subsidies and extensive food price support measures. In Hungary, for example, social spending on unemployment, health, education and pensions accounted for almost three-quarters of public spending (Parker 1993, 16).

An old Bulgarian proverb has it that 'there are passengers for every train'. Four main candidates stood at the station ready to accomplish the mammoth task of the restructuring of bankrupt or loss-making state enterprises and the transfer of ownership to the private sector: foreigners, existing managers, banks and other financial intermediaries, and new owner-managers. Although the foreign solution held great attractions, not least the new management techniques, up-to-date technologies and access to capital and markets which Western managers conveniently brought with them, it could never be a total answer because of the tendency of outside firms to pick and choose. Only the former GDR, whose economic rehabilitation was the prerogative of West Germany, could rely predominantly on this approach. Hungary made the mistake of expecting too much of foreign investment as the main driving force of privatization, but by 1993 the signs were that the flow of foreign funds was levelling off, partly because of the attractions of other East European markets and safer privatizations in France and Italy. Although existing managers might appear to be too steeped in communist ways, in fact many emerged who were able to adapt their management techniques, such as those involved in the Gdansk shipyards in Poland and the Czech electronics firm Tesla Piestany. Banks soon became major players in Czechoslovakia following the mass privatization intended to create a nation of shareholders. The first round of auctions sold 2000 firms to the public with 400 investment funds, many established by banks, taking the lion's share of the vouchers issued. The banks exercised control over firms through representation on their boards. The second wave of privatization in the summer of 1994 involved 862 state firms, completing the process, with the state retaining a stake in only 53 strategic firms, principally in the defence and utilities sectors. By the end of 1994 some 90 per cent of assets in the economy would be in private hands, marking out the Czech Republic as the leader in the field (Pomery 1994). Poland also intends to use holding companies to exert similar influence when it introduces mass privatization. The first privatization round, scheduled for 1994, was to involve over 360 state companies. Hungary tinkered with voucher schemes, but generally regarded mass privatization schemes as ineffective since they do not resolve the issue of management control and fail to generate new capital. Finally, new owner-managers have the advantage of daily supervision of individual firms. This class has increasingly emerged as state enterprises have sold assets, which enables budding entrepreneurs to construct new businesses (Parker 1993, 10, 15; Clegg 1993).

A constraint that all countries shared was an inadequate domestic banking sector which, saddled with debts inherited from the communist past, quickly proved insufficiently flexible to respond to the requirements of an expanding private sector. Many banks were reluctant to grant credit and when they did they charged usurious rates of interest. The Czechs took the lead in privatizing the banks, the prelude to which is necessarily the refinancing of inherited bad debts. Even so, it is yet to be seen whether privatized banks with healthy balance sheets will prove more responsive and sympathetic to the needs of the private sector. For instance, Ivnostenska Banka, based in Prague, exhibited the same reluctance to take risks, with commercial loans representing only one-twentieth of its 20 billion crowns ($670 million) capital. Clearly, it will take time to create a private banking sector on Western lines. But the achievement of this objective has been complicated and retarded by several factors, including the development of large budget deficits in Poland and Hungary, the effect of which has been to deprive the private sector of savings, the tendency of governments to cover bad loans to state firms, and inadequate bankruptcy laws, either too weak, as was true of the Czech Republic, or too harsh, such as in Hungary (Robinson and Denton 1993; *The Economist* 1993, 113–14).

BIG BANG VERSUS GRADUALISM: THE EXPERIENCE OF INDIVIDUAL COUNTRIES

Although they shared the same form of government over five decades, the economies of Eastern Europe were not as one, a fact which needed to be taken into account when individual regimes considered the pace and sequencing of reforms. Hungary and Poland were already some way down the reformist road, but the other countries had barely started the journey. The typical command economy was dominated by industry and agriculture with services only comprising around one-third of the whole, the reverse of the usual Western pattern. There were nevertheless variations on this theme – for instance, Czechoslovakia was far more industrial than Romania, where the agricultural sector still bulked large. Again, in Hungary, the services sector, which began to be developed in the 1970s, as well as pharmaceuticals and consumer electronics, were already more important in the economy than in the case of Poland where heavy industry (chemicals, heavy engineering, steel and shipyards) formed a much greater part of the whole (Kozminski 1992, 318).

The basic decision confronting the new regimes was whether to go all out for change (the big bang or shock therapy approach), or instead to elect for a more gradual reform strategy. These choices were not mutually exclusive and could interact since governments constantly faced the question of whether reforms should be speeded up or slowed down. The big bang approach involved price shocks of considerable magnitude as government subsidies were quickly removed and currencies substantially devalued. Political and economic considerations meant that a total package of reforms, involving the simultaneous introduction of all necessary measures, was only possible in the former GDR. Even there it did not produce a rapid turn-round since the massive costs involved generated inflation and led to recession in Germany as a whole.

The shock therapy route was favoured by Czechoslovakia and Poland. By 1992 Czech unemployment, at 2.5 per cent, was the lowest in the region, the result of the rapid growth of the private sector, with the creation of over 1 million jobs counteracting the labour shedding undertaken in the state-owned sector. The proceeds from privatization proved sufficient to promote the establishment of a special institution, the Konsolidacni Banka, to finance bad debt write-offs by state enterprises. Consumer and producer subsidies were eliminated over a two-year period and the budget deficit was reduced to under 1 per cent of GDP. VAT and other tax reforms were introduced at the start of 1993, including the continued reduction of corporation tax as part of the prime minister's expressed strategy of establishing 'a stable, low inflation, low tax environment for business' (Robinson 1993a).

Apart from that of the former East Germany, Poland's reform programme was the most ambitious. Driven by the need to avoid hyperinflation, price stabilization measures were implemented in January 1990 in the Balcerowicz programme and included a substantial devaluation of the zloty to achieve a realistic exchange rate, with the currency being rendered convertible for current account transactions. Government subsidies to producers and consumers were slashed from 17 per cent of GDP in 1989 to only 4 per cent within two years, wage rises were pegged, a substantial trade liberalization was undertaken, reducing trade protection to moderate tariffs, and plans were unveiled to privatize 1000 of the 7600 state enterprises. Privatization was scheduled to occur in two phases: a 'commercialization' stage in which state enterprises became joint-stock companies, followed by a sell-off of the shares within two years. As with Czechoslovakia, the results of Poland's crash programme were impressive: hyperinflation was quickly eliminated; the substantial budget deficit of 1989 became a surplus in 1990; exports were stimulated by the competitive devaluation; and shortages were eliminated (Collins and Rodrik 1992, 14–17).

With its tradition of reform, inherited from the days of 'goulash communism', Hungary had a head start and did not quite need to match the hectic pace set by Poland. Among the measures already in place were a two-tier banking system, a modern taxation structure, a foreign investment law based on the European standard, and a bankruptcy law. The state monopoly of foreign trade had already vanished. Hungary's approach was therefore more gradual, though not as inhibited as the Bulgarian or Romanian programmes. By 1993 three institutions were overseeing privatization and macroeconomic policy – the State Property Agency, the National Bank of Hungary and Allami Vagyonkezelo (AV RT), a state asset management corporation. Some enterprises made the mistake of assuming that the state would obligingly bail them out and engaged in export dumping, but a wave of bankruptcies in 1992 showed this assumption to be erroneous. When it came into power in June 1990, the conservative Hungarian Democratic Forum set itself the goal of privatizing half the state sector during its four-year term in office. After a promising start, the rate of sale of state assets slowed down sufficiently to make this goal unattainable. In 1989 there were about 2000 state enterprises of which, by September 1993, 273 had been sold outright, while majority shareholdings were disposed of in 144 cases and minorities in 71 others. A further 370 companies disappeared as a result of liquidation. By 1993 an estimated 36 per cent of the workforce was involved in the private sector, a percentage which is certain to increase once the utilities are privatized (Denton 1993b).

It is likely that Romania will come to be seen as the classic case of how not to advance towards a market economy. Romania suffered from the handicap of having the most centralized economy in Eastern Europe. It was asking a lot to try to set right the 25 years of economic mismanagement left by Ceausescu. As Denekas and Khan (1991, 30) note:

> Ceausescu's legacy was an economy plagued by an inefficient industrial structure and an almost totally obsolete capital stock, a completely disorganised system of production and distribution, a collectivised agricultural sector, a decaying infrastructure, and a population whose living standards had been forced steadily down to a level where even basic necessities – food, heating, electricity, and medical attention – were hard to come by. There is little doubt that the initial obstacles to reform in Romania were far worse than those faced by the other reforming East European countries.

A dynamic go-ahead leadership was required to unravel, repair and restructure the faltering Romanian economy. Unfortunately, the political complexion of the Romanian government, with former senior communists holding sway, frustrated rather than promoted the reform process. Although there was talk of 'a leap towards the market', it was very much a case of two steps forward and one step back. There was no concerted effort to subdue inflation, which had been the lowest in Eastern Europe in 1990, but by 1993 was running in triple figures. Because wages were indexed to inflation a vicious price spiral was created which the government partly offset through additional subsidies for essentials such as food and fuel. Not until the summer of 1993 were consumer subsidies eliminated together with the majority of price controls. The authorities were also sensitive to the political effects of job losses. Unemployment compensation entitlement was extended from six to nine months, after which period a new 'support allowance' was introduced, enabling claimants access to additional state support for a further 18 months (Jeffries 1992, 282).

Corruption also marred the image of capitalism in Romania. Several highly dubious schemes appeared, including 'The Enchanted Pocket' and 'Grandma's Pocket', which were designed to persuade the population to part with their well-earned money. The most successful pyramid-selling scheme, 'Caritas', attracted the equivalent of half the state's annual budget between June 1992 and the close of 1993, with its alluring promise to provide investors with a sevenfold return in three months. A local newspaper which printed the names of the winners saw its daily circulation increase from under 3000 to around 250 000. Such a massive fraud could only be sustained as long as the cash collected approximately doubled each month. By the end of 1993 the scheme was thoroughly discredited, with only a tiny proportion of existing investors being repaid. The 'Black Sea Bubble', as it became known, threatened to provoke widespread unrest among disgruntled investors (Barber 1994).

The gradual approach adopted to market reforms in Romania meant that by 1993 state-owned enterprises still accounted for 90 per cent of industrial production, a reflection of the authorities' reluctance to relinquish them because of the feared political consequences. The reformist government of Petre Roman was brought down in October 1991 after 6000 miners demonstrated in Bucharest over the failure of wages to match price increases and the spectre of unemployment. But the hands-off policy towards the public sector had serious consequences. State concerns continued to rake off most of the available credit, squeezing out the negligible private sector. Moreover, the delay in launching a mass privatization programme (first mooted in 1991) gave managers of state firms a golden opportunity to strip them of assets, thereby reducing their attraction to budding entrepreneurs. Similarly, the government's willingness to support thousands of workers in unproductive jobs often created labour shortages for private firms. The inefficiency of the state sector meant that although inter-enterprise debts were written off in

January 1992, by mid-1993 these had re-emerged, rising to about $2.4 billion, which represented 20 per cent of GDP. Again, enterprise reform legislation remained incomplete at this date. Four years after the removal of Ceausescu, the OECD was moved to comment that there was 'a lack of coherence' about Romanian reforms, occasioned by the reluctance to dent its political support through unpopular measures. 'The situation remains critical', the OECD concluded, 'with the foundations for a sustained recovery and transformation not yet laid' (Robinson 1993b).

The Bulgarian government faced a long uphill task in moving the emphasis away from energy-intensive industries to a more diversified and productive economy based on services, light engineering, a modernized agro-industrial sector and tourism. The situation was not helped by the internal bickering which dogged the first post-communist government and led to its collapse at the end of 1992. It was replaced by a coalition of technocrats who, in theory, were non-partisan, but in reality their support depended on the former communists of the Bulgarian Socialist Party who had already tasted power and whose influence remained strong.

Bulgaria's first privatization law had to be withdrawn within a few months of its introduction in the spring of 1991 because it was being abused by managers of state enterprises who took advantage of the lack of regulatory checks and engaged in extensive asset-stripping. Hidden or *nomenklatura* privatization often involved the establishment of private companies by the family and friends of managers of state-owned enterprises who sold the former products and assets at bargain-basement prices. A much improved privatization law was introduced in May 1992 which benefited from the experiences of Hungary, Poland and Czechoslovakia. Even so, the government's commitment was not as full-blooded as it might have been since at least 20 per cent of the shares of privatized industries were earmarked to be retained, partly to finance social security funds. A year later, tax reforms, including VAT, were still only in the pipeline. The slow march towards privatization was also evidenced by the failure to introduce other essential complementary legislation, such as the modernization of the banking and financial sectors (Robinson 1993d). By early 1994 the lack of political will to drive economic reform was evident in the fact that a bankruptcy law was still lacking, ministries had sold only 200 small businesses and a new mass privatization scheme was stalled in parliament (Marsh and Robinson 1994).

THE WEST'S RESPONSE

There was no prospect of a Marshall Aid style programme from the West despite the recognized magnitude of the transformations required in East

European economies. Several arguments were advanced against such an approach, including the fear that far from promoting reform such a policy would actually retard it. Between 1970 and 1981 East European countries attracted an annual inflow of $5.8 billion, but only succeeded in avoiding reforms and running up considerable external debts (see Chapter 8). When the European Bank for Reconstruction and Development (EBRD) was founded in April 1991, to assist economic development in Eastern Europe, its president suggested that 'These countries need 2,000 billion Ecus over twenty years to organise their economies to the level of the rest of the world, but the main point is that the money will come from the reorganisation of their own economies and their own savings'. Another argument against massive Western aid was that if it did not produce the hoped-for results then the West would be blamed and nationalism promoted. In turn, some nationalists did not welcome outside assistance and sympathized with a Russian politician who equated Western aid to 'free cheese in the mousetrap' (Jeffries 1993, 336, 346).

The main Western effort to assist Eastern Europe was embodied in the PHARE programme, which was established following the Paris summit of the G7 nations in July 1989 to assist East European countries intent on political and economic reform. At first limited to Poland and Hungary (hence the title which stands for 'Poland and Hungary – Assistance for Restructuring the Economy'), eventually the Czech and Slovak republics, Bulgaria and Romania were included in the programme. The PHARE scheme concentrated on key sectors of command economies to assist the transition process. Even so, the programme has been viewed as more of a gesture since its budget was inconsequential when compared with the total restructuring task. The same is true of the EBRD and the European Investment Bank, the EC's long-term financing institution (Johnson and Miles 1994; McRae 1994).

'Trade not aid' has been the West's motto in regard to the Third World. If there were a slogan for Eastern Europe it would be much more ambiguous. True, both ingredients have been present in the early 1990s, but the balance achieved has not been a happy one with neither aid nor trade being prescribed in satisfactory dosages. Indeed, the EC has preferred aid to trade. Lending to promote recovery in Eastern Europe by the European Investment Bank was increased to £1.34 billion at the close of 1993. The 'Visegrad Four' are hoping to achieve full membership of the European Union by the year 2000. In the spring of 1994 Poland and Hungary led the way by formally applying for membership. The Czech Trade and Industry Minister, Vladimir Dlouhy, suggested that a major factor in the formation of Cefta was the perceived need 'to convey to all Western countries our commitment to joining the trend towards free trade. We are sending a signal to Brussels – to the European community' (Butler 1994). The advantages of such a step are manifold: these and any other East European countries who are allowed to join would become part of an enormous free trade area and enjoy the benefits of collective security. At the December 1992 Edinburgh summit, the existing twelve EC members became committed in principle to allowing the East Europeans to join, but no specific timetable was set for entry. Although East European governments pointed to the examples of Greece and Portugal, whose shortcomings in meeting membership criteria were conveniently overlooked, on the other side of the coin the Community's richer states were concerned that the poorer members were finding it onerous to fulfil their duties. Admitting the East Europeans, it is argued, would simply add to the strain on the EC's regional fund. Unlike the four projected new members drawn from the European Free Trade Association in 1994, who would all be net contributors to the EC, the countries of Eastern Europe were liable to be net recipients and therefore less welcome.

In December 1991 treaties embodied in the 'Europe Agreements' provided for associate member status to Poland, Hungary and Czechoslovakia as a prelude to full membership; in 1993 Bulgaria and Romania were added to the list. It was envisaged that over a ten-year period trade barriers for industrial goods would be dismantled, leading to free trade between the two halves of Europe. But the fact that these agreements were not ratified by all EC members by the January 1993 deadline did not bode well. Indeed, instead of heralding free trade, the agreements were manipulated to the advantage of existing EC members through the provision that no less than 40 per cent of associate members' exports could be penalized by trade restrictions. The accords also permitted the EC to indulge in 'safeguard measures' if the level of imports from the East threatened local producers. EC governments were especially concerned at the impact on their home industries of 'sensitive' goods such as cheap chemicals, textiles, clothing and footwear, coal, farm products and iron and steel. Two vivid illustrations occurred in 1992. The Community's lifting of all steel quotas in March 1992 quickly triggered a large increase in East European exports which prompted the EC to slap restrictions on Czech steel and impose provisional anti-dumping duties on Croatian, Czech and Polish steel tubes. The East Europeans naturally complained that they were being penalized in exactly those areas where they enjoyed a competitive advantage. When, in April 1992, the EC banned imports of livestock and dairy products from Eastern Europe because of the outbreak of foot-and-mouth disease in former Yugoslavia, this was regarded by Easterners as an excuse for protectionism. The Czech farm minister went so far as to state that the ban 'restored the iron curtain'. He had a point. The last reported instances of the disease in Poland or Czechoslovakia dated back eighteen years, which could not be said of several EC members. The boycott lasted until the summer of 1992, during which time Poland, Europe's largest live cattle exporter, lost $50 million in potential beef sales (Parker 1993, 20–22; Rollo and Smith 1993). As Johnson (1993) puts it, the stricken cow which started the furore 'became the symbol of Western terror of eastern European imports'.

The Europe Agreements definitely ran in the EC's favour. To 1990 the EC had a trade deficit with Eastern Europe, but in that year it became a surplus and has remained so ever since. The EC's trade surplus with the region rose from 1.4 billion Ecu in 1991 to 2.5 billion Ecu in 1992. The same pattern is apparent in OECD trade: between 1989 and 1992 Eastern Europe increased the value of its exports to OECD countries by 43 per cent, but Eastern imports rose by 67 per cent, transforming the trading relationship in the OECD's favour from a small deficit to a large surplus. By 1993 Poland's trade gap threatened to exceed $2.2 billion and compelled the government to redirect hard currency intended to service the foreign debt to creditors in the EC (Traynor 1994a).

Ultimately the EC must make up its mind whether Eastern Europe is a friend to be courted or an enemy to be thwarted. In the early 1990s the EC's policy contained a mixture of both attitudes. For instance, Germany, which in 1992 accounted for 56 per cent of EC trade with the five main East European countries, wanted closer ties with Eastern Europe for political reasons, but fears for domestic jobs created hesitation. With hourly wages in the Czech and Slovak Republics, Hungary and Poland considerably below the West German levels, a government spokesman was prompted to remark: 'It is as if we had Hong Kong just 80 kilometres from Berlin.' The yawning trade gap between the EC and Eastern Europe ought to make the former more receptive to imports from the latter. What is certain is that without greater access to EC markets, Eastern Europe's efforts to bridge the performance gap with the West will be rendered much more difficult (Barber and Marsh 1993).

As Western firms increasingly invest in Eastern Europe, it is possible that the vexed issue of trade restrictions will be satisfactorily resolved as they will naturally seek an outlet for products produced in the East. Foreign direct investment flows to Eastern Europe (including Albania) rose from $2.3 billion in 1990 to $11 billion in 1992. The uneven geographical spread reflected the natural desire of Western businessmen to cherry-pick and inevitably some former communist states were judged to be more attractive investments than others. Bulgaria's geographical position, which makes it far removed from Western markets (although it is reasonably placed for the Middle East) put it at a clear disadvantage. And despite its status as one of the least indebted countries in Eastern Europe, Romania had a struggle to entice foreign investors because of the dilatory pace of its reforms. In fact foreign investors have been attracted to one of the most indebted nations. By 1993, post-communist Hungary had managed to draw in about half of the total foreign investment injected into Eastern Europe following the raising of the Iron Curtain. The Czech Republic, with its industrial traditions, modest external debt, open capital markets, sound monetary policies and relatively low inflation, was another magnet for foreign investors. So too was Poland because of its sheer size which, with its go-ahead reform policy, provided great potential. Its sizeable population represented a larger potential market than Austria, the Czech Republic, Hungary and Slovakia combined.

A pressing issue was the modernization of telecommunication networks whose inadequacy was identified by the OECD as Eastern Europe's worst infrastructure handicap *vis-à-vis* the improvement of exports. Communist regimes had not been keen on free communication and therefore bequeathed their successors antiquated telephone exchanges, with some dating back to the 1930s. Where the Western norm was around 40 lines per 100 inhabitants, for Eastern Europe the average was only 10–20. The installation of modern telecommunication networks provides Eastern Europe with an opportunity to leap-frog generations of development.

Most countries set about providing telephone utilities with digital switches and fibre-optic cable, utilizing Western manufacturers, such as Siemens, Northern Telecom and AT&T, for the equipment. In December 1993 a German–American consortium won the tender to purchase a 30 per cent stake in Matav, Hungary's state-owned telephone company, marking the largest privatization deal in Eastern Europe to that date. Hungary's minister of tele-communications predicted that Matav and its new partner would 'develop Hungary as an international hub for telecommunications in eastern central Europe' (Hooker 1993). The main focus across Eastern Europe has been on providing more landlines, which the OECD estimates will cost $129 billion by the millennium, to bring average line density up to 35 per 100. Although international institutions have proved sympathetic to this requirement (such as credits from the EBRD for the $150 million Gdansk project), the main funding so far has been domestic-based, with tariffs rising to help meet the enormous construction costs. The Polish state telecoms operator, Telekomunikacja, is intent on providing one-third of investment outlays from its own resources. Over the longer term, foreign equity investment will be necessary. The Matav example could prove that privatization is the best method of attracting substantial foreign investment and lead other countries to follow suit (Denton 1993a; Adonis, Denton and Bobinski 1993).

Apart from Czechoslovakia and Romania, the new post-communist governments inherited considerable external debt burdens from their predecessors. Poland was saddled with one of the largest debts in absolute terms. In March 1991 the Paris Club, consisting of seventeen major Western government creditors, agreed to write off in stages half of Poland's debts provided it met the IMF's standby criteria. The United States went further and forgave

70 per cent of government-to-government debts. In September 1993 Hungary concluded an eighteen-month credit package worth £320 million with the IMF, though this quickly ran into difficulties owing to the likelihood of overshooting the IMF's target budget deficit of 5.4 per cent of GDP in 1994. Some 80 per cent of Bulgaria's inherited $12 billion of external debt was owed to around 300 foreign banks. Such was the strain that in 1990 the repayment of capital and interest was suspended. Subsequently, the Paris Club agreed to restructure the official debt, though it was feared that the poor earning power of the Bulgarian economy might render such a gesture meaningless. Agreements with commercial banks have proved much harder to negotiate. Failure to achieve a sympathetic settlement with its commercial creditors undoubtedly constrained Bulgaria's reform process. The same was true, but to a much lesser extent, of Poland where the virtual default on the servicing of commercial debts in the autumn of 1989 produced substantial accumulated arrears, with the commercial bank debt standing at $13 billion by the end of 1993. There was hope of a settlement in the near future, which would enhance Poland's prospects of future bank borrowing (Cohen 1991, 246; IMF 1993, 59; Robinson 1994b). In March 1994, following four years of difficult negotiations, the leading commercial banks of the London Club agreed to cancel 42.5 per cent of Poland's total debts amounting to $13.1 billion. The deal allowed the Poles to spread their remaining repayments over a 30-year period and was 'viewed by western economists as the final adjustment needed for Poland, Europe's fastest-growing economy, to integrate thoroughly into the international economy' (Dunne 1994).

THE NATIONALITIES QUESTION

No sooner had the map of Europe been redrawn to take account of the collapse of communism than further adjustments were required based on destabilizing ethnic lines as nationalist and racist forces, which had simmered under socialism, now came to the boil, driven by ancient hatreds, rivalries and territorial claims. Without exception, East European countries regard themselves as victims of history. Perspectives naturally differ. For example, Hungarians look back nostalgically on the nineteenth century as a glorious period when they ruled most of the Danube, whereas the subject peoples understandably regard this era as one best forgotten. Again, Serbs, labelled by the world community as aggressors, equate their actions differently to reclaiming and defending territory that is historically theirs. All across Eastern Europe, the new regimes sought to replace communist icons with nationalist figures who emphasize their statehood: in Hungary, Admiral Horthy, the interwar regent who destroyed the communist threat in 1919, was reburied in a state ceremony; in Romania, Marshal Ion Antonescu, the wartime leader and figurehead of the Nazi Iron Guard, became the new hero; in Croatia, Ante Pavelic, leader of the puppet Nazi wartime state, is venerated. All these figures were Hitler's allies and their elevation to cult status marks a disturbing shift to the extreme right (Hockenos 1993; Monteflore 1994).

The different outcomes of nationality disputes (peaceful or violent) were influenced by the particular factors in each case. In January 1993 Czechoslovakia broke apart in a 'velvet divorce' with two republics being established in the Czech lands and Slovakia after 74 years of uneasy 'marriage'. The Czechs initiated the proceedings when they suggested a hyphen be added to the federation's title to read the 'Federal Republic of Czecho-Slovakia'. Several months of dispute passed before the idea was dropped, but by then Slovak resentments were being fanned by a former boxer, Vladimir Meciar. He overplayed his hand over the autonomy issue and the Czechs were more than happy to agree to a total separation. The grounds for the split rested on the differing economic progress of the two regions since 1989. Slovakia, which contained the bulk of the outmoded heavy engineering and arms sectors, was adversely affected by Prague's fast-paced economic reforms which Meciar's nationalist movement for a democratic Slovakia vehemently opposed. In economic terms, the Czechs had everything to gain from a separation: the size of their population was much greater, they had considerably more land, far less unemployment and were attracting the greater share of foreign investment, $550 million against Slovakia's $150 million in 1991 (Robinson 1992; Millar 1992; Sherwell 1992).

The economic consequences were apparent within a year of the 'velvet divorce'. While the two new currencies started out on level pegging, the Slovak crown soon began to depreciate more rapidly against the American dollar. Where the Czechs pressed on happily with privatization, the Slovaks hesitated, not wishing to add to their already high unemployment figures. Though the Deutsche Bank could describe the Czech Republic as having 'the best development potential of all countries in Eastern Europe' (Bridge 1993) this certainly was not true of Slovakia. As Robinson (1993e) perceives, 'Without rapid privatisation and higher foreign investment Slovakia's ability to build a less energy and raw material intensive economy more attuned to international trade will remain in doubt'. Growing dissatisfaction at the contrasting economic fortunes of the two parts of former Czechoslovakia resulted, in March 1994, in the toppling of Meciar as prime minister in a vote of no confidence amid allegations of Stalinist tendencies and corruption involving the sale of state enterprises. He went bitterly into opposition, determined to keep the nationalist flag flying and to rail against the substantial Hungarian minority (Traynor 1994b). The signs were, however, that, with independence achieved, Meciar would find a further political comeback diffi-

Source: D. Johnson and L. Miles, *Eastern Europe: economic challenges and business opportunities*, Hull: Hidcote Press, 1994.

Map 4   Eastern Europe in 1993

cult as 'From all sides people argue that the most important thing now is to make Slovakia work, and above all to get the economy up and running' (Robinson 1994a).

Hungary too was not without its ethnic problems. As many as one in four ethnic Hungarians live outside Hungary with sizeable minorities located in Romania, Serbia, Slovakia and the Ukraine. Developments in all four gave rise for concern. In Romania, the downfall of Ceausescu did not end the harassment of Hungarians, in addition to which there was discrimination against the largest Gypsy population in Europe and the rekindling of the anti-semitism of the interwar years. Slovakia's ethnic Hungarians, who made up 10 per cent of the total population, resented their treatment as an irredentist group and the Slovak government's resistance to adopting dual Hungarian–Slovak place names in areas where there is an ethnic Hungarian majority. They also wanted the removal of the Slovak suffix 'ova' which was affixed to married female Hungarian surnames. Slovakia's determination to assert itself was epitomized by its decision to proceed with the completion of the Gabčikova dam on the Danube without consulting Hungary. Although all the main Hungarian political parties ruled out ethnic border changes, it suited Meciar well to paint a picture of Hungary as a revisionist state out to create a 'Greater Hungary' through the recovery of lands lost in the Treaty of Trianon. By January 1994 the ethnic Hungarian minority in Slovakia was calling for the creation of a self-governing province and the situation threatened to turn violent (Bridge 1994). The ethnic Hungarians living in Serbia's northern Vojvodina province were represented by the League of Vojvodina Hungarians, which, alleging Serb discrimination, wanted an autonomous province centred on seven majority Hungarian towns. But since the ethnic Hungarians were not participating in the bloody civil war which gripped former Yugoslavia, it seems highly unlikely that their demand will be acceded to.

Yugoslavia imploded and the tangled web of ethnic conflict threatened to turn the country into a semi-permanent battlefield. Once begun, the civil war took on a life of its own with warring factions confronting each other – Croats against Muslims and Serbs, Muslims fighting Croats and Serbs, Serbs assailing Croats and Muslims. No sooner did one intra-ethnic struggle subside than another flared into life to sustain the bloody civil war. The spilling over of the Serb–Croatian conflict from Croatia into Bosnia-Herzegovina was a logical progression. Before hostilities began, the latter's jumbled Muslim–Serb–Croat population comprised 44, 32 and 17 per cent of the total respectively. Sandwiched between Croatia and Serbia, Bosnia-Herzegovina was bound to be affected by the proximate hostilities. The Serbs and Croats considered Bosnia-Herzegovina to be an artificial state ripe for dismantlement and to this end the Serbian Democratic Party in Bosnia declared three areas of Bosnia 'Serb Autonomous Regions' while the extreme Croatian

Party of Rights sought the annexation of Bosnia (Malcolm 1994b, 224–5). In March 1992, under EC pressure, a referendum was held on independence. Although 65 per cent of the electorate voted in favour, the fact that the Bosnian Serbs boycotted the proceedings meant that there was no ethnic consensus. Milošević had in fact begun sending arms to the Bosnian Serbs in 1991, who then started to deploy heavy artillery in strategic positions. Fighting immediately erupted after the referendum and once begun showed no signs of coming to an early end. Although the Serbs, having used their superior firepower to drive back the poorly armed Muslims and reduce their territory to small unconnected enclaves, controlled around 70 per cent of the disputed territory (as well as a quarter of Croatia) and had achieved most of their military aims by the summer of 1993, the Bosnian Muslims and Croats then began fighting each other for compensating territorial advantage (Barber 1992; Malcolm 1994a).

The West's reaction, particularly that of the EC, was half-hearted and arguably it worsened the situation. The EC's president, Jacques Delors, conceded that 'the Community is like an adolescent facing the crisis of an adult'. Determined not to become militarily involved, the West restricted itself to recognizing new states (Slovenia, Croatia, Bosnia-Herzegovina, Macedonia), playing the role of mediator, imposing an arms embargo on all parties and sanctions against Serbia and Montenegro alone, declaring 'safe areas' which were not adequately defended, and providing humanitarian aid for the afflicted civilian populations. None of these policies did anything to stop the slaughter which might have been achieved by earlier, decisive military intervention. No sooner were cease-fires agreed than they were broken, while peace talks rapidly collapsed as the parties persistently quarrelled over maps. Again, the UN's imposition of a universal arms embargo in September 1991 effectively discriminated against the Bosnian Muslims because the Serbs could draw on the considerable stockpiles of the former federal army. Even the sanctions imposed on Serbia backfired in allowing Milošević to claim that the country's economic ills were the result of a conspiracy of foreign powers. Although the Serbs proved willing to give some territory back to the Bosnian Muslims, the future status of Sarajevo (claimed by both Muslims and Serbs) remained a bone of contention. The provision of UN humanitarian supplies to sustain starving populations was increasingly frustrated by the resentment of other nationalities, who blocked and sometimes ransacked food convoys destined to feed their enemies, with the result that often only a small proportion of the aid reached its intended target (Malcolm 1994a; Traynor and Luce 1994).

Wherever the ethnic strife manifested itself, the economic and social consequences were profound: place names were literally wiped from the map and their populations 'ethnically cleansed'; economic infrastructures were destroyed; the destruction of the Old Bridge at Mostar, which had stood for 600 years, showed that nothing was sacrosanct in this conflict. By the summer of 1993 an estimated 140 000 people had died in Bosnia-Herzegovina and 2 million were rendered homeless by fleeing the fighting, the destruction of their homes and forced expulsions. Sarajevo, one of the UN's six Muslim 'safe areas', was subjected to a protracted siege by the Serbs which guaranteed it a place in the history books alongside other famous sieges such as Mafeking, Khartoum and Leningrad. In one important respect Sarajevo was different: it was supplied, albeit intermittently, by food-laden UN aircraft. At the same time, the besieging Serbs ensured that the free movement of people or commercial traffic was impossible, and that there were no normal water, gas or electricity supplies. Indeed, the city was reduced to a basic feudal-type existence. The need for water meant a daily trek by citizens with handcarts to springs beside the River Miljacka where they were exposed to Serb shell and sniper fire. Burying the victims became a daily ritual. By 1993 the average weight of a new-born child in Sarajevo had plummeted by 20 per cent while the average adult was 33 pounds lighter than before the siege (Block 1993).

While reluctant to intervene militarily in the Yugoslav civil war, the international community looked to exercise available economic levers to punish the perceived aggressor. In May 1992 sanctions were imposed by the UN against Serbia and her ally Montenegro which, in December 1991, had together formed a 'Third Yugoslavia'. Although pessimistic predictions that their economies would collapse within three months proved wide of the mark, gradually and inexorably the adverse effects of sanctions became more and more apparent, especially after loopholes were closed in April 1993. In September rationing was introduced on basic items such as cooking oil, flour, sugar and salt. By October Montenegro's inflation rate, at 1900 per cent, was the highest in the world, but it was soon exceeded by Serbia's. At the end of 1993, the Serb monthly inflation rate was running at 50 000 per cent, setting a new world record, eclipsing even that of Weimar Germany in the autumn of 1923. As in the latter case, the money printing presses went into overdrive as more and more worthless dinars came into circulation. Seventy years after the great inflation rocked Germany, the Milošević regime introduced the 1 million dinar note, which was quickly followed by the 50 million dinar note. Also echoing the German case, bartering and the use of foreign currency (principally the Deutschmark) became commonplace. Milošević also followed Weimar Germany in paying workers rendered idle by sanctions. Were it not for the existence of a black market, the blaming of the situation on the West, and the unifying rallying cry of a 'Greater Serbia', then the Milošević regime might soon have collapsed. As it was, in the elections of December 1993 a third of the electorate still supported the government and most parties campaigned on a nationalist platform. *The Economist*'s Belgrade correspondent (1993, 46) captured the defiant mood: 'On the eve of war, one Serb politician roared that Serbs would eat roots rather than surrender. The election saw a vote for roots.' In January 1994 a new economic programme saw the introduction of a 'new dinar' backed by hard currency. But although the pressure on the 1994 state budget was marginally eased by the intention to render 210 000 public employees redundant, a more extensive redundancy programme was seen as too politically risky by the regime. Moreover, other commitments suggested that it would be very difficult for the Milošević government to keep inflationary pressures in check for long – the need to sustain Serb forces in the field (estimated at 20 per cent of GDP in 1992), health care and the police force.

Sarajevo had been subjected to constant artillery bombardment since April 1992. Thousands died in the intervening period until, on 5 February 1994, a single Serb mortar claimed 68 victims and wounded 142 others shopping innocently in a Saturday market. The worldwide media attention and the resulting public indignation the tragedy attracted at last forced the UN and NATO to take action and an ultimatum was issued which threatened punitive air strikes if the Bosnian Serbs did not remove their heavy artillery from the hills surrounding the Bosnian capital. The world waited with bated breath, but after a dilatory initial response the Bosnian Serbs complied as best they could in the wintry conditions. Although Serb checkpoints remained around Sarajevo, the threat of daily shelling was lifted and the city's population could return to some semblance of normal living (Krushelnycky 1994; Vulliamy 1994b).

After the success over Sarajevo, the civil war entered a new phase with American diplomatic and military muscle seemingly having an impact where European efforts had palpably failed. Washington successfully brokered a Croatian–Bosnian general ceasefire and promoted a loose confederation between the two sides which was seen as a means of averting ethnic partition. NATO warplanes were engaged in action for the first time since the organization's founding and gave meaning to the no-fly zone by shooting down four trangressing Bosnian Serb Jastreb aircraft. Nonetheless, the Bosnian Serbs were allowed to harness their heavy artillery against the Muslim enclave of Gorazde, another 'safe area'. Only belatedly, after much suffering on the part of the virtually defenceless civilian population, did the West intercede, forcing the attackers to back off after a Sarajevo-style ultimatum. But from the Muslim perspective, the Bosnian Serbs were being allowed to move their exclusive weaponry to fight with another day (Stone 1994; Fairhall 1994).

The Serbs persistently drove a coach and horses through the West's half-hearted Bosnian policy, exposing the fact that there was a lack of unity and resources, especially ground troops. Some saw signs of the cold war being re-enacted in the Balkans with the United States taking the side of the Muslims and the Russians that of their traditional allies, the Serbs. The West's desire to maintain reasonable relations with Moscow and its lack of vital interests in the Balkans hammered another nail in Bosnia's coffin. The Croat–Muslim federation was largely meaningless without the willingness of the Bosnian Serbs to surrender substantial territorial gains. Yet they indicated that they would only consider joining if Bosnian Serb territory could be linked to Serbia proper. As one Serb official commented on the West's peace efforts: 'they don't know what to do with us'. As long as the UN and NATO avoids becoming deeply embroiled in the fight the Serbs can be confident of retaining a large proportion of their military gains. This factor will in turn make the Muslims reluctant to settle unless they are totally defeated. It can be argued that belated international action, far from limiting the dimensions of the conflict may, conversely, have stoked up the embers of war through giving the Muslims false hope of outside salvation and making the Serbs determined to complete their carve-up of Bosnia while they can.

Haunting questions remain. Can the shotgun wedding rapprochement between the Muslims and Croats hold? Will the Serbs be willing to give up enough territory to satisfy the Muslims without compromising their ambitious war aims? It is far from certain that a sustainable peace settlement can be attained given the conflicting agendas of the warring parties and the West's resolve not to become militarily embroiled as a combatant. The alternative of lifting the arms embargo, thereby allowing the Bosnian Muslims to redress the military imbalance, carried the risk of rendering Bosnia into a semi-permanent battleground. In short, there were no easy options or solutions.

THE LEGACIES OF THE PAST AS A MORTGAGE ON THE FUTURE

Eastern Europe's future is far from certain and it is haunted by the fear that it cannot escape from its grim past. The region suffers from various legacies, including the dominance of outside powers and an economic performance gap with the richer nations. There have not been long periods when the region has been left to its own devices. The burden of empire in Eastern Europe was borne successively by the Habsburg dynasty, the Third Reich and the Soviet Union. In 1918 a number of small independent states were created but it was only a matter of time before these new democracies were dominated by stronger powers. Whether the new-found freedoms of 1989 will prove to be more durable remains to be seen.

Central and Eastern Europe are sometimes referred to as 'the lands between'. Traditionally, the power vacuum that they represent has been filled by one or more of the great powers. A military threat, if it materializes once again, looks most likely to emanate from Russia, especially if reforms fail to deliver prosperity to the average Russian within a few years. When the Soviet Union was disintegrating, there was rejoicing that the Russian threat seemed to have disappeared forever. One inspired critic (Mortimer 1990) sounded a note of caution and asked the hypothetical question: 'But what if there emerged, like Nazi Germany from Weimar, a "paranoid" Russian nationalist regime, in a country which, whatever else changed, was likely to remain a thermonuclear power?' Three years later this speculation assumed greater poignancy when, in the Russian parliamentary elections of December 1993, a hard-line neo-fascist party, ironically called the Liberal Democrats and led by Vladimir Zhirinovsky, gained the the majority of seats. The success of his nationalistic rhetoric, which was suffused with wild threats and outlandish promises, quickly drew comparisons with Hitler and earned him the titles of 'Mad Vlad' and a potential 'Hitler with H-bombs'. It could be that the Russian economy has until 1996, when Zhironovsky will contest the presidency, to bring prosperity to the majority, to avoid the country from falling into the hands of an extremist whose future actions are uncertain and particularly worrying for Central and Eastern Europe as well as for the West (Rees-Mogg 1993).

As for Germany, her interest in Central and Eastern Europe looks likely to be purely economic in character. Once Germany, the region's most important trading partner, escapes from the mire of recession and again becomes the economic power-house of Europe, then Central and Eastern Europe should stand to benefit. But there are also dangers. When Czechoslovakia split apart some cynics suggested that the Czech Republic should be renamed 'Eastern Germany' because its economic ties would attach it firmly to the German-speaking core of Europe. Hohensee (1993, 100) poses the questions which the next few years should begin to answer: 'Will Germany serve as a bridge between the two Europes and help integrate the East European economies into the European Community? Or will Germany come to dominate a *Balkanised* Eastern Europe culturally and economically as it turns into a German sphere of influence?'

Another scenario was foreshadowed by a *Financial Times* leader of 2 September 1989: 'If the superpowers are retreating from Europe, might we be heading back towards the old intra-European power struggles, with all their terrifying destructive potential?' This question assumes even greater poignancy following events in former Yugoslavia. Bismarck once suggested that the Balkans were not worth the bones of even a single Pomeranian grenadier, yet within a few decades troubles in the region had sparked off the First World War. In October 1993 the French president, François Mitterrand, warned that conflicts in the Balkans could cause a European war early in the next century. There are certainly dangers of this if the Yugoslav civil war is allowed to spread outside Bosnia-Herzegovina. Should Milošević be replaced by the ultra-nationalist Serbian Renewal Party, which demands the annexation of Macedonia and the mass expulsion of Albanians from Kosovo, then Bulgaria, Greece, Albania or Turkey might well become militarily involved. During the nineteenth century, Bulgaria and Serbia went to war three times over Macedonia, which the Greeks today insist on calling Skopje to distinguish it from the Greek territory of the same name. In February 1994, in an effort to try to compel Macedonia to change its name and drop the use of the Vergina star, an ancient Greek symbol, on its flag, Greece imposed an economic blockade against the former Yugoslav republic. This followed the recognition of Macedonia by other EC members and the United States. In the end, it may indeed take substantial outside military intervention, aimed at rolling back Serb conquests, to bring the conflict to an end and stop it from spreading or flaring up again. Left to its own devices, the Bosnian civil war could run and run.

For Eastern Europe as a whole, much will depend on the creation of dynamic free market economies which are able to compete successfully in the world economy. The evidence is not encouraging for, as Good (1993, 1) remarks, 'even a rudimentary knowledge of European economic history demonstrates that the source of economic backwardness in Central and Eastern Europe lies deep in the past, not simply in the post-1945 cold war era'. On the basis of his new estimates, Good (1993, 10) demonstrates that 'the current lag of Central and Eastern Europe was already deeply entrenched in the nineteenth century'. Table 10.2 shows that despite more than a century of economic growth, Central and Eastern Europe continued to lag behind the United States' performance by a wide margin. Significantly Austria produced the best performance of the Central and Eastern countries. It gained from being more industrialized than Hungary within the Austro-Hungarian Empire in the pre-1914 period, experiencing a rate of industrialization comparable to that of France, and after 1945 Austria was spared from being ensnared by communism and clearly benefited from contact with the Western democracies with their free market economies. By contrast, 'Second Yugoslavia' (1945–91) was never fully embraced by the West (although Western aid helped to produce impressive growth rates in the 1950s), not least because it continued to favour communism. Yugoslav economic performance suffered accordingly in the long run. The whole region is still clearly afflicted by the entrails of the experience of over four decades of economic mismanagement under communism. As Good (1993, 12) comments, 'The data do hint at a special legacy of communism in perpetuating this lag'. Romania, which remained hopelessly attached to the Stalinist variant long after it had gone out of style, looks destined to suffer most: 'The prewar legacy of economic

Table 10.2   Indices of GDP per capita in Europe and the United States,
1870, 1910, 1987 (present-day, post-1989 boundaries, US =
100)

Country	1870	1910	1987
United States	100.0	100.0	100.0
North-West			
United Kingdom	113.4	80.6	69.3
Belgium	87.5	65.7	64.8
Netherlands	88.9	62.9	67.5
France	65.4	49.2	70.6
Germany	54.1	49.3	73.4
Switzerland	73.6	58.7	76.4
Northern			
Denmark	68.8	63.0	74.1
Finland	39.8	32.9	70.2
Norway	51.2	39.9	87.3
Sweden	54.5	48.4	77.6
Mediterranean			
Italy	52.1	40.3	66.7
Portugal	40.0	22.2	42.6
Spain	48.5	41.4	47.3
Greece	–	20.9	34.7
Central and Eastern			
Austria	59.4	51.0	64.4
Czechoslovakia	45.7	41.9	46.0
Hungary	30.2	35.2	44.3
Poland	23.9	21.4	30.1
Yugoslavia	19.0	20.4	30.2
Romania	21.7	23.3	28.8
Bulgaria	–	18.8	32.9
Russia (Soviet Union)	38.6	26.2	44.0

Source: Good (1993, 27), revised in the light of communication from Professor Good dated
8th July 1994

underdevelopment and the Ceausescu legacy of exploitation stand to haunt Romania for quite some time' (Gilberg 1992, 297).

The legacy of Western mistrust and suspicion of Eastern Europe needs to be overcome if the latter is ever to succeed in closing the performance gap. Roberts (1992) suggests that the ideal solution would be for the EC to assume the mantle of the Austro-Hungarians as benign overlords by allowing the East Europeans to join the club in the near future. Then 'Czechs, Slovaks, Serbs, Croats, and Trans-Carpathian Ruthenians could unite in deriding, serving and defrauding Brussels'. The position adopted by the West to the brave new world to its east is fundamental to the latter's future prospects. The immediate signs are not promising. In an address to the Council of Europe, Václav Havel, the Czech president, expressed his frustration at the turn of events:

> Europe today lacks an ethos; it lacks imagination; it lacks generosity; it lacks the ability to see beyond the horizon of its own particular interests, be they partisan or otherwise, and to resist the pressure from various lobbying groups. There is no real identification in Europe with the meaning and purpose of integration (Wistrich 1993).

Since the demise of communism there have been a succession of what Eyal (1993) characterizes as 'make-believe institutions' put forward by the West to placate the East as a substitute for the genuine article: the Conference on Security and Cooperation in Europe, the OECD's Partners in Transition Programme, NATO's North Atlantic Cooperation Council, and latterly the Partnership for Peace promoting joint military exercises within NATO, but with no certainty of eventual full membership, which the East Europeans see as essential to their security. At a time of recession and rising unemployment, the threat of competition from the East clearly disturbs the members of the EC, notwithstanding diplomatic blandishments to the contrary. The membership of the European Economic Area, the world's largest free trade zone, established in January 1994, did not include any East European country, and while the conclusion of the Uruguay Round of the GATT in December 1993 may lead to fewer trade impediments between Eastern and Western Europe, it is equally possible that the EC will resort characteristically to anti-dumping measures and import quotas to restrict the increasing competition posed by low-cost East European goods.

Czechoslovakia apart, a further legacy which the East Europeans have to overcome is that of a lack of democratic traditions. Long-term economic progress is in danger of coming to grief through the election of anti-reform or reactionary governments by electorates who are weary of the sacrifices required. Already, the evidence suggests that it will take at least a decade for the leading East European countries to achieve free market economies in all respects. And this is on the assumption that their populations continue to support fast-track reforms. As Coyle (1992, 66) observes:

> Although the new governments began with an enormous amount of goodwill, countries that started out with no unemployment, no inflation, no absolute property, now have all of these. There are goods in the shops but few can afford them. The few that can flaunt it.

The time lag before the positive effects of economic reforms manifest themselves in improved standards of living for the majority ensures that reformist governments are exceedingly vulnerable at election times. Indeed, of the initial post-communist governments, only that in Hungary survived for a full four-year term. Even in Poland, which in the mid-1990s promises to become the fastest growing economy in Europe, the reformist government proved vulnerable, falling in September 1993 to a left-wing coalition led by the Polish Peasant Party and the post-communist Left Democratic Alliance. Bobinski (1993) commented at the time, 'the social pressures the government faces will be difficult to contain, as Poles continue to yearn for the marked improvement in their standard of living that the overthrow of the communist regime in 1989 promised, but failed, to bring'. This is true of Eastern Europe as a whole with the trend moving clearly in the direction of the election of populist parties on the left and the right.

By 1994 a picture was emerging which pointed to the likelihood of a division of the countries studied into leaders and laggards: those with the best prospects had western borders with Germany or Austria (Poland, the Czech Republic, Hungary, Slovenia), while those with the bleakest prospects (Bulgaria, the Slovak Republic, Romania, most of former Yugoslavia) generally looked eastwards towards the former USSR. If this projection is borne out, then it will repeat the pre-1914 situation which led Lampe (1989, 193) to conclude that 'the experience of the southern and eastern Habsburg periphery suggests that these borderlands did not share fully in the monarchy's fairly impressive economic growth and integration between 1815–1914'. Slovakia's long-term future could well be tied to that of neighbouring Ukraine which supplies enriched iron pellets from Krivoi Rog to sustain the east Slovakian Steel Works as well as Russian gas fed by pipeline under Ukrainian soil (Robinson 1992). Slovenia, on the other hand, is geographically well placed to maintain its historic lead as the best performing Yugoslav republic. Free from the ravages of war and located between Italy, Austria, Hungary and Romania, Slovenia searched for new export markets to replace those lost in former Yugoslavia through the civil war and UN sanctions against Serbia, once a source of cheap raw materials. Slovenia's relatively open economy allowed some companies to compete successfully in Western markets while its small population of 2 million eased the pressures of increased unemployment arising from job shedding as firms adjusted to the loss of former export markets. By 1994 steady growth was projected, the new currency (the tolar) was stable, inflation was falling and the budget deficit and external debt were both manageable, providing an ideal framework for privatization and attracting foreign investment (Silber 1994). The contrast with Serbia could not have been more stark. Just before the civil war erupted the massive Elektronska Industrija factory was on the point of producing 1 million television sets for domestic and international consumption, but by early 1994 it was unable to procure imported parts or to export a single product. Where Slovenian unemployment was 15 per cent, 60 per cent of Serb workers in industry, services and administration were without a job and most economic activity existed in the black market (*The Economist* 1994).

Over time, Central Europe, with its more Western traditions, stands the best chance of being integrated fully into Western Europe. On 28 January 1994, speaking on the theme of the creation of a *Grande Europe,* Delors suggested that 'Vienna, Budapest, Warsaw and other towns are just as much poles of European culture as Berlin, Paris, Brussels, Amsterdam and London' (Marshall 1994). Early in 1994, following American encouragement, the Czech Republic, Hungary and Poland applied to join the OECD, a further indication that they had been singled out as prospective full members of the Western club (Trofimov 1994). Another indication of this trend is Hungary's new M1 motorway, which, when completed, will stretch from Budapest and link up with Austria's A4 motorway which leads into Vienna.

As of old, the great imponderable is the future of Russia and the Balkans. Moscow's decision to despatch 400 peace-keeping Russian troops to Sarajevo in February 1994 marked the reassertion of a cherished 'historic' mission to defend fellow Slavs in the Balkans and could yet lead to greater Russian involvement in the region. The shock results of Russia's 1993 elections led both to a slowdown in its economic reforms and a new assertiveness abroad which reflected the desire to placate the nationalists at home through being considered once again a great power to be reckoned with as before. Russia has a great imperial tradition which could yet see it try to re-establish some of its old borders, especially if market reforms prove unsustainable. Russian instability could, in turn, retard East European reforms. On the other hand, a menacing Russia might, paradoxically, provide real impetus to the integration of Eastern Europe into the European economy because of the West's need for stable and strong buffer countries to keep any new Russian threat at a distance. The eventual end of the civil war in former Yugoslavia will bring into question the economic viability of the ethnically determined carve-up which takes place, recreating the situation of 1918, albeit on a smaller scale. 'We think of the region as an ethnic mosaic', a former premier of rump Yugoslavia warned the West, 'but it has also become a mosaic of mini-economies, none of which is likely to survive on its own.' He advocated, as others had done in the past, an international programme to foster regional economic cooperation as a means to end the ethnic struggle, thereby providing the embattled civilian populations with the hope of a better future than their demagogic leaders can offer. Otherwise he feared that 'we will never see an end to chronic ethnic strife in the region' (Panic 1994). The conundrum, however, is that such an aid package looks unlikely to materialize, if at all, until the fighting ceases for good. George Bernard Shaw once quipped that 'We learn from history that we learn nothing from history'. If the turbulent economic record of Eastern Europe demonstrates anything, it is that history repeats itself, that the future can only be determined by reference to the past, that accumulated hatreds, deep suspicions and rivalries do not remove themselves either within or outside the region, but return under certain conditions to shape and determine the course of events. And so it will be again as further travails lie ahead.

References

Adam, J. (1993), *Planning and market in Soviet and East European thought, 1960s–1992*, London: Macmillan.

Adonis, A., N. Denton and C. Bobinski (1993), 'The West rings in changes in Eastern Europe', *Financial Times*, 1 October.

Aldcroft, D.H. (1977), *From Versailles to Wall Street, 1919–1929*, London: Allen Lane.

Aldcroft, D.H. (1980), *The European economy 1914–1980*, London: Croom Helm.

Aldcroft, D.H. (1988), 'Eastern Europe in an age of turbulence, 1919–1950', *Economic History Review*, 41.

Aldcroft, D.H. (1989), 'The decline of Europe: trade and reconstruction in the 1920s', *European University Institute Papers*, 136/89, 11.

Aldcroft, D.H. (1991a), 'Origins of world war II', *The Economic Review*, 8, January.

Aldcroft, D.H. (1991b), 'Destabilising influences in the European economy in the 1920s', in C. Holmes and A. Booth (eds), *Economy and society: European industrialisation and its social consequences. Essays presented to Sidney Pollard*, Leicester: Leicester University Press.

Aldcroft, D.H. (1993a), 'Depression and recovery: the Eastern European experience', in W.R. Garside (ed.), *Capitalism in Crisis: international responses to the great depression*, London: Pinter Publishers.

Aldcroft, D.H. (1993b), *The European economy 1914–1990*, London: Routledge.

Aliber, R.Z. (1962), 'Speculation in the foreign exchanges: the European experience, 1919–1926', *Yale Economic Essays*, 2.

Almond, M. (1992), *The rise and fall of Nicolae and Elena Ceausescu*, London: Chapmans.

Alpert, P. (1951), *Twentieth century economic history of Europe*, New York: Schuman.

Ambrosius, G. and W.H. Hubbard (1989), *A social and economic history of twentieth century Europe*, Cambridge, Mass.: Harvard University Press.

Apponyi, A. (1928), *Justice for Hungary: review and criticism of the Treaty of Trianon*, London: Longmans Green.

Artaud, D. (1973), *La reconstruction de l'Europe 1919–1929*, Paris: Presses Universitaires de France.

Ascherson, A. (1987), *The struggle for Poland*, London: Michael Joseph.

Ash, T.G. (1993), *In Europe's name: Germany and the divided continent*, New York: Random House.

Aslund, A. (1992), *Post-communist economic revolutions: How big a bang?* Washington DC: The Center for Strategic & International Studies.

Bairoch, P. (1976), 'Europe's gross national product: 1800–1975', *Journal of European Economic History*, 5.

Bairoch, P. (1991), 'How and not why; economic inequalities between 1800 and 1913: some background figures', in J. Batou (ed.), *Between development and underdevelopment: the precocious attempts at industrialization at the periphery 1800–1870*, Geneva: Librairie Droz.

Bairoch, P. (1993), *Economics and world history: myths and paradoxes*, Hemel Hempstead: Harvester-Wheatsheaf.

Balfour, M. (1981), *The adversaries: America, Russia and the open world 1941–62*, London: Routledge & Kegan Paul.

Banac, I. (1988), *The national question in Yugoslavia: origins, history, politics*, Ithaca: Cornell University Press.

Bandera, V.N. (1964), *Foreign capital as an instrument of national economic policy: a study based on the experience of east European countries between the two world wars*, The Hague: Nijhoff.

Barber, A. (1994), 'Romanians storm city as scam ruins millions', *The Independent on Sunday*, 16 January.

Barber, A., C. Bellamy and B. Cathcart (1992), 'Bosnia: A plain person's guide to the new tragedy of the Balkans', *Independent on Sunday*, 16 August.

Barber, L. and D. Marsh (1993), 'Morsels from a groaning table', *Financial Times*, 7 June.

Basch, A. (1944), *The Danube Basin and the German economic sphere*, London: Kegan Paul, Trench, Trubner.

Baumont, M. (1946), *La faillité de la paix (1918–1939)*, Paris: Presses Universitaires de France.

Behr, E. (1992), *'Kiss the hand you cannot bite': the rise and fall of the Ceausescus*, London: Penguin.

Belgrade correspondent (1993), 'Roots of war', *The Economist*, 25 December.

Bell, J.D. (1977), *Peasants in power. Alexander Stambolski and the Bulgarian Agrarian National Union, 1899–1923*, Princeton: Princeton University Press.

Bencze, I. and E.V. Tajti (1972), *Budapest: an industrial–geographical approach*, Budapest: Akademiai Kiado.

Bentley, R. (1992), *Research and technology in the former German Democratic Republic*, Boulder, Col.: Westview Press.

Berend, I.T. and G. Ranki (1969), 'The economic problems of the Danube region at the break-up of the Austro-Hungarian monarchy', *Journal of Contemporary History*, 4.

Berend, I.T. (1974), 'Investment strategy in East-Central Europe', in H. Daems and H. van der Wee (eds), *The rise of managerial capitalism*, The Hague: Nijhoff.

Berend, I.T. (1985), 'Agriculture', in M.C. Kaser and E.A. Radice (eds), *The economic history of eastern Europe 1919–1975. Vol I. Economic structure and performance between the wars*, Oxford: Oxford University Press.

Berend, I.T. (1986), 'The historical evolution of Eastern Europe as a region', *International Organisation*, 40.

Berend, I.T. and G. Ranki (1958), 'The German economic expansion in Hungary', *Acta Historica*, 5.

Berend, I.T. and G. Ranki (1974a), *Economic development in East Central Europe in the 19th and 20th centuries*, New York: Columbia University Press.

Berend, I.T. and G. Ranki (1974b), *Hungary: a century of economic development*, Newton Abbot: David & Charles.

Berend, I.T. and G. Ranki (1982), *The European periphery and industrialization*, Cambridge: Cambridge University Press.

Berend, I.T. and G. Ranki (1985), *The Hungarian economy in the twentieth century*, London: Croom Helm.

Bernasek, M. (1970), 'Czechoslovak planning 1945–48', *Soviet Studies*, July.

Berov, L. (1983), 'Inflation and deflation policy in Bulgaria during the period between world war I and world war II', in N. Schmukler and E. Marcus (eds), *Inflation through the ages*, New York: Brooklyn College Press.

Beyen, J.W. (1951), *Money in maelstrom*, London, Macmillan.

Bialer, S. (1986), *The Soviet paradox: external expansion, internal decline*, London: Tauris.

Bicanic, B. (1973), *Economic policy in socialist Yugoslavia*, Cambridge: Cambridge University Press.

Black, C.E. et al. (1992), *Rebirth: a history of Europe since world war II*, Boulder, Col.: Westview Press.

Blanchard, et al. (1993), *Post-communist reform: pain and progress*, London: the MIT Press.

Block, R. (1993), 'Theatre of conflict', *The Independent*, 28 October.

Bobinski, C. (1993), 'Poles look to new cabinet to deliver', *Financial Times*, 11 November.

Bonnell, A.T. (1940), *German control over international economic relations 1930–1940*, Urbana, Ill.: University of Illinois Press.

Boyce, R. and E.M. Robertson (1989), *Paths to war: new essays on the origins of the second world war*, Basingstoke: Macmillan.

Brada, J.C. (1985), 'Soviet subsidization of Eastern Europe: the primacy of economics over politics?' *Journal of Comparative Economics*, 9.

Brada, J.C., E.A. Hewett and T.A. Wolf (1988), *Economic adjustment and reform in Eastern Europe and the Soviet Union*, London: Duke University Press.

Bridge, A. (1993), 'Slovakia rues high cost of its "velvet divorce"', *The Independent*, 31 December.

Bridge, A. (1994), 'Hungarians demand own province in Slovakia', *The Independent*, 7 January.

Brown, B. (1988), *Monetary chaos in Europe: the end of an era*, London: Croom Helm.

Brown, J.F. (1990), 'Hope and uncertainty in Eastern Europe', *SAIS Review*, 10.

Brown, J.F. (1988), *Eastern Europe and communist rule*, Durham: Duke University Press.

Brus, W. (1986), 'Postwar reconstruction and socio-economic transformation', in M.C. Kaser and E.A. Radice (eds), *The economic history of Eastern Europe 1919–1975. Vol. II. Interwar policy, the war and reconstruction*, Oxford: Oxford University Press.

Brzezinski, Z. (1988), 'Special address', *Problems of Communism*, 38.

Bullock, A. (1991), *Hitler and Stalin: parallel lives*, London: Harper Collins.

Bunce, V. (1985), 'The empire strikes back: The transformation of the eastern bloc from a Soviet asset into a Soviet liability', *International Organization*, 39.

Burke, J.F. (1993), 'Romanian and Soviet intelligence in the December revolution', *Intelligence and National Security*, 8.

Butler, H. (1941), *The lost peace: A personal impression*, London: Faber and Faber.

Butler, R. (1968), 'The peace treaty settlement of Versailles 1918–1933', in C.L. Mowat (ed.), *The shifting balance of world forces, 1898–1945*, Cambridge: Cambridge University Press.

Butler, R. (1994), 'Visegrad Four reap the rewards of united front', *The European*, 25 February–3 March.

Cagan, P. (1956), 'The monetary dynamics of hyperinflation', in M. Friedman (ed.), *Studies in the quantity theory of money*, Chicago: University of Chicago Press.

Cairncross, A.K. (1986), *The price of war: British policy on German reparations 1941–1949*, Oxford: Blackwell.

Carter, B. and F. Singleton (1982), *The economy of Yugoslavia*, London: Croom Helm.

Carter, F.W. (ed.) (1993), *Environmental problems in Eastern Europe*, London: Routledge.

Chafetz, G.R. (1993), *Gorbachev, reform, and the Brezhnev doctrine: Soviet policy toward Eastern Europe, 1985–1990*, London: Praeger Publishers.

Childs, D. (1987), *East Germany to the 1990s: can it resist glasnost?* London: The Economist.

Cipkowski, P. (1991), *Revolution in Eastern Europe*, Chichester: John Wiley & Sons.

Cipolla, C.M. (ed.) (1976), *The Fontana economic history of Europe vol.5: the contemporary economies, part two*, London: Collins/Fontana.

Clegg, N. (1993), 'Hungary's privatisation falters after flying start', *Financial Times*, 19 October.

Clough, S.B., T. Moodie and C. Moodie (eds) (1969), *Economic history of Europe: twentieth century*, London: Macmillan.

Cohen, D. (1991), 'The solvency of Eastern Europe' in European Commission, *European Economy: The path of reform in Central and Eastern Europe*, Brussels: EEC.

Collins, S.M. and D. Rodrik (1992), *Eastern Europe and the Soviet Union in the world economy*, Washington DC: Institute for International Economics.

Condliffe, J.B. (1941), *The reconstruction of world trade: a survey of international economic relations*, London: Allen & Unwin.

Constantinescu, N.N. (1964), 'The exploitation and pillage of the Romanian economy by Hitler Germany in 1939–44', *Revue Roumaine d'Histoire*, 3.

Cottrell, P.L. (1983), 'Aspects of western equity investment in the banking systems of East Central Europe', in A. Teichova and P.L. Cottrell (eds), *International Business and Central Europe, 1918–1939*, Leicester: Leicester University Press.

Coyle, D. (1992), 'Eastern Europe', *Investor's Chronicle*, 1 May.

Crampton, R.J. (1987), *A short history of modern Bulgaria*, Cambridge: Cambridge University Press.

Crawshaw, S. (1992), *Goodbye to the USSR: the collapse of Soviet power*, London: Bloomsbury.

Cupitt, R.T. (1993), 'The political economy of arms exports in post-communist societies: The case of Poland and the CSFR', *Communist and Post-Communist Studies*, 26.

Cviic, C. (1992), *Remaking the Balkans*, London: Pinter.

Daly, E. (1994), 'Serbs query economic miracle', *The Independent*, 30 April.

Danaillow, G.T. (1932), *Les effects de la guerre en Bulgarie*, Paris: Presses Universitaires de France.

Davis, J.S. (1920), 'World currency experience during the war and in 1919', *Review of Economics and Statistics*, 2.

Davis, J.S. (1923), 'Economic and financial progress in Europe', *Review of Economics and Statistics*, 5.

Davis, J.S. (1924), 'Economic and financial progress in Europe 1923–24', *Review of Economics and Statistics*, 6.

Davis, J.S. (1925), 'Economic and financial progress in Europe 1924–25', *Review of Economics and Statistics*, 7.

Davy, R. (1992), *European détente: a reappraisal*, London: The Royal Institute of International Affairs.

Dawisha, K. (1990), *Eastern Europe, Gorbachev and reform*, Cambridge: Cambridge University Press, 2nd edition.

Dawisha, K. and P. Hanson (eds) (1981), *Soviet–East European dilemmas: Coercion, competition and consent*, London: Heinemann.

De Nevers, R. (1990), *The Soviet Union and Eastern Europe: the end of an era*, London: The International Institute for Strategic Studies.

Deldycke, T., H. Gelders and J.M. Limbor (1968), *The working population and its structure: international historical statistics*. Vol. I, Brussels: Université Libre de Bruxelles.

Denekas, D.G. and M.S. Khan (1991), *The Romanian economic reform programme*, Washington DC: IMF.

Denton, N. (1993a), 'Poised on the verge of recovery', *Financial Times*, 17 November.

Denton, N. (1993b), 'Starting from scratch', *Financial Times*, 18 October.

Djordjevic, D. (1992), 'The Yugoslav Phenomenon', in J. Held (ed.), *The Columbia History of Eastern Europe in the Twentieth Century*, New York: Columbia University Press.

Dockrill, M.L. and J.D. Goold (1981), *Peace without promise: Britain and the Paris Peace Conference, 1919–1923*, London: Batsford.

Doder, D. (1993), 'Yugoslavia: new war, old hatreds', *Foreign Policy*, no.91.

Donald, R. (1928), *The tragedy of Trianon*, London: Thornton Butterworth.

Dovring, F. (1965), *Land and labour in Europe in the twentieth century*, The Hague: Nijhoff.

Drabek, Z. (1985), 'Foreign trade performance and policy', in M.C. Kaser and E.A. Radice (eds) *The economic history of Eastern Europe, 1919–1975. Vol. I. Economic structure and performance between the wars*, Oxford: Oxford University Press.

Dragnich, A.N. (1983), *The first Yugoslavia: search for a viable political system*, Stanford, Ca.: Hoover Institution Press.

Drewnowski, J. (1982), *Crisis in the East European economy: the spread of the Polish disease*, London: Croom Helm.

Dubček, A. (1993), *Hope dies last: the autobiography of Alexander Dubček*. London, Harper Collins.

Dunne, H. (1994), 'Polish reach accord to cancel 42pc of debt', *The Daily Telegraph*, 12 March.

Dyker, D.A. (1990), *Yugoslavia: socialism, development and debt*, London: Routledge.

Economist (1938a), 'Germany's clearing debts', 3 December.

Economist (1938b), 'Germany's trade offensive', 5 November.

Economist (1938c), 'Great Germany and South-eastern Europe', 14 May.

Economist (1939a), 'The fight for Romanian trade', 3 June.

Economist (1939b), 'Jugoslavia's self-sufficiency', 2 September.

Economist (1993), 'One little piggy went to market – but starved', 27 November.

Economist (1994), 'The sanctions alternative', 12 February.

Ehrlich, E. (1973), 'Infrastructure and an international comparison of relationships with indicators of development in Eastern Europe, 1920–1950', *Oxford Papers in East European Economics*, 33.

Ehrlich, E. (1985), 'Infrastructure', in M.C. Kaser and E.A. Radice (eds), *The economic history of Eastern Europe, 1919–1975. Vol. I. Economic structure and performance between the wars*, Oxford: Oxford University Press.

Eichengreen, B. (1992a), 'The origins and nature of the Great Slump revisited', *Economic History Review*, 45.

Eichengreen, B. (1992b), *Golden fetters: the gold standard and the great depression, 1919–1939*, Oxford: Oxford University Press.

Einzig, P. (1935), *World finance since 1914*, London: Kegan Paul, Trench, Trubner.

Einzig, P. (1938), *Bloodless invasion: German economic penetration into the Danubian states and the Balkans*, London: Duckworth.

Ellis, H.S. (1939), 'Exchange control in Austria and Hungary', *Journal of Economics*, 54.

Ellis, H.S. (1941), *Exchange control in central Europe*, Cambridge, Mass.: Harvard University Press.

Eyal, J. (1993), 'Blackballed by the Nato club', *The Independent*, 8 December.

Fairhall, D. (1994), 'Eternally optimistic British commanders build peace out of Bosnian conflict's dying spasms', *The Guardian*, 5 April.

Fallenbuchl, Z.M. (1986), 'East–West trade in capital goods since 1970', *Studies in Comparative Communism*, XIX.

Falush, P. (1976a), 'The Hungarian hyperinflation of 1945–46', *National Westminster Bank Quarterly Review*, August.

Falush, P. (1976b), 'The monetary collapse of the Hungarian pengo', *International Currency Review*, 8.

Financial Times (1990), 'East Europe in ferment', 24 January.

Financial Times (1992), 'The post-postwar era', 2 September.

Fischer-Galati, S. (1970), *Twentieth century Romania*, New York: Columbia University Press.

Fischer-Galati, S. (1992), 'Eastern Europe in the Twentieth Century: "Old Wine in New Bottles"', in J. Held (ed.), *The Columbia History of Eastern Europe in the twentieth century*, New York: Columbia University Press.

Fishburn, D. (1994), *The world in 1994*, London: *The Economist* Publications.

Fisher, A.G.B. (1939), 'The German trade drive in South-eastern Europe', *International Affairs*, 18.

Fowkes, B. (1993), *The rise and fall of communism in Eastern Europe*, London: Macmillan.

Friedman, P. (1974), *The impact of trade destruction on national incomes: a study of Europe, 1924–1938*, Gainsville: University Presses of Florida.

Friedman, P. (1976), 'The welfare costs of bilateralism: German–Hungarian trade 1933–38', *Explorations in Economic History*, 13.

Friedman, P. (1978), 'An econometric model of national income, commercial policy and the level of international trade: the open economies of Europe, 1924–1938', *Journal of Economic History*, 38.

Frydman, R., A. Rapaczynski and J.S. Earle (1993), *The privatisation process in Eastern Europe*, London: Central European University Press.

Galbraith, J.K. (1989), 'Assault', *The Guardian*, 16 December.

Gati, G. (1990), *The bloc that failed: Soviet–East European relations in transition*, Indianapolis: Indiana University Press.

Gerschenkron, A. (1966), *Economic backwardness in historical perspective*, London: Pall Mall Press.

Gilberg, T. (1992), 'The multiple legacies of history: Romania in the year 1990', in J. Held (ed.), *The Columbia history of eastern Europe in the twentieth century*, New York: Columbia University Press.

Gitz, B.R. (1992), *Armed forces and political power in Eastern Europe*, New York: Greenwood.

Glenny, M. (1993), *The fall of Yugoslavia*, London: Penguin, 2nd edition.

Glenny, M. (1993), *The rebirth of history: Eastern Europe in the age of democracy*, London: Penguin, 2nd edition.

Gomulka, S. (1986), *Growth, innovation and reform in Eastern Europe*, Brighton: Wheatsheaf.

Good, D.F. (1984), *The economic rise of the Habsburg Empire, 1750–1914*, Berkeley, Ca.: University of California Press.

Good, D.F. (1993), 'The economic lag of Central and Eastern Europe: Evidence from the late nineteenth-century Hapsburg Empire', *Working papers in Austrian Studies*, 93–7, College of Liberal Arts, University of Minnesota.

Gordon, R.J. (1982), 'Why stopping inflation may be costly: evidence from fourteen historical episodes', in R.E. Hall (ed.), *Inflation: causes and effects*, Chicago: University of Chicago Press.

Gorecki, R. (1935), *Poland and her economic development*, London: Allen & Unwin.

Greenberg, S. (1993), 'Czechs to face moment of truth', *The Guardian*, 30 October.

Griffith, W.E. (ed.) (1989), *Central and Eastern Europe: the opening curtain?* Boulder, Col.: Westview Press.

Gruber, J. (1924), *Czechoslovakia: a survey of economic and social conditions*, New York: Macmillan.

Gustafson, T. and D. Yergin (1993), *Russia 2010: What it means for the world*, London: Random House.

Halasz, A. (1928), *New Central Europe in economical maps*, Budapest: R. Gergely.

Halecki, O. (1978), *A history of Poland*, London: Routledge & Kegan Paul.

Hanak, P. (1992), 'Hungary 1918–1945', in J. Held (ed.), *The Columbia history of Eastern Europe in the twentieth century*, New York: Columbia University Press.

Harris, S.E. (1936), *Exchange depreciation: its theory and its history 1931–35, with some consideration of related domestic policies*, Cambridge: Mass.: Harvard University Press.

Hauner, M. (1986), 'Military budgets and the armaments industry', in M.C. Kaser and E.A. Radice (eds), *The economic history of Eastern Europe 1919–1975. Vol. II. Interwar policy, the war and reconstruction*, Oxford: Oxford University Press.

Heilperin, M.A. (1931), *Le problème monétaire d'après-guerre et sa solution en Pologne, en Autriche et en Tchécoslovaquie*, Paris: Recueil Sirey.

Held, J. (1980), *The modernization of agriculture: rural transformation in Hungary 1848–1975* (East European monographs 63), New York: Columbia University Press.

Held, J. (ed.) (1992), *The Columbia history of Eastern Europe in the twentieth century*, New York: Columbia University Press.

Heller, A. and F. Feher (1990), *From Yalta to glasnost*, London: Blackwell.

Hertz, F. (1947), *The economic problem of the Danubian states. A study in economic nationalism*, London: Gollancz.

Heuser, H. (1939), *Control of international trade*, London: Routledge.

Hiden, J. (1977), *Germany and Europe 1919–1939*, London: Longman.

Hilton Young E. (1924), *Report on financial conditions in Poland*, London: Waterloo & Sons.

Hocevar, T. (1965), *The structure of the Slovenian economy 1848–1963*, New York: Studia Slovenica.

Hockenos, P. (1993), *Free to hate: The rise of the right in post-communist Eastern Europe*, London: Routledge.

Hoffman, E. (1993), *Exit into History: a journey through the new Eastern Europe*, London: Heinemann.

Hohensee, H. (1993), 'The return to diversity in Eastern Europe', *Contemporary European history*, 2.

Holloway, D. and M.O. Sharp (eds) (1984), *The Warsaw Pact: alliance in transition?* London: Macmillan.

Holzman, F.D. (1987), *The economics of Soviet bloc trade and finance*. Boulder, Col.: Westview Press.

Hooker, L. (1993), 'Western group plugs into Hungarian phone network', *The Guardian*, 20 December.

Hoptner, J.B. (1962), *Yugoslavia in crisis, 1934–1941*, New York: Columbia University Press.

Horsman, G. (1988), *Inflation in the twentieth century: evidence from Europe and North America*, Hemel Hempstead: Harvester-Wheatsheaf.

Howerd, M. (1989), 'The legacy of the first world war', in R. Boyce and E.M. Robertson (eds), *Paths to war: new essays on the origins of the second world war*, Basingstoke: Macmillan.

Hughes, G. and P. Hare (1991), 'Competitiveness and industrial restructuring in Czechoslovakia, Hungary and Poland', *European Economy*, 2.

Hutchings, R.L. (1983), *Soviet–East European relations: consolidation and conflict, 1968–1980*, Madison: University of Wisconsin Press.

IMF (1993), *World economic outlook*, Washington DC: IMF, May.

IMF Survey (1993), 'Seminar explores sequencing of reforms in former socialist economies', 11 January.

Irvine, J.A. (1993), *The great question: partisan politics in the formation of the Yugoslav socialist state*, Boulder, Col.: Westview Press.

Irving, D. (1978), *The war path: Hitler's Germany 1933–9*, London: Michael Joseph.

Jack, D.T. (1927), *The restoration of European currencies*, London: P.S. King & Son.

Jackson, M.R. and J.R. Lampe (1983), 'The evidence of industrial growth in South Eastern Europe before the second world war', *East European Quarterly*, 16.

Jacobs, R.L. (1977), 'Hyperinflation and the supply of money', *Journal of Money, Credit and Banking*, 9.

Jacobson, J. (1983), 'Is there a new international history of the 1920s?', *American Historical Journal*, 88.

Janos, C. (1982), *The politics of backwardness in Hungary 1825–1945*, Princeton: Princeton University Press.

Jaszi, O. (1929), *The dissolution of the Habsburg monarchy*, Chicago: University of Chicago Press.

Jaszi, O. (1935), 'The economic crisis in the Danubian states', *Social Research*, 2.

Jedruszczak, H. (1972), 'Land reform and economic development in the people's democracies of Europe', *Studia Historiae Oeconomicae*, 7.

Jeffries, I. (1993), *Socialist economies and the transition to the market: a guide*, London: Routledge.

Jeffries, I. (ed.) (1992), *Industrial reform in socialist countries: from restructuring to revolution*, Aldershot: Edward Elgar.

Jelavich, B. (1983), *History of the Balkans. Vol. 2 twentieth century*, Cambridge: Cambridge University Press.

Jelavich, C. and B. (1977), *The establishment of the Balkan national states, 1804–1920*. Seattle: University of Washington Press.

Job, C. (1993), 'Yugoslavia's ethnic furies', *Foreign Policy*, no.92.

Johnson, B. (1993), 'Europe's new iron curtain', *The Sunday Telegraph*, 7 November.

Johnson, D. and L. Miles (1994), *Eastern Europe: economic challenges and business opportunities*, Hull: Hidcote Press.

Johnson, O.V. (1985), *Slovakia 1918–1938: education and the making of a nation*, New York: Columbia University Press.

Johnson, P.M. (1989), *Redesigning the communist economy: the politics of economic reform in Eastern Europe*, Berkeley: University of California Press.

Joint Committee Report (1986), *East European economies: slow growth in the 1980s*, Washington DC: Government Printing Office.

Jones, F. Elwyn (1937), *Hitler's drive to the East*, London: Gollancz.

Joseph, P. (ed.) (1987), *The economies of Eastern Europe and their foreign economic relations*, Brussels: NATO.

Kaiser, D.E. (1980), *Economic diplomacy and the origins of the second world war: Germany, Britain, France and Eastern Europe, 1930–1939*, Princeton: Princeton University Press.

Kanet, R.E., D.N. Miner and T.J. Resler (1992), *Soviet foreign policy in transition*, Cambridge: Cambridge University Press.

Kaser, M.C. and E.A. Radice (eds) (1985), *The economic history of Eastern Europe 1919–1975. Vol I. Economic structure and performance between the wars*, Oxford: Oxford University Press.

Kaser, M.C. and E.A. Radice (eds) (1986), *The economic history of Eastern Europe 1919–1975. Vol. II. Interwar policy, the war and reconstruction*, Oxford: Oxford University Press.

Kaser, M.C. (ed.) (1986), *The economic history of Eastern Europe 1919–1975 Vol. III. Institutional change within a planned economy*, Oxford: Oxford University Press.

Kavan, Z. and B. Wheaton (1993), *The velvet revolution: Czechoslovakia 1988–1991*, Boulder, Col.: Westview Press.

Kavka, F. (1960), *An outline of Czechoslovak history*, Prague: Orbis.

Keegan, W. (1993), *The spectre of capitalism: the future of the world economy after the fall of communism*, London: Vintage.

Kemeny, G. (1952), *Economic planning in Hungary 1947–1949*, London: Royal Institute of International Affairs.

Kerek, M. (1940), 'Agricultural land reform in Hungary', *Hungarian Quarterly*, 6.

Keren, M. and G. Ofer (1993), *Trials of transition: Economic reform in the former communist bloc*, Boulder, Col.: Westview Press.

Keynes, J.M. (1919), *The economic consequences of the peace*, London: Macmillan.

Keynes, J.M. (1922), *A revision of the treaty*, London: Macmillan.

Kiraly, B.K., P. Pastor and I. Sanders (eds) (1982), *War and society in East Central Europe, Vol. VI: Essays on world war I: total war and peacemaking, a case study of Trianon*, New York: Brooklyn College Press.

Kirk, D. (1946), *Europe's population in the interwar years*, Geneva: League of Nations.

Kitchen, M. (1988), *Europe between the wars: a political history*, London: Longman.

Kofman, J. (1981), 'The political role of big business circles in Poland between the two world wars', *Acta Poloniae Historica*, 43.

Kofman, J. (1990), 'Economic nationalism in East–Central Europe in the interwar period', in H. Szlajfer (ed.), *Economic nationalism in East–Central Europe and South America*, Geneva: Droz.

Kolodko, G.W. (1993), 'From recession to growth in post-communist economies: expectations versus reality', *Communist and Post-Communist Studies*, 26.

Komlos, J. (1983), *The Habsburg monarchy as a customs union*, Princeton: Princeton University Press.

Komlos, J. (1989), *Nutrition and economic development in the eighteenth-century Habsburg Monarchy: an anthropometric study*, Princeton: Princeton University Press.

Korbonski, A. (1992), 'Poland: 1918–1990', in J. Held (ed.), *The Columbia history of Eastern Europe in the twentieth century*, New York: Columbia University Press.

Koszui, J.P. (1932), *Les efforts de restauration financière de la Bulgarie (1922–1931)*, Paris: Presses Universitaires de France.

Koves, A. (1985), *The CMEA countries in the world economy: Turning inwards or turning outwards*, Budapest: Akademiai Kiado.

Koves, A. (1992), *Central and East European economies in transition*, Boulder, Col.: Westview Press.

Kozminski, A.K. (1992), 'Transition from planned to market economy: Hungary and Poland compared', *Studies in Comparative Communism*, XXV.

Kramer, J.M. (1991), 'Eastern Europe and the "energy shock" of 1990–91', *Problems in Communism*, XL.

Kramer, M. (1992), 'Eastern Europe goes to market', *Foreign Policy*, no.86.

Krejci, J. (1977), 'The Czechoslovak economy during the years of systematic transformation 1945–49', *Jahrbuch der Wirtschaft Osteuropas*, 7.

Krushelnycky, A. (1994), 'Hope that died in a shellblast', *The European*, 11–17 February.

Kulischer, E.M. (1948), *Europe on the move: war and population changes 1917–1947*, New York: Columbia University Press.

Lampe, J. (1989), 'Imperial borderlands or capitalist periphery? Redefining Balkan backwardness, 1520–1914', in D. Chirot (ed.), *The origins of backwardness in Eastern Europe: Economics and politics from the Middle Ages until the early twentieth century*, Berkeley: University of California Press.

Lampe, J.R. (1980), 'Unifying the Yugoslav economy 1918–1921: misery and early misunderstandings', in D. Djordjevic (ed.), *The creation of Yugoslavia, 1914–18*. Santa Barbara, Ca.: Clio Books.

Lampe, J.R. (1986), *The Bulgarian economy in the twentieth century*, London: Croom Helm.

Lampe, J.R. and M.R. Jackson (1982), *Balkan economic history 1550–1950*, Bloomington: Indiana University Press.

Landau, Z. (1983), 'Inflation in Poland after world war I', in N. Schmukler and E. Marcus (eds), *Inflation through the ages*, New York: Brooklyn College Press.

Landau, Z. (1984), 'Poland's finance policy in the years of the Great Depression (1930–35),', *Acta Poloniae Historica*, 49.

Landau, Z. (1992), 'The economic integration of Poland, 1918–23', in P. Latawski (ed.), *The reconstruction of Poland, 1914–23*, Basingstoke: Macmillan.

Landau, Z. and J. Tomaszewski (1985), *The Polish economy in the twentieth century*, London: Croom Helm.

League of Nations (1920), *Currencies after the war: a survey of conditions in various countries*, Geneva: League of Nations.

League of Nations (1922), *The general transport situation in 1921*, Geneva: League of Nations.

League of Nations (1926), *The financial reconstruction of Hungary*, Geneva: League of Nations.

League of Nations (1927), *Tariff level indices*, Geneva: League of Nations.

League of Nations (1928), *Bulgarian stabilization loan*, Geneva: League of Nations.

League of Nations (1930a), *Economic work of the League of Nations: report and draft resolution presented by the second committee to the assembly*, Geneva: League of Nations.

League of Nations (1930b), *Principles and methods of financial reconstruction work undertaken under the auspices of the League of Nations*, Geneva: League of Nations.

League of Nations (1931), *The agricultural crisis*, 2 vols, Geneva: League of Nations.

League of Nations (1932a), *Conference for the restoration of Central and Eastern Europe*, Stresa: League of Nations.

League of Nations (1932b), *World economic survey, 1931–32*, Geneva: League of Nations.

League of Nations (1933a), *World economic survey, 1932–33*, Geneva: League of Nations.

League of Nations (1933b), *World production and prices, 1925–1932*, Geneva: League of Nations.

League of Nations (1935a), *Enquiry into clearing agreements*, Geneva: League of Nations.

League of Nations (1935b), *World economic survey 1934–35*, Geneva: League of Nations.

League of Nations (1937), *Money and banking 1936/37*, Geneva: League of Nations.

League of Nations (1938), *Report on exchange control*, Geneva: League of Nations.

League of Nations (1939a), *European conference on rural life 1939: the capital and income of farms in Europe as they appear from farm accounts for the years 1927–28 to 1934–35*, Geneva: League of Nations.

League of Nations (1939b), *European conference on rural life 1939: population and agriculture with special reference to agricultural overpopulation*, Geneva: League of Nations.

League of Nations (1941), *Europe's trade*, Geneva: League of Nations.

League of Nations (1942a), *Commercial policy in the interwar period*, Geneva: League of Nations.

League of Nations (1942b), *The network of world trade*, Geneva: League of Nations.

League of Nations (1943a), *Agricultural production in continental Europe during the 1914–18 war and the reconstruction period*, Geneva: League of Nations.

League of Nations (1943b), *Europe's overseas needs 1919–1920 and how they were met*, Geneva: League of Nations.

League of Nations (1943c), *Quantitative trade controls: their causes and nature*, Geneva: League of Nations.

League of Nations (1943d), *Relief deliveries and relief loans 1919–1923*, Geneva: League of Nations.

League of Nations (1943e), *The transition from war to peace economy: report of the delegation on economic depressions Part I*, Geneva: League of Nations.

League of Nations (1943f), *Trade relations between free market and controlled economies*, Geneva: League of Nations.

League of Nations (1944), *International currency experience: lessons of the interwar period*, Geneva: League of Nations.

League of Nations (1945a), *Economic stability in the postwar world: report of the delegation on economic depression Part II*, Geneva: League of Nations.

League of Nations (1945b), *Industrialisation and foreign trade*, Geneva: League of Nations.

League of Nations (1945c), *League of Nations reconstruction schemes in the interwar period*, Geneva: League of Nations.

League of Nations (1945d), *Transport problems which arose from the war of 1914–18 and the work of restoration undertaken in this field by the League of Nations*, Geneva: League of Nations.

League of Nations (1946a), *The course and control of inflation: a review of monetary experience in Europe after world war I*, Geneva: League of Nations.

League of Nations (1946b), *Food, famine and relief 1940–46*, Geneva: League of Nations.

Lee, C.H. (1969), 'The effects of the depression on primary producing countries', *Journal of Contemporary History*, 4.

Lee, S.J. (1987), *The European dictatorships 1918–1945*, London: Methuen.

Leslie, R.F. (ed.) (1980), *The history of Poland since 1863*, Cambridge: Cambridge University Press.

Lethbridge, E. (1985), 'National income and product', in M.C. Kaser and E.A. Radice (eds), *The economic history of Eastern Europe 1919–1975. Vol I. Economic structure and performance between the wars*, Oxford: Oxford University Press.

Lewis, W.A. (1949), *Economic survey 1919–1939*, London: Allen & Unwin.

Liepmann, K. (1938), *Tariff levels and the economic unity of Europe*, London: Allen & Unwin.

Lodge, O. (1941), *Peasant Life in Jugoslavia*, London: Seeley, Service & Co. Ltd.

Logio, G.C. (1932), *Rumania: its history, politics and economics*, Manchester: Sherratt and Hughes.

Logio, G.C. (1936), *Bulgaria: past and present*, Manchester: Sherratt and Hughes.

Loveday, A. (1931), *Britain and world trade*, London: Longmans Green.

Macartney, C.A. (1934), *National states and national minorities*, Oxford: Oxford University Press.

Macartney, C.A. (1937), *Hungary and her successors: the Treaty of Trianon and its consequences 1919–1937*, London: Oxford University Press.

Macartney, C.A. (1939), *The Danube Basin*, Oxford: Clarendon Press. Oxford Pamphlets on World Affairs, no. 10.

Macartney, C.A. (1942), *Problems of the Danube Basin*, Cambridge: Cambridge University Press.

Macartney, C.A. and A.W. Palmer (1962), *Independent Eastern Europe*, London: Macmillan.

Maddison, A. (1973), *Economic policy and performance in Europe, 1913–1970*, London: Collins/Fontana.

Madgearu, V. (1930), *Rumania's new economic policy*, London: P.S. King.

Magas, B. (1993), *The destruction of Yugoslavia: tracing the break-up 1980–92*, London: Verso.

Maier, C.S. (1979), 'The truth about the treaties', *Journal of Modern History*, 51, March.

Maier, C.S. (1981), 'The two postwar eras and the conditions for stability in twentieth century Western Europe', *American Historical Review*, 86.

Major, I. (1993), *Privatization in Eastern Europe: A critical approach*, Aldershot: Edward Elgar.

Malcolm, N. (1994a), 'The betrayal of Bosnia', *The Sunday Telegraph*, 23 January.

Malcolm, N. (1994b), *Bosnia: a short history*, London: Macmillan.

Marks, S. (1976), *The illusion of peace: international relations in Europe 1918–1933*, London: Macmillan.

Marrese, M. and J. Vanous (1983), *Soviet subsidization of trade with Eastern Europe*, Berkeley: University of California Press.

Marsh, V. and A. Robinson (1994), 'Bulgaria closer to debt reduction pact', *Financial Times*, 29 March.

Marshall, A. (1994), 'EU drives east towards a "greater Europe"', *The Guardian*, 29 January.

Mason, D.S. (1992), *Revolution in East-Central Europe: the rise and fall of communism and the cold war*, Boulder, Col.: Westview Press.

Mastropasqua, C. and V. Rolli (1993), 'Industrial countries' protectionism with respect to Eastern Europe: The impact of the Association Agreement concluded with the EC on the exports of Poland, Czechoslovakia and Hungary', *Temi di discussione del Servizio Studi*, no.188, Gennaio: Banca d'Italia.

McElvoy, A. (1992), *The saddled cow: East Germany's life and legacy*, London: Faber and Faber.

McRae, H. (1994), 'EBRD faces a life out of the limelight', *The Independent*, 19 April.

Millar, P. (1992), 'Czecho..slovakia', *The Sunday Times*, 21 June.

Milward, A. (1977), *War, Economy and Society, 1939–1945*, London, Allen Lane.

Mitrany, D. (1930), *Land and the peasant in Rumania: the war and agrarian reform (1917–1921)*, London: Oxford University Press.

Mitrany, D. (1936), *The effect of the war in Southeastern Europe*, New Haven: Yale University Press.

Mitrany, D. (1948), 'Land tenure: Eastern Europe and Near East', *Encyclopedia of the Social Sciences*, 9.

Mlynarski, F. (1926), *The international significance of the depreciation of the zloty in 1925*, Warsaw: The Polish Economist.

Mocsy, I.I. (1983), *War and society in East Central Europe*, Vol. XII. *The effects of world war I. The uprooted: Hungarian refugees and their impact on Hungary's domestic politics, 1918–1921*, New York: Brooklyn College Press.

Momtchiloff, N. (1944), *Ten years of controlled trade in South-eastern Europe*, Cambridge: Cambridge University Press.

Montias, J.M. (1966), 'Economic nationalism in Eastern Europe: forty years of continuity and change', *Journal of International Affairs*, 20.

Montefiore, S.S. (1994), 'Cult of horror-story heroes', *The Sunday Telegraph*, 16 January.

Moore, W.E. (1945), *Economic demography in Eastern and Southern Europe*, Geneva: League of Nations.

Morgan, O.S. (ed.) (1933), *Agricultural systems of Middle Europe*, New York: Macmillan.

Mortimer, E. (1990), 'From Yalta to Ditchley', *Financial Times*, 26 June.

Moulton, H.G. and L. Pasvolsky (1932), *War debts and world prosperity*, Washington DC: Brookings Institution.

Munk, F. (1940), *The economics of force*, New York: George W. Stewart.

Munting, R. (1972), 'A comparative survey of land reforms after the first world war', *Oxford Papers in East European Economics*, 18.

Myant, M. (1993), *Transforming socialist economies: the case of Poland and Czechoslovakia*, Aldershot: Edward Elgar.

Newman, K.J. (1970), *European democracy between the wars*, London: Allen & Unwin.

Newman, W.J. (1968), *The balance of power in the interwar years, 1919–1939*, New York: Random House.

North, D.C. (1962), 'International capital movements in historical perspective', in R.F. Mikesell (ed.), *U.S. private and government investment abroad*, Eugene: University of Oregon Books.

Nötel, R. (1974), 'International capital movements and finance in Eastern Europe, 1919–1949', *Vierteljahrschrift für Sozial- und Wirtschaftsgeschichte*, 61.

Nötel, R. (1984), 'Money, banking and industry in interwar Austria and Hungary', *Journal of European Economic History*, 13.

Nötel, R. (1986), 'International credit and finance', in M.C. Kaser and E.A. Radice (eds), *The economic history of Eastern Europe 1919–1975. Vol. II. Interwar policy, the war and reconstruction*, Oxford: Oxford University Press.

Notestein, F.W. et al. (1944), *The future population of Europe and the Soviet Union*, Geneva: League of Nations.

Oaky, R. (1990), *Crisis in Eastern Europe: roots and prospects*, London: The Social Market Foundation.

Orde, A. (1990), *British policy and European reconstruction after the first world war*, Cambridge: Cambridge University Press.

Organization for European Economic Cooperation (OEEC) (1960), *Industrial Statistics, 1900–1959*, Paris: OEEC.

Overy, R. (1989), *The road to war*, London: Macmillan.

Panic, M. (1994), 'Self-interest the key to peaceful Balkans', *The European*, 1–7 January.

Parker, J. (1993), 'A survey of Eastern Europe', *The Economist*, 13 March.

Pasvolsky, L. (1928), *Economic nationalism of the Danubian states*, London: Allen & Unwin.

Pasvolsky, L. (1930), *Bulgaria's economic position*, Washington DC: Brookings Institution.

Pearson, R. (1983), *National minorities in Eastern Europe 1848–1945*, London: Macmillan.

Perman, D. (1962), *The shaping of the Czechoslovak state. Diplomatic history of the boundaries of Czechoslovakia, 1914–1920*, Leiden: E.J. Brill.

Political and Economic Planning (1945), *Economic development in S.E. Europe*, London: Political and Economic Planning.

Pollard, S. (1981), *Peaceful conquest: the industrialisation of Europe 1760–1970*, Oxford: Oxford University Press.

Polonsky, A. (1975), *The little dictators: the history of Eastern Europe since 1918*, London: Routledge & Kegan Paul.

Pomery, C. (1994), 'Czechs become nation of share chasers', *The European*, 18–24 March.

Pond, E. (1993), *Beyond the wall: Germany's road to unification*, London: Brookings Institution.

Ponikowski, W. (1930), 'Polish agricultural land organisation since the world war', *Annals of the American Academy of Political and Social Science*, 150.

Pravda, A. (ed.) (1992), *The end of the outer empire: Soviet–East European relations in transition, 1985–90*, London: Royal Institute of International Affairs.

Prestina, D. (1992), *Regional development in Communist Yugoslavia: Success, failure and consequences*, Boulder, Col.: Westview Press.

Pryor, Z.P. (1973), 'Czechoslovak economic development in the interwar period', in V.S. Mamatey and R. Luza (eds), *A history of the Czechoslovak Republic 1918–1948*, Princeton: Princeton University Press.

Pryor, Z.P. (1979), 'Czechoslovak fiscal policies in the great depression', *Economic History Review*, 32.

Pryor, Z.P. and F.L. Pryor (1975), 'Foreign trade and interwar Czechozlovak economic development 1918–1938', *Vierteljahrschrift für Sozial- und Wirtshaftsgeschichte*, 62.

Pundeff, M. (1992), 'Bulgaria', in J. Held (ed.), *The Columbia history of Eastern Europe in the twentieth century*, New York: Columbia University Press.

Radice, E.A. (1986), 'Territorial changes, population movements and labour supplies', in M.C. Kaser and E.A. Radice (eds), *The economic history of Eastern Europe, 1919–1975. Vol. II. Interwar policy, the war and reconstruction*, Oxford: Oxford University Press.

Rady, M. (1992), *Romania in turmoil: A contemporary history*, London: I.B. Tauris.

Ranki, G. (1964), 'Problems of the development of Hungarian industry 1900–44', *Journal of Economic History*, 24.

Ranki, G. (1983a), *Economic and foreign policy: the struggle of the great powers for the hegemony of the Danube Valley 1919–1939*, New York: Columbia University Press.

Ranki, G. (1983b), 'Inflation in Hungary', in N. Schmukler and E. Marcus (eds), *Inflation through the ages*, New York: Brooklyn College Press.

Ranki, G. (1983c), 'Inflation in post-World War I East-Central Europe', in N. Schmukler and E. Marcus (eds), *Inflation through the ages*, New York: Brooklyn College Press.

Ranki, G. and J. Tomaszewski (1986), 'The role of the state in industry, banking and trade', in M.C. Kaser and E.A. Radice (eds), *The economic history of Eastern Europe, 1919–1975. Vol. II. Interwar policy, the war and reconstruction*, Oxford: Oxford University Press.

Rasin, A. (1923), *Financial policy of Czechoslovakia during the first year of its history*, London: Clarendon Press.

Ratesh, N. (1991), *Romania: The entangled revolution*, London: Praeger Publishers.

Raupach, H. (1969), 'The impact of the great depression in Eastern Europe', *Journal of Contemporary History*, 4.

Rees-Mogg, W. (1993), 'Russia's bad tidings', *The Times*, 16 December.

Revenz, G. (1990), *Perestroika in Eastern Europe: Hungary's economic transformation, 1945–1988*, Boulder, Col.: Westview Press.

Richardson, D. (1990), 'How food has changed the face of Europe', *Financial Times*, 9 January.

Roberts, A. (1992), 'No, Europe is not replaying 1914', *Sunday Telegraph*, 21 June.

Roberts, H.L. (1951), *Rumania: political problems of an agrarian state*, New Haven: Yale University Press.

Robinson, A. (1992), 'Parting is such sweet sorrow', *Financial Times*, 30 December.

Robinson, A. (1993a), 'A rich diet of adjustment', *Financial Times*, 24 March.

Robinson, A. (1993b), 'OECD fears for faltering Romanian reforms', *Financial Times*, 27 July.

Robinson, A. (1993c), 'Bulgaria: re-emerging – if slowly', *Financial Times*, 5 May.

Robinson, A. (1993d), 'Why progress has been slow', *Financial Times*, 5 May.

Robinson, A. (1993e), 'Adventure in statehood', *Financial Times*, 2 November.

Robinson, A. (1994a), 'Meciar skulks in Slovakia's political wings', *Financial Times*, 5 April.

Robinson, A. (1994b), 'Will the boom continue in central Europe?', *Financial Times*, 10 January.

Robinson, A. and N. Denton (1993), 'Clean-up prior to going on sale', *Financial Times*, 15 September.

Robinson, J. et al. (1943), *Were the minorities treaties a failure?* New York: Antin Press.

Rollo, J. and A. Smith (1993), 'The political economy of Eastern Europe's trade with the European Community: Why so sensitive?', *Economic Policy*, 16.

Rose, W.J. (1939), *Poland*, Harmondsworth: Penguin Books.

Roskin, M.G. (1991), *The rebirth of East Europe*, Englewood Cliffs: Prentice Hall.

Rosner, J. (1934), 'Measures to combat the depression and unemployment in Poland', *International Labour Review*, 30.

Ross, G. (1983), *The great powers and the decline of the European states system 1914–1945*, London: Longman.

Roszkowski, W. (1986), 'Poland's economic performance between the two world wars', *East European Quarterly*, 20.

Roszkowski, W. (1987), 'Large estates and small farms in the Polish agrarian economy between the wars (1918–1938)', *Journal of European Economic History*, 16.

Roszkowski, W. (1989), 'The growth of the state sector in the Polish economy in the years 1918–1926', *Journal of European Economic History*, 18.

Rothschild, J. (1974), *East Central Europe between the two world wars*, Seattle: University of Washington Press.

Rothschild, J. (1989), *Return to Diversity. A political history of East Central Europe since world war II*, Oxford: Oxford University Press.

Roucek, J.S. (1932), *Contemporary Roumania and her problems: a study in modern nationalism*, Stanford, Ca.: Stanford University Press.

Roucek, J.S. (1939), *The politics of the Balkans*, New York: McGraw-Hill.

Royal Institute of International Affairs (1936), *The Balkan states: a review of the economic and financial development of Albania, Bulgaria, Greece, Roumania and Yugoslavia since 1919*, London: Oxford University Press.

Royal Institute of International Affairs (1937), *The problem of international investment*, Oxford: Oxford University Press.

Royal Institute of International Affairs (1939), *South Eastern Europe: a political and economic survey*, London: Oxford University Press.

Royal Institute of International Affairs (1940), *South-eastern Europe: a brief survey*, London: Oxford University Press.

Sanders, I.T. (1949), *Balkan Village*, Lexington: University of Kentucky Press.

Schlesinger, R. (1945), *Federalism in Central and Eastern Europe*, London: Kegan Paul, Trench, Trubner.

Schönfeld, R. (1975), 'Die Balkanländer in der Weltwirtschaftskrise', *Vierteljahrschrift für Sozial- und Wirtschaftsgeschichte*, 62.

Schopflin, G. (1993), *Politics in Eastern Europe 1945–1992*, Oxford: Blackwell.

Schwartz, H. (1973), *Eastern Europe in the Soviet shadow*, London: Abelard-Schuman.

Selbourne, D. (1990), *Death of the dark hero: Eastern Europe 1987–90*, London: Jonathan Cape.

Selucky, R. (1991), 'From capitalism to socialism', in H. Gordon Skilling (ed.), *Czechoslovakia 1918–88: seventy years from independence*, London: Macmillan.

Seton-Watson, H. (1946), *Eastern Europe between the wars 1918–1941*, Cambridge: Cambridge University Press.

Seton-Watson, H. (1950), *The East European revolution*, London: Methuen.

Seton-Watson, H. (1977), *Nations and states*, London: Methuen.

Sharp, A. (1991), *The Versailles settlement: peacemaking in Paris, 1919*, Basingstoke: Macmillan.

Shen, R. (1992), *The Polish economy: legacies from the past, prospects for the future*, London: Praeger Publishers.

Sherwell, P. (1992), 'Slovakia is born – the poor relation', *The Daily Telegraph*, 31 December.

Silber, L. (1994), 'Small, scenic and flexible', *Financial Times*, 12 April.

Silverman, D.P. (1982), *Reconstructing Europe after the Great War*, Cambridge, Mass.: Harvard University Press.

Simons, T.M. (1993), *Eastern Europe in the postwar world*, Basingstoke: Macmillan, 2nd edition.

Simpson, J. (1992), *The darkness crumbles: despatches from the barricades*, London: Hutchinson, 2nd edition.

Singleton, F. and B. Carter (1982), *The economy of Yugoslavia*, London: Croom Helm.

Skilling, H.G. (1991), *Czechoslovakia 1918–88*, Oxford: Macmillan.

Smith, A.H. (1983), *The planned economies of Eastern Europe*, London: Macmillan.

Smith, L. (1936), 'The zloty, 1924–35', *Journal of Political Economy*, 44.

Sokolovsky, J. (1990), *Peasants and power: state autonomy and the collectivization of agriculture in Eastern Europe*, Oxford: Westview Press.

Somogyi, L. 'Introduction' in L. Somogyi (ed.) (1993), *The political economy of the transition process in Eastern Europe*, Aldershot: Edward Elgar.

Sontag, R.J. (1971), *A broken world, 1919–1939*, New York: Harper & Row.

Spigler, J. (1986), 'Public finance', in M.C. Kaser and E.A. Radice (eds), *The economic history of Eastern Europe 1919–1975. Vol. II, Interwar policy, the war and reconstruction*, Oxford: Oxford University Press.

Spulber, N. (1959), 'The role of the state in economic growth in Eastern Europe since 1860' in H.G. Aitken (ed.), *The state and economic growth*, New York: Social Science Research Council.

Spulber, N. (1966), *The state and economic development in Eastern Europe*, New York: Random House.

Stambrook, F.G. (1963), 'A British proposal for the Danubian states: the customs union project of 1932', *The Slavonic and East European Review*, 42.

Stevens, J.N. (1985), *Czechoslovakia at the crossroads: the economic dilemmas of communism in postwar Czechoslvakia*, New York: Columbia University Press.

Stone, N. (1992), 'The eagle's curse', *The Sunday Times*, 9 August.

Stone, N. (1994), 'US brings hope of Bosnian peace where Europe failed', *The Sunday Times*, 13 March.

Svennilson, I. (1954), *Growth and stagnation in the European economy*, Geneva: United Nations.

Swain, G. and N. (1993), *Eastern Europe since 1945*, London: Macmillan.

Swain, N. (1992), *Hungary: the rise and fall of feasible socialism*, London: Verso.

Sword, K. (ed.) (1990), *The Times guide to Eastern Europe*, London: Times Books.

Syklos, P.L. (1991), 'Fiscal policy and inflationary expectations: the Hungarian tax pengo experiment of 1946', *Journal of European Economic History*, 20.

Sylla, R. and G. Toniolo (eds) (1991), *Patterns of European industrialization: the nineteenth century*, London: Routledge.

Tampke, J. (1983), *The people's republics of Eastern Europe*, London: Croom Helm.

Taylor, J. (1952), *The economic development of Poland 1919–1950*, Ithaca, NY: Cornell University Press.

Teichova, A. (1981), 'Structural changes and industrialisation in interwar Central-East Europe', in P. Bairoch and M. Levy-Leboyer (eds), *Disparities in economic development since the industrial revolution*, London: Macmillan.

Teichova, A. (1983), 'A comparative view of inflation of the 1920s in Austria and Czechoslovakia', in N. Schmukler and E. Marcus (eds), *Inflation through the ages*, New York: Brooklyn College Press.

Teichova, A. (1985), 'Industry', in M.C. Kaser and E.A. Radice (eds), *The economic history of Eastern Europe 1919–1975. Vol. I. Economic structure and performance between the wars*, Oxford: Oxford University Press.

Teichova, A. (1988), *The Czechoslovak economy 1918–1980*, London: Routledge.

Teichova, A. (1989), 'East–Central and South-East Europe 1919–1939', in P. Mathias and S. Pollard (eds), *The Cambridge economic history of Europe. Vol. VIII. The industrial economies: the development of economic and social policies*, Cambridge: Cambridge University Press.

Temperley, H.W.V. (1920), *A history of the Peace Conference of Paris*, Vol. 1, London: Hodder & Stoughton.

Temperley, H.W.V. (1921), *A history of the Peace Conference of Paris*, Vol. IV, London: Hodder & Stoughton.

Tennenbaum, H. (1944), *Central and Eastern Europe in the world economy*, London: Barnard & Westwood.

Thompson, D. (1966), *Europe since Napoleon*, Harmondsworth: Penguin.

Thompson, M. (1992), *A paper house: The ending of Yugoslavia*, London: Vintage.

Tiltman, H.H. (1934), *Peasant Europe*, London: Jarrolds.

Timoshenko, V. (1933, 1983), *World agriculture in depression*, Ann Arbor: University of Michigan. Reprinted by Garland Publishing, New York, 1983.

Tittenbrun, J. (1993), *The collapse of 'real socialism' in Poland*, London: Janus Publishing Company.

Tomasevich, J. (1949), 'Foreign economic relations', in R.J. Kerner (ed.), *Yugoslavia*, Berkeley, Ca.: University of California Press.

Tomasevich, J. (1955), *Peasants, politics and economic change in Yugoslavia*, Stanford, Ca.: Stanford University Press.

Tomaszewski, J. (1977), 'Some problems of the capital formation and investment in the capitalist societies of East–Central Europe', *Acta Poloniae Historica*, 25.

Tracey, M. (1964), *Agriculture in Western Europe: crisis and adaptation since 1880*, London: Cape.

Traynor, I. (1994a), 'Eastern dismay as EU exploits the post-communist markets', *The Guardian*, 1 January.

Traynor, I. (1994b), '"Velvet divorce" brings triumph and tears in its wake', *The Guardian*, 19 March.

Traynor, I. and E. Luce (1994), 'Talks fail to solve war of the maps', *The Guardian*, 20 January.

Trofimov, Y. (1994), 'Visegrad nations join their first Western club', *The European*, 1–7 January.

Turnock, D. (1974), *An economic geography of Romania*, London: G. Bell & Sons.

Turnock, D. (1986), *The Romanian economy in the twentieth century*, London: Croom Helm.

Tyson, L.D. (1980), *The Yugoslav economic system and its performance in the 1970s*, Berkeley: University of California.

United Nations (1947), *Financial needs of devastated countries: interim report*, Lake Success: United Nations.

United Nations (1948), *Foreign exchange position of devastated countries*, New York: United Nations.

United Nations (1949a), *International capital movements during the interwar period*, New York: United Nations.

United Nations (1949b), *Statistical Yearbook 1948*, New York: United Nations.

United Nations (1950), *Economic survey of Europe in 1949*, Geneva: League of Nations.

United Nations (1987), *Economic survey of Europe in 1986–1987*, New York: United Nations.

United Nations (1989), *Economic survey of Europe in 1988–1989*, New York: United Nations.

United Nations (1990), *Economic survey of Europe in 1989–1990*, New York: United Nations.

United Nations (1991a), *Economic survey of Europe in 1990–1991*, New York: United Nations.

United Nations (1991b), *Economic Commission for Europe bulletin*, 43.

United Nations (1992), *Economic survey of Europe in 1991–1992*, New York: United Nations.

Van Brabant, J.M. (1989), *Economic integration in Eastern Europe: a handbook*, London: Harvester-Wheatsheaf.

Volgyes, I. (1991), *Hungary in revolution 1918–1919*, Lincoln: Nebraska University Press.

Vulliamy, E. (1994a), *Seasons in hell: understanding Bosnia's war*, London: Simon & Schuster.

Vulliamy, E. (1994b), 'Sophisticated Sarajevo tortured and broken', *The Guardian*, 10 February.

Wadekin, K.E. (1982), *Agrarian policies in communist Europe*, The Hague: Allanheld, Osmun & Co.

Wallace, W.V. and R.A. Clarke (1986), *Comecon trade and the West*, London: Pinter.

Waller, M. (1993), *The end of the communist power monopoly*, Manchester: Manchester University Press.

Warriner, D. (1940), *Eastern Europe after Hitler*, Fabian Research Series, London: Gollancz.

Warriner, D. (1964), *Economics of peasant farming*, London: Frank Cass, 2nd edition.

Wellisz, L. (1938), *Foreign capital in Poland*, London: Allen & Unwin.

Williams, D. (1963), 'The 1931 financial crisis', *Yorkshire Bulletin of Economic and Social Research*, 15.

Williams, F. (1993), 'E Europe in trouble if Uruguay Round fails', *Financial Times*, 10 December.

Williamson, J. (1993), 'Why did output fall in Eastern Europe?' in L. Somogyi (ed.), *The political economy of the transition process in Eastern Europe*. Aldershot: Edward Elgar.

Wiskemann, E. (1938), *Czechs and Germans: a study of the struggle in the historic provinces of Bohemia and Moravia*, London: Oxford University Press.

Wistrich, R. (1993), 'The rebirth of nationalism', BBC Radio Three series, part 1, December.

Woytinsky, W.S. and E.S. (1953), *World population and production*, New York: Twentieth Century Fund.

Wright, M. (ed.) (1989), *Soviet Union: the challenge of change*, London: Longman.

Wynot, E.D. (1983), *Warsaw between the world wars: profile of the capital city in a developing land, 1919–1939*, East European Monographs, Boulder, Col.: distributed by Columbia University Press, New York.

Yates, P.L. (1959), *Forty years of foreign trade*, London: Allen & Unwin.

Yeager, L.B. (1966), *International monetary relations: theory, history and policy*, New York: Harper & Row.

Yeager, L.B. and Associates (1981), *Experiences with stopping inflation*, Washington DC: American Enterprise Institute.

Yovanovich, D. (1930), *Les effets économiques et sociaux de la guerre en Serbie*, Paris: Presses Universitaires de France.

Zagoroff, S.D. et al. (1955), *The agricultural economy of the Danubian countries 1933–45*, Stanford, Ca.: Stanford University Press.

Zarnowski, J. (ed.) (1983), *Dictatorships in East–central Europe 1918–1939*, Warsaw: Zaklad Navodowy im. Ossoliskich.

Zauberman, A. (1964), *Industrial progress in Poland, Czechoslovakia and East Germany, 1937–1962*, London: Oxford University Press.

Zauberman, A. (1976), 'Russia and Eastern Europe, 1920–1970', in C.M. Cipolla (ed.), *The Fontana Economic History of Europe, Vol.6, Part 2, Contemporary economies*, London: Collins/Fontana.

Zweig, F. (1944), *Poland between the wars: a critical study of social and economic changes*, London: Secker & Warburg.

Index

Afghanistan 170, 193
Agrarian reform 99
Agricultural holdings 27–8
  structure of 74
Agriculture 17, 98, 99
  backwardness of 46–7, 76
  collectivization drive 118–25
  crisis in 72
  debt burden 72, 74
  dependence on 18, 46, 47, 48
  EC boycott 219–20
  efficiency of 73, 76
  export subsidies 66, 75
  farm debts 59–60
    relief of 74
  farm incomes decline 59, 72, 76
  landless labourers 20
  modernization of 75–6
  output 93, 102, 103
  policy 73–5
  price support schemes 75
  problems in 1970s and 1980s 173–4
  productivity levels 46
  recovery of 28
  returns on capital 72
  size of undertakings 19
  structure of holdings 74
  structure of production 75
  surplus manpower 89
  tax burden 45, 46
  technical improvements 75
  terms of trade 72
  weaknesses of 46–8
Agrominimum 122
Albania 88, 132, 139, 143, 220, 231
Allami Vagyonkezelo (AV RT) 215
Allied Supreme Council 15
Alsace-Lorraine 89
American Relief Administration 15–16
Apel, Erich 115
Ascherson, A. 167

Associations (or trusts) 116–17
AT & T 221
Austria–Hungary 35
  economic performance 231
  intra-regional trade 50
  loss of internal market 50
Austria 3, 4, 7, 8, 9, 10, 11, 16, 24, 28,
  37, 39, 86, 195, 221, 235
  Anschluss with Germany 66
Austro-Hungarian Empire xi–xii, 1, 3, 4,
  5, 6, 8, 9, 10, 12, 25, 28, 70, 84
Ayrian race 90

Balance of power xii–xiii, 6, 128
Balcerowicz, Leszek 208
Balcerowicz programme 214–15
Balkan federation schemes 133
Balkan Wars 4, 200, 230
Balkans 17, 18, 20, 31, 34, 46, 48, 52,
  54, 61, 71, 80, 130
  agricultural diversification 46
  currency stabilization 40
  export earnings decline 59
  growth rate 79
  housing 80
  manufacturing production 61, 78–9
  regressive tax system 71–2
  shift away from cereals 75
  structure of income 79
  surplus manpower in agriculture 74
  tax distortions 72
  use of fertilisers 76
Banac, I. 10
Bandera, V.N. 53
Banking sector 106, 117, 213
Bankruptcy laws 213
Basch, A. 67
Battle of Kosovo (1389) 202
Baumont, M. 17
Belgium 11
  income per capita indices 84

Berend, I.T. 25, 54, 80
Berliet bus plant 164
Berlin 89, 96
Berlin Wall 112, 189, 190, 191, 195, 196, 197
Bessarabia 4, 88, 96
Bierut, Boleslaw 97
Big bang approach 214
Bismarck, Otto 131, 195, 230
Black market (second economy) 126, 174
Black Sea 169
Black Sea Bubble 216
Bohemia–Moravia 4, 5, 7, 88, 131, 167
Boom (later 1920s) 42–5
Bosnia 4, 88
Bosnia-Herzegovina 172, 202, 203, 225, 226, 227
Bosnian Muslims 201, 226, 228, 229
Brandt, Willy 158
Brasov riots (1987) 190
Brezhnev Doctrine 150, 192–4
Brezhnev, Leonid 136
    attempts to revitalise CMEA 136–7
    attitude towards Czech reforms 148–9
    Gorbachev attacks policies 178
Brown, J.F. 179, 182
Brus, W. 99
Brzezinski, Zbigniew 189
Budapest 7
Bukovina 4, 88, 96
Bulgaria 1, 3, 4, 8, 9, 10, 11, 16, 27, 28, 29, 41, 44, 60, 68, 86, 88, 90, 91, 96, 98, 99, 101, 102, 107, 108, 113, 116, 125
    attitude towards Soviet reforms 181–2, 189
    capital inflow decline 56
    collectivization in 120, 124–5
    credit agreement with Soviet Union 132
    currency stabilization 40
    effort to improve living standards 159
    exchange control 64, 66
    extent of indebtedness 161, 171
    falls into debt trap 187
    faltering economic reform 217
    farm debts, relief of 74
    German trade share 67
    import of Canadian wheat 124
    income per capita indices 83, 84
    industrial production 103
    inflation 34
    inherited debt 222
    land reform 19, 20
    loyal Soviet ally 132, 143
    manufacturing production 61, 79
    national income 61, 103
    privatization drive 217
    recycles Soviet oil 167
    refugees 10
    revolution (1989) 197
    shift away from cereals 76
    state ownership 77
    tariff policy 30
    use of fertilisers 76
    war effects 15
Bulgarian Socialist Party 197, 217
Bulgarian–Yugoslav plan 133
Bush, George 193
Business methods 45
Butler, H. 85

Camp of National Unity 71
Canada 43, 124, 158
Capital 47
    accumulation 47, 82
    constraints 47
    cost of 36
Cartels 77–8
Ceausescu, Elena 200
Ceausescu family 159, 198
Ceausescu, Nicolae 179
    downfall of 199–200
    hostile response to Gorbachev's reforms 181
    legacy 215, 231, 233
    megalomaniacal policies 190–91, 198
Central Europe 235
    future integration prospects 235
Central European Free Trade Agreement (Cefta) 200
Centrally planned economy 105
    weaknesses of 109–11
Cereals 48–9
    expansion of 48–9
    exports 49
    oversupply 49
    stocks 49

Chamberlain, Neville 149
Charter 77 189, 198
Chetniks 201
Christian Democrats 196
Clearing agreements 66
Cold war 131, 133, 178, 193, 228
Collectivization 99, 118–25
Combines 180
Cominform (Communist Information
    Bureau) 119, 128, 131
Command economy 106, 211
Commission on International Policy
    183
Commodity Credit Corporation 160
Commodity prices 40, 42
    fall in 57, 58–9
Communist Information Bureau
    (Cominform) 99
Communist parties 130
    lack of support for 130
Communist regimes 96
    reasons for 97–8
Conference on Security and Cooperation
    in Europe 206, 233
Consumption 103–4
Corruption 216
Council for Mutual Economic Assist-
    ance (CMEA/Comecon) 98, 117,
    130, 135, 148, 164
    CMEA six's growing trade deficit
        with the Soviet Union 175
    decline of 192
    effect of demise 208
    efforts to transform 183–7
    formation of 133–4
    intra-CMEA trade 134–5
    lack of strategy on technology
        imports 162–3
    trade with America 157
    transformation of 136–7
    winding up of 204, 207–8
Council of Europe 194
Coyle, D. 234
Cracow 78
Croatia 88, 202, 203, 225, 226
Croatian Party of Rights 225–6
Croats 10, 201
Currencies, non-convertible nature for
    export 160–61
Currency convertibility 211

Currency depreciation 32, 33, 36–40,
    64, 65, 66
Currency instability 24
Currency stabilization 36–41, 42
    dates of 38
    gold exchange standard 37
    methods of 37–8
Czech Communist Party 146
Czech Republic 212, 218, 221, 223, 234
Czecho-Slovak Cereals Company 75
Czechoslovak–Polish trade agreement
    133
Czechoslovakia: 1, 3, 4, 5, 7, 9, 10, 11,
    16, 25, 31, 40, 41, 42, 44, 45, 48,
    51, 58, 59, 60, 61, 81, 82, 86, 93,
    96, 99, 102, 105, 107–8, 109, 115,
    116, 119, 125, 126, 127, 130, 131,
    132, 133, 134, 135, 136, 138, 139,
    140, 154, 161, 173, 185–6, 187,
    207, 208, 209, 221, 230, 233
    agricultural policy 46
    agricultural subsidies 75
    agriculture 102–3, 120–21
    annexation of 87–8
    cartels 77
    collectivization in 121
    consumption 103
    credit agreement with Soviet Union
        132–3
    currency stabilization 38–9
    Czech attitude towards Gorbachev
        179, 181–2, 189, 190
    defence expenditure 70, 71
    defence sector 141, 142–3
    defence spending and economic
        recovery in 1930s 71
    deteriorating relations with Soviet
        Union 192
    discrimination against minorities 9
    exchange control 64
    export earnings 59
    favourable energy arrangements with
        Soviet Union 168
    fiscal policy 69
    five-year plan reforms 112–13
    German trade share 67
    import substitution 75
    income per head 83, 84
    industrial policies 82
    industrial production 103

industrial recovery 35
inflation 34
integration problems 8
international markets 51, 53
investment programme 78
land reform 18–19, 20
loss of comparative advantage 82
manufacturing production 61, 78, 79
marketing of agricultural products 75
military build-up 70
national income 61, 103
nature of post-communist recession
     209–10
Prague Spring 146–51
privatization drive 212–13
progress of reform 214
real wages 35
relief aid 100–101
revolution (1989) 197–8
Soviet withdrawal from 204
stagnation in income per capita 83
state ownership 77
structure of income 79
tariff policy 30
use of fertilisers 76
war losses 14
'velvet divorce' 223
Czechs 9, 134, 135, 147, 213, 223, 233

Dalmatian Islands 96
Danube 198, 200, 222
Danubian customs union 5
Danubian federation 5, 63
Danubian region 51
Danubian states 84
Danzig 88
Debt burdens 65
   relief of 65, 74
Defence 140–41
   defence industries 141–3
   defence of Soviet bloc 139–43
   expenditure 63, 70
   increasing burden of 192–3
Delors, Jacques 226, 235
Denekas, D.G. and M.S. Khan 215
Denmark 76
   income per capita indices 84
Depression 21
   (1920–21) 21, 33
   (1930s) impact of 58–62

   1931 crisis 60–61
Détente 157–62
Deutsche Bank 223
Dimitrov 98
Dlouhy, Vladimir 218
Dobrogea 88
Dobrudja 4
Dracula, Count 198
Dubček, Alexander
   arrest and exile 150
   becomes Czech leader 146–7
   inspirational figure 198
   marks invasion anniversary 190
   meetings with Brezhnev 148–9

East Germany (German Democratic
     Republic GDR) 98, 102, 107, 113,
     114, 115, 116, 125, 126, 130, 132,
     133, 136, 139, 176
   attitude towards *glasnost* and
     perestroika 180–81
   collectivization in 123–4, 125
   consumption squeezed 103–4
   decadent lifestyles of leadership 196
   defence sector 141–2, 192–3
   effect of higher prices for Soviet oil
     168–9
   heavy industry programmes falters 110
   imports of western technology 163
   lack of innovation 185–6
   motor car industry 187–8
   New Economic System 117
   new course 111–12
   problems with agriculture 173–4
   recession in 192
   relations with West Germany 158,
     159, 160, 161, 170–71, 180, 191
   reparations to Soviet Union 101
   repression in 190
   revolution (1989) 195–7
   second five-year plan 111–12
   shortage of consumer goods 188
   strategic importance to USSR 138
   supports invasion of Czechoslovakia
     149–50
   uprising (1953) 110, 143–4
   see also Germany
East–West split 96
Eastern Europe xi–xiii, 110, 137, 204,
     206, 220

adopts the Soviet command economy 105–9
agrarian incomes 59
agricultural crisis 72–3
agricultural policies 73–5
agriculture 17, 46–8, 75–6, 93, 98, 102, 103
armies 139, 140
authoritarian regimes 58, 84
backwardness of 6, 83
balance of payments 55
budgetary problems 69
capital losses after second world war 91–2
cartels 77–8
cereals 48–9
changes in regimes 86
clearing agreements 66
coalition governments 97
collectivization 118–20
commodity exports 48, 52
communist regimes 97–8
conflict of interests on modernization 82
consumption 103–4
currency depreciation 32, 33, 36–40
currency protection 64–5
currency stabilization 36–41
debt burdens 56, 59, 60, 65
debt problems 169–72
decline in capital imports 56–7, 60
defence expenditure 63, 70
defence issues 139–43
definition 1
deflationary measures 69–72
dependence on agriculture 18, 46–8
depression 58–62
devastation after first world war 11–15
  after second world war 91–2
disorganization after second world war 93, 102
division of after second world war 94–6
domination by Germany 87–91
dual structure 81–2
economic performance 113, 118, 125–6, 175–6, 185, 187, 191–3, 207–10
economic structure 213–14

ethnic diversity 8–9, 9–10
ethnic problems 8–9
exchange control 64, 65, 66
expansion in later 1920s 44–7
export earnings 56, 59, 60
export premia 66, 75
exports 48, 49, 52, 59
extent of progress in interwar years 83
external accounts protected 64–5, 77
fall of communism 177, 179, 183, 194
farm debts 74
farm incomes depressed 76
fiscal policies 69–72
fiscal problems 29, 33, 37–40, 60
foreign capital in 52–7
frontier changes after second world war 95–6, 102
future prospects 229–36
gap between East and West 83–4, 126
German trade penetration 66–8
import-led growth 156–7, 162–3, 167
importance to Soviet Union 131–2
imports into 16, 94
income gains 83
income per capita indices 84
industrial development, need for 28, 29, 30
industrial policies 29–32, 41, 45, 76–82
industrial production 102–3
industrial structure 81
inflation 32–6
infrastructures 71
insolvency 60–61
intra-regional trade 50–51
investment programmes 78
land reform 17–20, 27–8, 74, 98, 99
legacy of economic backwardness 231–3
manufacturing production 44, 61
modernization of agriculture 75–6
monetary policies 69–72
national income 61, 103
nationalism 30–31, 63
Nazi agents 68
neglect of agriculture 173–4
new trading links 51
nostrification 63
output decline 93

overvaluation of currencies 65
peasant incomes 72–3
planning 99–100
policy determinants 62–3
policy options 62
population changes 3, 4, 5, 27, 73, 83, 96, 102
post-communist regimes 210
post-communist requirements 218–19
post second world war outlook 94
power vacuum in 5, 6
price falls 58–9
promotion of industry 76–82
public relief measures 69–70
rebellions in 143–51
reconstruction plans 99
reconstruction problems 24–5, 26, 28–9, 41, 100–104
recovery after first world war 23, 41
  after second world war 102–4
relationship to the world economy 168
relief assistance 26, 96, 100–101
reparations 101–2
revolutions 191–2
seeks import-led growth 156–7
share of world trade 68
short-term indebtedness 56
shortages 93–4
socialization of economies 98, 99–100
Soviet dominance 128–33
Soviet subsidies 138, 154
state control 80
state ownership 76, 77
structural problems 47
tariff policies 29–30
tax burden 71–2
tax yields 69
taxation structure 71–2
terms of trade 49–50, 59
territorial changes 3, 4, 5
trade regulation 29–30, 64, 65
vulnerability of 47, 58, 84, 85
Western banks' policy towards 160–62, 170, 222
Eco-Glasnost 197
Economic reforms
  in 1960s 113–18
  in 1990s 210–13

political implications 211–12, 233–4
Economic System of Socialism 117
Edinburgh summit 219
Eichengreen, B. 6
Einzig, P. 35
Electric power 163
Elektronska Industrija factory 235
Ellis, H.S. 50
Emigration 27
Employment 125–6, 115–16
Energy
  energy guzzling industries 154, 176
  energy shocks and Eastern Europe 166–9
  favourable Soviet pricing formula 167
  revised Soviet prices 168–9
Ethnic cleansing 200–201, 226–7
Europe 61
  attitudes towards 94–5
  balance of power in 84
  division of after second world war 94–6
  expansion in activity 42–5
  income per capita indices 84
  recovery 22–4
  security of 84–5
Europe agreements 219–20
European Bank for Reconstruction and Development (EBRD) 218, 221
European Coal and Steel Community 134
European Consultative Commission 85
European Economic Area 233
European Economic Community (EEC), subsequently European Community (EC) then European Union (EU)
  attitude towards the new Eastern Europe 218–20, 233
  comparisons with CMEA 134
  effects of tariffs on Yugoslavia 172
  expansion of 87
  Yugoslavia's commercial agreement with 162
European Free Trade Association 219
European Investment Bank 218
Exchange control 64, 65
  effects of 65
  relaxation of 66
Exchange control countries 65
Exchange rate 211

Export Administration Act (1969) 160
Export–Import Bank 160
Export premia 66, 75
Extensive growth 106, 114
Eyal, J. 233

Famine 15
Federal Reserve Bank (New York) 57
First World War
  devastation caused by 11–15
  impact of 1
  reconstruction 15–17
Fiscal policies 69–72
  deflationary stance of 69–72
  regressive nature of 71–2
  tax yields 69
Fiscal problems 29, 33, 37–40, 69, 60
Five-year plans
  achievements of in early 1980s 175–6
  changed directions 111–13
  initial plans 106–9
Food output 43
Food prices 59
Food rationing 111–12
Foreign capital 44, 52–7, 80
  borrowing costs 55
  curtailment of 56–7
  debt service burden 56, 57
  flow of 52, 56–7
  instability 53–4, 56–7
  motives for 55
  need for 52–3
  preferences in post-communist
    Eastern Europe 220–21
  role of 53, 56–7
  short-term funds 55–6
  utilization of 53–4, 55, 56–7
France 11, 12, 42, 52, 84, 85, 196, 198,
  212
  income per capita indices 84
French revolution, parallels of 1989
  situation 177, 198

Galbraith, Kenneth 207
General Agreement on Tariffs and Trade
  (GATT) 159, 165, 233
German Reich *see* Germany
Germans 9–10
Germany 3, 4, 11, 16, 24, 37, 42, 51, 52,
  70, 85, 95–6, 97, 207
    attitude towards Eastern Europe 82,
      84, 85, 230
    currency reform 102
    division of 96
    domination of Eastern Europe by 87–
      91
    drive for European hegemony 58
    exploitation of Eastern Europe 90–91
    income per capita indices 84
    infiltration of Nazi agents in Eastern
      Europe 68
    manipulation of cartel system 78
    Nazi Germany 86–9
    New Order for Europe 89
    rearmament 77
    trade with Eastern Europe 66–8, 220
Gerö, Ernö 145
Gierek, Edward 152
Glasnost 178, 180, 181, 182, 189
Goebbels, Josef 128
Gold standard 27, 42
  collapse of 64
  exchange standard 36–41
  gold bloc countries 65
Gomulka, Wladyslaw 144–5, 151–2
Good, D.F. 231–3
Gorbachev, Mikhail
  attitude of Eastern European leaders
    towards 179–83
  encourages dismantlement of Soviet
    empire 192–4
  initiates reforms 177–9
  see also Glasnost and *Perestroika*
Gottwald, Klement 98
Grande Europe 235
Greater Hungary 225
Greater Siberia 227
Greece 4, 66, 109, 187, 231
Grosz, Karoly 183

Halecki, O. 97
Hard currency foreign debt
  efforts to resolve 221–2
  growth of 170–73
  influence on 1989 revolutions 192
Havel, Václav 177, 198, 233
Heavy industry lobby 165, 185
Helsinki accords 158, 199
Herzegovina 4, 88
Hitler, Adolf 6, 10, 70, 71, 200, 201

and conquest of Europe 86–91
Hoffman, E. 189–190
Holzman, F.D. 154–5
Honecker, Erich 180, 181, 183, 195–6
Hong Kong 220
Hungarian Central Statistical Office 114
Hungarian Democratic Forum 195, 215
Hungarian Planning Office 133
Hungarian Revolution (1956) 144–6
Hungary 1, 3, 4, 7, 8, 9, 10, 11, 16, 17,
    24, 26–7, 28, 37, 40, 41, 44, 45, 50,
    51, 60, 74, 81, 86, 88, 91, 99, 107,
    108, 119, 120, 133, 135, 139, 140,
    141, 150, 159, 168, 185, 186, 190,
    192, 208, 209, 218, 219, 231, 234,
    235
  agricultural output 72
  attitude towards Soviet reforms 182,
      183
  availability of consumer goods 112,
      174, 187
  capital inflow decline 56
  cartels 77
  changed trading relationship with
      Moscow 175
  clearing agreements 66
  collectivization experience 122–3
  currency stabilization 39
  deflationary policy 69
  economic problems on the eve of
      revolution (1989) 192
  effects of peace treaty 7
  ethnic problems 225
  exchange control 64
  export earnings, fall in 59
  falling labour productivity 176
  farm debts 59
  fiscal reform 39
  German trade share 67
  hyperinflation 32, 33–4, 39
  import-led growth strategy 163, 164
  importance to Soviet Union 132, 138
  inadequate reforms 188–9
  income per capita indices 84
  industrial expansion in second world
      war 91
  industrial production 103
  industry 7, 45
  investment programme 70, 78
  land reform 19, 20
  leads withdrawal from Warsaw Pact
      204
  manufacturing production 61, 79
  national income 61, 103
  New Economic Mechanism 116, 117
  over-reliance on foreign investment
      212
  overambitious five-year plan (1950–
      54) 108
  peasant incomes 73
  post-communist economic develop-
      ments 213–14
  post-inflation depression 34
  real wages 34, 35
  reform programme 215
  refugees 10
  renewal of nationalism 190, 222–3
  reparations to Soviet Union 101, 102
  revised plan goals 112, 114, 115
  revolution (1989) 144, 194–5
  state ownership 77
  tariffs 30
  wartime destruction 14, 92, 96
Husák, Gustav 151, 179
Hyperinflation 24, 32, 37, 39, 214–15

Ikarus buses 175, 208
Iliescu, Ion 200
Import-led growth 154–5, 156–7, 162–5,
    169–73
Import licences 164
Industrial development 107
  assistance for 31
  need for 28, 29, 30
Industrial policies 29–32
  defects of 31
  results of 41
Industrial production 42–3, 102, 103
  indices 23, 43
Inflation 22, 24, 32–6, 102, 192
  aid to reconstruction 32–6
  benefits of 33–4
  causes of 32
  disadvantages of 34–6
  effect on savings 36
  following the 1973 oil price shock
      166–7, 202, 227
  hits Romania 216
  hyperinflation 24, 32, 37, 39, 214–15
  impact on income distribution 35

resource misallocation 35
Infrastructure investment 71
Innovation 114, 185
Intensive growth 106, 114
International lending 26–7, 44, 52–7, 80
   decline in 60
International Monetary Fund (IMF) 159,
   165, 172, 212
Iran 199
Iron Curtain 128, 195
Istrian peninsula 96
Italy 4, 42, 51, 96, 109, 212
Ivnostenska Banka 213

Jackson, M.R. 79
Jakes, Milos 180, 197
Japan 160, 185
Jaruzelski, Wojciech 153, 182–3, 190
John Paul II, Pope 152
Joint Technical Committee (Warsaw
   Pact) 142
Joint venture schemes with western
   firms 185
July Concept 182

Kádár János 146, 180, 183, 195
Katowice steel plant 16
Keegan, W. 168
Khrushchev, Nikita 111, 113, 115, 139,
   144–6
Kingdom of Serbs, Croats and Slovenes
   4
   see also Yugoslavia
Kolakowski, Leszek 179
Kolodko, G.W. 210
Kombinate 180
Komlos, J. 6
Konsolidacni Banka 214
Korean War 100, 111, 135
Kosovo, 172, 202
Kramer, M. 209
Kremlin 127, 145
Krenz, Egon 196
Kulaks 122
Kun, Bela 14, 19, 145

L-29 AERO trainer 142
Labour productivity 108, 176
Labour shortages 125–6
Labour surplus 108

Lada motor cars 192
Lampe, J.R. 79, 234
Land reform 17–20, 98, 99
   defects of 19–20, 74
   extent of 18–19
   impact of 27–8
   objectives 18
Landau, Z. 25
Latvia 12
Lausanne, Treaty of 3
League of Communists of Yugoslavia
   202
League of Nations 17, 22, 26, 34, 39,
   72, 85
   reconstruction schemes 39, 40, 41
League of Vojvodina Hungarians 225
Left Democratic Alliance 234
Lewis, W.A. 22
Liberal Democrats 230
Liberman, Yevsai 113
Lithuania 40, 96
Lloyd George, David 206
Locarno Pact 42
Lodz 13
London Club 222
Loveday, A. 42
Luxembourg 89
Lvov 78

Macedonia 4, 172, 202, 203, 226, 231
Machine tractor stations (MTS) 120
Maginot Line 196
Magyars 10
Market economy 153–4, 211
Marrese, M. and Vanous, J. controversy
   over thesis 137–9
Marshall Aid 101, 132, 133, 217
Marxism–Leninism (or Marxist–
   Leninism) 128, 148, 190
Matav 221
Meciar, Vladimir 223
Middle East 169, 220
MIG-23 fighter aircraft 140
Miljacka, river 227
Mill, John Stuart 147
Miloševič, Slobodan 202, 203, 226, 227,
   231
Ministry of Commerce and Industry 77
Mittag, Gunter 115
Mitterand, François 230–31

Mocsy, I.I. 10
Monetary policies 69–72
Montenegro 4, 88, 172, 202, 226, 227
Moore, W.E. 47
Moscow 95, 99

Nagy, Imre 110, 123, 145–6
National Bank of Hungary 215
National income 45, 61, 93, 103–4
National Salvation Front 199, 200
national minorities 9–10
Nationalization 106, 108
Nationalism 30–31, 63, 190
Nationalities question 222–9
Nazi Germany *see* Germany
Neues Forum 196
Netherlands
    income per capita indices 84
Neuilly, Treaty of 3, 4
New Economic Mechanism (NEM) 117
New Economic Model 115
New Economic Policy 116
New Economic System (NES) 117
New Order for Europe 89
    failure to consolidate 89–90
New World Order 206
Newly industrialised countries (NICs)
    187
Nomenklatura 182
North Atlantic Cooperation Council 233
North Atlantic Treaty Organization
    (NATO) 139, 140, 141, 193, 228,
    229, 233
Northern Telecom 221
Norway 86
Nostrification 31, 76, 80, 82
Nötel, R. 55, 61
Novotny, Antonin 146, 147
Nyers, Rezso 115

Oder-Neisse line 139, 151, 158, 204
Opposition Round Table 194
Orenburg natural gas project 137
Organization for Economic Develop-
    ment and Co-operation (OECD)
    208, 217, 220, 221, 233, 235
Organization for International Economic
    Cooperation 204
Organization for Petroleum Exporting
    Countries (OPEC) 161, 166, 168

Ostpolitik 158
Ottoman Empire 202
Output decline 207–10
Overy, R. 71

Paris Charter 206
Paris Club 221, 222
Partners in Transition (OECD) 233
Partnership for Peace 233
Pauker, Ana 98
Pavelic, Ante 201, 223
Peace settlement
    defects of 4–5, 6, 7, 8, 9, 10
    terms of 1, 3–4
Peasantry 122–3
    decline in incomes 72
    effects of inflation on 36
    grievances re tax burden 76
    majority element in 1950s 105
    tax burden of 71–2, 76
People's democracies in Eastern Europe
    130
Perestroika 178, 180, 182, 189, 196
Pilsudski, General 40, 71
Pilzen 70
Planning 99, 100, 104
Poland 1, 3, 4, 5, 8, 9, 10, 11, 16, 17, 24,
    25, 28, 30, 41, 44, 45, 50, 59, 60,
    74, 81, 91, 97, 99, 101, 107, 108,
    109, 120, 130, 132, 136, 140, 145,
    175, 176, 186, 210, 212
    agricultural production difficulties
        125, 173
    anti-reform stance 115, 188
    anti-Soviet rising (1953) 144
    applies for EU membership 218
    applies for OECD membership 235
    benefits from Soviet subsidies 138
    big bang approach 214–15
    capital inflow decline 56
    cartels 77
    collectivization in 122
    conquest by Germany 88, 89
    costs of import-led growth 170
    currency stabilization 39–40
    debt negotiations 222
    defence expenditure 70, 71
    defence industry 135, 142, 204
    deflationary policies 69
    disillusionment with communism 188

exchange control 64, 66
falling industrial production 209
fiscal reform 40
five-year plan (1956–60) 112
German trade share 67
hyperinflation 32, 33, 39
import-led growth 164, 156, 159, 163, 170
income per capita indices 84
industrial production 103
inflation-ravaged economy 192
integration problems 8, 25–6
investment programme 70, 78
joint venture schemes 185
laggard status 114, 115, 118
land reform 19, 20
manufacturing production 61, 79
national income 61, 103
political fallout from economic reforms 234
pollution in 168
post-inflation depression 34, 35
price support schemes 75
real wages 35
reform programme 214–15
relations with EC 219–20
relief aid 102
response to Gorbachev 182–3
shortage of consumer goods 169
social unrest 36
state ownership 30, 77
subjugation of armed forces by Soviets 139
suffers from American import ban 133
surplus manpower in agriculture 74
uprising (1956) 144–5
war devastation 12–13, 92, 93, 96
workers' revolts 151–3
see also Solidarity
Poland and Hungary: Assistance for Restructuring the Economy (PHARE) 218
Polish Communist Party 153
Polish defence sector 141
Polish disease 164
Polish October 144
Polish Peasant Party 234
Polish Research Institute 210
Political consequences of post-1989 reforms 211–12

Political Consultative Commission (Warsaw Pact) 141
Pollard, S. 92
Pollution 167–8
Population 3, 17, 18, 27, 45, 73, 83, 96, 102
dependent on agriculture 18
growth of 45
war losses 11–12
Portugal 187
Potsdam 96
Prague Spring 146–51, 190
Pravda 113, 150
Preustroistvo 182
Primary commodities, output of 43, 44
overdependence on 48
prices 42, 49–50, 58–9
Private sector 212
Privatization 211–13, 217
Public opinion 189–91

Quixote, Don 196

Raisin, Alois 38
Rákosi, Mátyás 98, 110
Ranki, G. 25, 54, 50
Raw materials 43
prices of 59
Reagan, Ronald 178
Recession 191–2, 207–10, 233
Reconstruction
plans for 99
reconstruction problems 24–5, 26, 28–9, 41, 42, 100–104
relief aid 15–17, 26, 96, 100–101
Red Army 128, 129, 131, 139
Refolution 195
Reform substitution 159
Refugees 10
Reparations 14, 101–2, 132, 133
Revolutions in Eastern Europe
economic background to 191–2
see also individual country headings
Roberts, A. 233
Roman Catholic Church 152
Romania 1, 3, 4, 8, 9, 10, 11, 16, 18, 19, 28, 31, 41, 44, 49, 60, 86, 88, 90, 91, 99, 107, 108, 114, 125, 130, 133, 134, 213, 221, 223, 225, 234
agriculture 134, 173, 174

anti-reform stance 115, 118
cartels 77
Ceausescu legacy 231–3
CMEA policy 136, 137, 186
collectivization in 124
corruption 31–2
currency stabilization 31–2
deteriorating standard of living 190–91
effect of ostracism from USSR on oil import bill 169
excessive energy consumption of industries 176
exchange control 64
export earnings, fall in 59
farm debts 74
foreign capital 54
foreign debt repayment and its ramifications 171
German trade share 67
import-led growth strategy 163, 164–5
income per capita indices 84
industrial policy 31
industrial production 103
infiltration of Nazi agents 68
integration problems 8
investment programme 78
laggard economy 115, 118, 124
manufacturing production 61, 79
membership of IMF and World Bank 164
most favoured nation status with US 160
national income 61, 103
pollution levels 168
price support schemes 75
reduced Soviet interest in 138–9
reform programme 215–17, 220
relations with Moscow 132, 138–9, 140, 204
reparations to Soviet Union 101, 102
rescheduling of debt 171
resists *glasnost* and *perestroika* 180, 181
revolution (1989) 198–200
Stalinist economy 116
state ownership 77
tariff policy 30
war losses 14, 96

Romanian Communist Party 199
Rothschild, J. 54, 58, 67, 89, 97
Ruhr 42
Rural population 113–14
Rural Solidarity 152
Russia
    possible future threat to Eastern Europe 230, 235
    revolution 18
    see also Soviet Union
Ruthenia 20, 88

SALT I 158
SALT II 158
Sarajevo 227, 228, 235
Savings 36, 80, 82
Saudi Arabia 184
Schwartz, H. 5
Second World War 5
    devastation by 91–2, 93, 102
    division of Europe after 94–6
    reconstruction plans 99
    reconstruction problems 100–4
    recovery after 102–4
    territorial changes 95–6
    Yugoslavia's experience 201
Second Yugoslavia 231
Sector A industries (heavy industry) 107, 108, 110, 119, 213–14
Sector B industries (consumer or light industries) 107, 108, 110, 213–14
Securitate 199
Self-determination 3, 5
Self-sufficiency 44
Serb Autonomous Regions 225
Serb Democratic Party 225
Serb Renewal Party 231
Serbia 3, 4, 88, 202, 225, 227, 235
    inflation 227
    war losses 11–12
Serbs 9, 201, 202, 203, 222
Seton-Watson, Hugh 201
Sèvres, Treaty of 3
Shah of Iran 169
Shaw, George Bernard 236
Shock therapy approach *see* Big bang approach
Shortage economy 187–8
Show trials 131
Siberia 137

Siemens 221
Silesia (Austrian) 4
Skoda works 70, 143
Slansky, Rudolf 131
Slovakia 4, 10, 88, 91, 96, 218, 223, 225, 234
    military output 91
Slovakian Communist Party 147
Slovaks 9, 147, 223
Slovenes 10
Slovenia 4, 88, 172, 202, 203, 226, 234–5
Smith, A.H. 133
Social sector 108
Social Unity Party (SED) 111
Socialism in one country 130
Solidarity
    comes to power 194
    crushing of 153
    formation of 152–3
    reasserts itself 100
Sontag, R.J. 5
South-East Asia 153
Southern Europe 81, 187
Soviet Department for Liaison with the Communists and Workers' Parties of Socialist Countries 183
Soviet Ministry of Defence 140
Soviet Union (USSR) 4, 13, 24, 28, 37, 40, 43, 50, 70, 77, 88, 89, 90, 100, 102, 105, 116, 125, 133, 139, 140, 141, 146, 158, 159, 162, 169, 187
    attitude to Polish crisis 151, 153
    change of emphasis under Khrushchev 113
    changes energy formula 168
    CMEA policy 134, 135, 136–7, 175, 184–5, 192, 204–5, 208
    economic decline in 183–4
    economic exploitation of Eastern Europe 132, 154
    empire in Eastern Europe 128–30
    faltering Soviet economy 177–8, 183
    features of Soviet command economy 106–7, 109–11
    future attitude towards Eastern Europe 230, 235
    import-led growth strategy 156
    importance of individual countries to 131–2
    motives for *détente* 154–5, 160
    planning model 98, 99
    policy on Eastern Europe 101, 102–4, 192–4
    position in Europe 97
    reaction to Prague Spring 148–51
    reparations from Eastern Europe 101
    response to 1956 rebellions in Eastern Europe 143–6
    strategy on Europe 94–5, 96
    subsidization of Eastern Europe 130, 137–8, 154, 167
    superpower status 128
    see also Brezhnev Doctrine; Brezhnev, Leonid; Council for Mutual Economic Assistance; *Glasnost*; Gorbachev, Mikhail; Khrushchev, Nikita; *Perestroika*; Stalin, Josef; Warsaw Pact
Spain 187
Spulber, N. 44
Sputnik 189
St Germain, Treaty of 3
Staatssicherheit (Stasi) 190
Stalin, Josef
    effects of death 105, 111, 143–4
    high Stalinism 130–35
    identifies two world markets 134
Standard of living
    and *détente* 159
    cause of pressure for reform 157
    compared with western norms 187–8
    decline in under initial five-year plans 109–10
    greater emphasis on the consumer 111–13
    growing consumerism 174
    lack of choice in socialist countries 106, 110
    see also Black market; Shortage economy
Star Wars programme 178
State Department (US) 144
State intervention 30
Strikes (in Poland) 190
Strong, Benjamin 57
Structure of enterprise 45
Successor states, problems of 7–8
Sudeten lands 88
Suez Canal 173

Sweden 71
income per capita indices 84

T-54/55 tank 140
T-72 tank 142
Tariffs 64
protectionist policies 29–30
TASS (Soviet news agency) 153
Taxation
changes required in market economy
210–11
corporation tax in Czechoslovakia 214
peasant grievances re burden of
taxation 76
regressive nature of 71–2
Technological gap with the West 154–5,
157, 162–5, 178
Telecommunications 221
Telekomunikacja 221
Terms of trade 49–50
Tesla Piestany 212
Textile industry 7
Third World 161, 173, 218
Third Yugoslavia 227
Tiltman, H.H. 9
Tito, Josip Broz 97, 109, 131, 146, 172,
201–2
Tocqueville, Alexis de 177
Tomasevich, J. 71
Tomaszewski, J. 79
Trabant motor car 187–8
Trade regulation 29–30, 64, 65
effects of 65
Trans-Carpathian Ruthenians 233
Transport equipment 163
Transylvania 4, 20, 88
Trianon, Treaty of 3, 7, 10, 28, 225
Trusts *see* Associations
Turkey 3, 109, 140, 197, 231
Turkish Empire 1
Turnock, D. 80
Twentieth Congress of the Soviet
Communist Party 144

Ukraine 88, 225, 234
Ulbricht, Walter 98, 143, 148
Unemployment
benefits 178
in Hungary 110
in Slovenia 234–5

of rural population 20
rise in 117
Union of Democratic Forces 197, 212
United Kingdom 11, 26, 42, 51, 52, 57,
59, 65, 84, 85, 95, 196, 207
income per capita indices 84
United Nations (UN) 226, 227, 228, 229
United Nations Convention on Refugees
195
United Nations Economic Commission
for Europe 209
United Nations Relief and Rehabilitation
Administration (UNRRA) 100, 101
United States 15, 26, 43, 51, 52, 53, 59,
65, 95, 96, 109, 112, 140, 157–8,
178, 196, 207
changing attitude towards Romania
181
foreign lending 56–7, 60
imposes sanctions on Poland 153
initiates new arms race 178
involvement in *détente* 160
perceived weaknesses of military
involvement in Korea 135
superpower status 128
trading relations with Eastern Europe
133
Upper Silesia 26, 89
Ustashi 200

Varga Commission 112
Verrechnungseinheit 161
Versailles, Treaty of 3
see also Peace settlement
Visegrad Four 210, 218
Voivodina 124
Vojvodina 202

Wages real 35
Walesa, Lech 152
Wandel durch Annaherung 159
Warriner, D. xi, 80
Warsaw 13, 78
Warsaw Letter 149
Warsaw Pact
and events in Poland 153
formation of 140
intervention in Czechoslovakia 149–50
outdated weaponry 193
Soviet dominance of 140

Soviet Union's financial contribution
158
termination of 204
Weimar Germany 227, 230
West Germany
growing trade with Eastern Europe
160
see also Germany; East Germany
Western banks
credit policy towards Eastern Europe
160–62
negotiations with Eastern Europe 222
revised attitudes on default 170
see also International Monetary Fund;
World Bank
Western Europe 166, 178
Western powers
attitude towards Eastern Europe 84,
217–22
détente with 156
Eastern Europe's development lag
with 126
Eastern Europe's need for Western
technology 154–5, 162–5
reaction to war in former Yugoslavia
226
Western strategy 169
Western Thrace 4
Woodward, S. 211
Workers' committees 116–17
Workers' Defence Committee 152
World Bank
attitude towards Yugoslavia's import
strategy 163–4
possible loan to Czechoslovakia 148
rescheduling agreement with Yugoslavia 173
World communist revolution 128

Yalta 96
Yeager, L.B. 37
Yom Kippur War 167
Young Poland Movement 152
Yugoslav Communist Party 203
Yugoslav National Army (YNA) 203,
226
Yugoslavia 1, 3, 4, 7, 9, 10, 11, 16, 18,
19, 25, 41, 44, 49, 60, 105, 125,
140

agricultural developments 109, 119,
122, 124
asserts independence from USSR 131
capital inflow decline 56
civil war in 203, 225–9, 231, 234–6
conquest by Germany 88
contrast with typical socialist
economy 117–18, 108–9
currency stabilization 40
deflationary policy 69
disintegration of 200–203
early reforms 116, 117–18
establishment of socialist state 97
ethnic composition of 10
exchange control 64
failure to collectivize agriculture 119
farm debts 59, 74
German trade share 67
impact of oil shocks 171–3
income per capita indices 84
industrial production 103
industrial workers 80
inflation 34, 166–7, 171–3, 202
integration problems 8
investment programme 78
manufacturing production 61, 79
Ministry of Commerce and Industry
77
misuse of western technology imports
163–4, 165
national income 61, 103
planning 99
plum trade with Germany 68
relations with the Soviet Union 131,
132, 183
relaxation of macro policy 70
relief aid 101
stagnation in income per capita 83
state ownership 77
structural shifts 79
structure of capital formation 72
textile factories 81
wartime losses 92, 93

Zauberman, A. 104
Zeiss works 132
Zhdanov, Andrei 128
Zhirinovsky, Vladimir 230
Zhivkov, Todor 143, 179, 187, 197